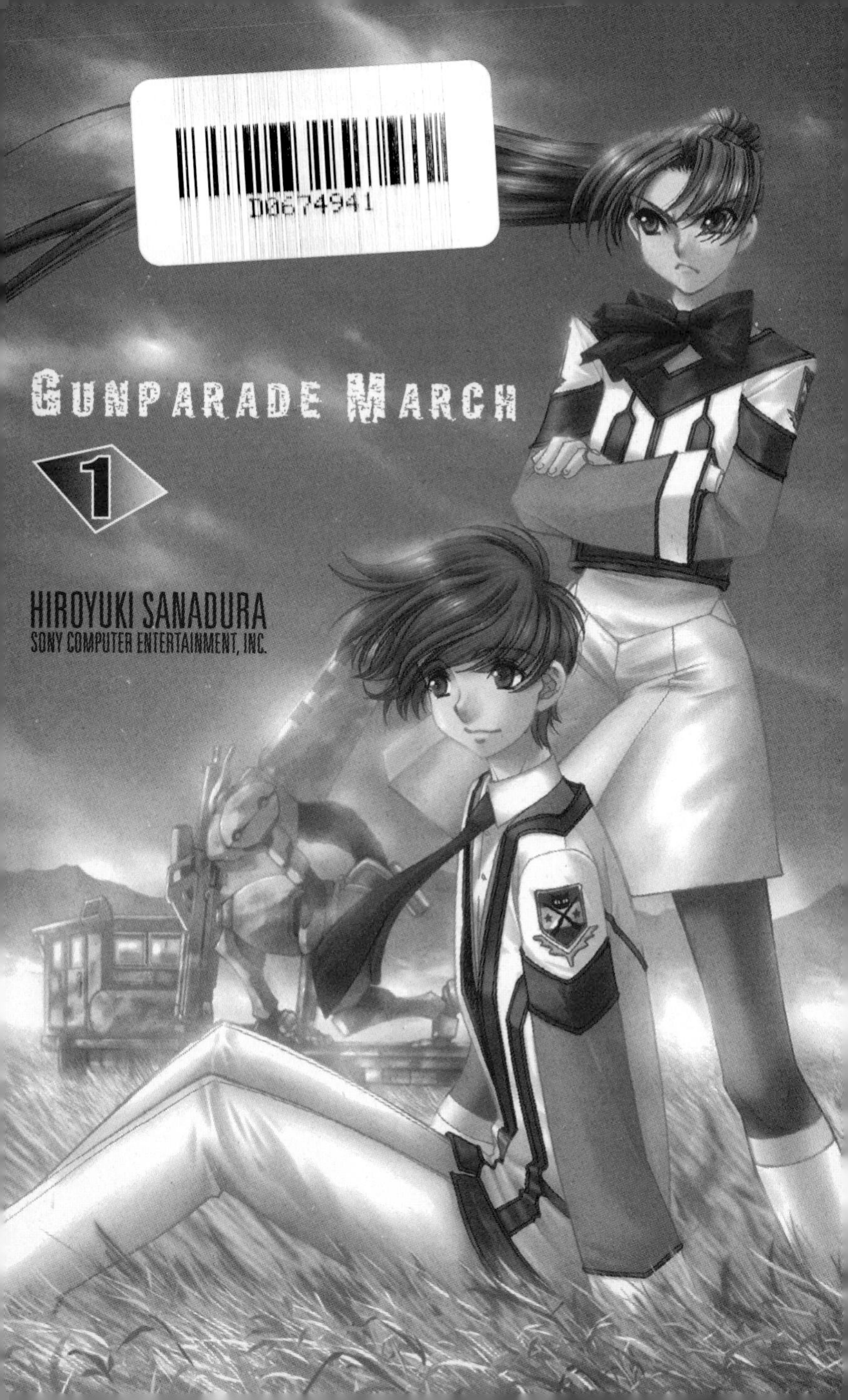
GUNPARADE MARCH
1
HIROYUKI SANADURA
SONY COMPUTER ENTERTAINMENT, INC.

CONTENTS

episode #1

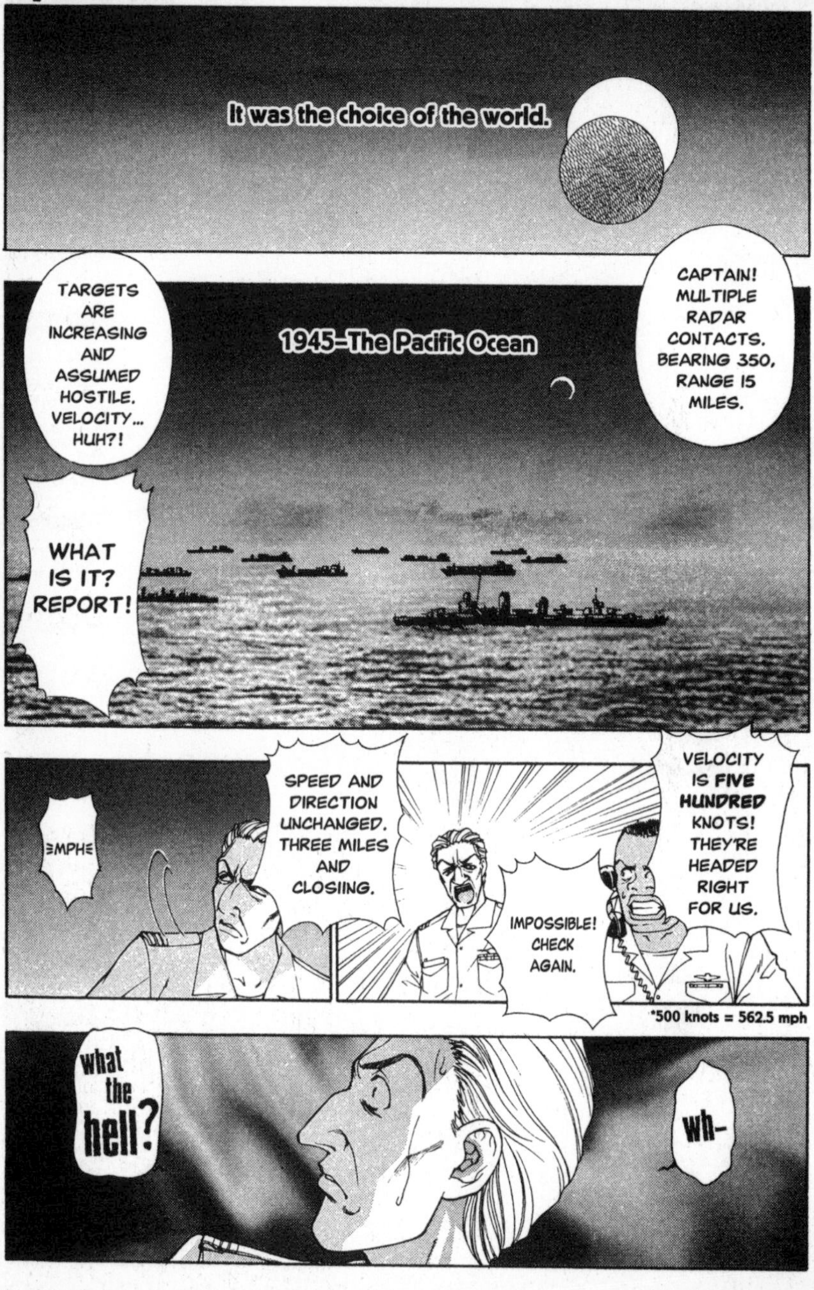
It was the choice of the world.
1945–The Pacific Ocean
CAPTAIN! MULTIPLE RADAR CONTACTS. BEARING 350, RANGE 15 MILES.
TARGETS ARE INCREASING AND ASSUMED HOSTILE. VELOCITY... HUH?!
WHAT IS IT? REPORT!
VELOCITY IS FIVE HUNDRED KNOTS! THEY'RE HEADED RIGHT FOR US.
IMPOSSIBLE! CHECK AGAIN.
SPEED AND DIRECTION UNCHANGED. THREE MILES AND CLOSIING.
EMPH
wh-
what the hell?

*500 knots = 562.5 mph

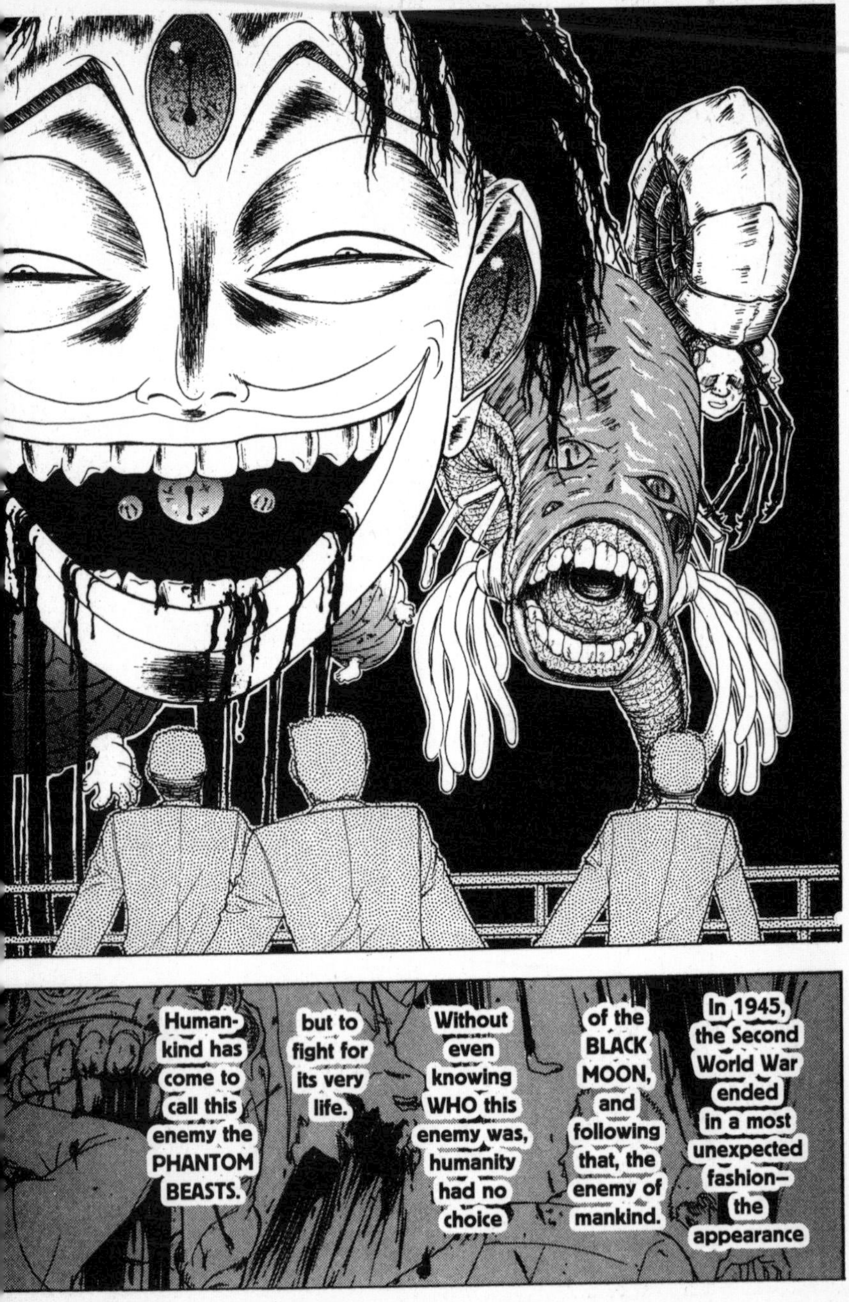
In 1945, the Second World War ended in a most unexpected fashion— the appearance
of the BLACK MOON, and following that, the enemy of mankind.
Without even knowing WHO this enemy was, humanity had no choice
but to fight for its very life.
Human-kind has come to call this enemy the PHANTOM BEASTS.

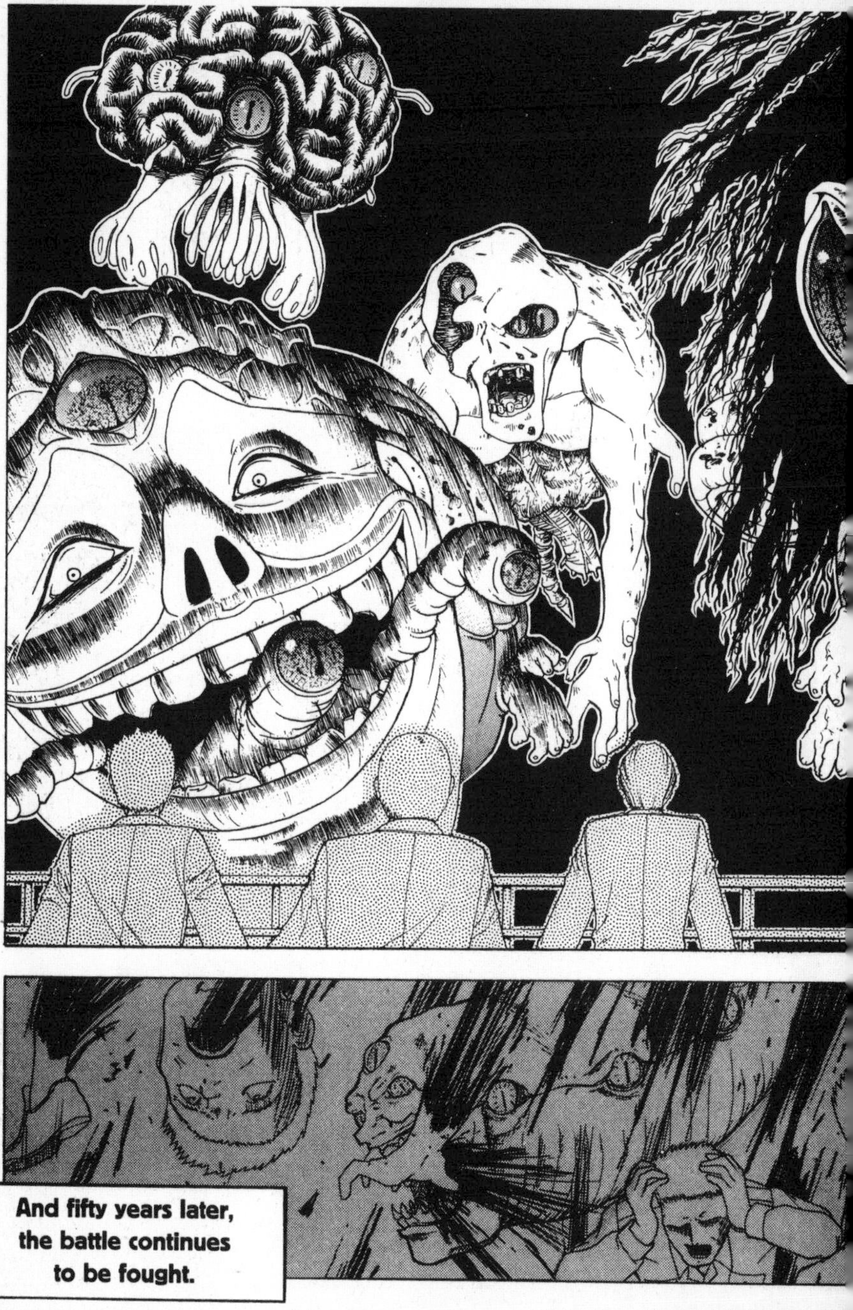
And fifty years later, the battle continues to be fought.

In 1998, a tragic loss occurred...
in the fight against the Phantom Beasts.
On the Yashiro Plain in Kyushu, the Self-Defense Forces deployed the sum total of its forces in combat.
They were 480,000 against the Phantom Beasts' 14 MILLION.
Humanity managed to win through the use of biological weaponry. But 80% of the surrounding land was destroyed,
and 300,000 lives were lost.
In 1999,
Two bills were passed by the Diet.

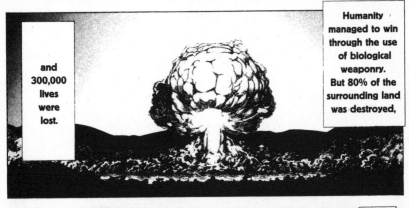

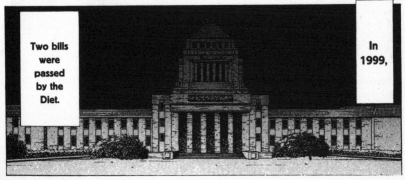

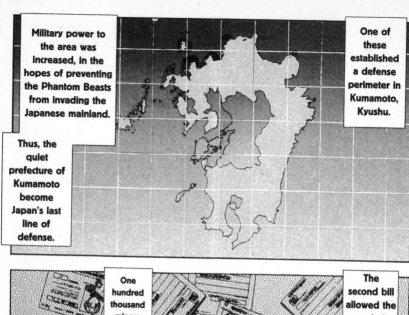

One of these established a defense perimeter in Kumamoto, Kyushu.
Military power to the area was increased, in the hopes of preventing the Phantom Beasts from invading the Japanese mainland.
Thus, the quiet prefecture of Kumamoto become Japan's last line of defense.
The second bill allowed the conscription of minors into the military,
with children from the ages of 14 to 17 being pulled from school.
One hundred thousand minors were put into active service,
and deployed to Kumamoto to buy time for the re-organization of the adult military forces.
The government believed that most of these young soldiers…
would be killed before year's end.
This is the story of those children who were…
dragged into the war against the Phantom Beasts.

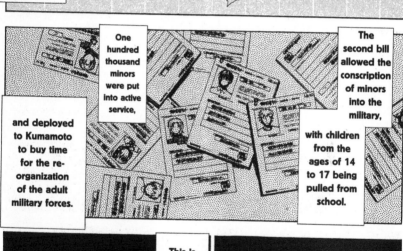

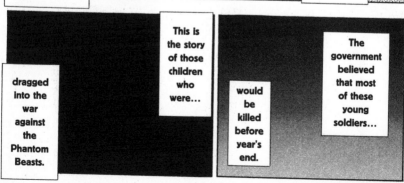

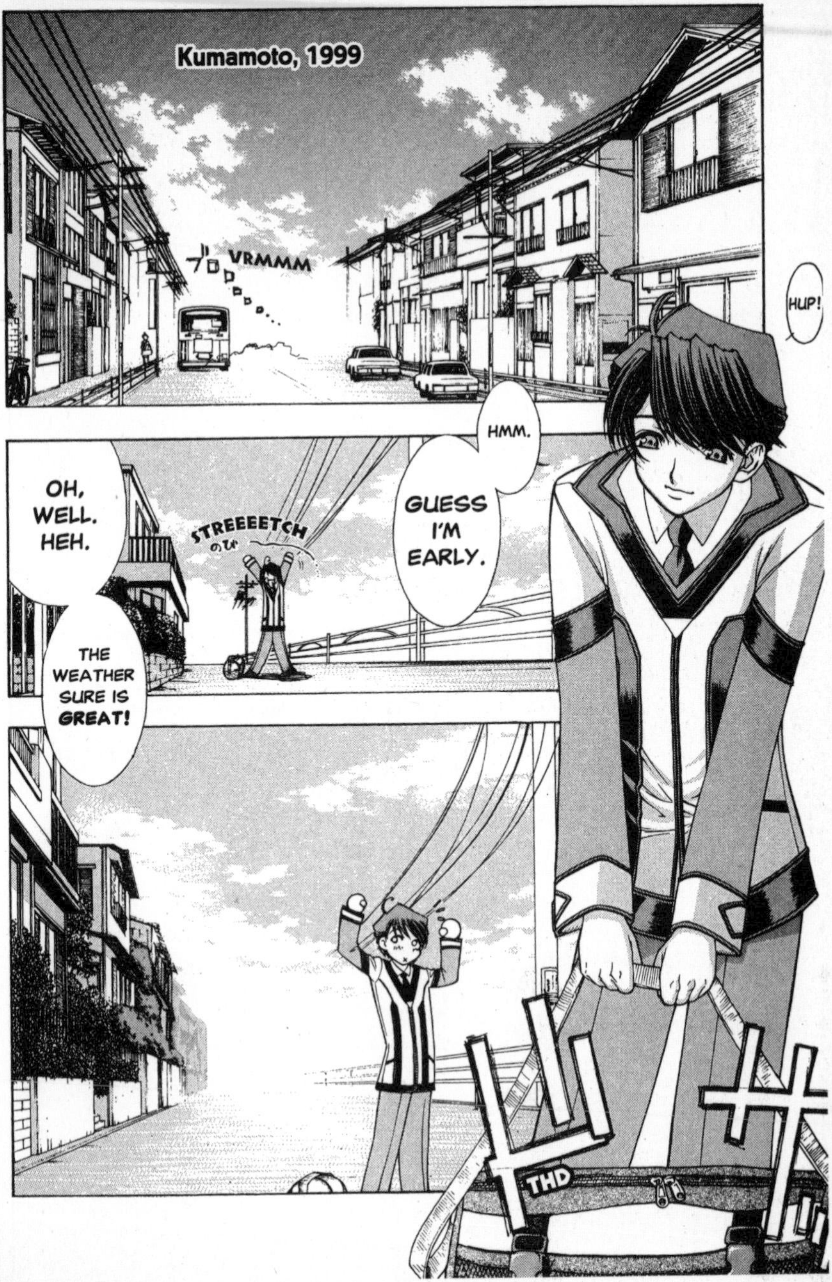
Kumamoto, 1999
ブロロロロ… VRMMM
HUP!
HMM.
GUESS I'M EARLY.
STREEEETCH のび
OH, WELL. HEH.
THE WEATHER SURE IS GREAT!
THD

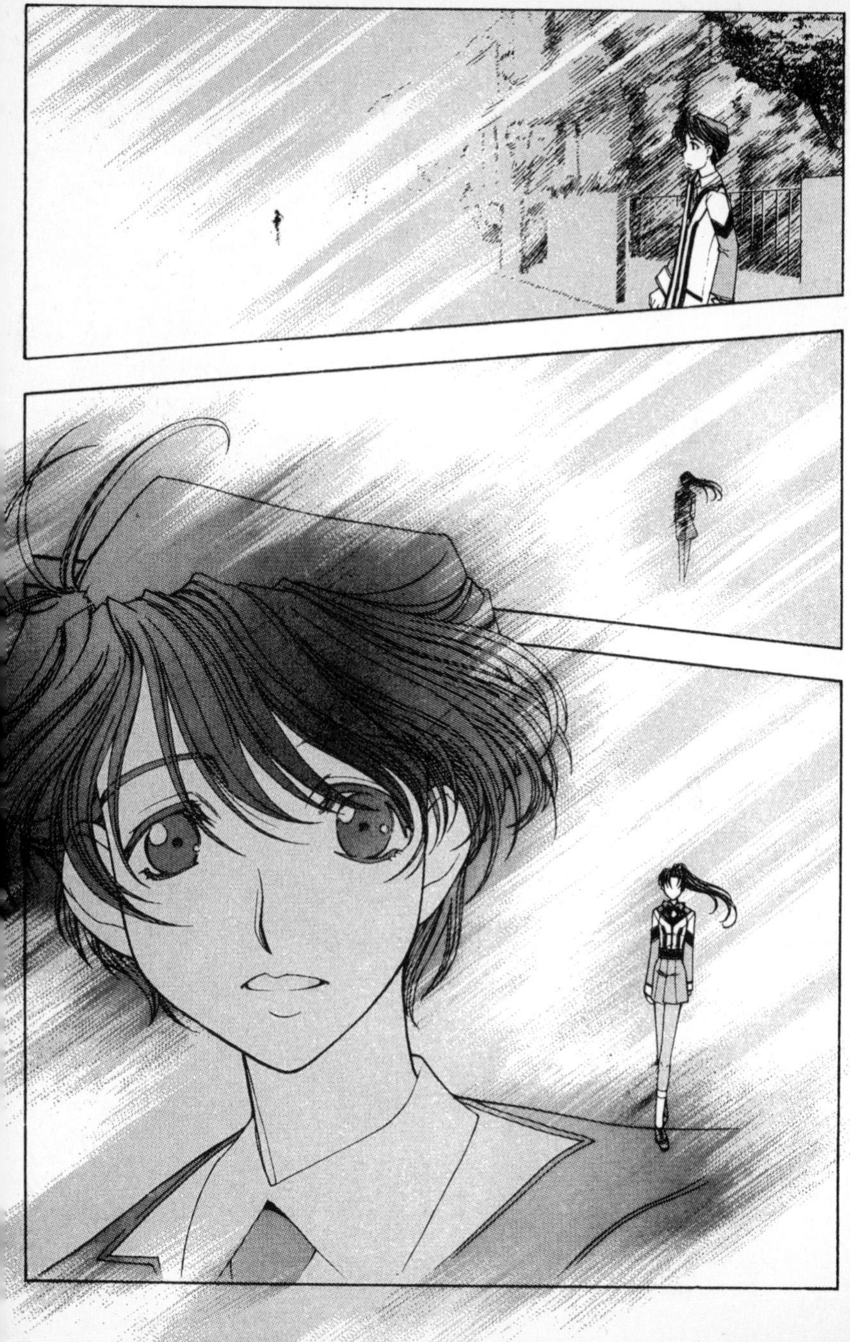

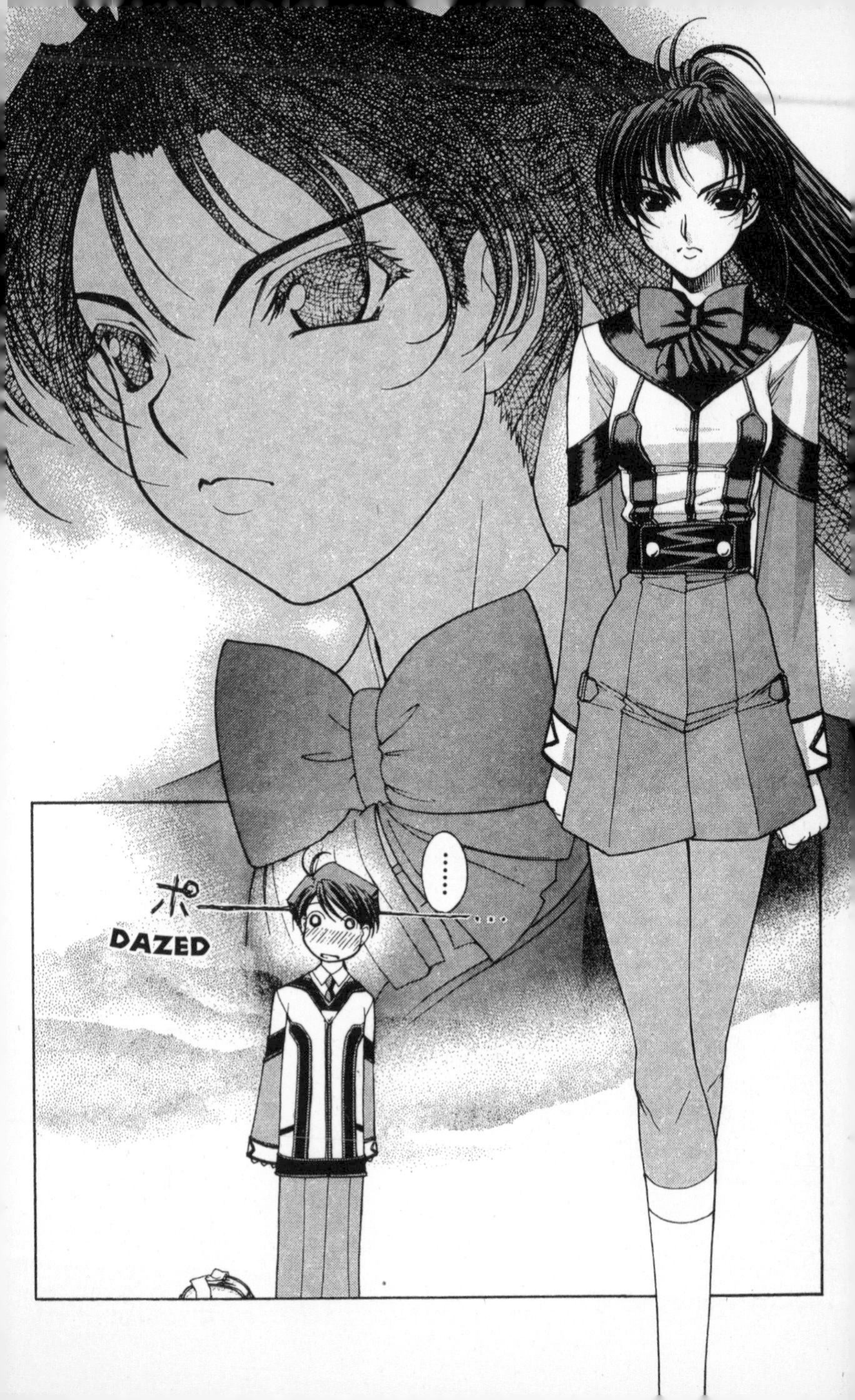

......
ポ
DAZED

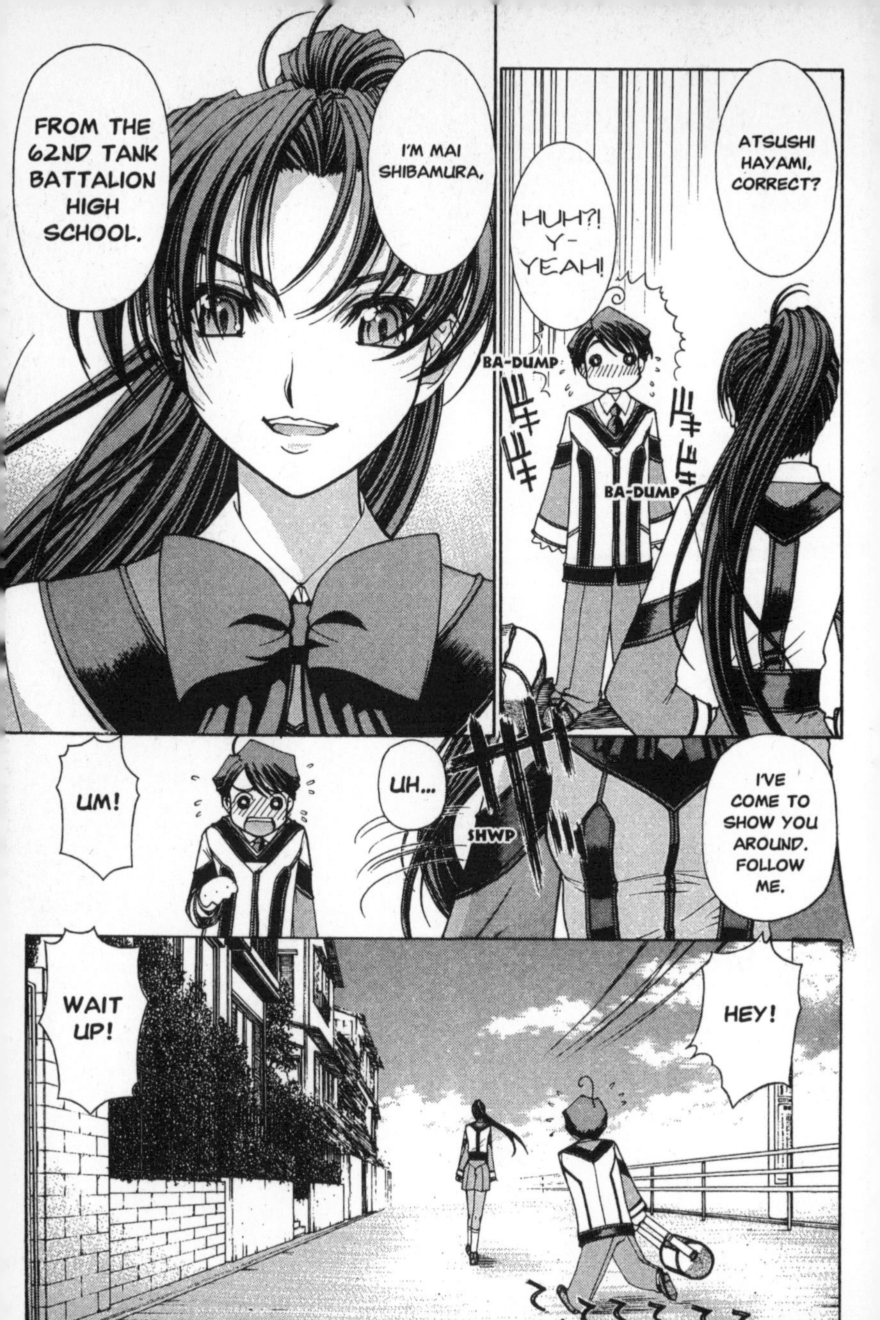
ATSUSHI HAYAMI, CORRECT?
HUH?! Y-YEAH!
BA-DUMP
BA-DUMP
I'M MAI SHIBAMURA,
FROM THE 62ND TANK BATTALION HIGH SCHOOL.
I'VE COME TO SHOW YOU AROUND. FOLLOW ME.
SHWP
UH...
UM!
HEY!
WAIT UP!
thp thp thp

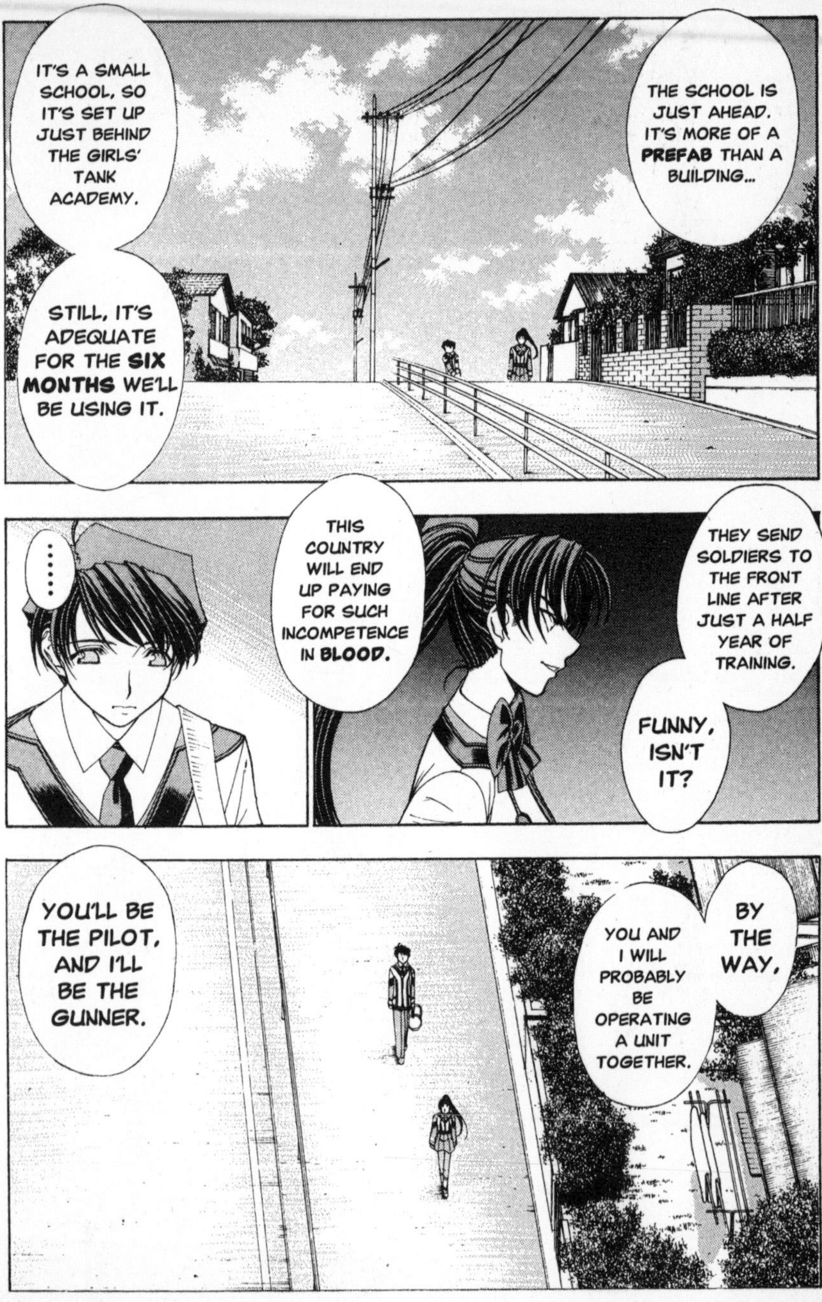
THE SCHOOL IS JUST AHEAD. IT'S MORE OF A PREFAB THAN A BUILDING...
IT'S A SMALL SCHOOL, SO IT'S SET UP JUST BEHIND THE GIRLS' TANK ACADEMY.
STILL, IT'S ADEQUATE FOR THE SIX MONTHS WE'LL BE USING IT.
THEY SEND SOLDIERS TO THE FRONT LINE AFTER JUST A HALF YEAR OF TRAINING.
FUNNY, ISN'T IT?
THIS COUNTRY WILL END UP PAYING FOR SUCH INCOMPETENCE IN BLOOD.
......
BY THE WAY,
YOU AND I WILL PROBABLY BE OPERATING A UNIT TOGETHER.
YOU'LL BE THE PILOT, AND I'LL BE THE GUNNER.

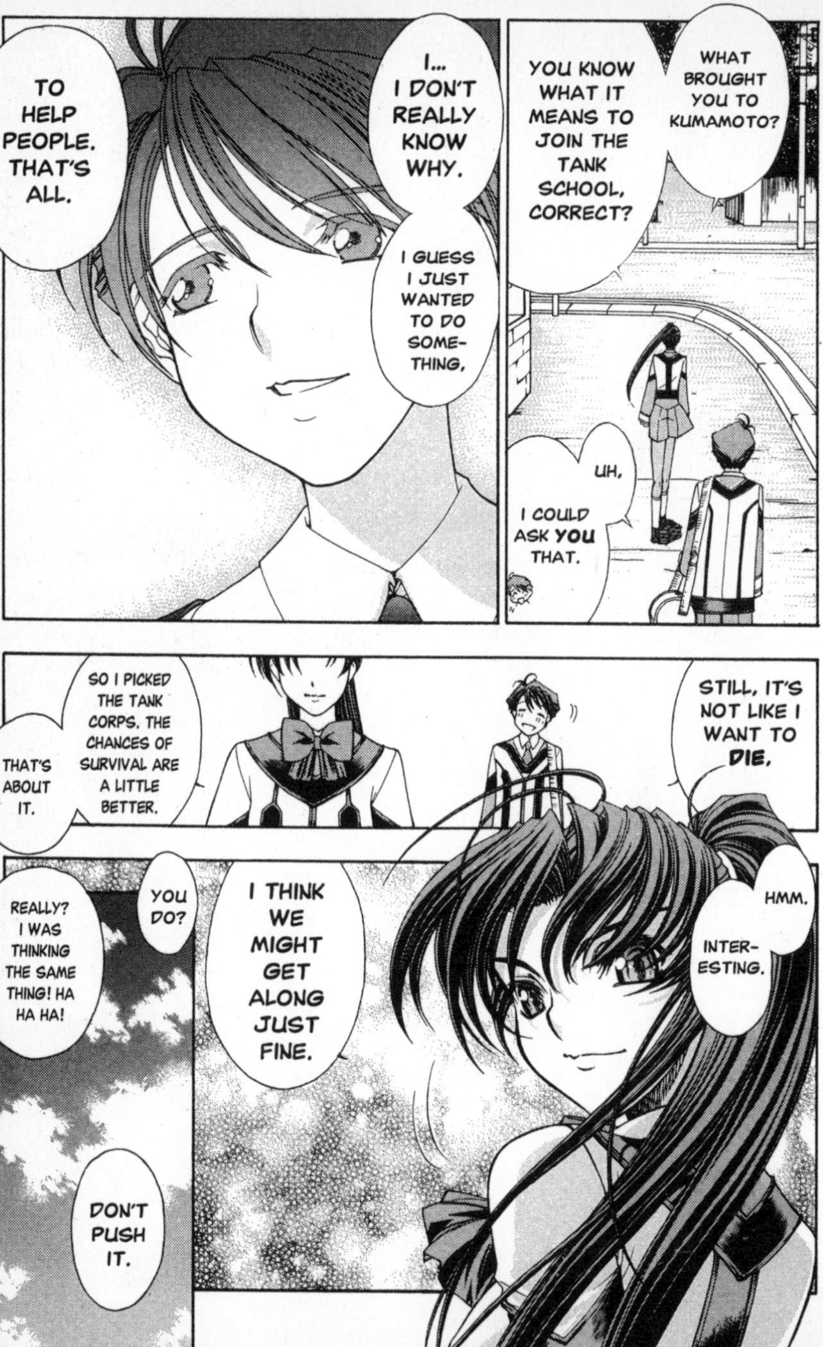
WHAT BROUGHT YOU TO KUMAMOTO?
YOU KNOW WHAT IT MEANS TO JOIN THE TANK SCHOOL, CORRECT?
UH,
I COULD ASK **YOU** THAT.
I... I DON'T REALLY KNOW WHY.
I GUESS I JUST WANTED TO DO SOME-THING,
TO HELP PEOPLE. THAT'S ALL.
STILL, IT'S NOT LIKE I WANT TO **DIE,**
SO I PICKED THE TANK CORPS. THE CHANCES OF SURVIVAL ARE A LITTLE BETTER.
THAT'S ABOUT IT.
HMM.
INTER-ESTING.
I THINK WE MIGHT GET ALONG JUST FINE.
YOU DO?
REALLY? I WAS THINKING THE SAME THING! HA HA HA!
DON'T PUSH IT.

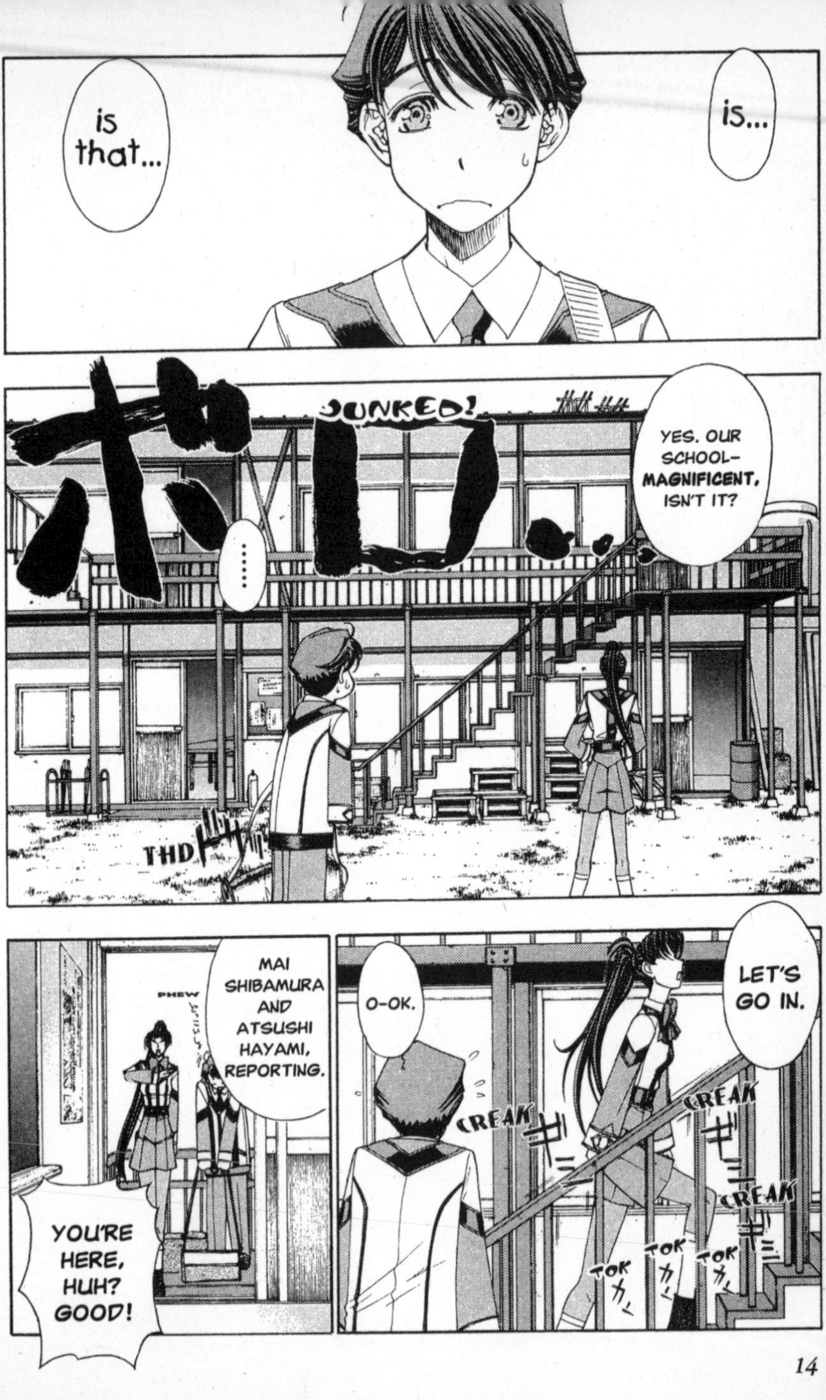
is...
is that...
ボロ
JUNKED!
YES. OUR SCHOOL—MAGNIFICENT, ISN'T IT?
......
THD
LET'S GO IN.
CREAK
CREAK
CREAK
O-OK.
TOK
TOK
TOK
MAI SHIBAMURA AND ATSUSHI HAYAMI, REPORTING.
PHEW
YOU'RE HERE, HUH? GOOD!

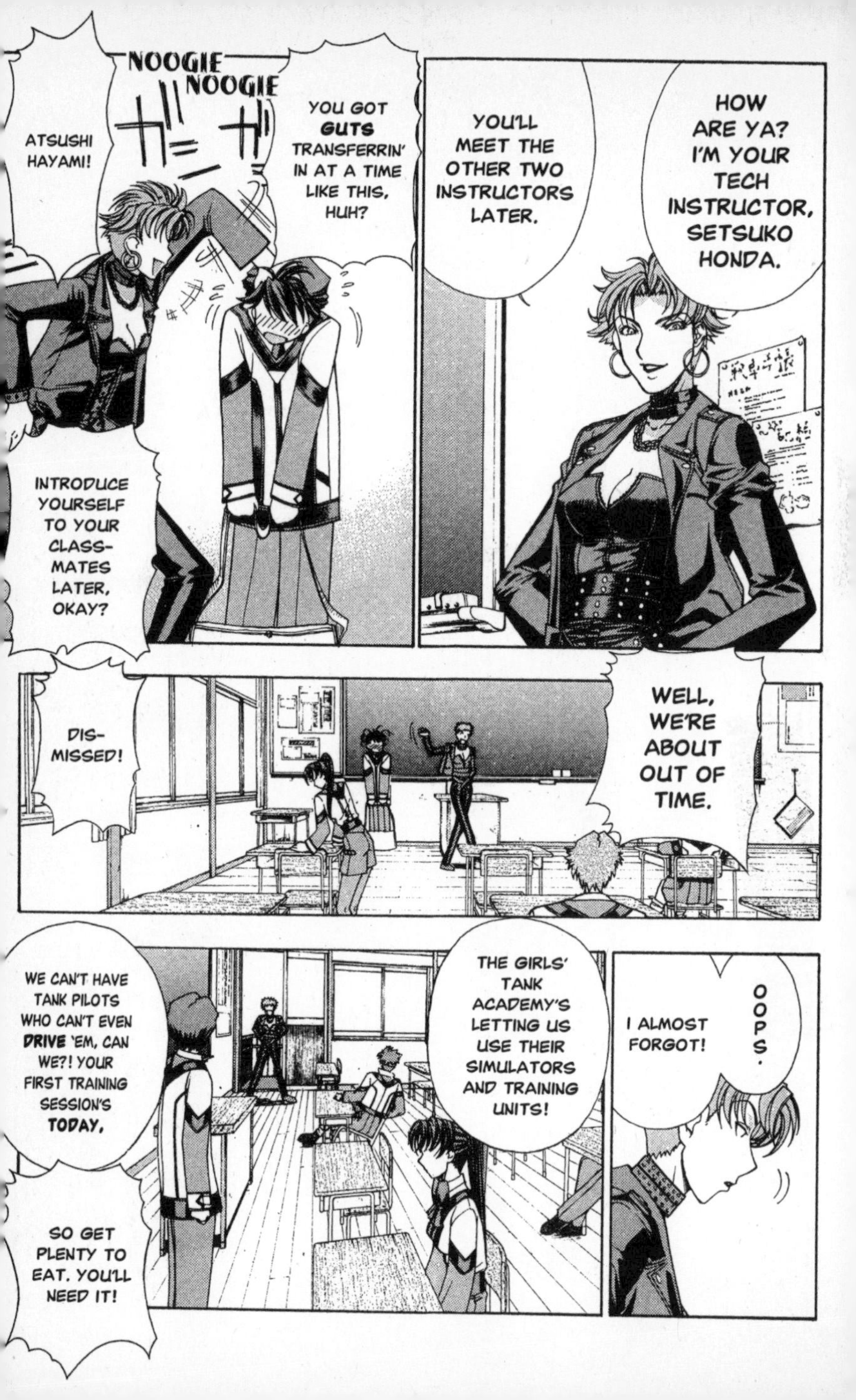
HOW ARE YA? I'M YOUR TECH INSTRUCTOR, SETSUKO HONDA.
YOU'LL MEET THE OTHER TWO INSTRUCTORS LATER.
ATSUSHI HAYAMI!
NOOGIE NOOGIE
YOU GOT **GUTS** TRANSFERRIN' IN AT A TIME LIKE THIS, HUH?
INTRODUCE YOURSELF TO YOUR CLASS-MATES LATER, OKAY?
WELL, WE'RE ABOUT OUT OF TIME.
DIS-MISSED!
OOPS.
I ALMOST FORGOT!
THE GIRLS' TANK ACADEMY'S LETTING US USE THEIR SIMULATORS AND TRAINING UNITS!
WE CAN'T HAVE TANK PILOTS WHO CAN'T EVEN **DRIVE** 'EM, CAN WE?! YOUR FIRST TRAINING SESSION'S **TODAY**,
SO GET PLENTY TO EAT. YOU'LL NEED IT!

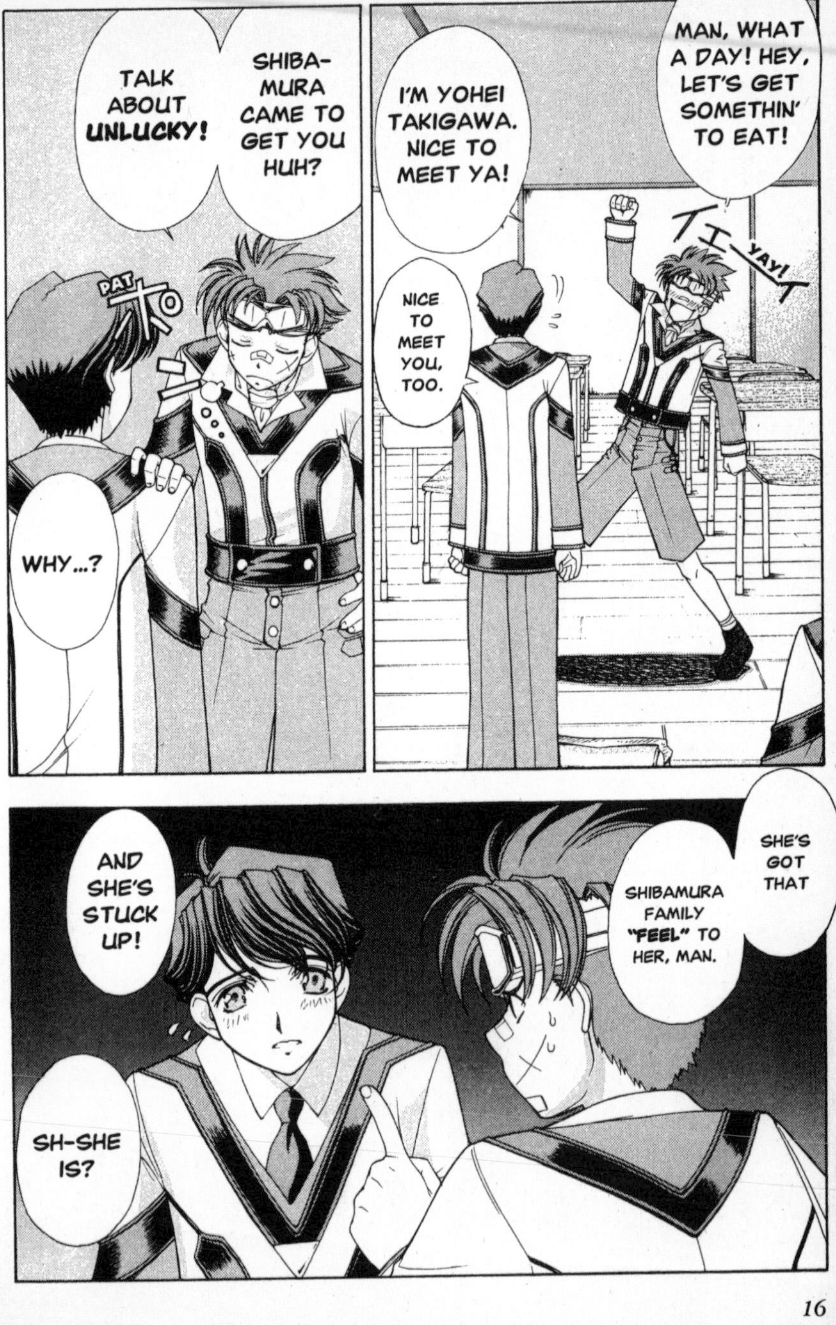
MAN, WHAT A DAY! HEY, LET'S GET SOMETHIN' TO EAT!
YAY!
I'M YOHEI TAKIGAWA. NICE TO MEET YA!
NICE TO MEET YOU, TOO.
SHIBA-MURA CAME TO GET YOU HUH?
TALK ABOUT UNLUCKY!
PAT
WHY...?
SHE'S GOT THAT
SHIBAMURA FAMILY "FEEL" TO HER, MAN.
AND SHE'S STUCK UP!
SH-SHE IS?

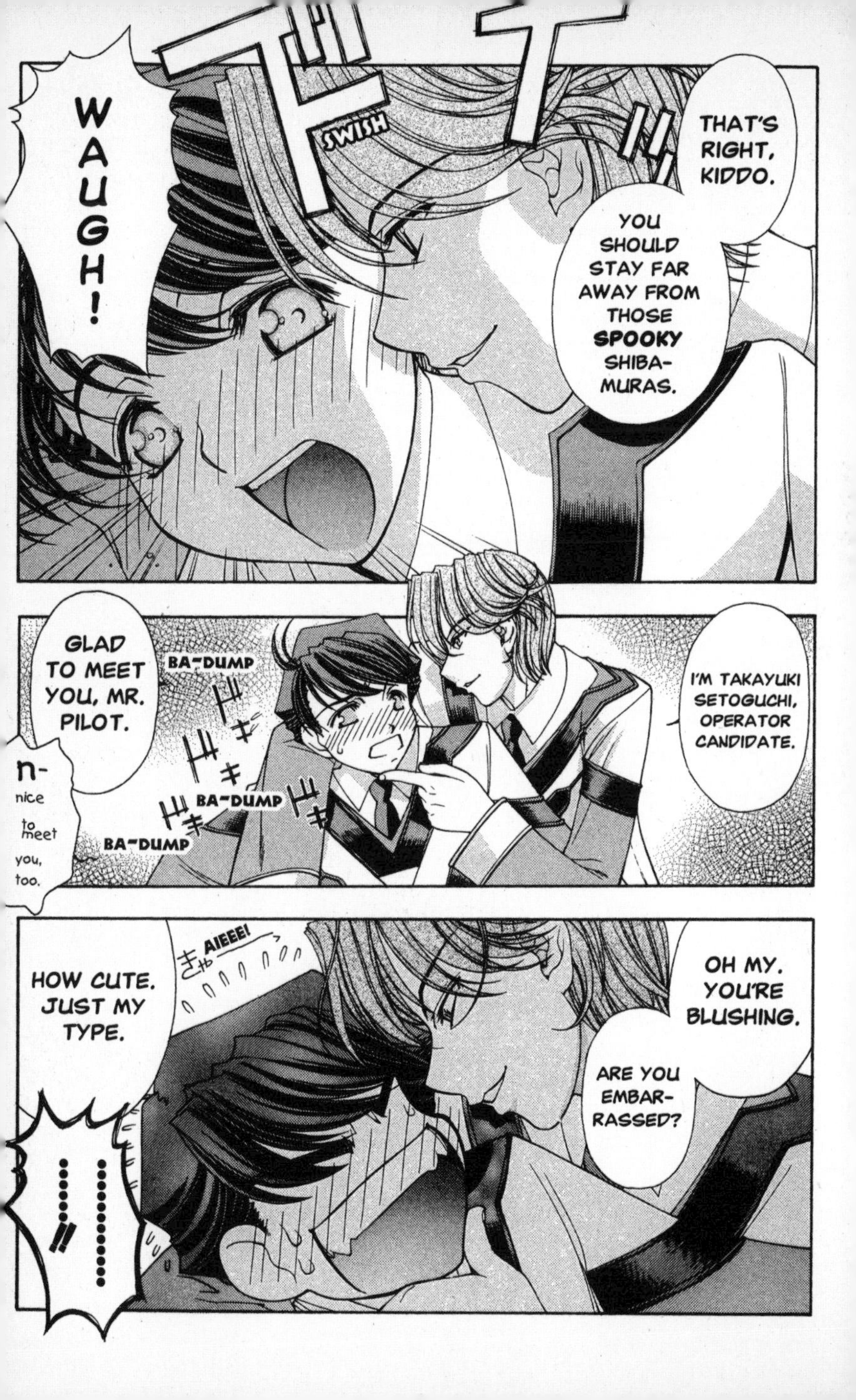
SWISH
THAT'S RIGHT, KIDDO.
YOU SHOULD STAY FAR AWAY FROM THOSE SPOOKY SHIBA-MURAS.
WAUGH!
I'M TAKAYUKI SETOGUCHI, OPERATOR CANDIDATE.
GLAD TO MEET YOU, MR. PILOT.
BA-DUMP
BA-DUMP
BA-DUMP
n- nice to meet you, too.
OH MY. YOU'RE BLUSHING.
ARE YOU EMBAR-RASSED?
AIEEE!
HOW CUTE. JUST MY TYPE.
..........!!

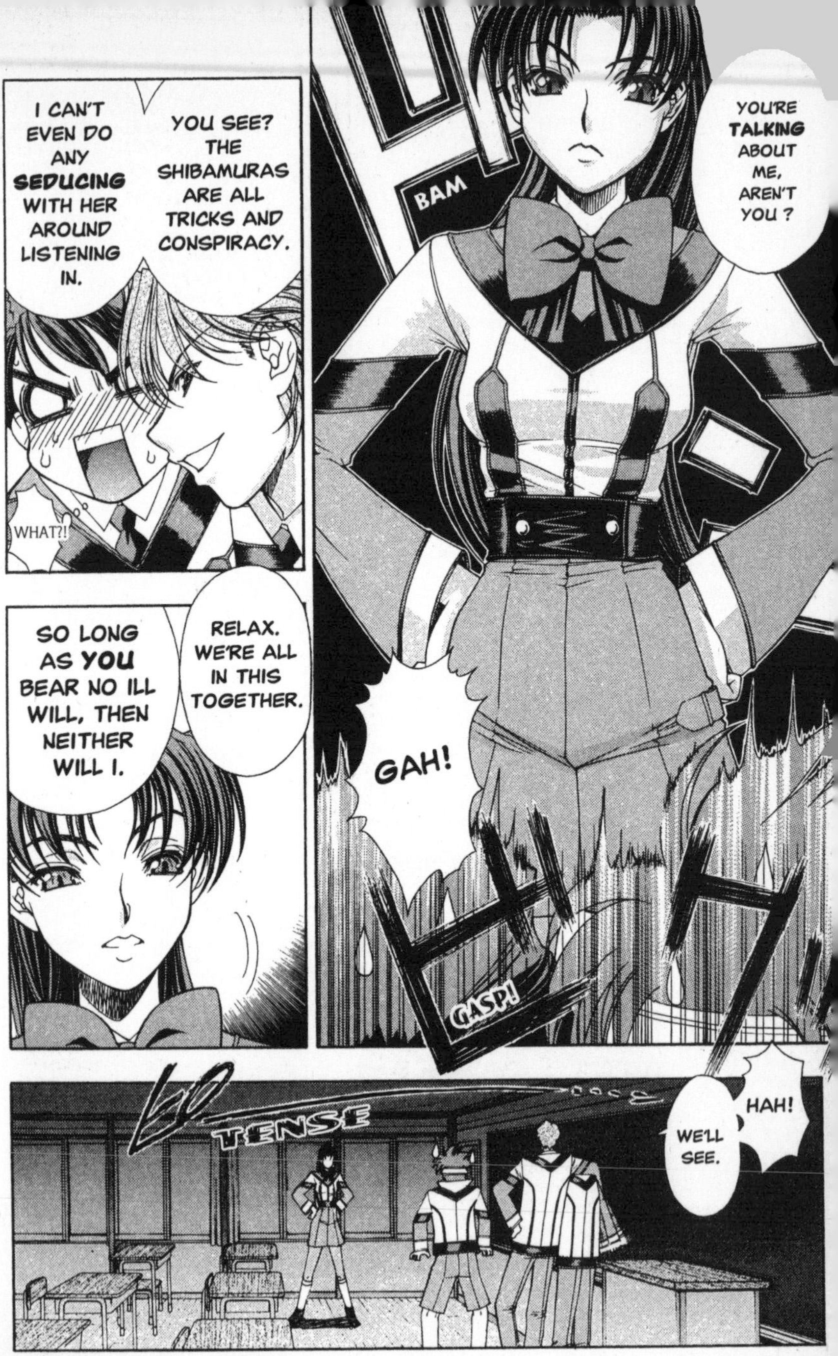
YOU SEE? THE SHIBAMURAS ARE ALL TRICKS AND CONSPIRACY.
I CAN'T EVEN DO ANY SEDUCING WITH HER AROUND LISTENING IN.
WHAT?!
BAM
YOU'RE TALKING ABOUT ME, AREN'T YOU ?
GAH!
GASP!
RELAX. WE'RE ALL IN THIS TOGETHER.
SO LONG AS YOU BEAR NO ILL WILL, THEN NEITHER WILL I.
TENSE
HAH!
WE'LL SEE.

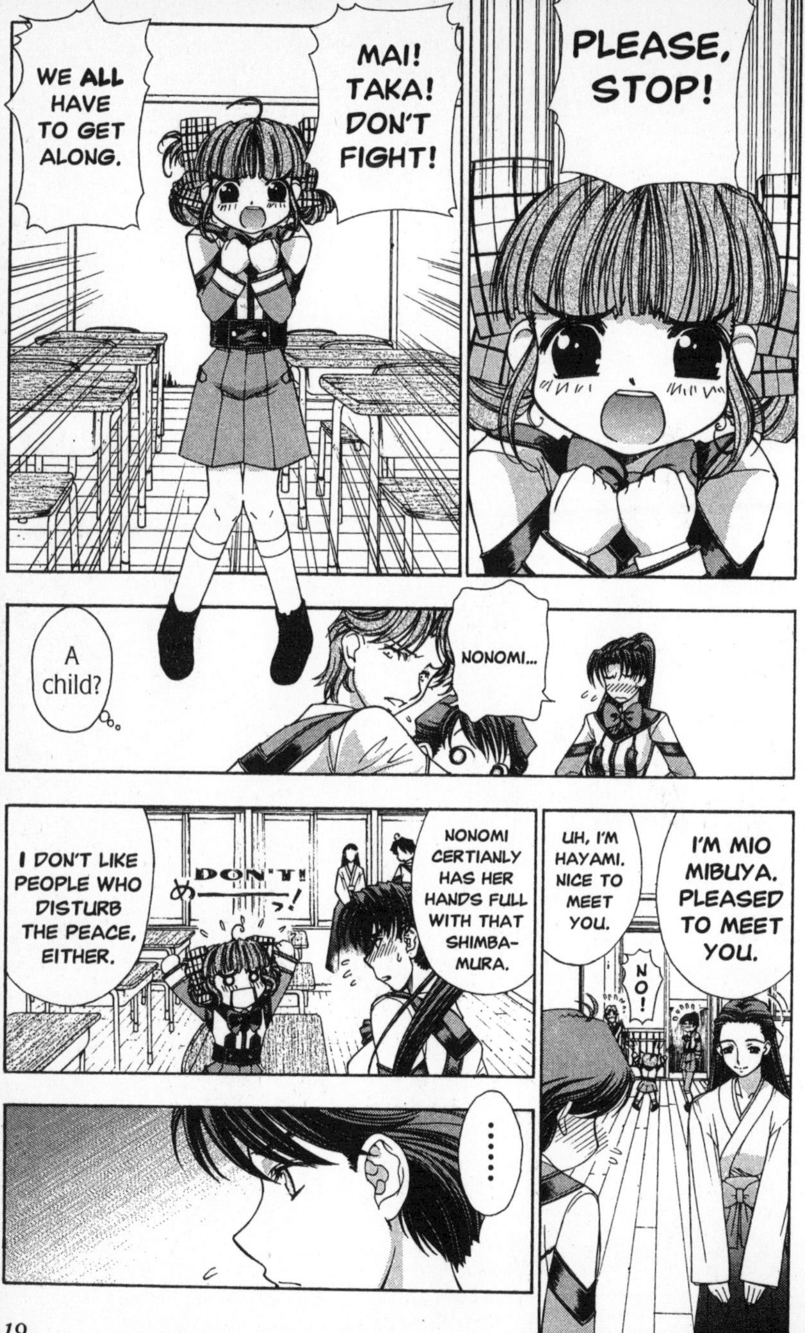
MAI! TAKA! DON'T FIGHT!
WE ALL HAVE TO GET ALONG.
PLEASE, STOP!
A child?
NONOMI...
I DON'T LIKE PEOPLE WHO DISTURB THE PEACE, EITHER.
DON'T!
NONOMI CERTIANLY HAS HER HANDS FULL WITH THAT SHIMBA-MURA.
I'M MIO MIBUYA. PLEASED TO MEET YOU.
UH, I'M HAYAMI. NICE TO MEET YOU.
NO!
......

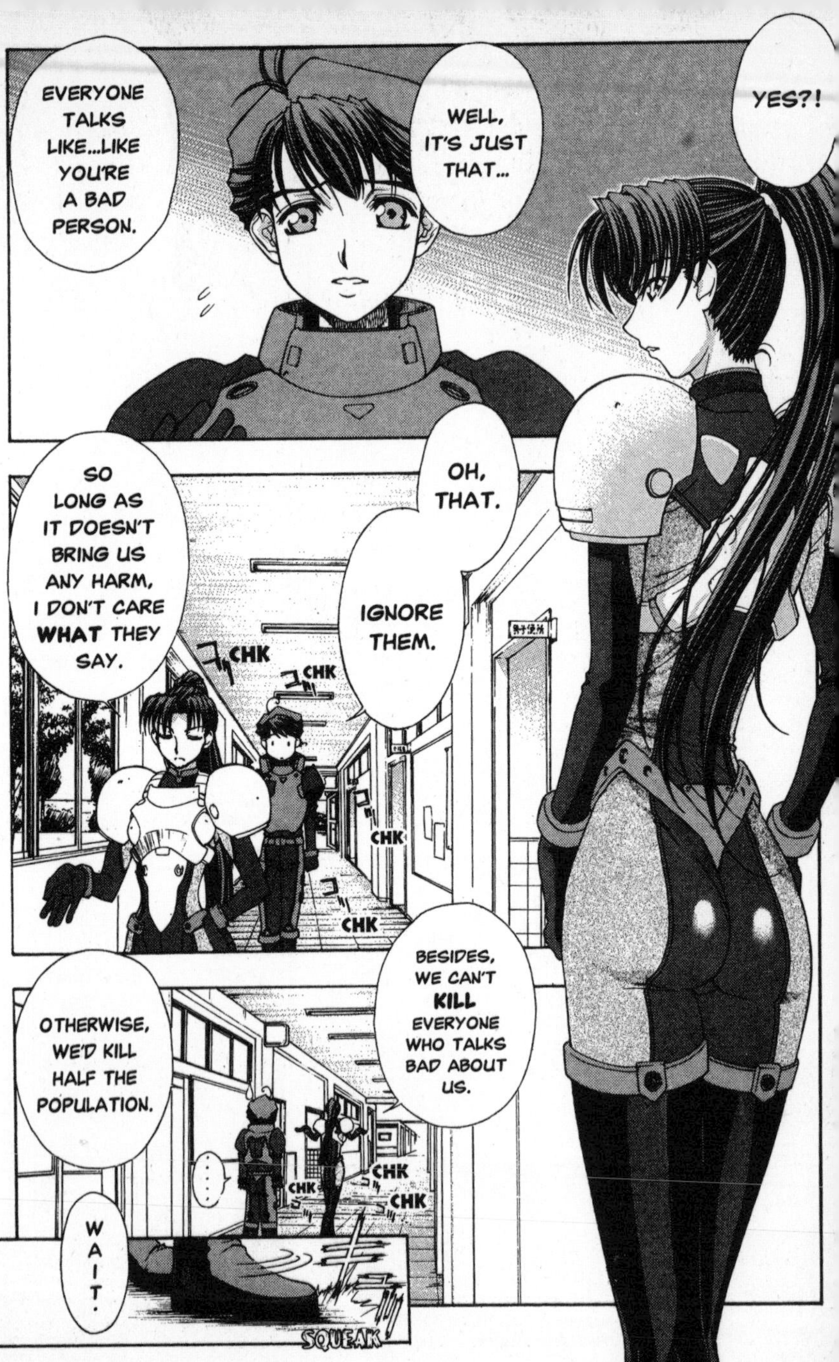
YES?!
WELL, IT'S JUST THAT...
EVERYONE TALKS LIKE...LIKE YOU'RE A BAD PERSON.
OH, THAT.
IGNORE THEM.
SO LONG AS IT DOESN'T BRING US ANY HARM, I DON'T CARE **WHAT** THEY SAY.
CHK
CHK
CHK
CHK
BESIDES, WE CAN'T **KILL** EVERYONE WHO TALKS BAD ABOUT US.
OTHERWISE, WE'D KILL HALF THE POPULATION.
.....
CHK
CHK
CHK
WAIT.
SQUEAK

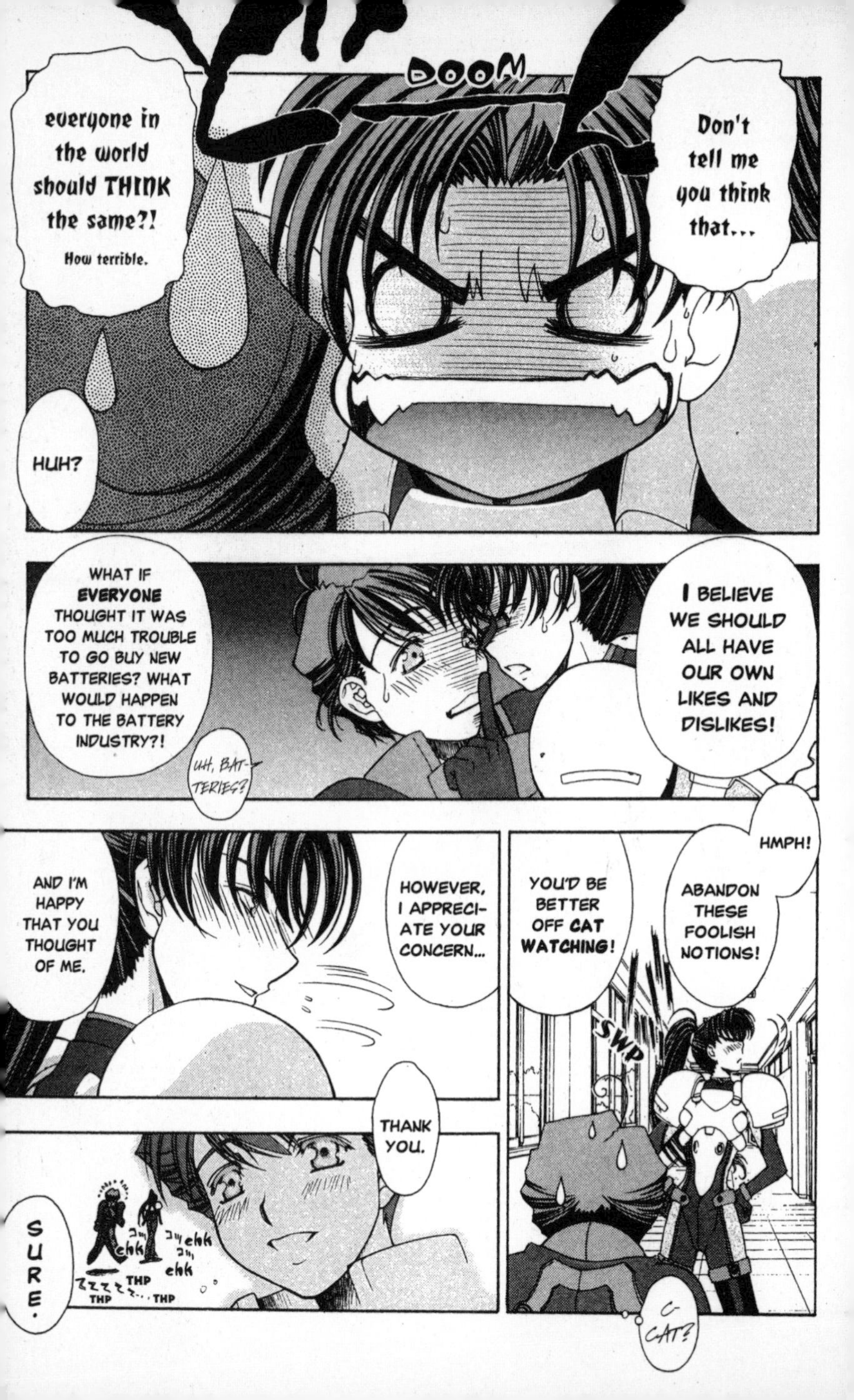

DOOM
Don't tell me you think that...
everyone in the world should THINK the same?!
How terrible.
HUH?
I BELIEVE WE SHOULD ALL HAVE OUR OWN LIKES AND DISLIKES!
WHAT IF EVERYONE THOUGHT IT WAS TOO MUCH TROUBLE TO GO BUY NEW BATTERIES? WHAT WOULD HAPPEN TO THE BATTERY INDUSTRY?!
UH, BATTERIES?
HMPH!
ABANDON THESE FOOLISH NOTIONS!
YOU'D BE BETTER OFF CAT WATCHING!
SWP
C-CAT?
HOWEVER, I APPRECIATE YOUR CONCERN...
AND I'M HAPPY THAT YOU THOUGHT OF ME.
THANK YOU.
SURE.
ehk
ehk
ehk
THP
THP
THP

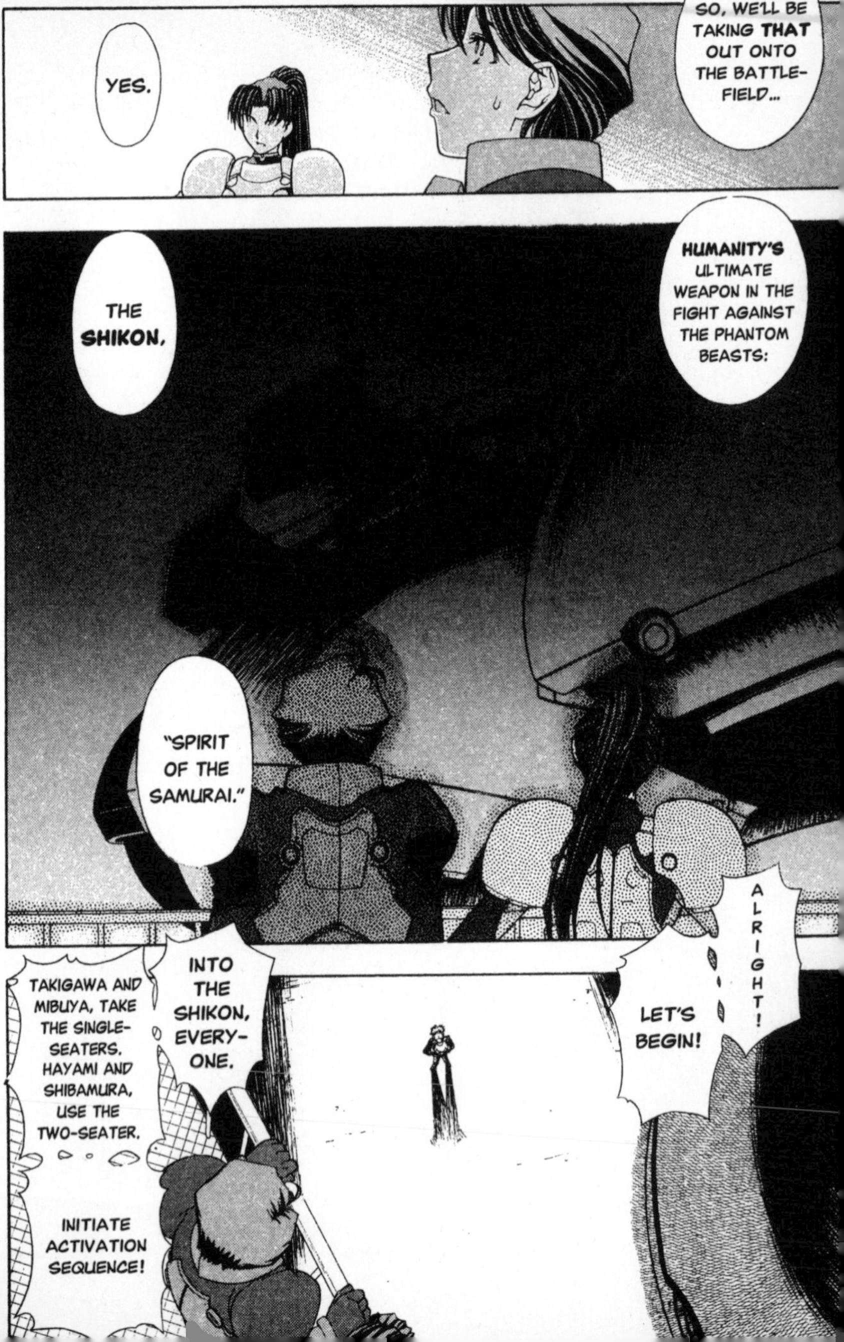
SO, WE'LL BE TAKING THAT OUT ONTO THE BATTLE-FIELD...
YES.
HUMANITY'S ULTIMATE WEAPON IN THE FIGHT AGAINST THE PHANTOM BEASTS:
THE SHIKON,
"SPIRIT OF THE SAMURAI."
ALRIGHT!
LET'S BEGIN!
INTO THE SHIKON, EVERY-ONE.
TAKIGAWA AND MIBUYA, TAKE THE SINGLE-SEATERS. HAYAMI AND SHIBAMURA, USE THE TWO-SEATER.
INITIATE ACTIVATION SEQUENCE!

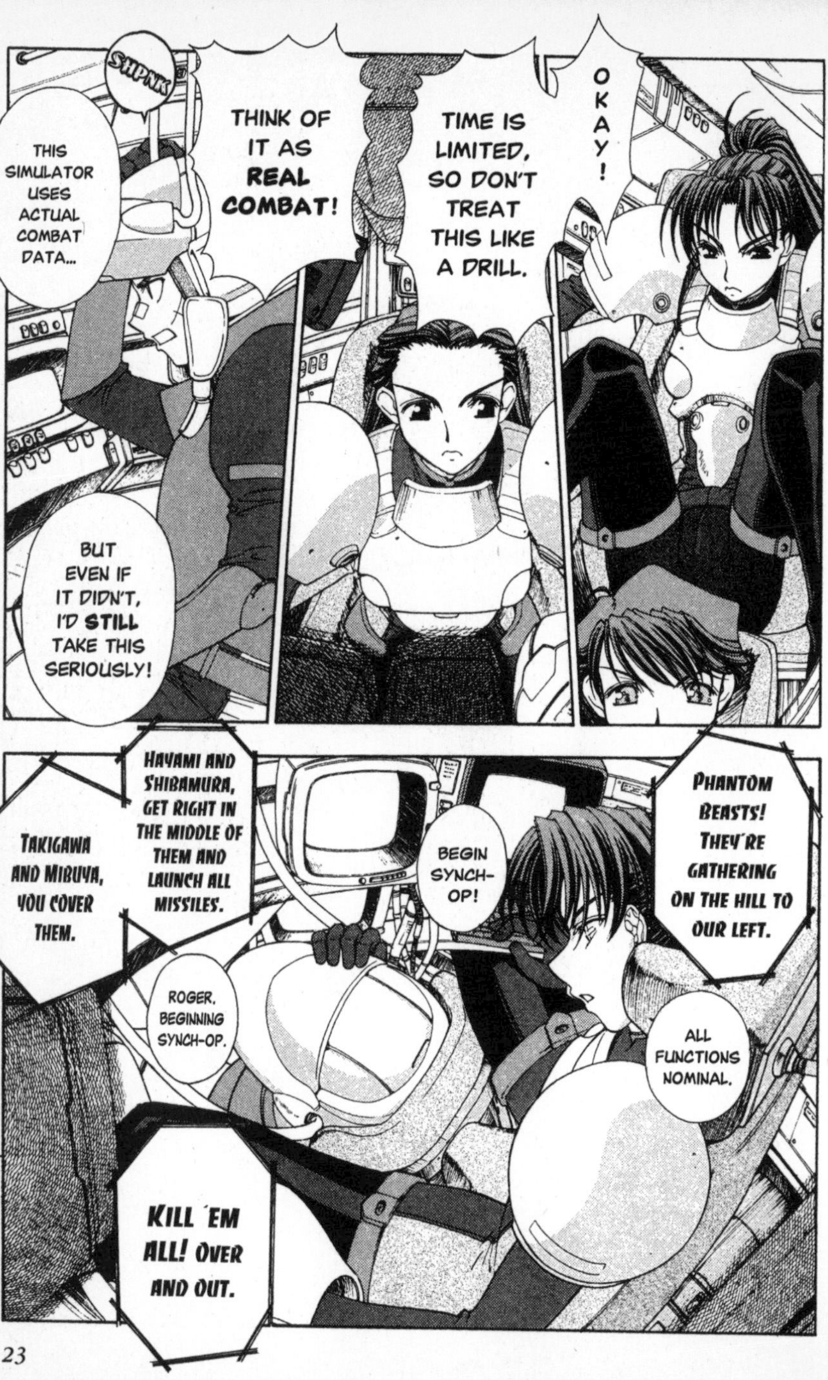
OKAY!
TIME IS LIMITED, SO DON'T TREAT THIS LIKE A DRILL.
THINK OF IT AS REAL COMBAT!
SHPNK
THIS SIMULATOR USES ACTUAL COMBAT DATA...
BUT EVEN IF IT DIDN'T, I'D STILL TAKE THIS SERIOUSLY!
PHANTOM BEASTS! THEY'RE GATHERING ON THE HILL TO OUR LEFT.
BEGIN SYNCH-OP!
HAYAMI AND SHIBAMURA, GET RIGHT IN THE MIDDLE OF THEM AND LAUNCH ALL MISSILES.
TAKIGAWA AND MIBUYA, YOU COVER THEM.
ALL FUNCTIONS NOMINAL.
ROGER. BEGINNING SYNCH-OP.
KILL 'EM ALL! OVER AND OUT.

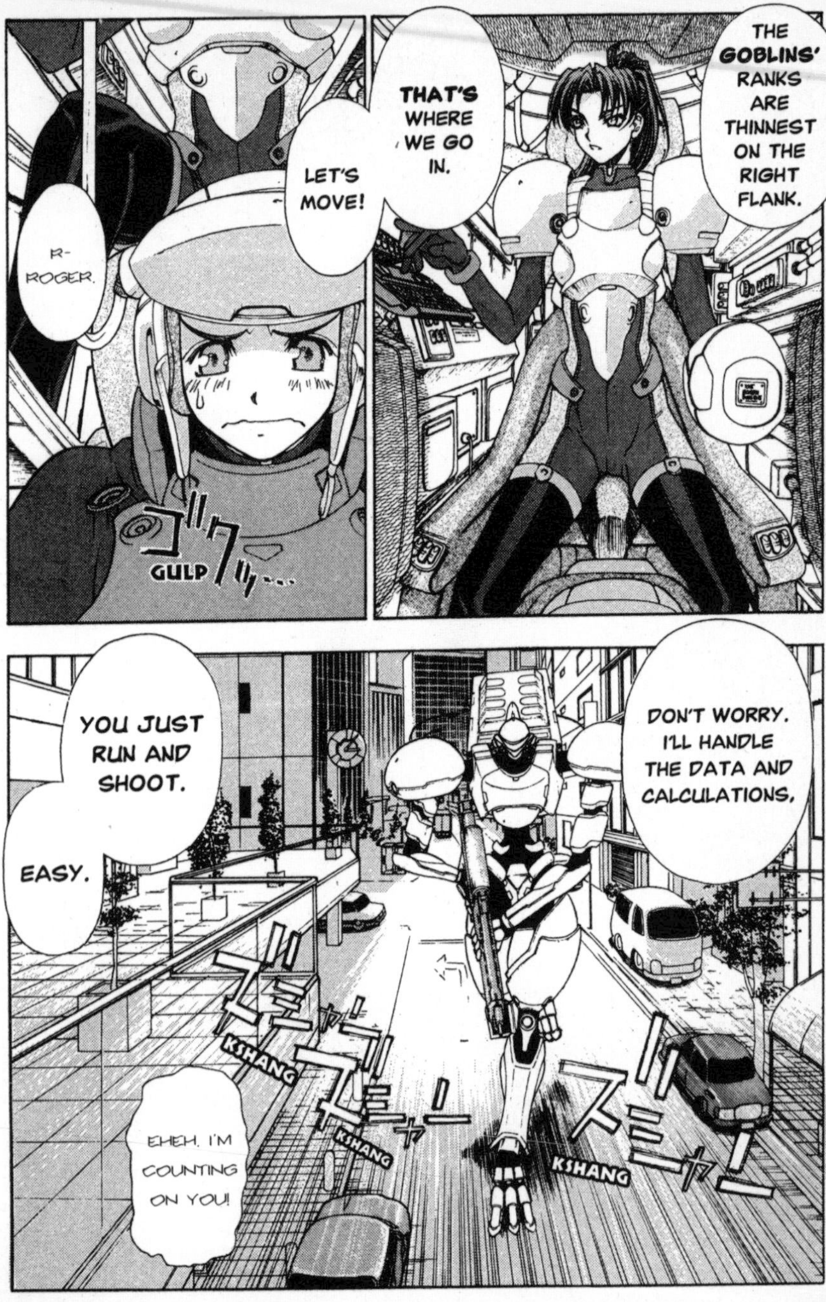
THE GOBLINS' RANKS ARE THINNEST ON THE RIGHT FLANK.
THAT'S WHERE WE GO IN.
LET'S MOVE!
R-ROGER.
GULP
DON'T WORRY. I'LL HANDLE THE DATA AND CALCULATIONS,
YOU JUST RUN AND SHOOT.
EASY.
KSHANG
KSHANG
KSHANG
EHEH, I'M COUNTING ON YOU!

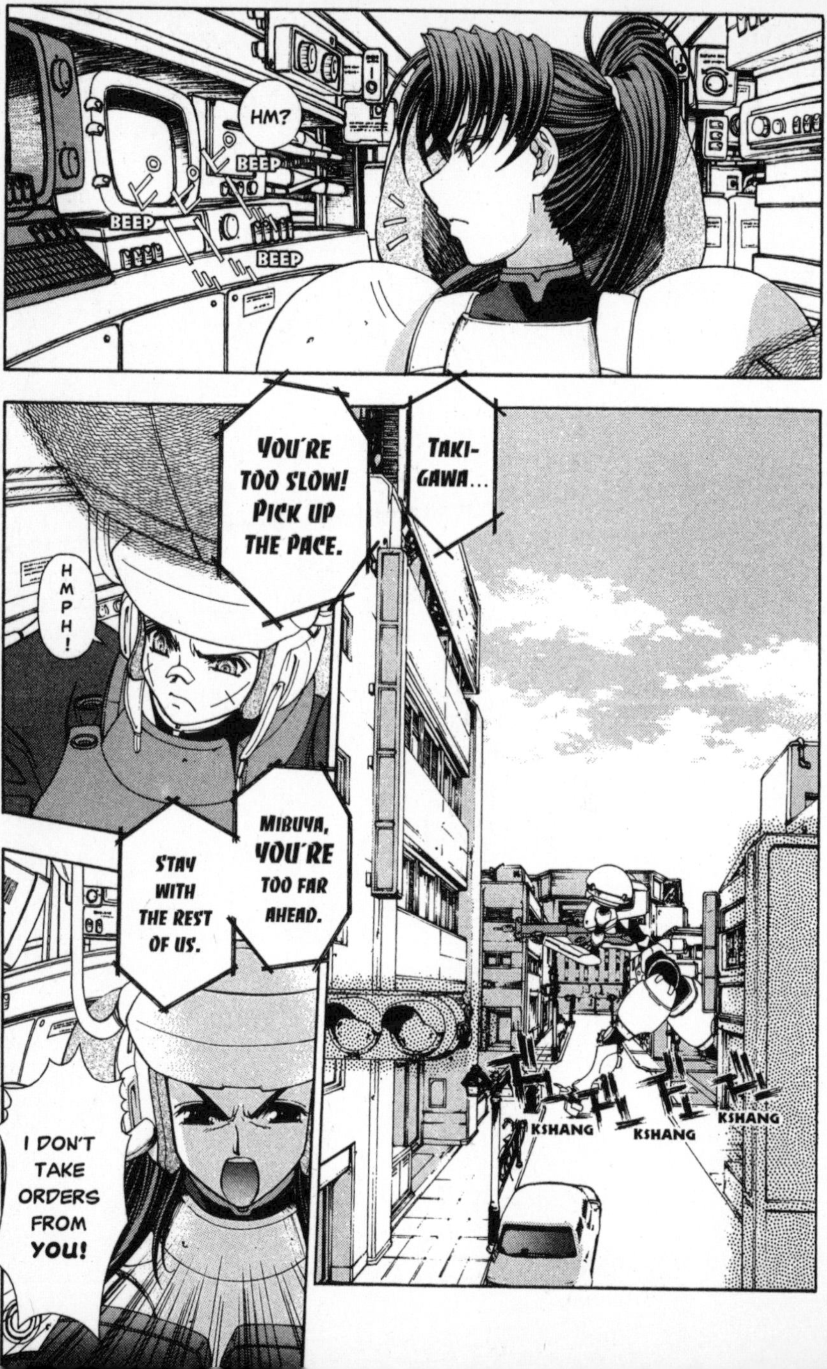
HM?
BEEP
BEEP
BEEP
TAKI-GAWA...
YOU'RE TOO SLOW! PICK UP THE PACE.
HMPH!
MIBUYA, YOU'RE TOO FAR AHEAD.
STAY WITH THE REST OF US.
KSHANG
KSHANG
KSHANG
I DON'T TAKE ORDERS FROM YOU!

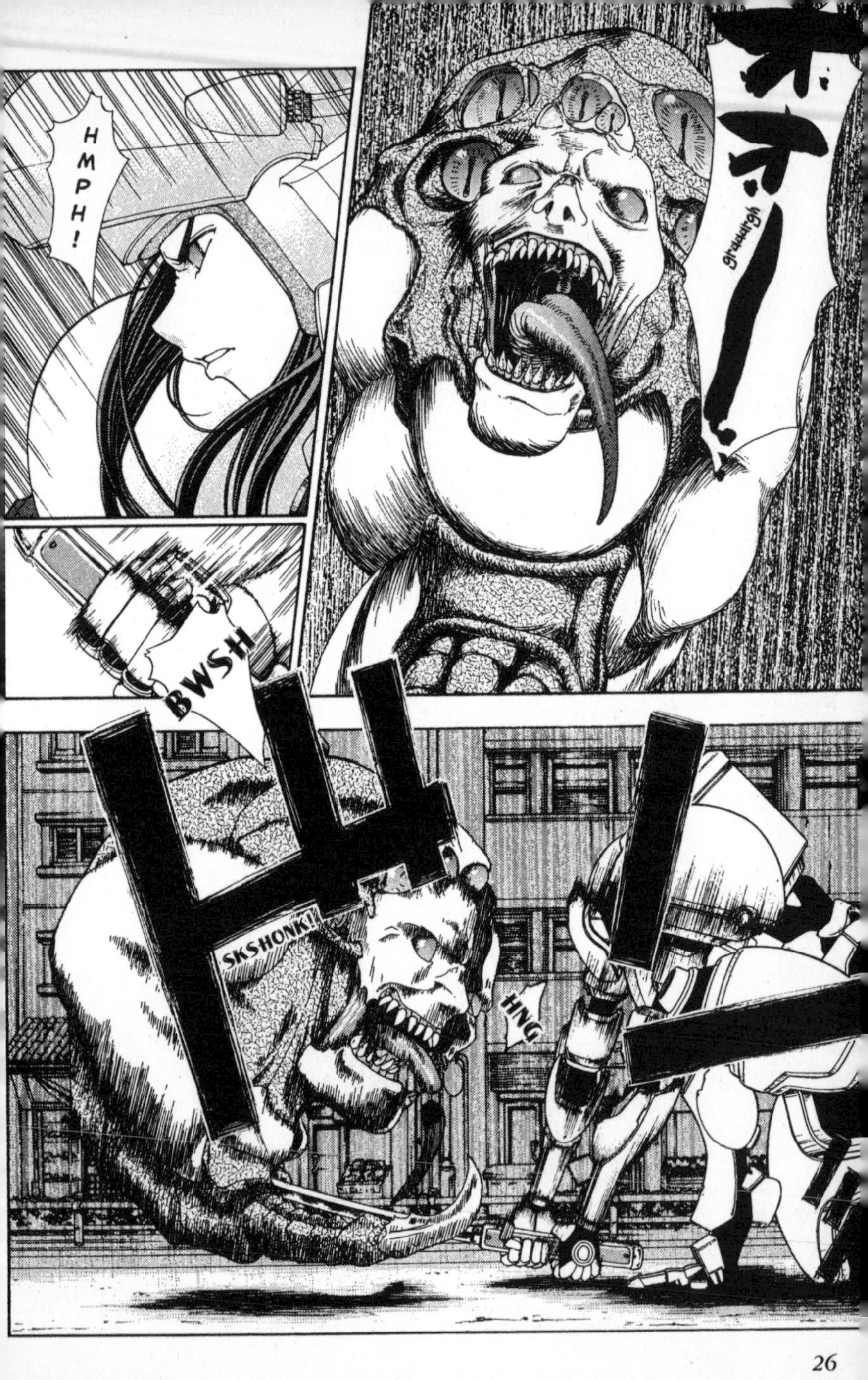
graaaargh
HMPH!
BWSH
SKSHONK!
HNG

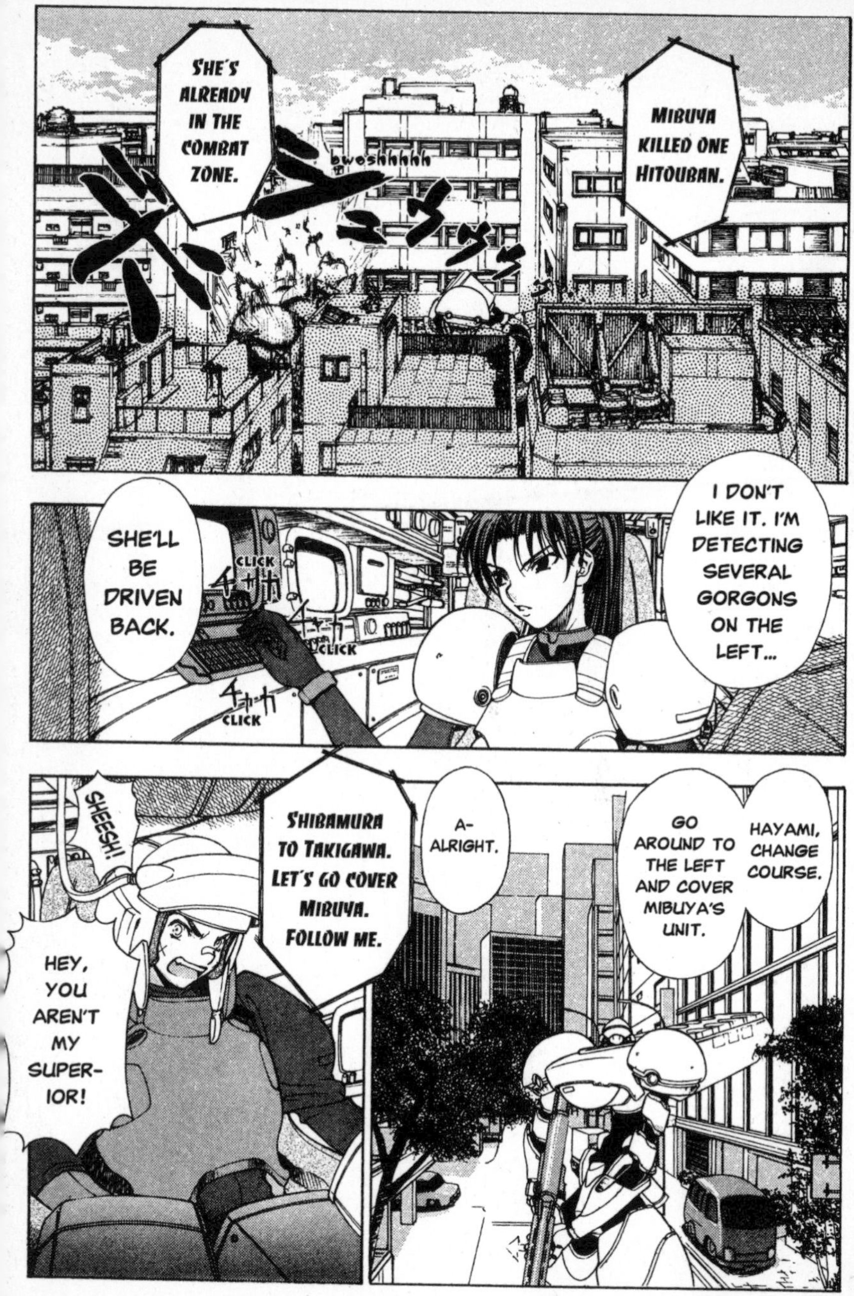
Mibuya killed one Hitouban.
bwoshhhhh
She's already in the combat zone.
I DON'T LIKE IT. I'M DETECTING SEVERAL GORGONS ON THE LEFT...
CLICK
CLICK
CLICK
SHE'LL BE DRIVEN BACK.
HAYAMI, CHANGE COURSE.
GO AROUND TO THE LEFT AND COVER MIBUYA'S UNIT.
A- ALRIGHT.
Shibamura to Takigawa. Let's go cover Mibuya. Follow me.
SHEESH!
HEY, YOU AREN'T MY SUPER- IOR!

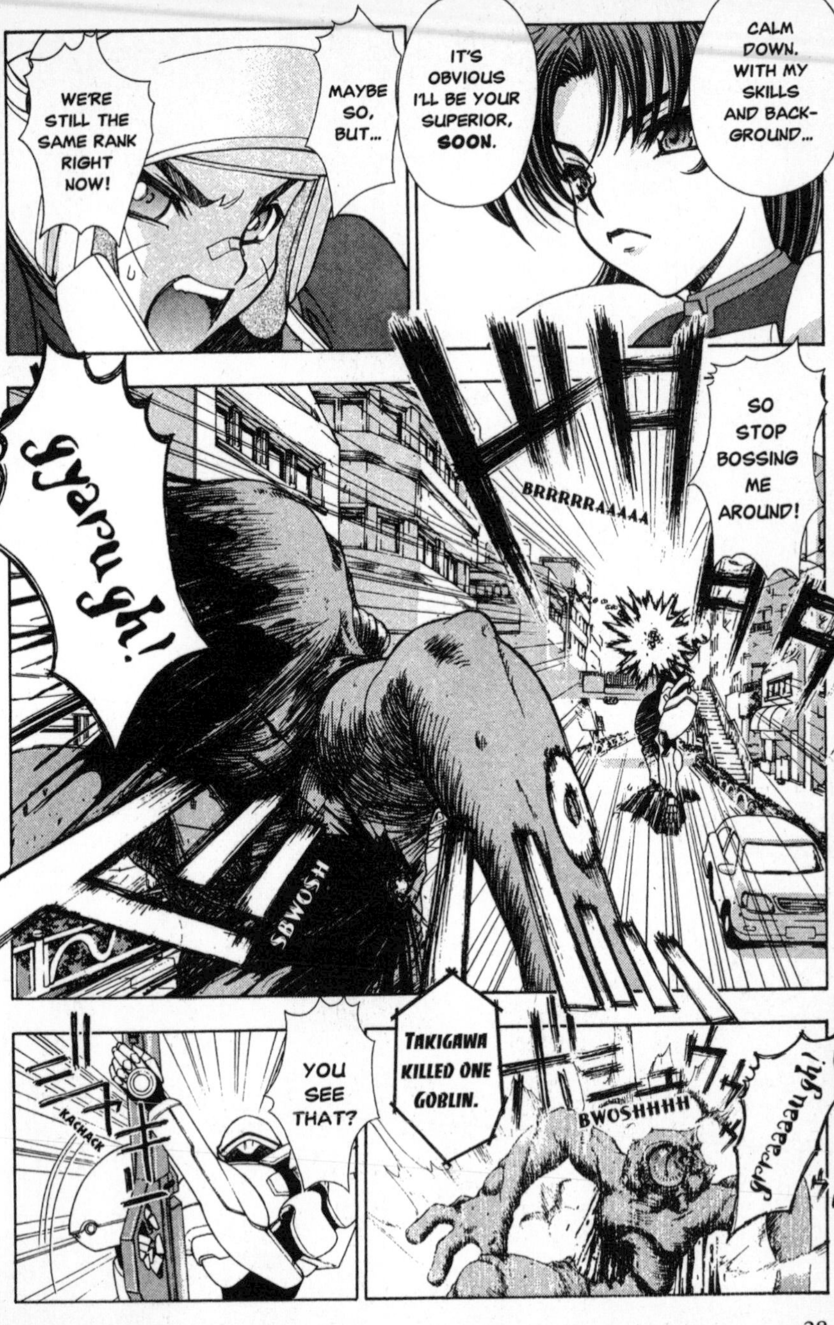

CALM DOWN. WITH MY SKILLS AND BACK-GROUND...
IT'S OBVIOUS I'LL BE YOUR SUPERIOR, SOON.
MAYBE SO, BUT...
WE'RE STILL THE SAME RANK RIGHT NOW!
SO STOP BOSSING ME AROUND!
BRRRRRAAAAA
gyarugh!
SBWOSH
gyaeeeaugh!
BWOSHHHH
TAKIGAWA KILLED ONE GOBLIN.
YOU SEE THAT?
KACHACK

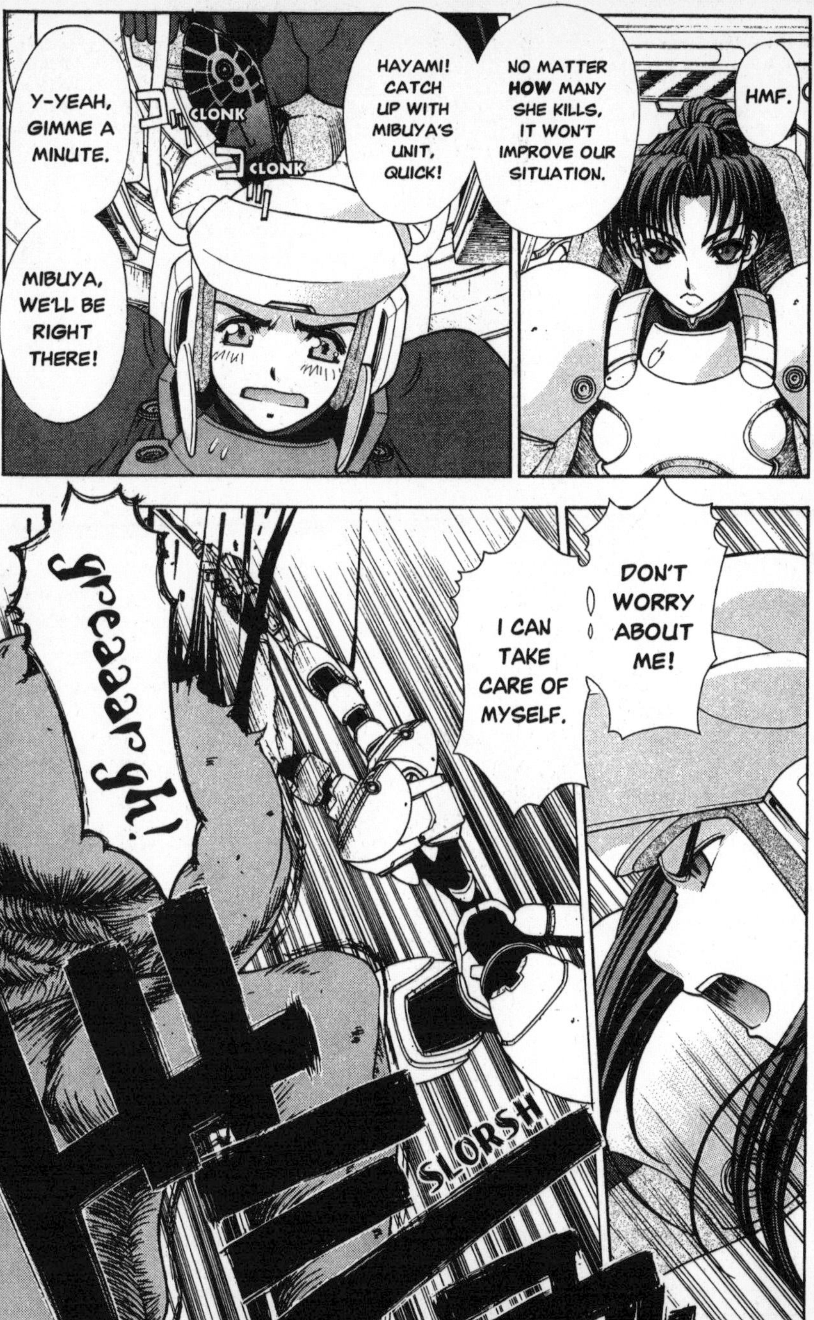
HMF.
NO MATTER HOW MANY SHE KILLS, IT WON'T IMPROVE OUR SITUATION.
HAYAMI! CATCH UP WITH MIBUYA'S UNIT, QUICK!
CLONK
CLONK
Y-YEAH, GIMME A MINUTE.
MIBUYA, WE'LL BE RIGHT THERE!
DON'T WORRY ABOUT ME!
I CAN TAKE CARE OF MYSELF.
greaaargh!
SLORSH

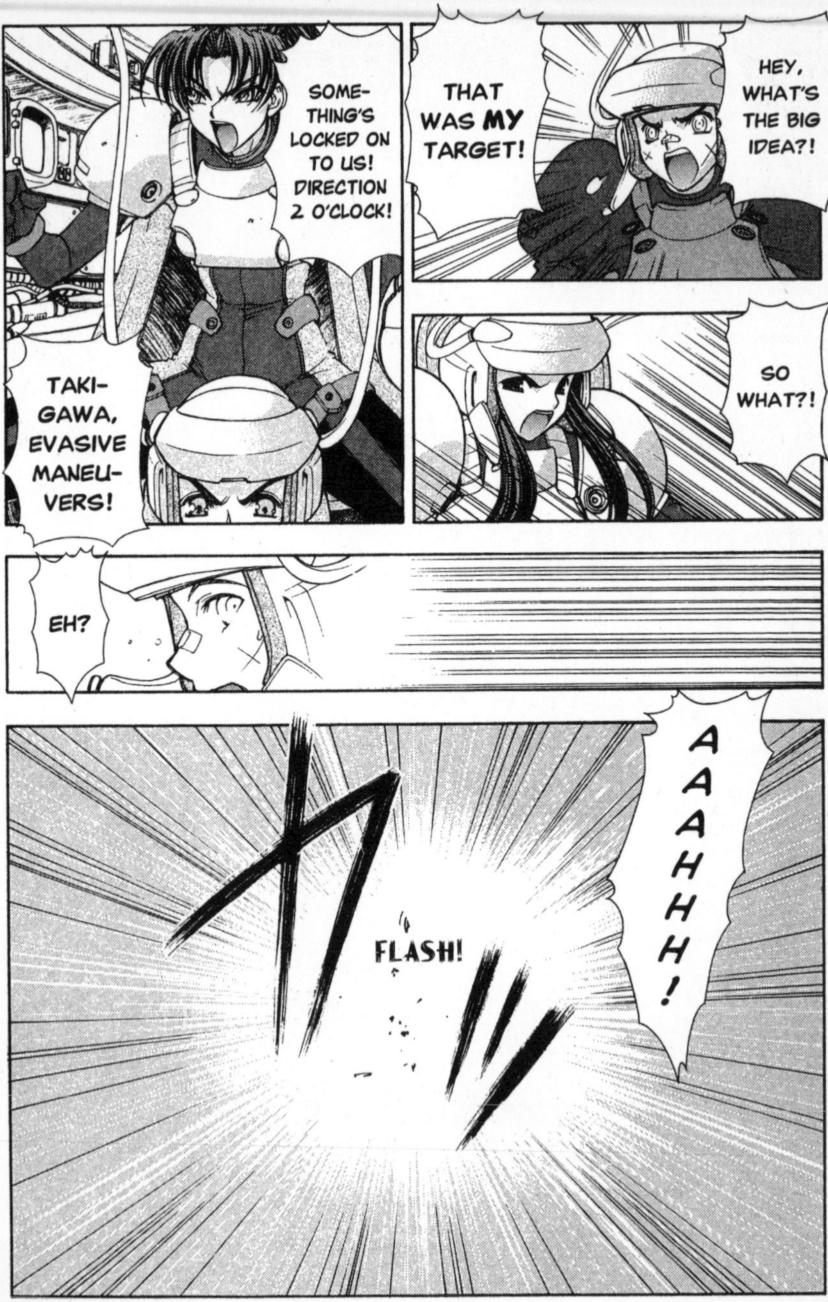
HEY, WHAT'S THE BIG IDEA?!
THAT WAS MY TARGET!
SO WHAT?!
SOME-THING'S LOCKED ON TO US! DIRECTION 2 O'CLOCK!
TAKI-GAWA, EVASIVE MANEU-VERS!
EH?
AAAAHHH!
FLASH!

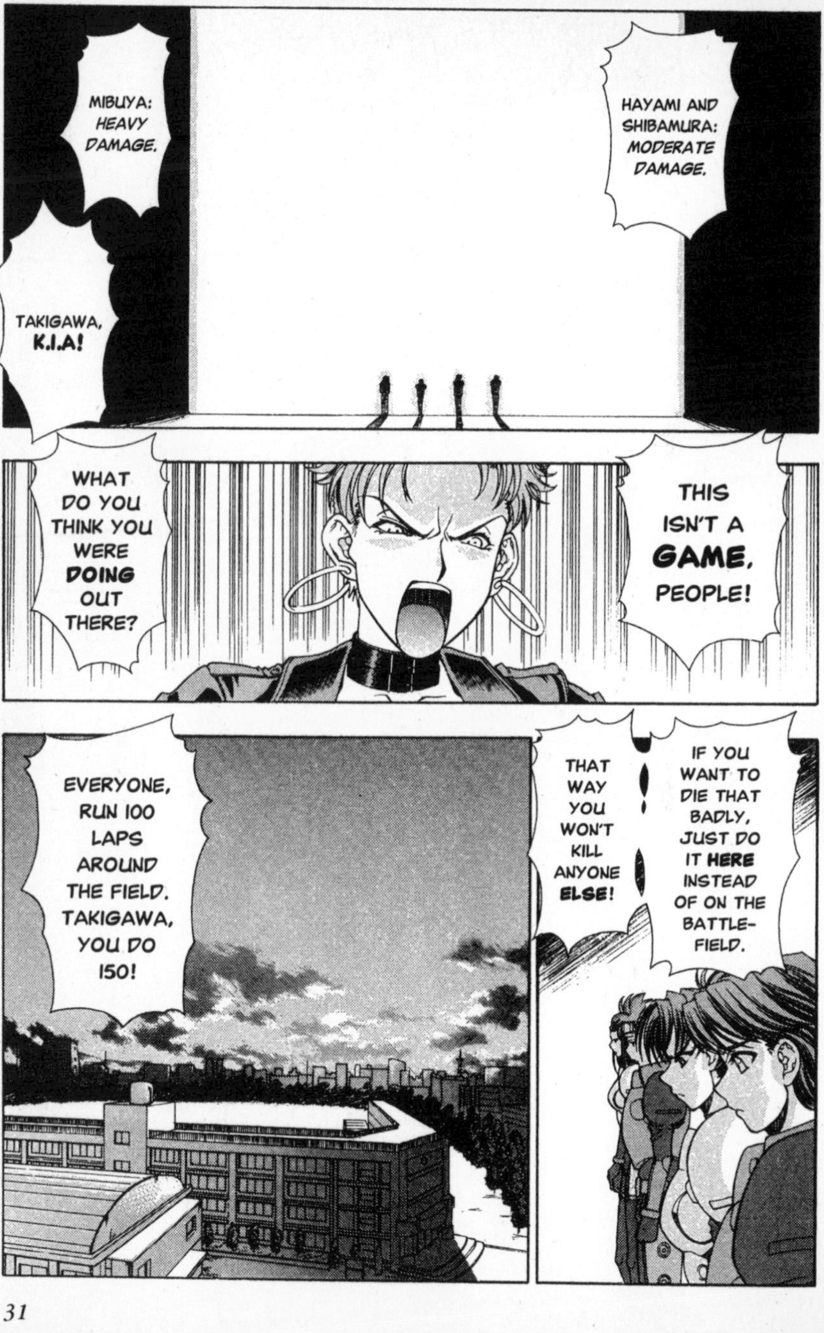
MIBUYA: HEAVY DAMAGE.
HAYAMI AND SHIBAMURA: MODERATE DAMAGE.
TAKIGAWA, K.I.A!
WHAT DO YOU THINK YOU WERE DOING OUT THERE?
THIS ISN'T A GAME, PEOPLE!
EVERYONE, RUN 100 LAPS AROUND THE FIELD. TAKIGAWA, YOU DO 150!
IF YOU WANT TO DIE THAT BADLY, JUST DO IT HERE INSTEAD OF ON THE BATTLE-FIELD.
THAT WAY YOU WON'T KILL ANYONE ELSE!

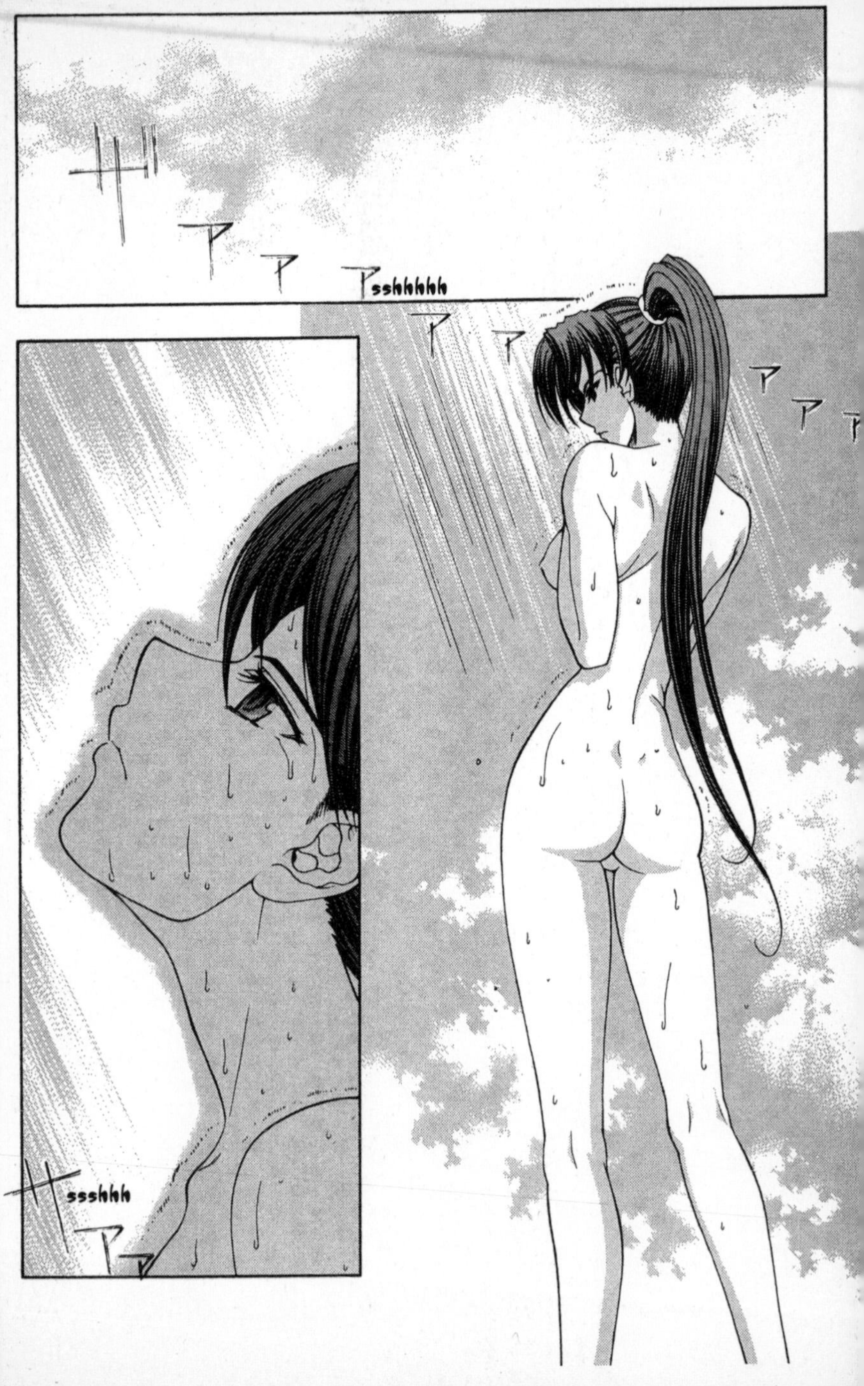
ザァァァ
sshhhhh
ァァァァァ
ザァァ
ssshhh

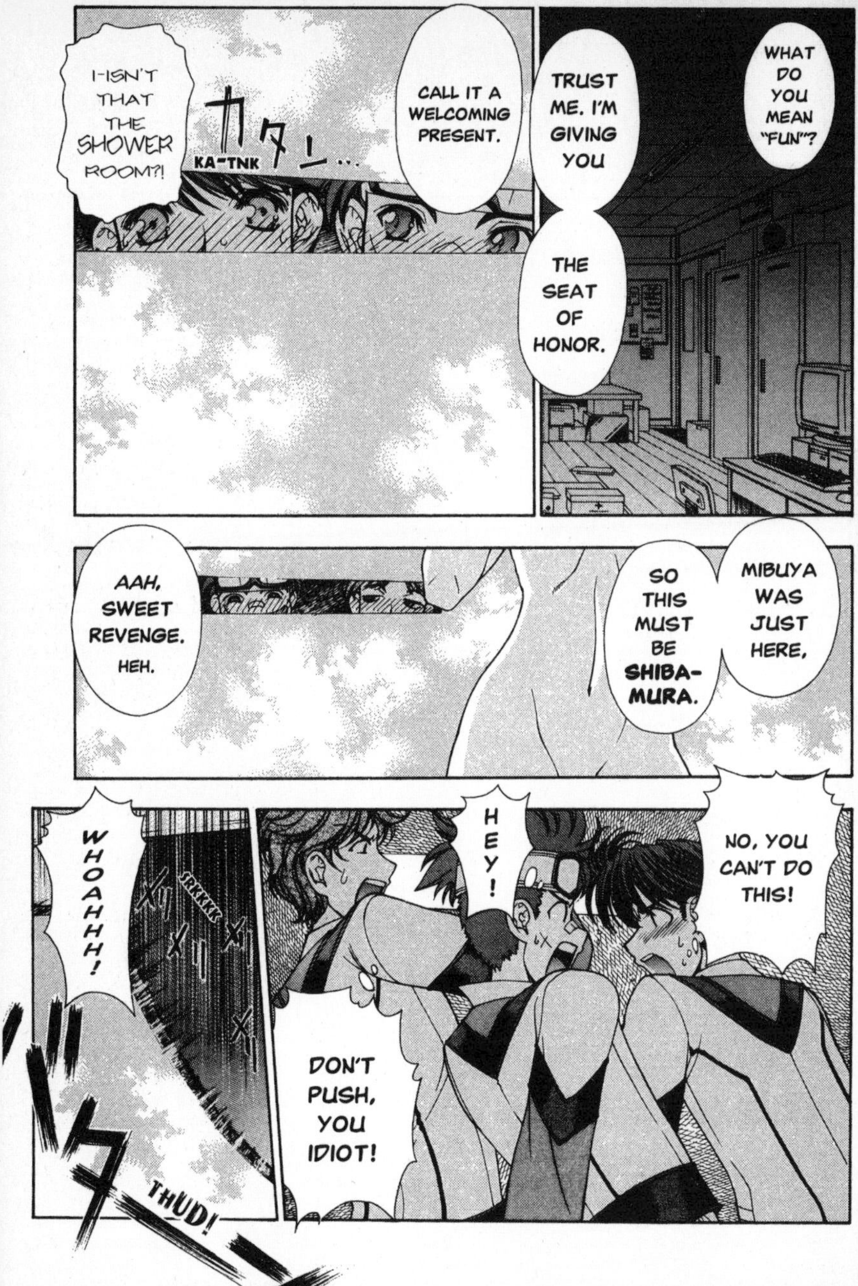
WHAT DO YOU MEAN "FUN"?
TRUST ME. I'M GIVING YOU
THE SEAT OF HONOR.
CALL IT A WELCOMING PRESENT.
KA-TNK
I-ISN'T THAT THE SHOWER ROOM?!
MIBUYA WAS JUST HERE,
SO THIS MUST BE SHIBA-MURA.
AAH, SWEET REVENGE. HEH.
NO, YOU CAN'T DO THIS!
HEY!
DON'T PUSH, YOU IDIOT!
WHOAHHH!
SRKKKK
THUD!

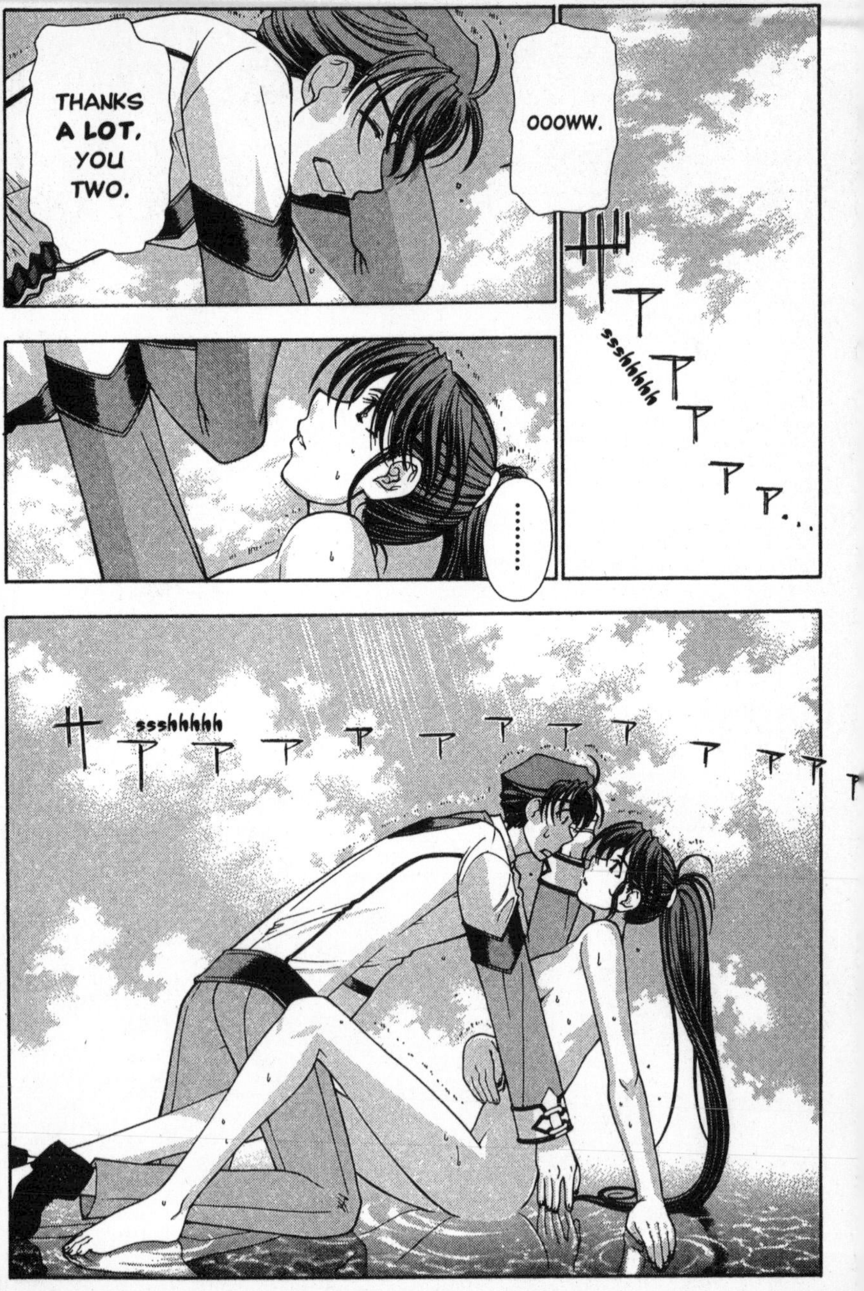
OOOWW.
ssshhhhh
THANKS A LOT, YOU TWO.
....
ssshhhhh

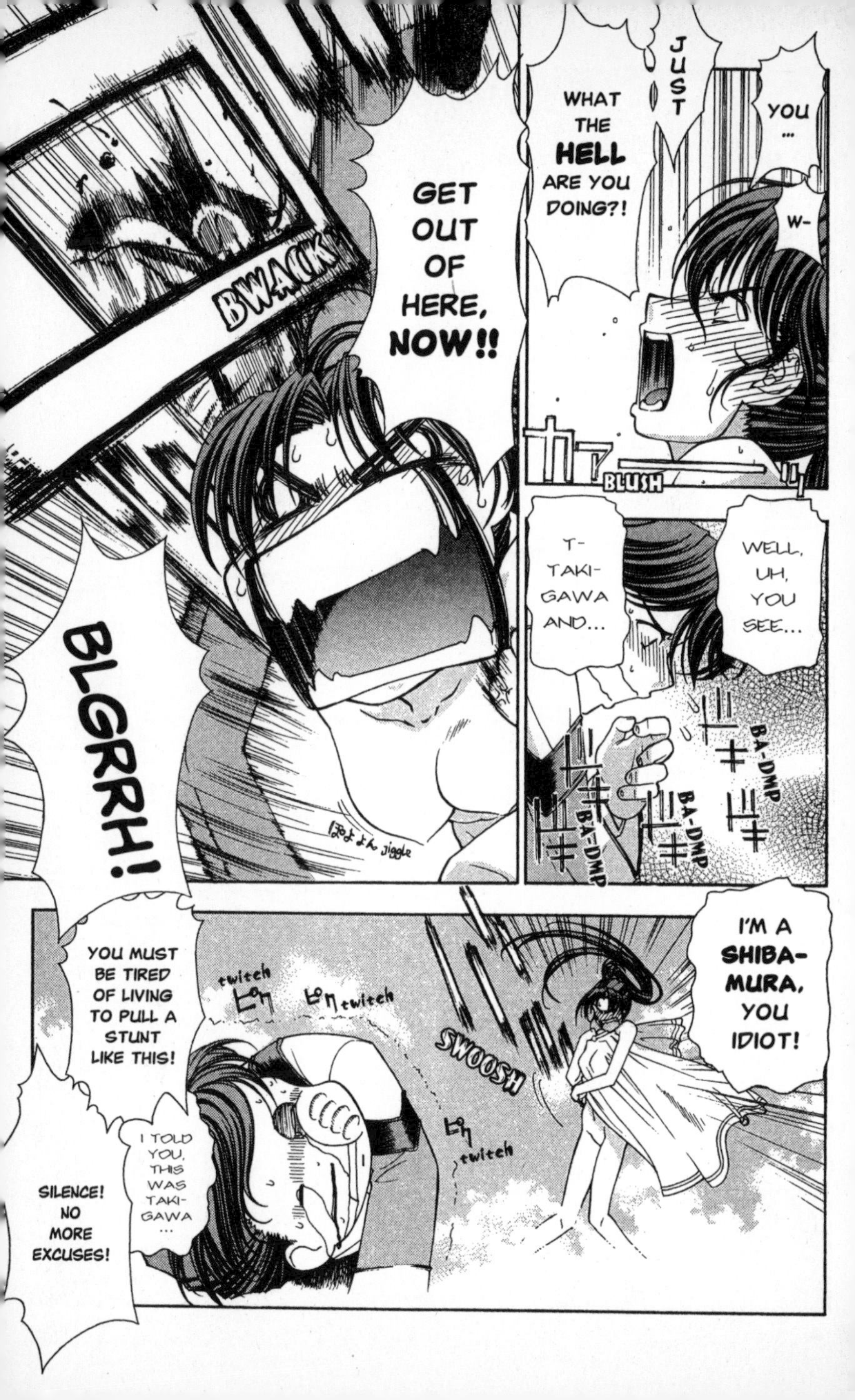
YOU ... W-
JUST
WHAT THE HELL ARE YOU DOING?!
BLUSH
GET OUT OF HERE, NOW!!
BWACK
WELL, UH, YOU SEE...
T-TAKI-GAWA AND...
BA-DMP
BA-DMP
BA-DMP
BA-DMP
jiggle
BLGRRH!
I'M A SHIBA-MURA, YOU IDIOT!
SWOOSH
twitch
twitch
twitch
YOU MUST BE TIRED OF LIVING TO PULL A STUNT LIKE THIS!
I TOLD YOU, THIS WAS TAKI-GAWA ...
SILENCE! NO MORE EXCUSES!

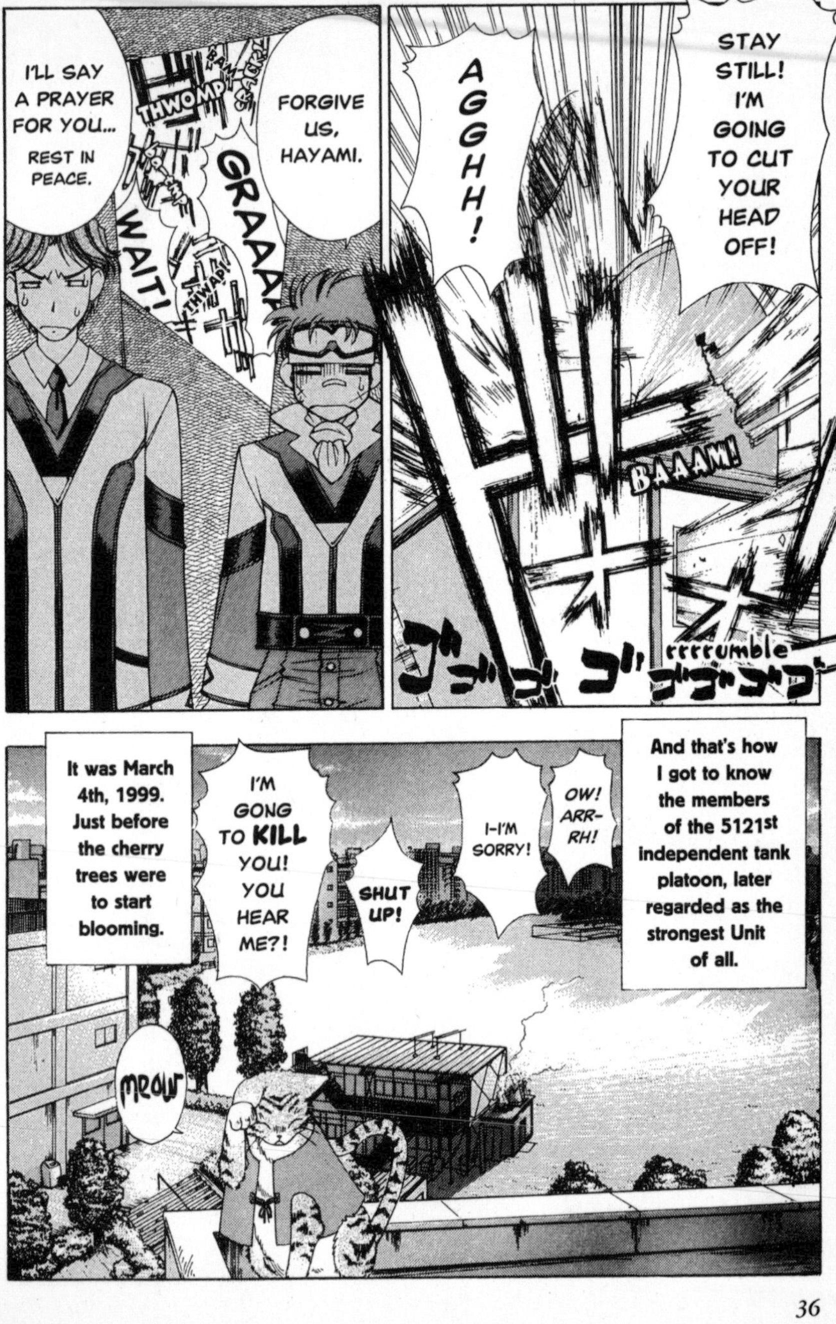
STAY STILL! I'M GOING TO CUT YOUR HEAD OFF!
AGGHH!
BAAAM!
rrrrumble
ゴゴゴ ゴ ゴゴゴゴ
FORGIVE US, HAYAMI.
GRAAAA
WAIT!
THWOMP!
BAM
CRACK
THWAP!
I'LL SAY A PRAYER FOR YOU...
REST IN PEACE.
And that's how I got to know the members of the 5121st independent tank platoon, later regarded as the strongest Unit of all.
OW! ARR-RH!
I-I'M SORRY!
SHUT UP!
I'M GONG TO KILL YOU! YOU HEAR ME?!
It was March 4th, 1999. Just before the cherry trees were to start blooming.
meow

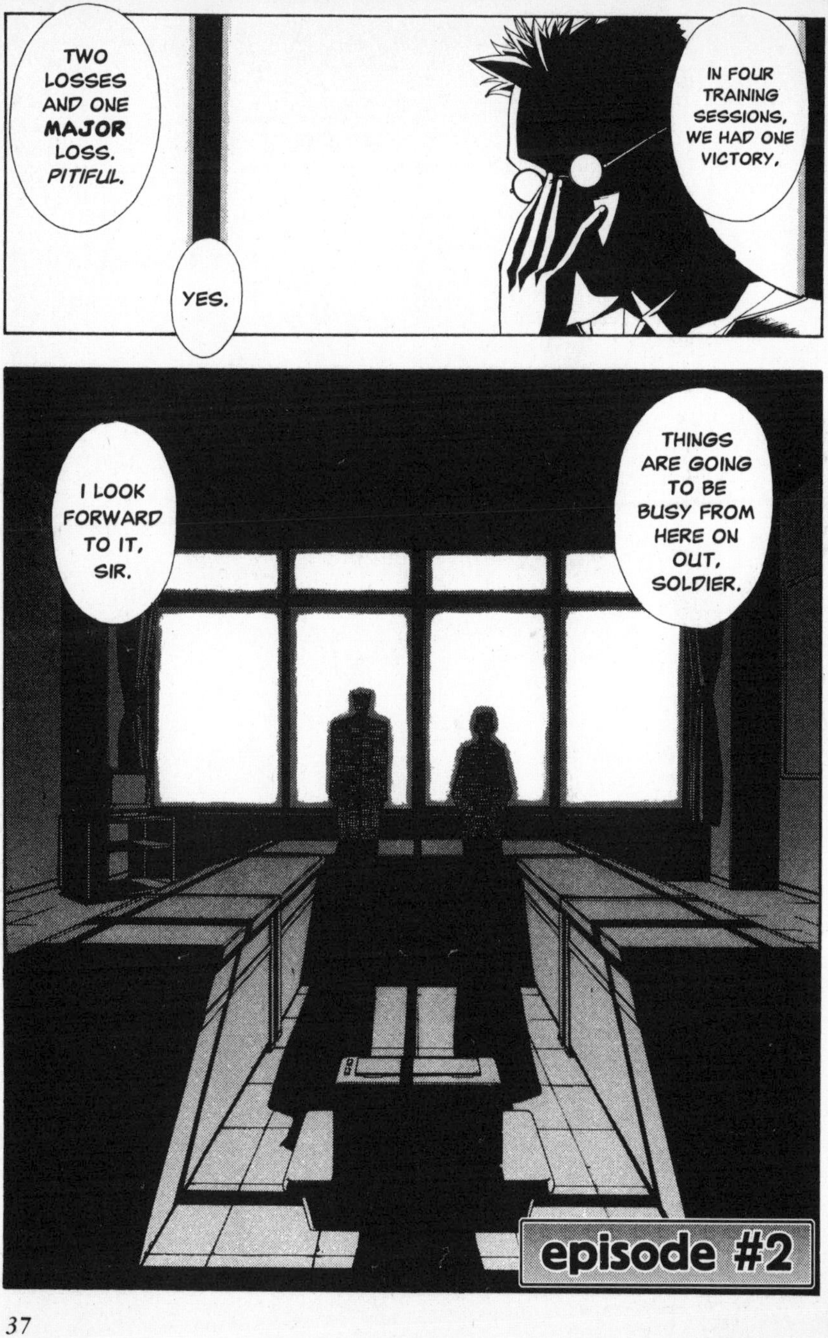
IN FOUR TRAINING SESSIONS, WE HAD ONE VICTORY,
TWO LOSSES AND ONE MAJOR LOSS. PITIFUL.
YES.
THINGS ARE GOING TO BE BUSY FROM HERE ON OUT, SOLDIER.
I LOOK FORWARD TO IT, SIR.
episode #2

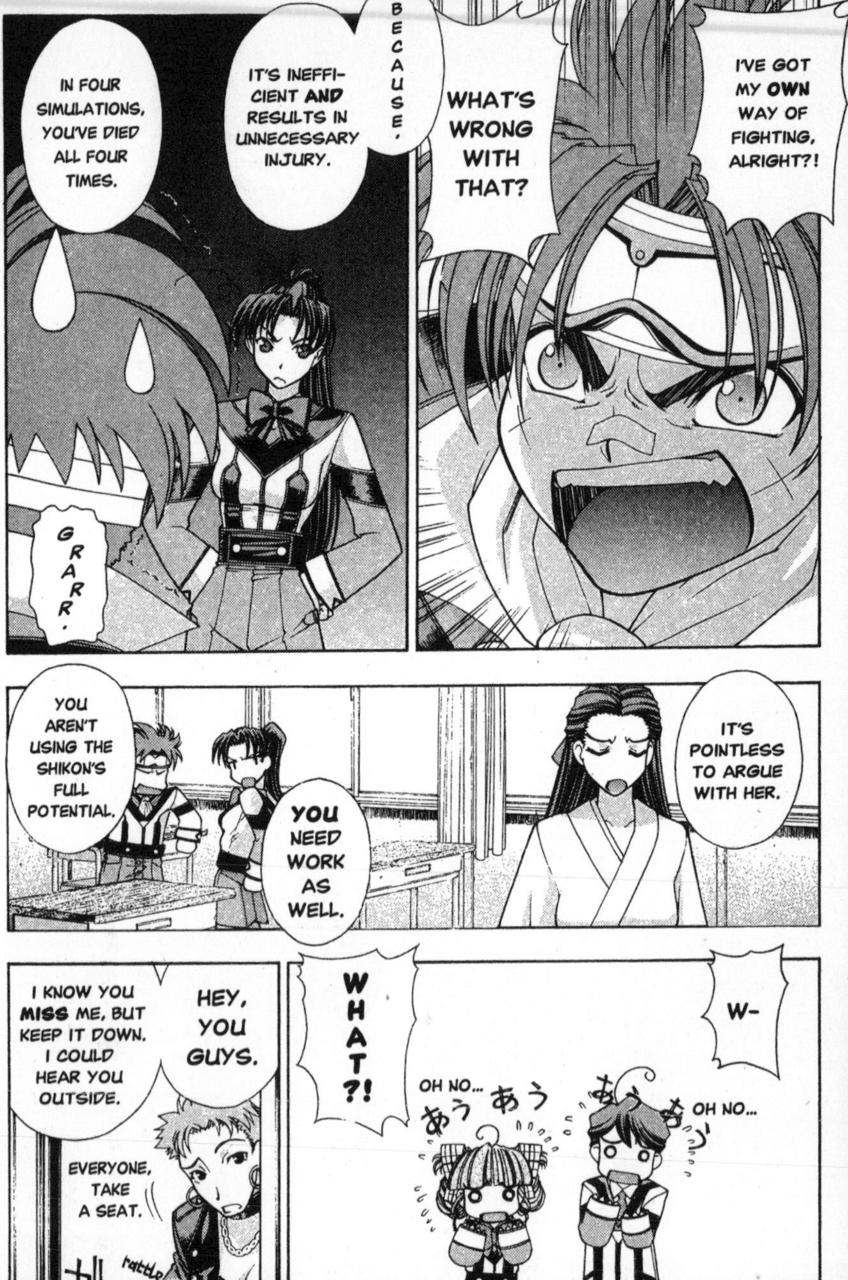
I'VE GOT MY OWN WAY OF FIGHTING, ALRIGHT?!
WHAT'S WRONG WITH THAT?
BECAUSE,
IT'S INEFFICIENT AND RESULTS IN UNNECESSARY INJURY.
IN FOUR SIMULATIONS, YOU'VE DIED ALL FOUR TIMES.
GRARR.
IT'S POINTLESS TO ARGUE WITH HER.
YOU NEED WORK AS WELL.
YOU AREN'T USING THE SHIKON'S FULL POTENTIAL.
W-
WHAT?!
OH NO...
OH NO... あう あう
HEY, YOU GUYS.
I KNOW YOU MISS ME, BUT KEEP IT DOWN. I COULD HEAR YOU OUTSIDE.
EVERYONE, TAKE A SEAT.
ガラ ガラ ガラ
rattle rattle rattle

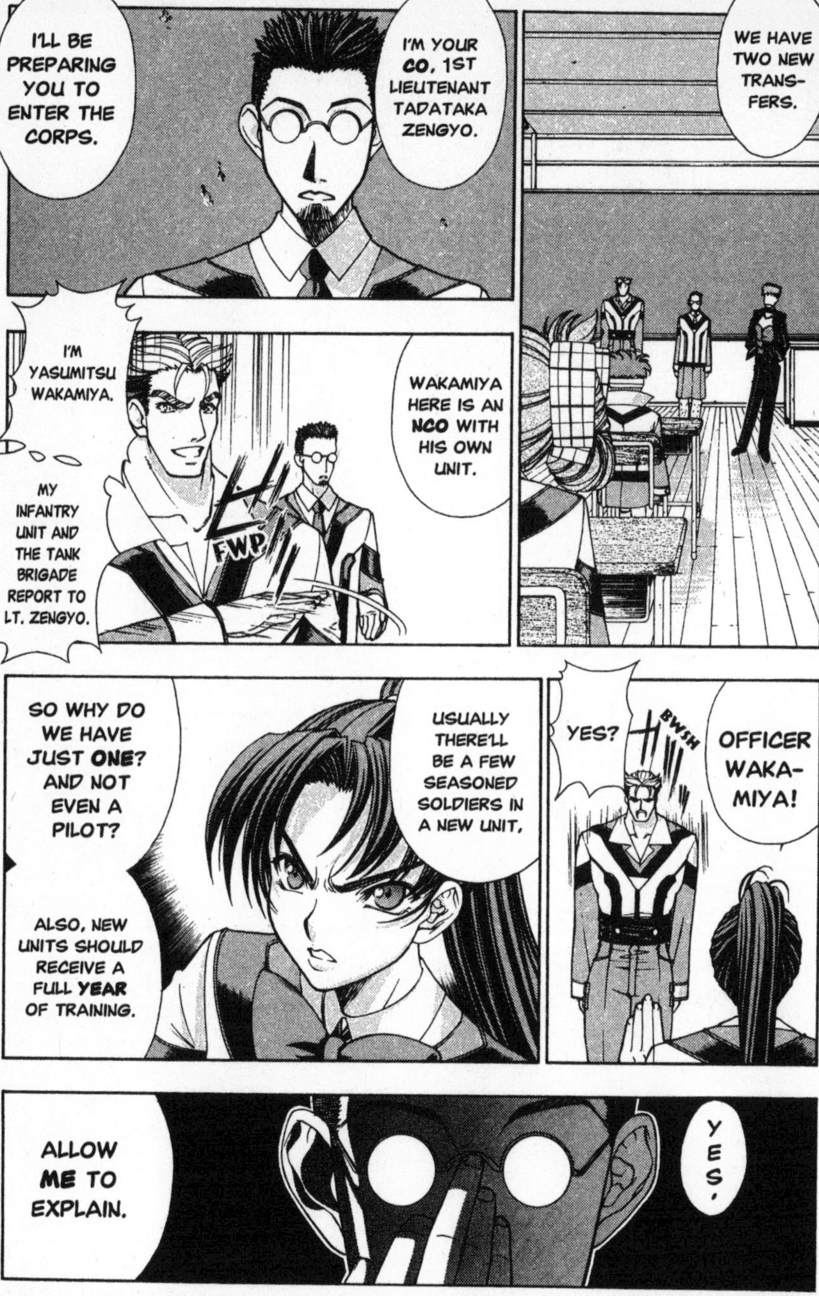
WE HAVE TWO NEW TRANS-FERS.
I'M YOUR CO, 1ST LIEUTENANT TADATAKA ZENGYO.
I'LL BE PREPARING YOU TO ENTER THE CORPS.
WAKAMIYA HERE IS AN NCO WITH HIS OWN UNIT.
FWP
I'M YASUMITSU WAKAMIYA.
MY INFANTRY UNIT AND THE TANK BRIGADE REPORT TO LT. ZENGYO.
OFFICER WAKA-MIYA!
BWSH
YES?
USUALLY THERE'LL BE A FEW SEASONED SOLDIERS IN A NEW UNIT,
SO WHY DO WE HAVE JUST ONE? AND NOT EVEN A PILOT?
ALSO, NEW UNITS SHOULD RECEIVE A FULL YEAR OF TRAINING.
YES.
ALLOW ME TO EXPLAIN.

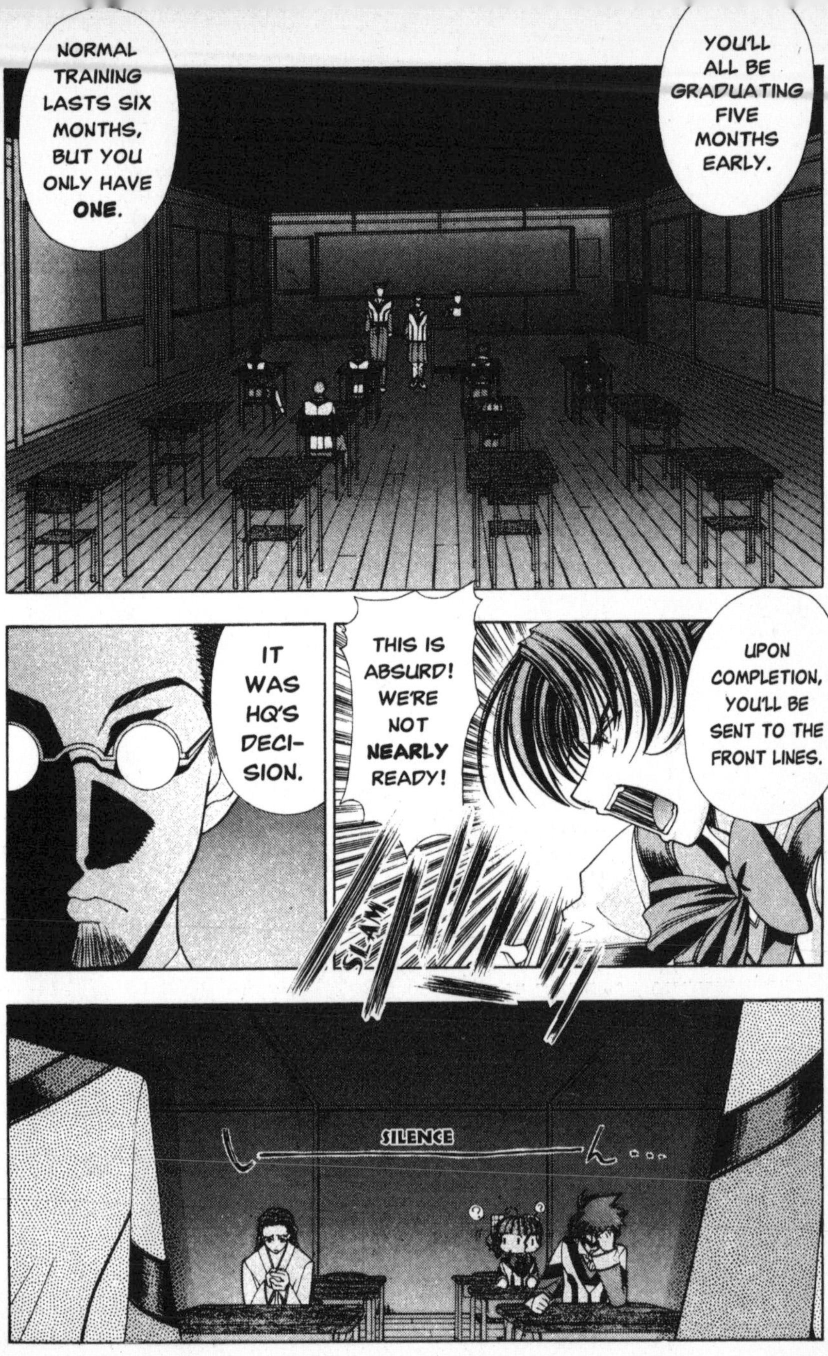
YOU'LL ALL BE GRADUATING FIVE MONTHS EARLY.
NORMAL TRAINING LASTS SIX MONTHS, BUT YOU ONLY HAVE ONE.
UPON COMPLETION, YOU'LL BE SENT TO THE FRONT LINES.
THIS IS ABSURD! WE'RE NOT NEARLY READY!
SLAM
IT WAS HQ'S DECI- SION.
SILENCE

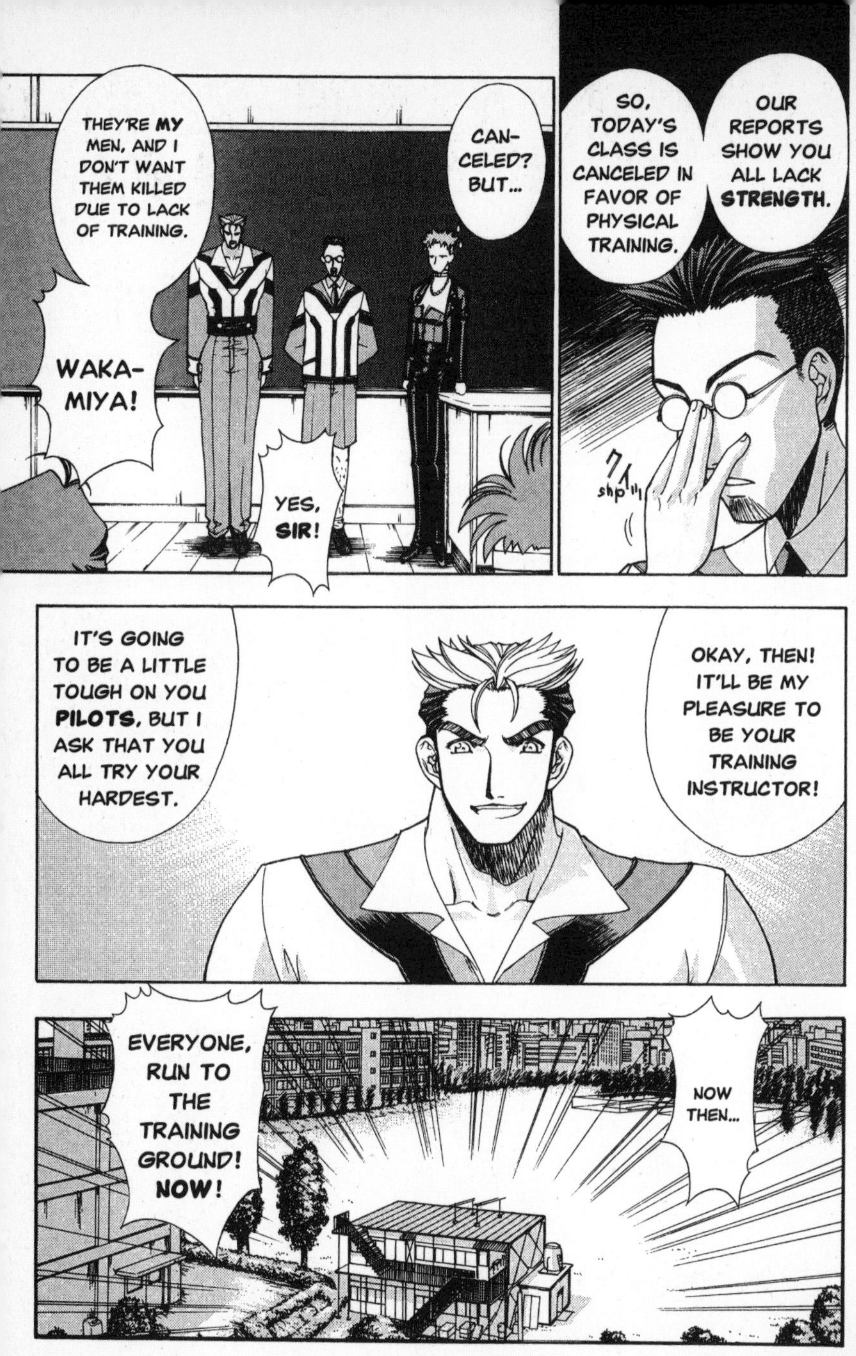
OUR REPORTS SHOW YOU ALL LACK STRENGTH.
SO, TODAY'S CLASS IS CANCELED IN FAVOR OF PHYSICAL TRAINING.
クイ
shp
CAN-CELED? BUT...
WAKA-MIYA!
THEY'RE MY MEN, AND I DON'T WANT THEM KILLED DUE TO LACK OF TRAINING.
YES, SIR!
OKAY, THEN! IT'LL BE MY PLEASURE TO BE YOUR TRAINING INSTRUCTOR!
IT'S GOING TO BE A LITTLE TOUGH ON YOU PILOTS, BUT I ASK THAT YOU ALL TRY YOUR HARDEST.
NOW THEN...
EVERYONE, RUN TO THE TRAINING GROUND! NOW!

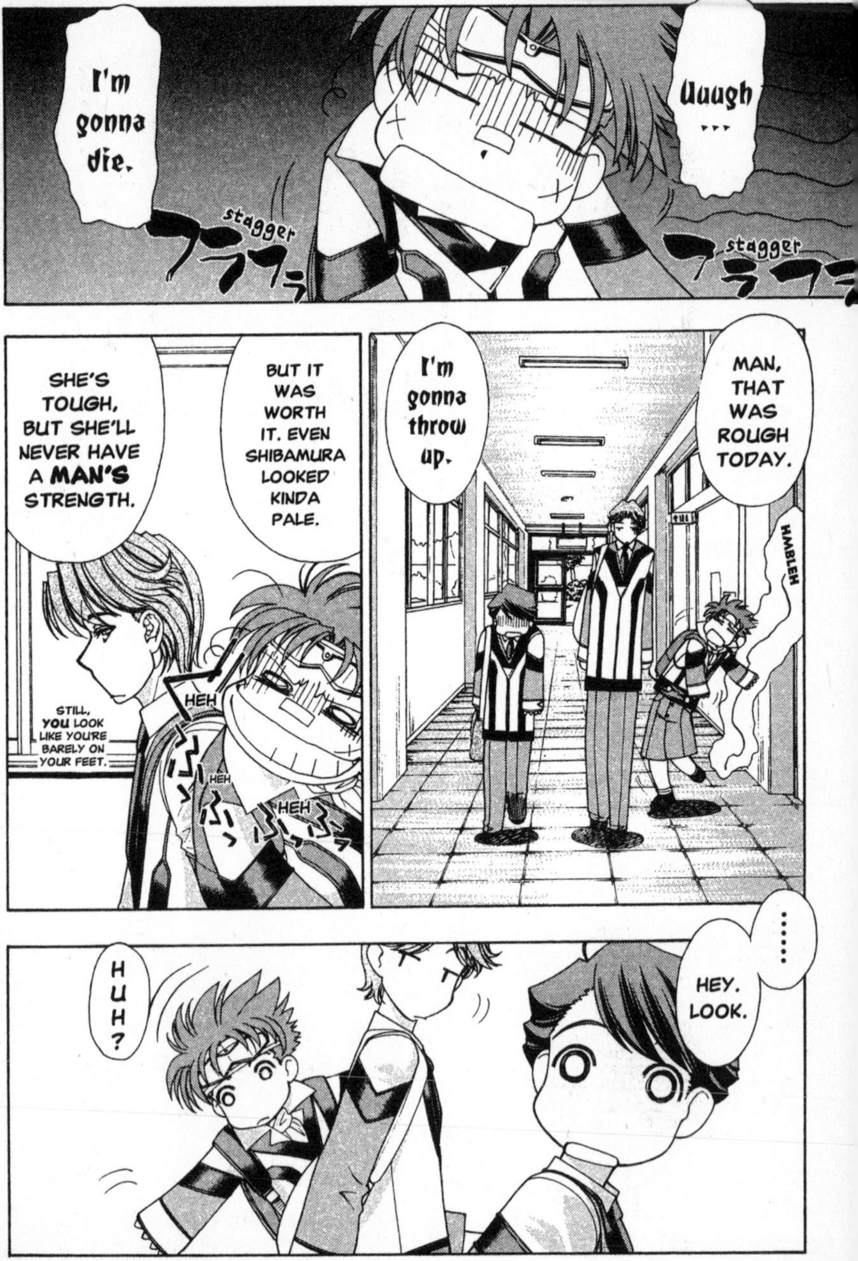
Uuugh ...
I'm gonna die.
stagger
stagger
MAN, THAT WAS ROUGH TODAY.
HMBLEH
I'm gonna throw up.
BUT IT WAS WORTH IT. EVEN SHIBAMURA LOOKED KINDA PALE.
SHE'S TOUGH, BUT SHE'LL NEVER HAVE A MAN'S STRENGTH.
HEH
HEH
HEH
STILL, YOU LOOK LIKE YOU'RE BARELY ON YOUR FEET.
......
HEY. LOOK.
HUH?

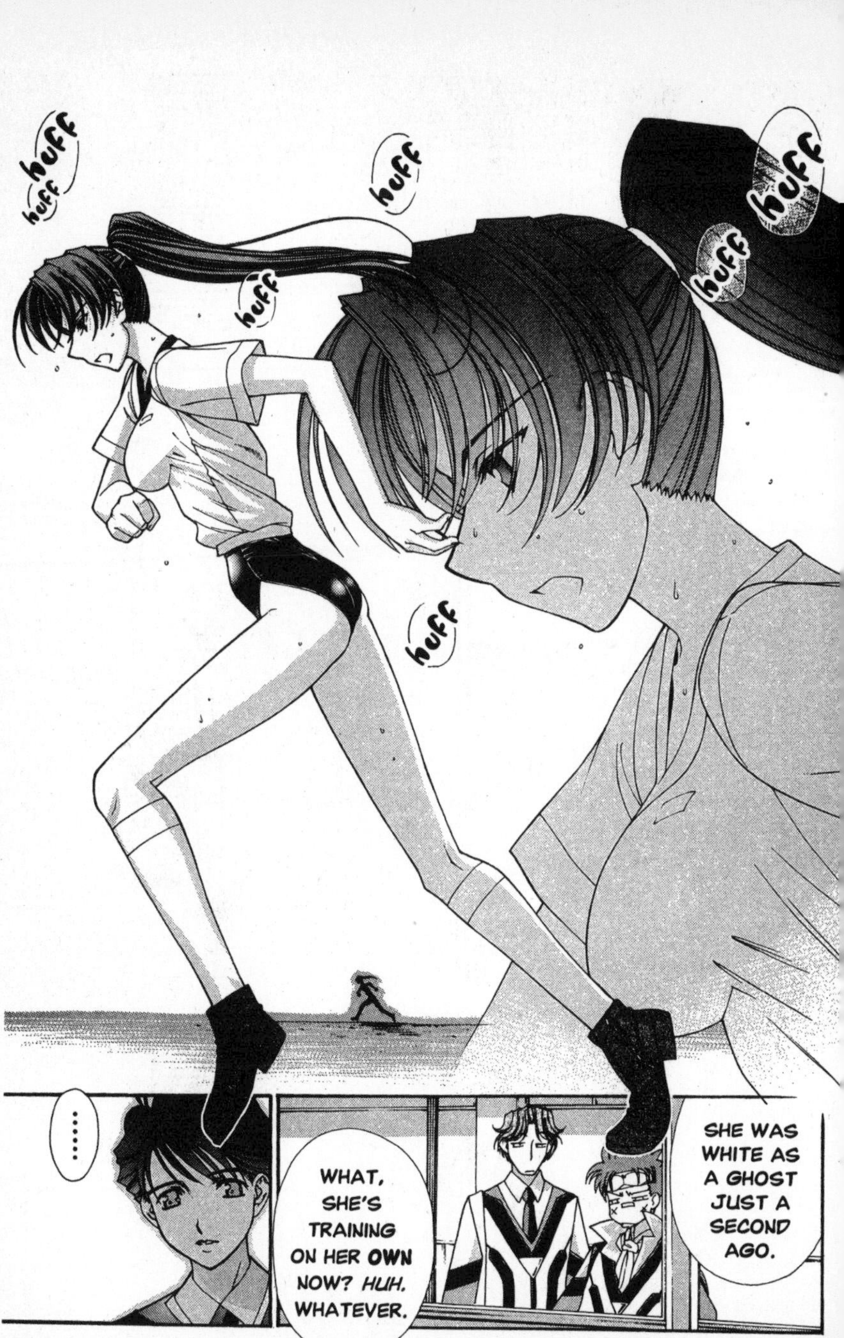
huff
huff
huff
huff
huff
huff
huff
SHE WAS WHITE AS A GHOST JUST A SECOND AGO.
WHAT, SHE'S TRAINING ON HER OWN NOW? HUH. WHATEVER.
......

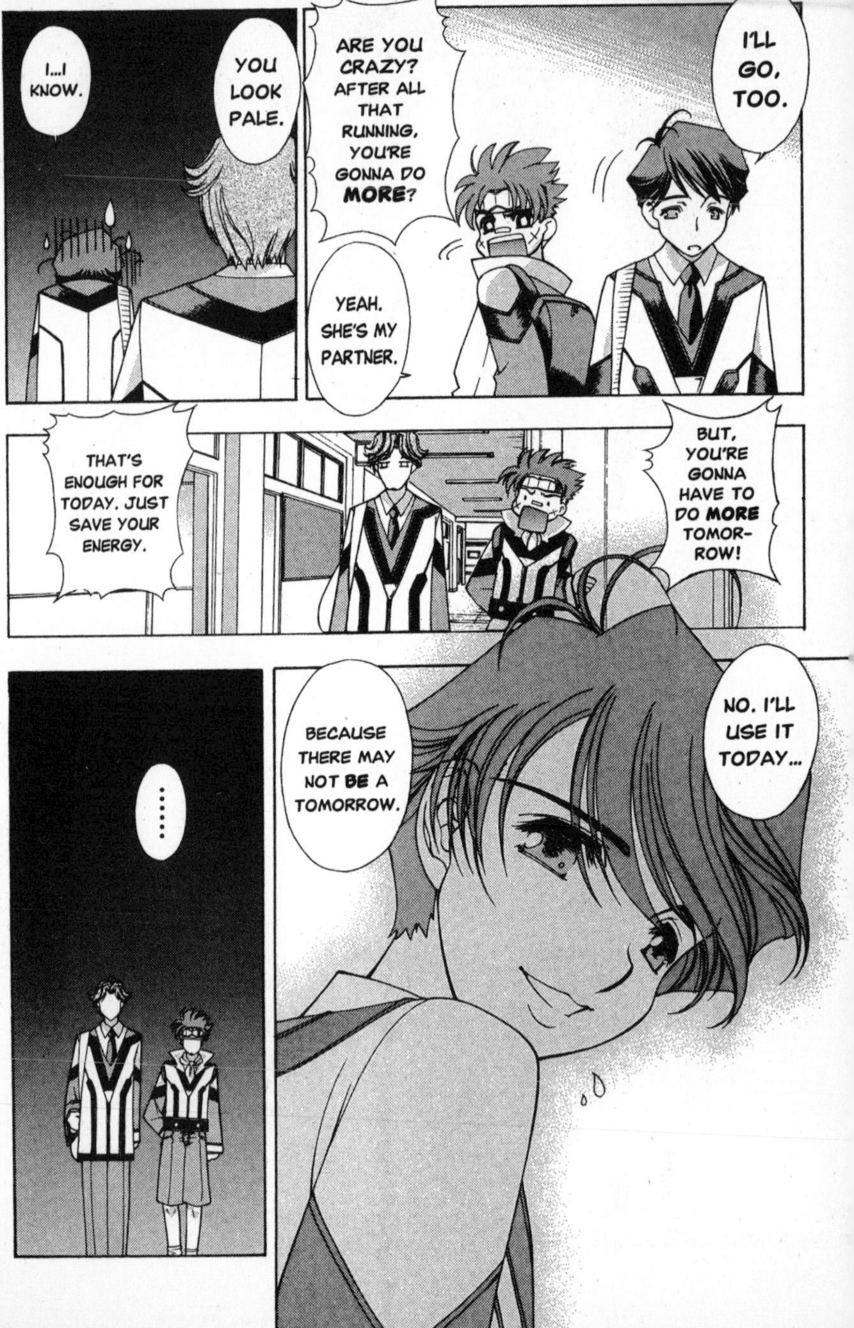
I'LL GO, TOO.
ARE YOU CRAZY? AFTER ALL THAT RUNNING, YOU'RE GONNA DO **MORE**?
YEAH. SHE'S MY PARTNER.
YOU LOOK PALE.
I...I KNOW.
BUT, YOU'RE GONNA HAVE TO DO **MORE** TOMORROW!
THAT'S ENOUGH FOR TODAY. JUST SAVE YOUR ENERGY.
NO. I'LL USE IT TODAY...
BECAUSE THERE MAY NOT **BE** A TOMORROW.
......

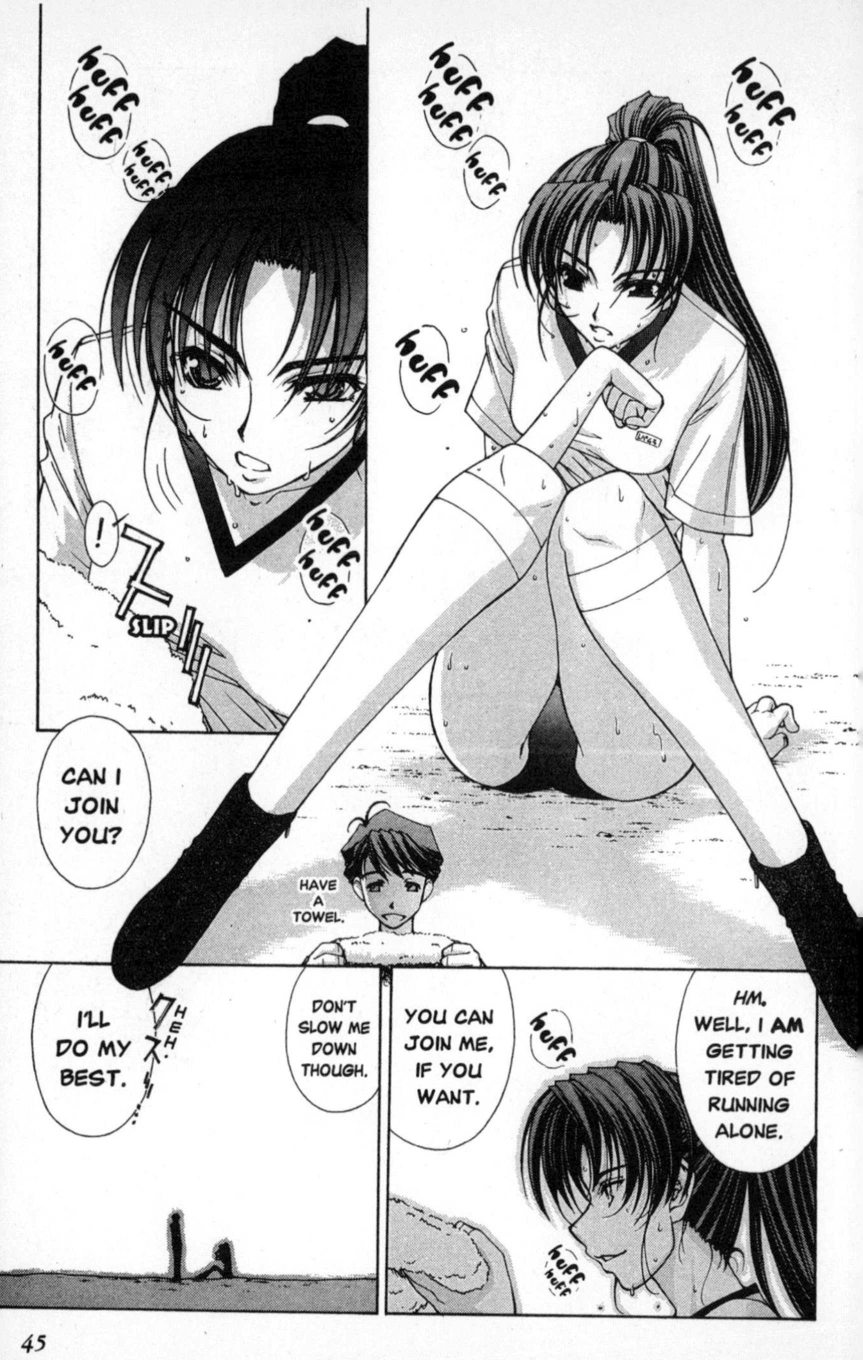
huff huff
huff
huff huff
huff
huff huff
huff huff
huff
!
SLIP
huff huff
CAN I JOIN YOU?
HAVE A TOWEL.
HM. WELL, I AM GETTING TIRED OF RUNNING ALONE.
huff
huff huff
YOU CAN JOIN ME, IF YOU WANT.
DON'T SLOW ME DOWN THOUGH.
HEH.
I'LL DO MY BEST.

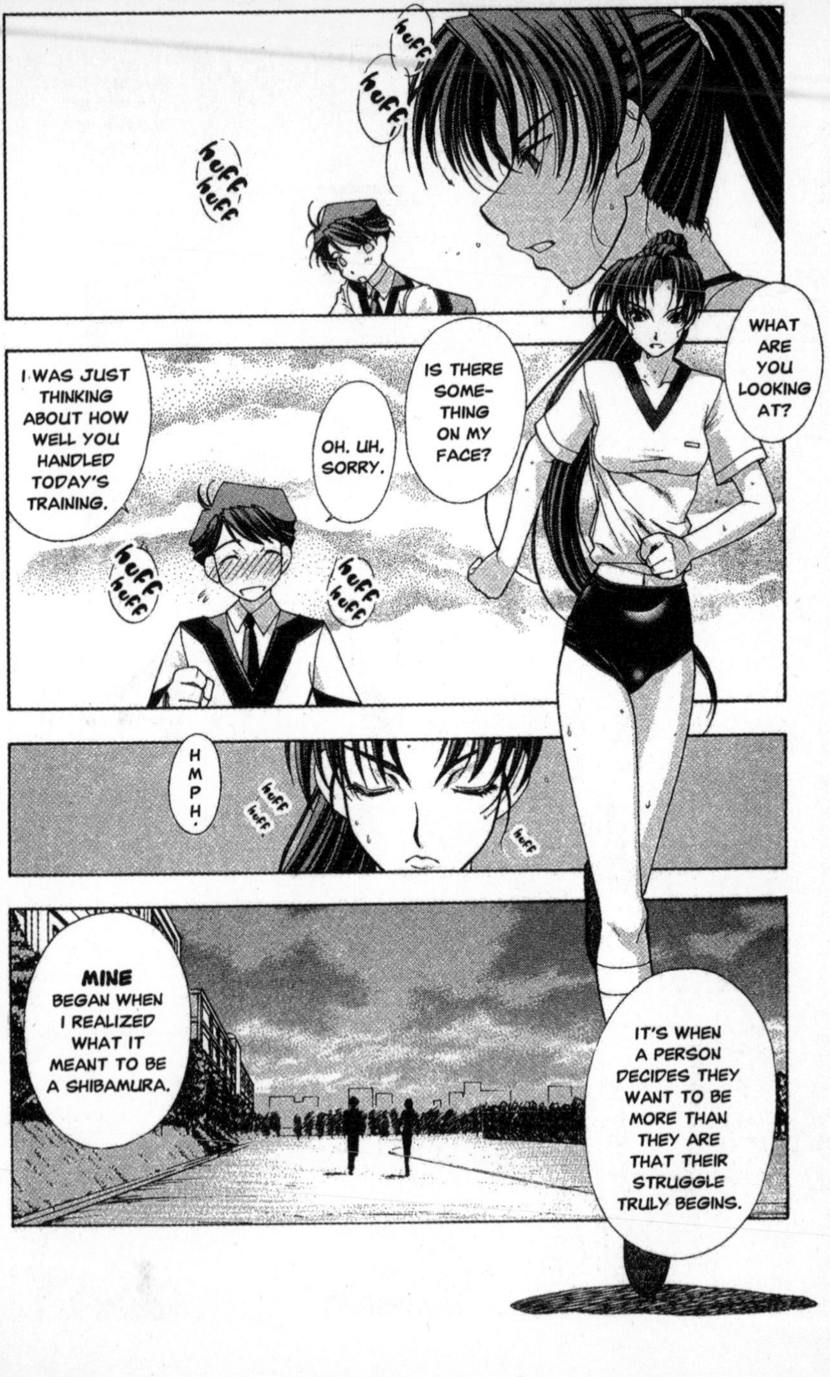
huff huff
huff huff
WHAT ARE YOU LOOKING AT?
IS THERE SOME- THING ON MY FACE?
OH. UH, SORRY.
I WAS JUST THINKING ABOUT HOW WELL YOU HANDLED TODAY'S TRAINING.
huff huff
huff huff
HMPH.
huff huff
huff
IT'S WHEN A PERSON DECIDES THEY WANT TO BE MORE THAN THEY ARE THAT THEIR STRUGGLE TRULY BEGINS.
MINE BEGAN WHEN I REALIZED WHAT IT MEANT TO BE A SHIBAMURA.

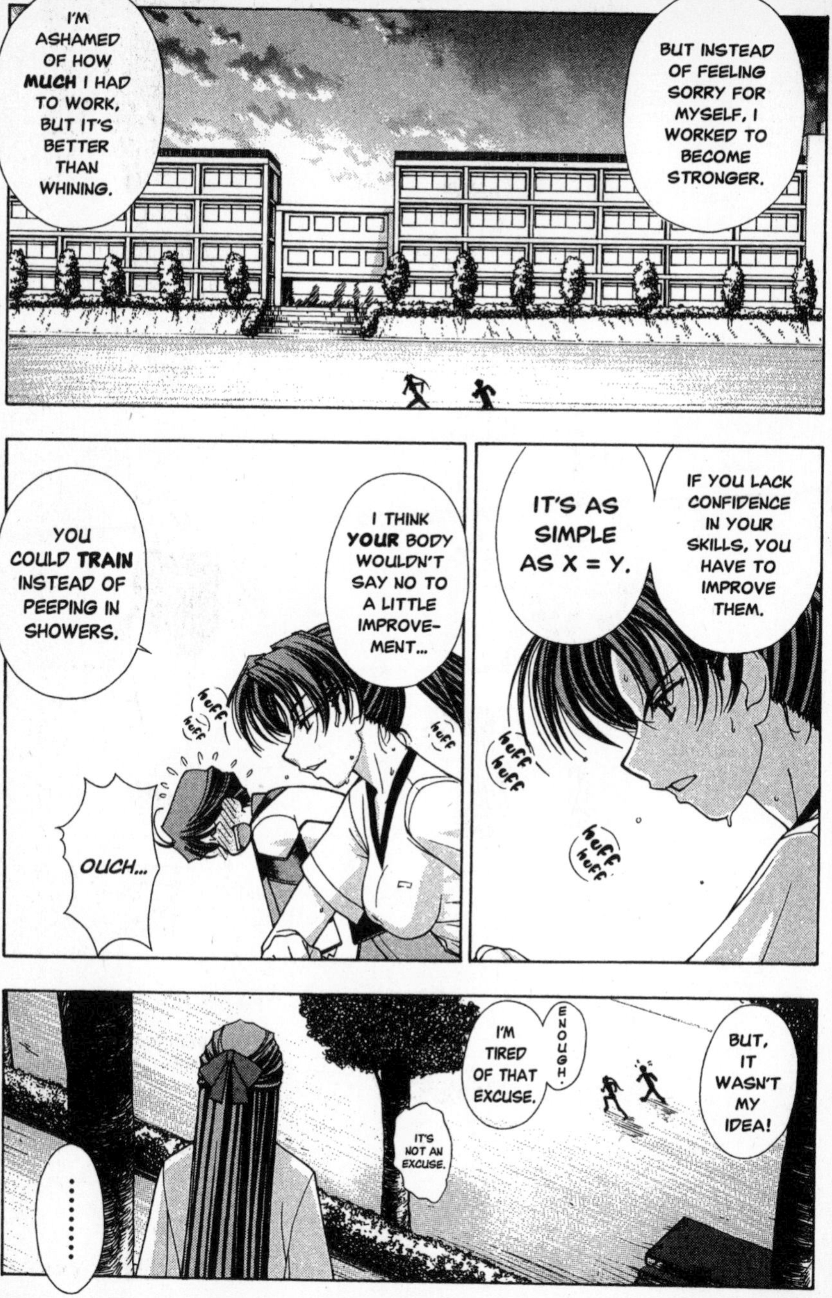

BUT INSTEAD OF FEELING SORRY FOR MYSELF, I WORKED TO BECOME STRONGER.
I'M ASHAMED OF HOW MUCH I HAD TO WORK, BUT IT'S BETTER THAN WHINING.
IF YOU LACK CONFIDENCE IN YOUR SKILLS, YOU HAVE TO IMPROVE THEM.
IT'S AS SIMPLE AS X = Y.
huff huff
huff huff
huff
I THINK YOUR BODY WOULDN'T SAY NO TO A LITTLE IMPROVEMENT...
huff huff
YOU COULD TRAIN INSTEAD OF PEEPING IN SHOWERS.
OUCH...
BUT, IT WASN'T MY IDEA!
ENOUGH.
I'M TIRED OF THAT EXCUSE.
IT'S NOT AN EXCUSE.
....

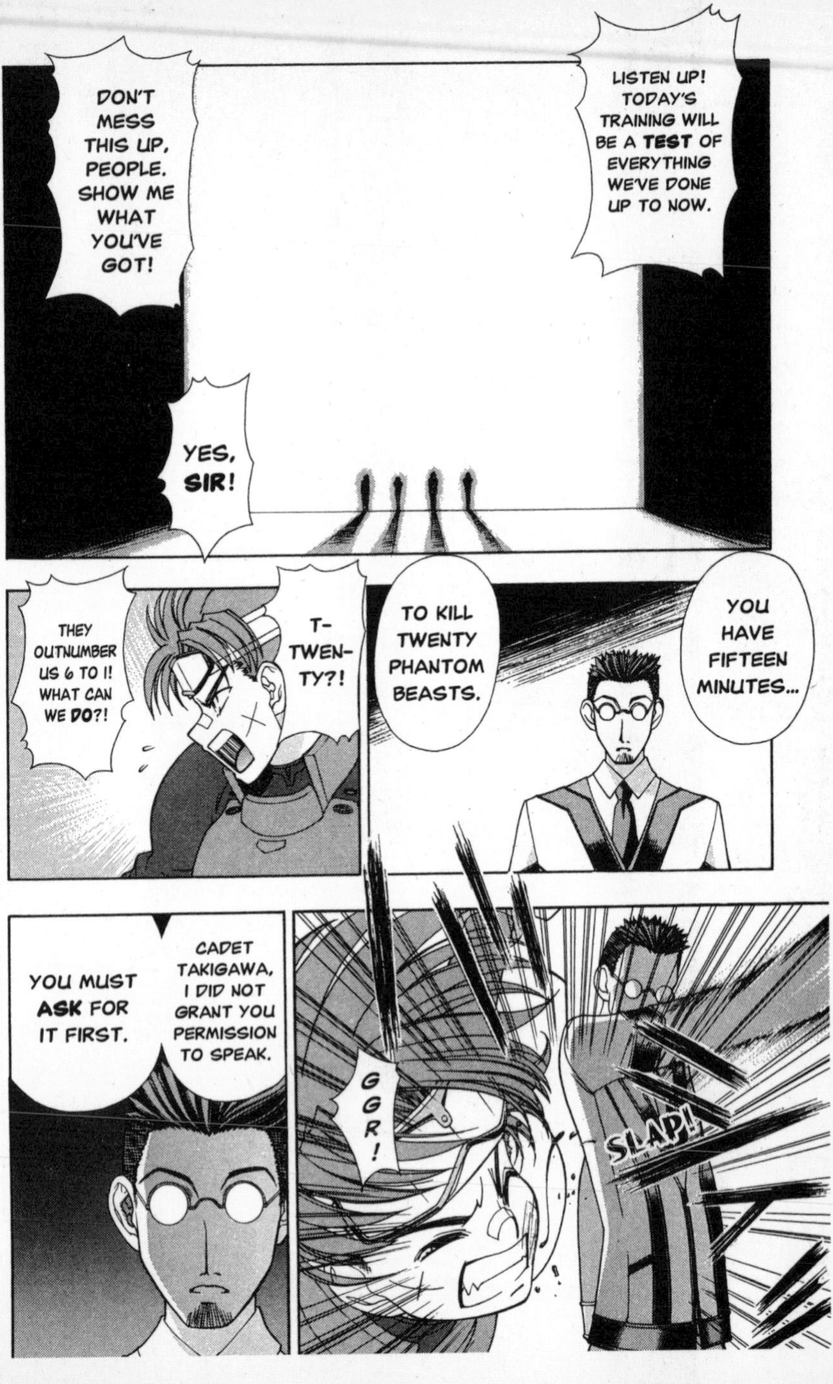
LISTEN UP! TODAY'S TRAINING WILL BE A TEST OF EVERYTHING WE'VE DONE UP TO NOW.
DON'T MESS THIS UP, PEOPLE. SHOW ME WHAT YOU'VE GOT!
YES, SIR!
YOU HAVE FIFTEEN MINUTES...
TO KILL TWENTY PHANTOM BEASTS.
T-TWEN-TY?!
THEY OUTNUMBER US 6 TO 1! WHAT CAN WE DO?!
SLAP!
GGR!
CADET TAKIGAWA, I DID NOT GRANT YOU PERMISSION TO SPEAK.
YOU MUST ASK FOR IT FIRST.

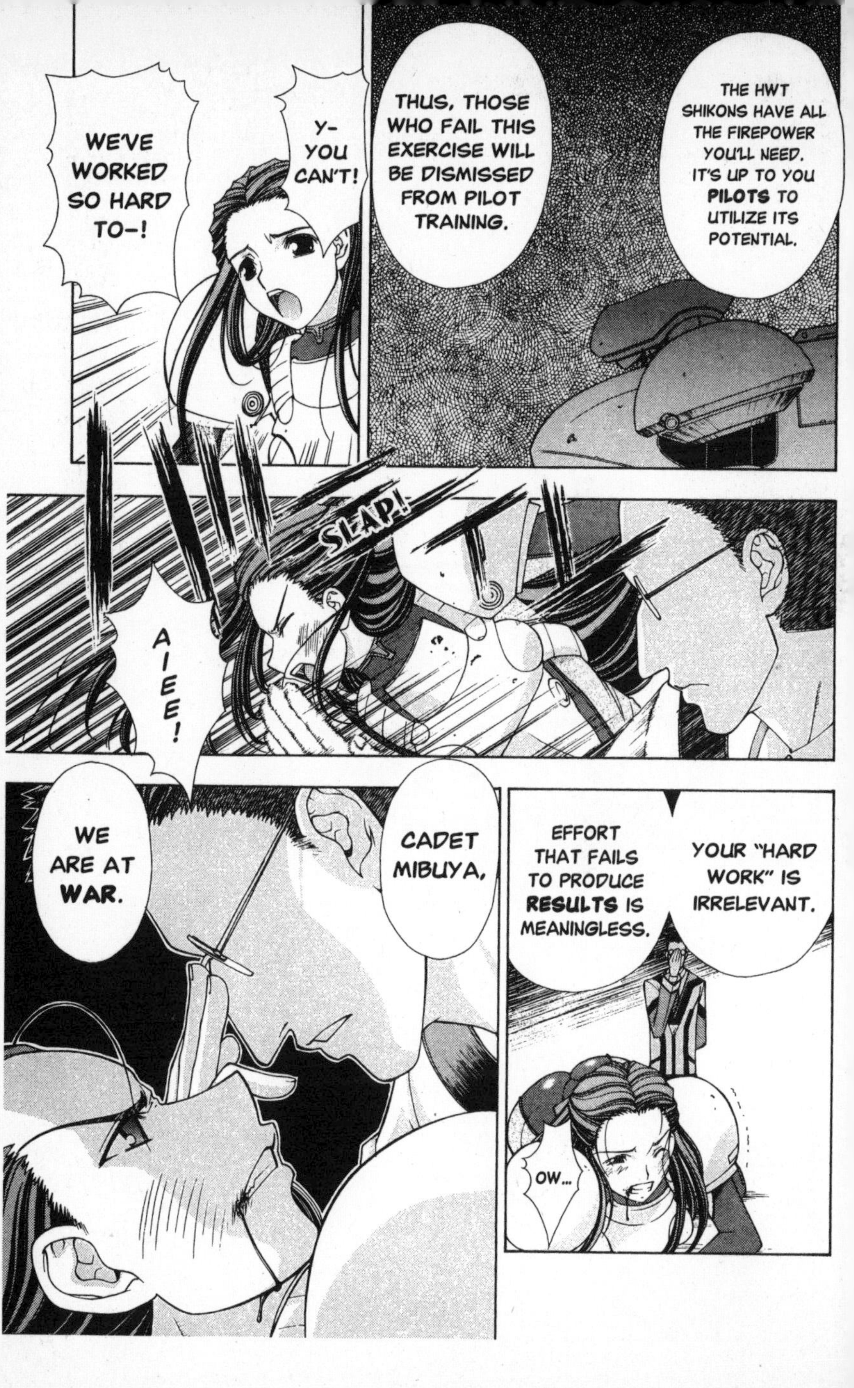
THE HWT SHIKONS HAVE ALL THE FIREPOWER YOU'LL NEED. IT'S UP TO YOU PILOTS TO UTILIZE ITS POTENTIAL.
THUS, THOSE WHO FAIL THIS EXERCISE WILL BE DISMISSED FROM PILOT TRAINING.
Y-YOU CAN'T!
WE'VE WORKED SO HARD TO-!
SLAP!
AIEEE!
YOUR "HARD WORK" IS IRRELEVANT.
EFFORT THAT FAILS TO PRODUCE RESULTS IS MEANINGLESS.
OW...
CADET MIBUYA,
WE ARE AT WAR.

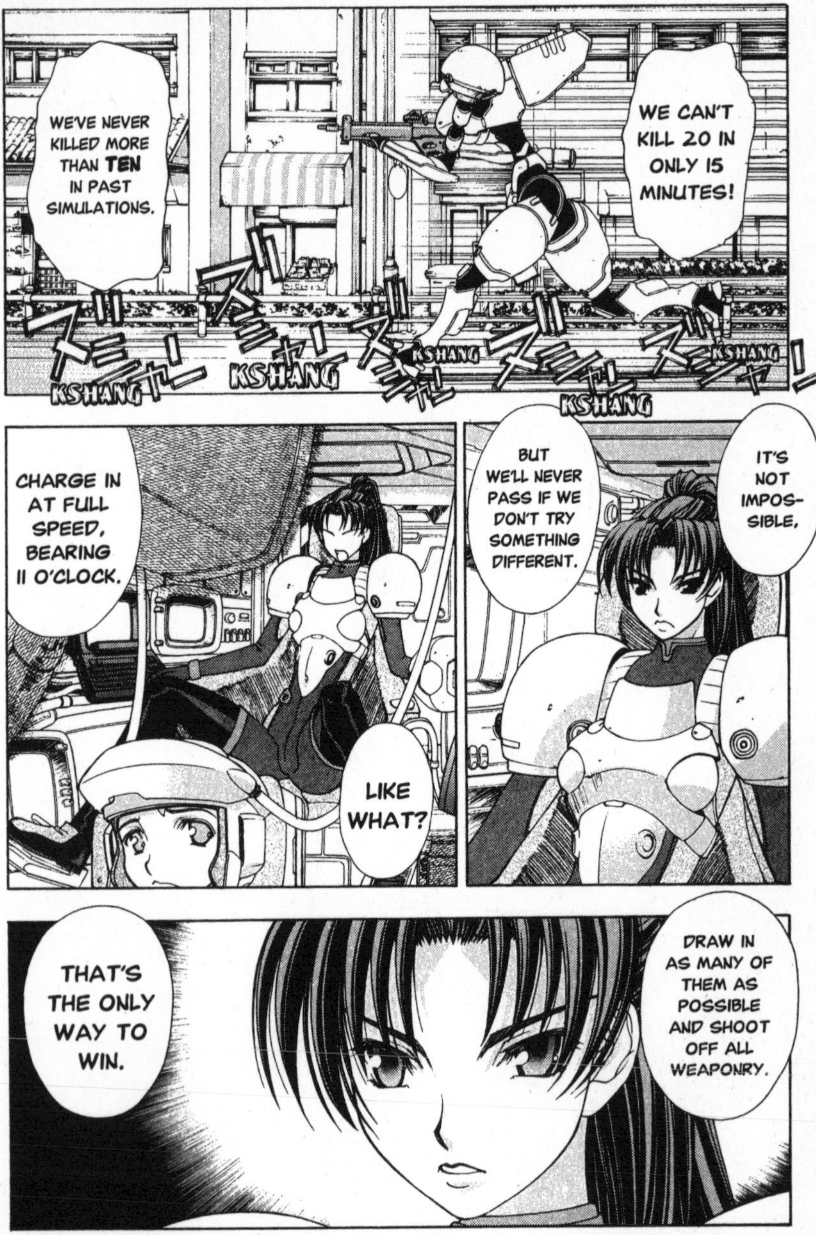
WE CAN'T KILL 20 IN ONLY 15 MINUTES!
WE'VE NEVER KILLED MORE THAN TEN IN PAST SIMULATIONS.
KSHANG
KSHANG
KSHANG
KSHANG
KSHANG
IT'S NOT IMPOSSIBLE,
BUT WE'LL NEVER PASS IF WE DON'T TRY SOMETHING DIFFERENT.
LIKE WHAT?
CHARGE IN AT FULL SPEED, BEARING 11 O'CLOCK.
DRAW IN AS MANY OF THEM AS POSSIBLE AND SHOOT OFF ALL WEAPONRY.
THAT'S THE ONLY WAY TO WIN.

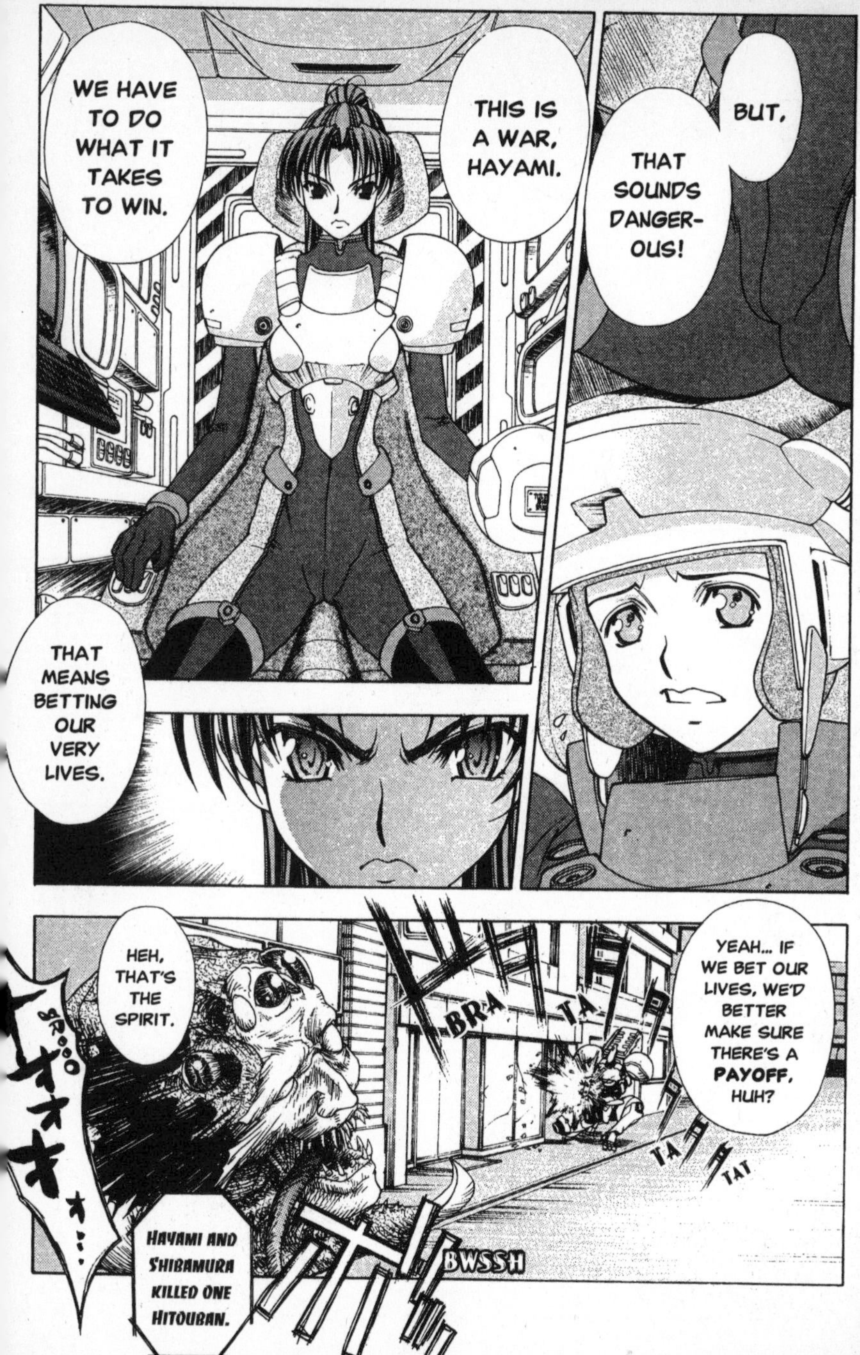
BUT,
THAT SOUNDS DANGER-OUS!
THIS IS A WAR, HAYAMI.
WE HAVE TO DO WHAT IT TAKES TO WIN.
THAT MEANS BETTING OUR VERY LIVES.
YEAH... IF WE BET OUR LIVES, WE'D BETTER MAKE SURE THERE'S A **PAYOFF**, HUH?
BRA
TA
TA
TAT
HEH, THAT'S THE SPIRIT.
BWSSH
HAYAMI AND SHIBAMURA KILLED ONE HITOUBAN.

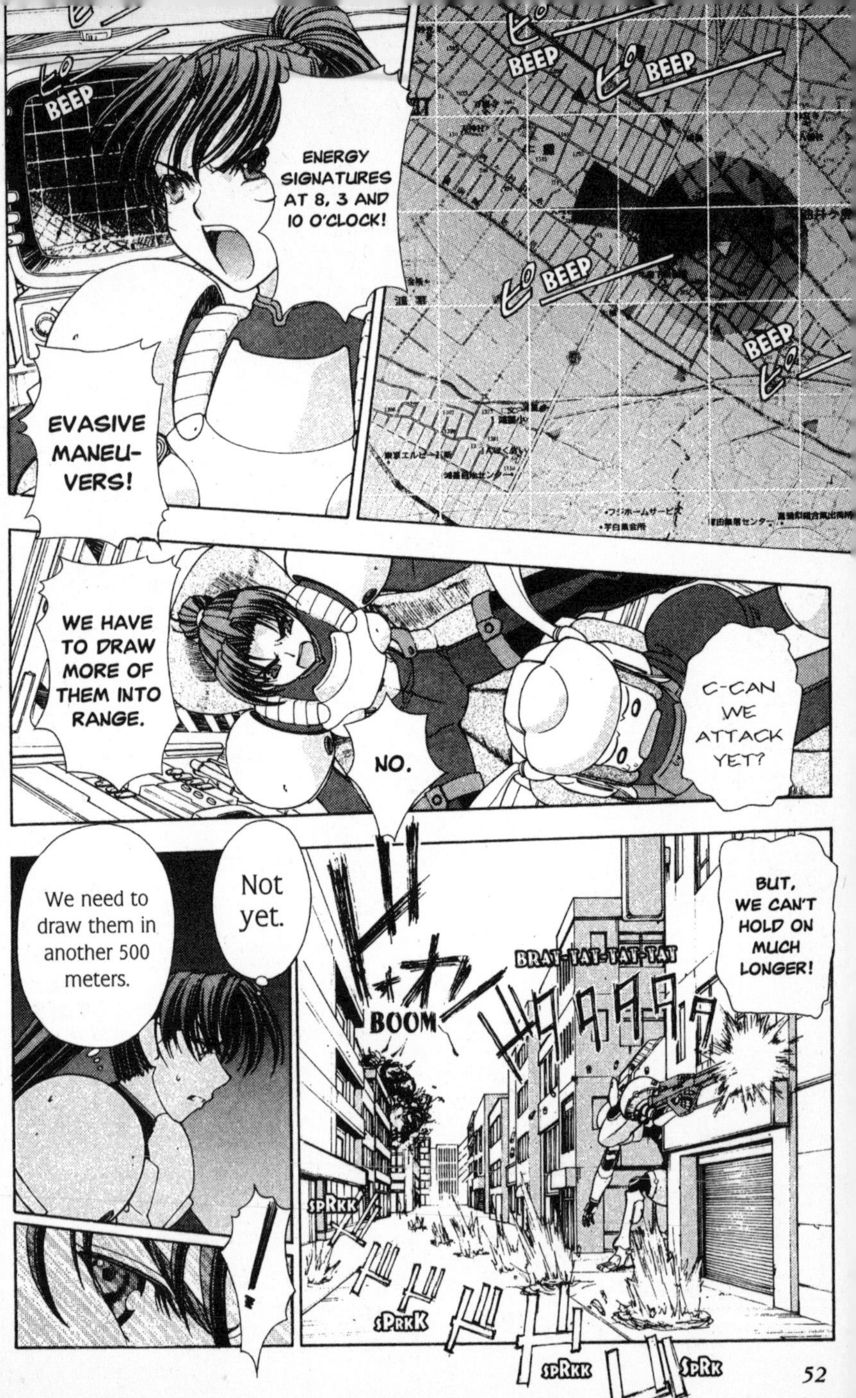
BEEP
BEEP
BEEP
BEEP
BEEP
ENERGY SIGNATURES AT 8, 3 AND 10 O'CLOCK!
EVASIVE MANEU-VERS!
C-CAN WE ATTACK YET?
NO.
WE HAVE TO DRAW MORE OF THEM INTO RANGE.
BUT, WE CAN'T HOLD ON MUCH LONGER!
BRAT-TAT-TAT-TAT
BOOM
SPRKK
SPRKK
SPRKK
SPRK
Not yet.
We need to draw them in another 500 meters.
!

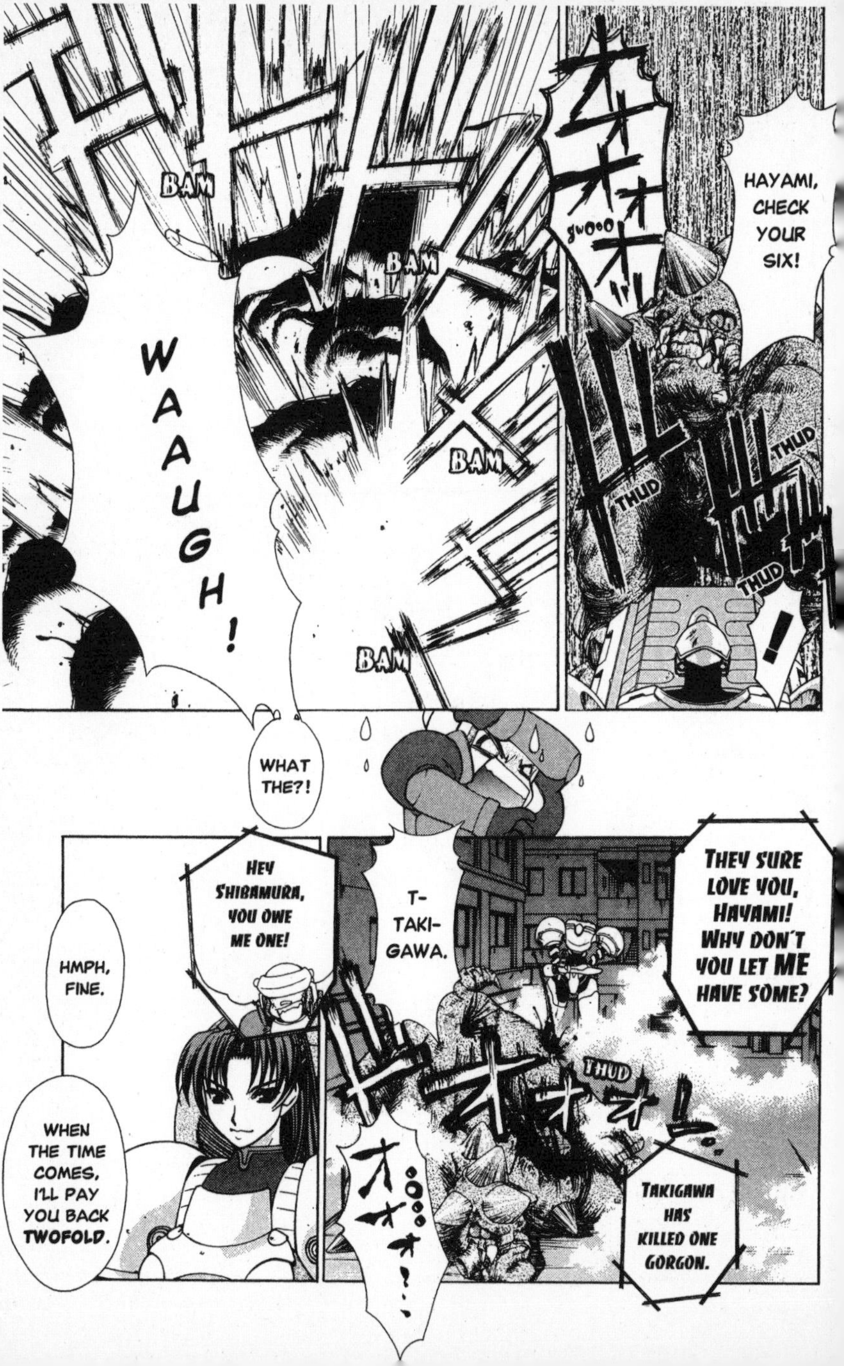
HAYAMI, CHECK YOUR SIX!
GWOOO
THUD
THUD
THUD
!
BAM
BAM
BAM
BAM
WAAUGH!
WHAT THE?!
THEY SURE LOVE YOU, HAYAMI! WHY DON'T YOU LET ME HAVE SOME?
T-TAKI-GAWA.
THUD
OOOO
TAKIGAWA HAS KILLED ONE GORGON.
HEY SHIBAMURA, YOU OWE ME ONE!
HMPH, FINE.
WHEN THE TIME COMES, I'LL PAY YOU BACK TWOFOLD.

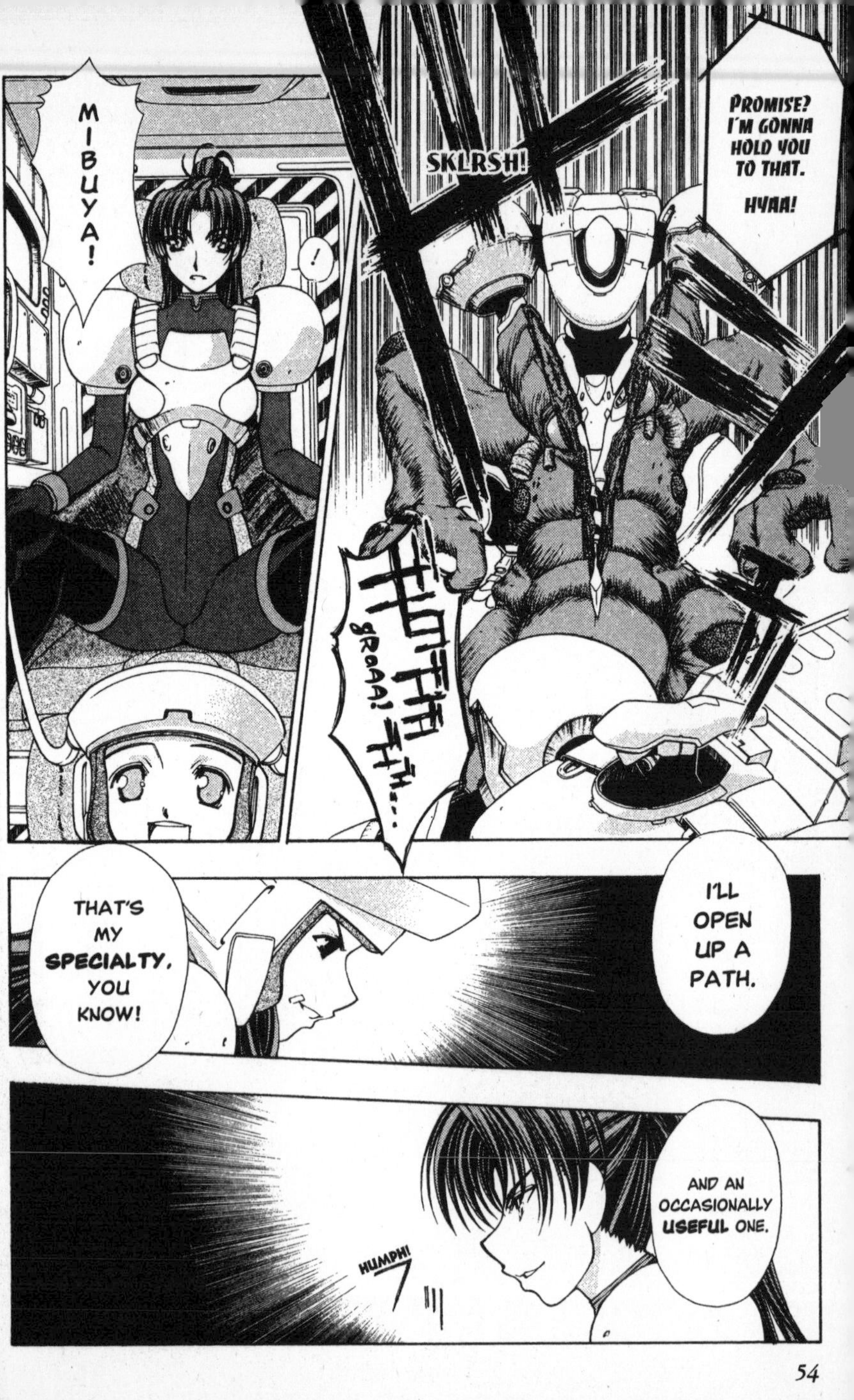
PROMISE? I'M GONNA HOLD YOU TO THAT.
HYAA!
SKLRSH!
MIBUYA!
!
GROAA!
I'LL OPEN UP A PATH.
THAT'S MY SPECIALTY, YOU KNOW!
AND AN OCCASIONALLY USEFUL ONE.
HUMPH!

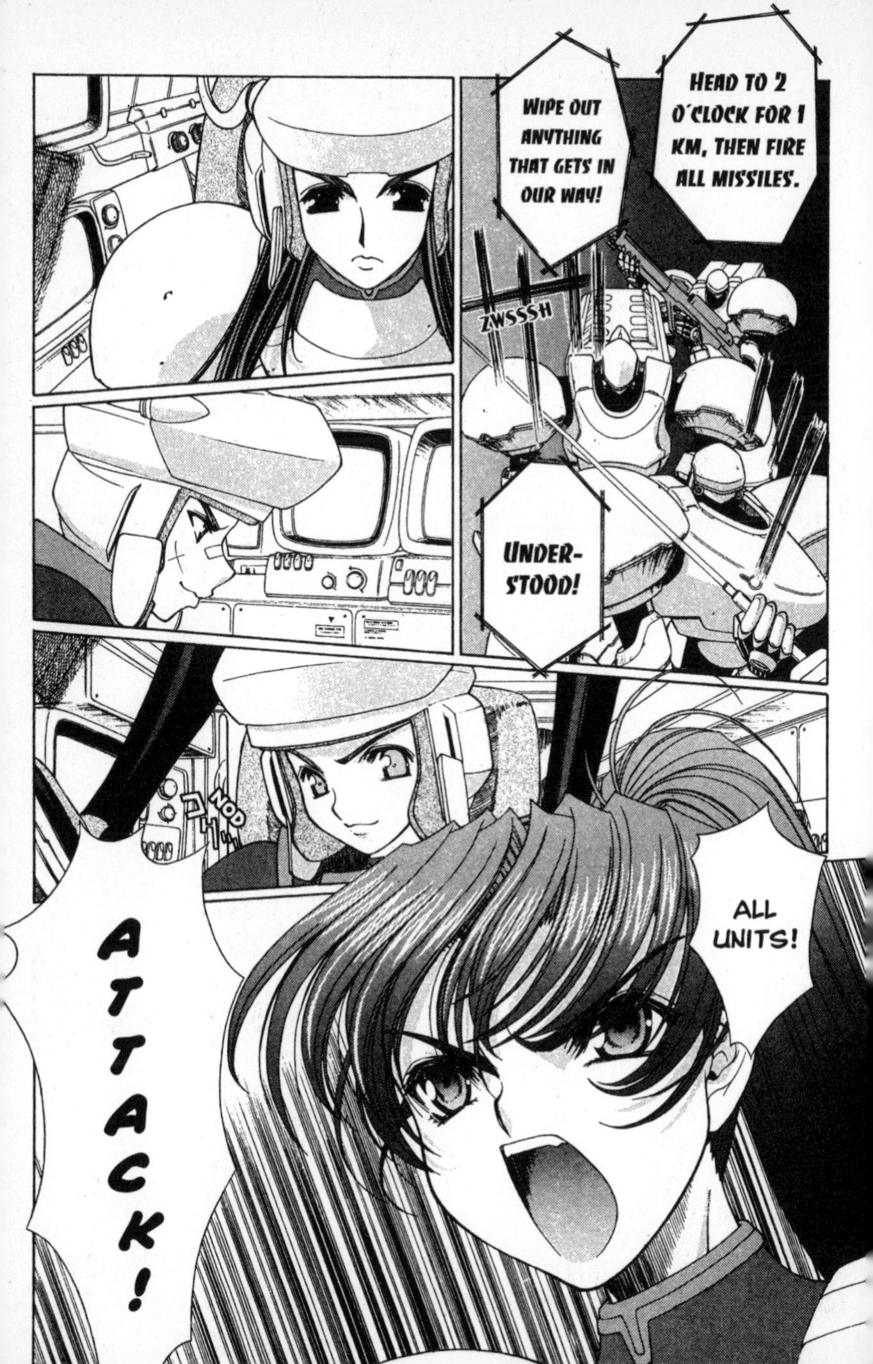
HEAD TO 2 O'CLOCK FOR 1 KM, THEN FIRE ALL MISSILES.
WIPE OUT ANYTHING THAT GETS IN OUR WAY!
ZWSSSH
UNDER-STOOD!
NOD
ALL UNITS!
ATTACK!

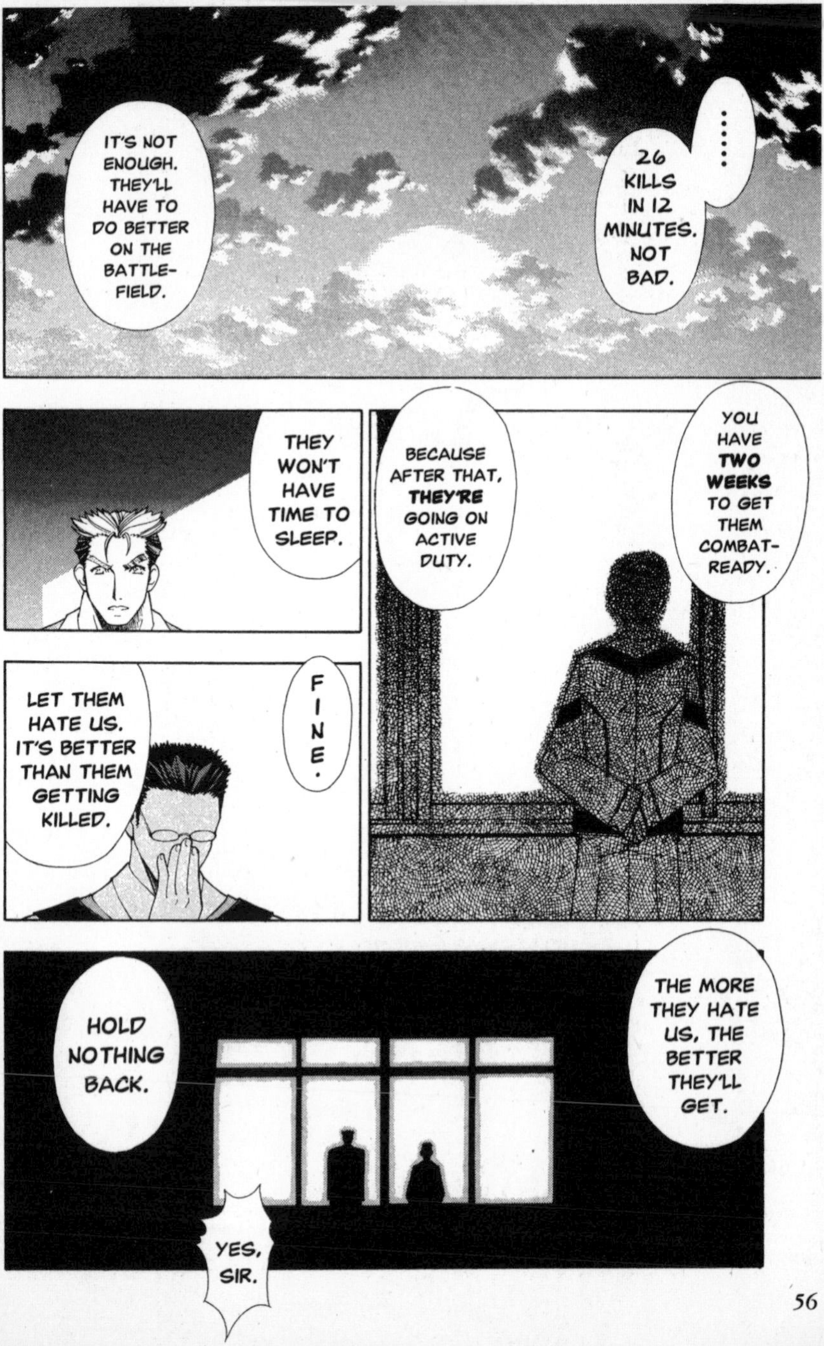
......
26 KILLS IN 12 MINUTES. NOT BAD.
IT'S NOT ENOUGH. THEY'LL HAVE TO DO BETTER ON THE BATTLE-FIELD.
YOU HAVE TWO WEEKS TO GET THEM COMBAT-READY.
BECAUSE AFTER THAT, THEY'RE GOING ON ACTIVE DUTY.
THEY WON'T HAVE TIME TO SLEEP.
FINE.
LET THEM HATE US. IT'S BETTER THAN THEM GETTING KILLED.
THE MORE THEY HATE US, THE BETTER THEY'LL GET.
HOLD NOTHING BACK.
YES, SIR.

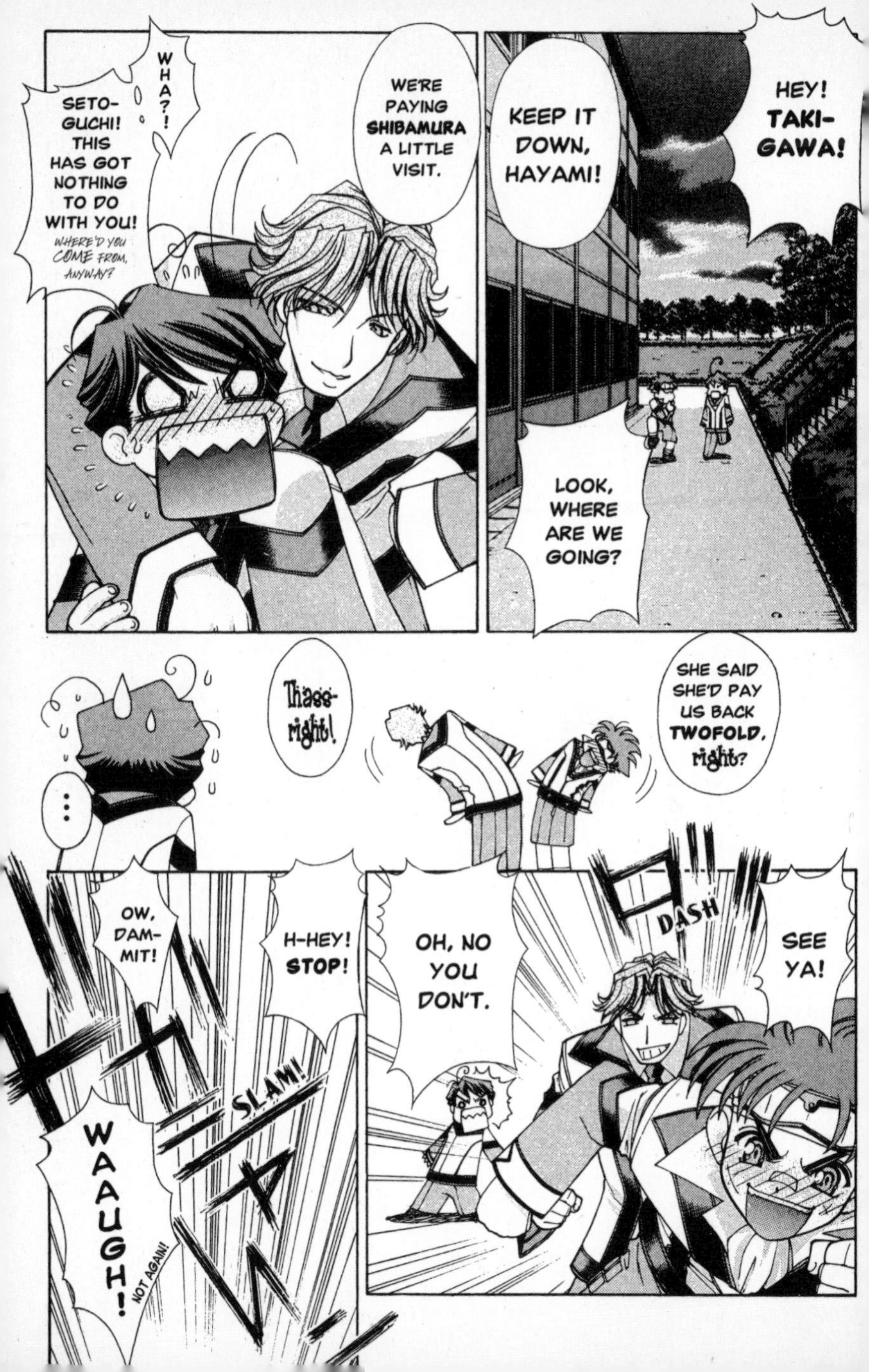
HEY! TAKI-GAWA!
KEEP IT DOWN, HAYAMI!
LOOK, WHERE ARE WE GOING?
WE'RE PAYING SHIBAMURA A LITTLE VISIT.
WHA?!
SETO-GUCHI! THIS HAS GOT NOTHING TO DO WITH YOU!
WHERE'D YOU COME FROM, ANYWAY?
SHE SAID SHE'D PAY US BACK TWOFOLD, right?
Thass-right!
...
SEE YA!
DASH
OH, NO YOU DON'T.
H-HEY! STOP!
OW, DAM-MIT!
SLAM!
WAAUGH!
NOT AGAIN!

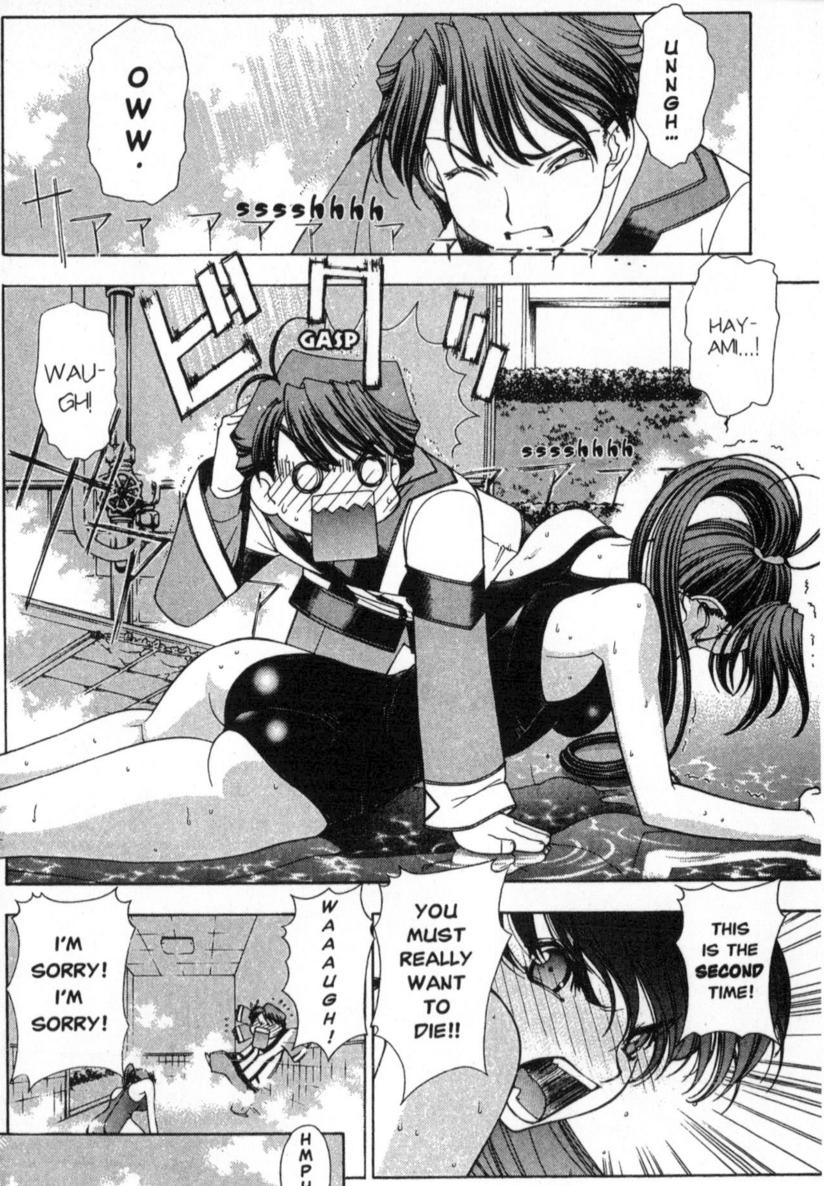
UNNGH...
OWW.
sssshhhh
HAY-AMI...!
GASP
WAU-GH!
sssshhhh
THIS IS THE SECOND TIME!
YOU MUST REALLY WANT TO DIE!!
WAAAAUGH!
I'M SORRY! I'M SORRY!
HMPH!

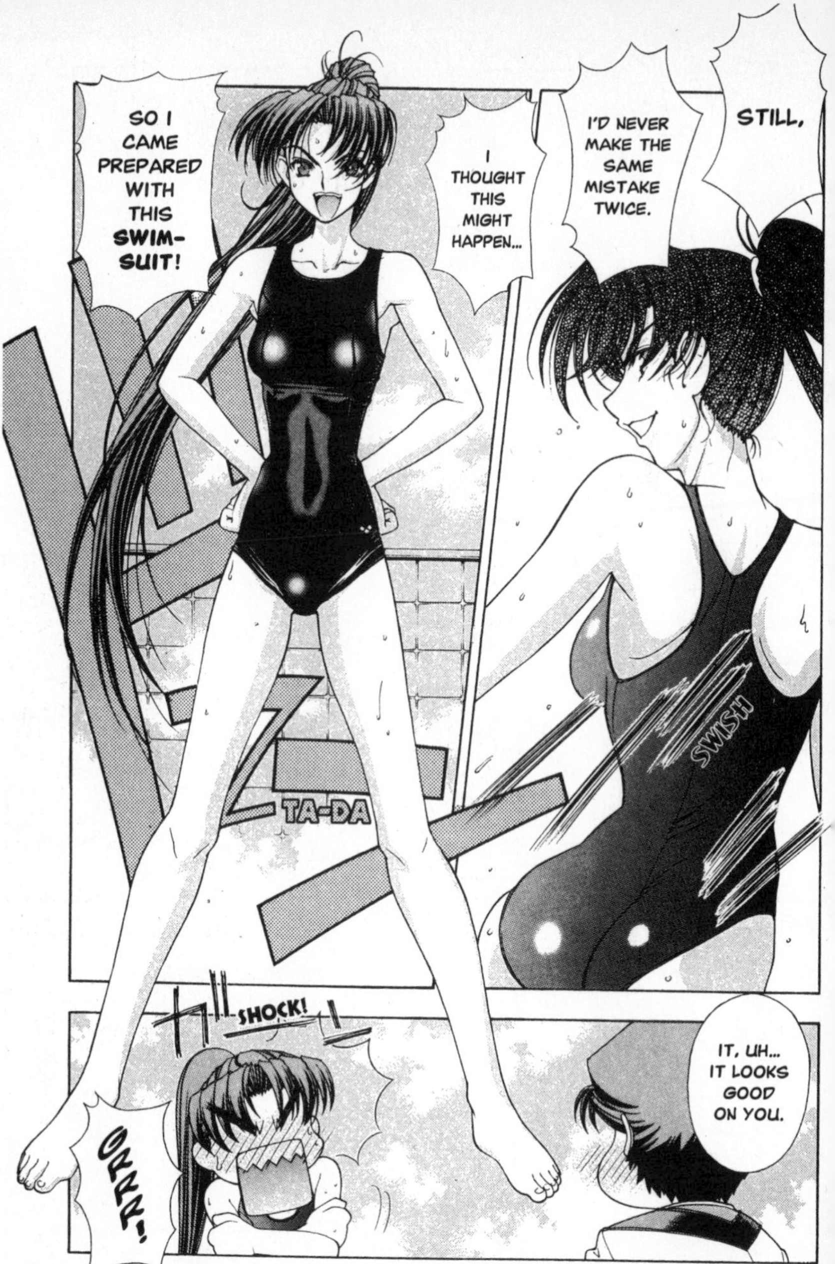
STILL,
I'D NEVER MAKE THE SAME MISTAKE TWICE.
I THOUGHT THIS MIGHT HAPPEN...
SO I CAME PREPARED WITH THIS SWIM-SUIT!
TA-DA
SWISH
IT, UH... IT LOOKS GOOD ON YOU.
SHOCK!
GRRR!

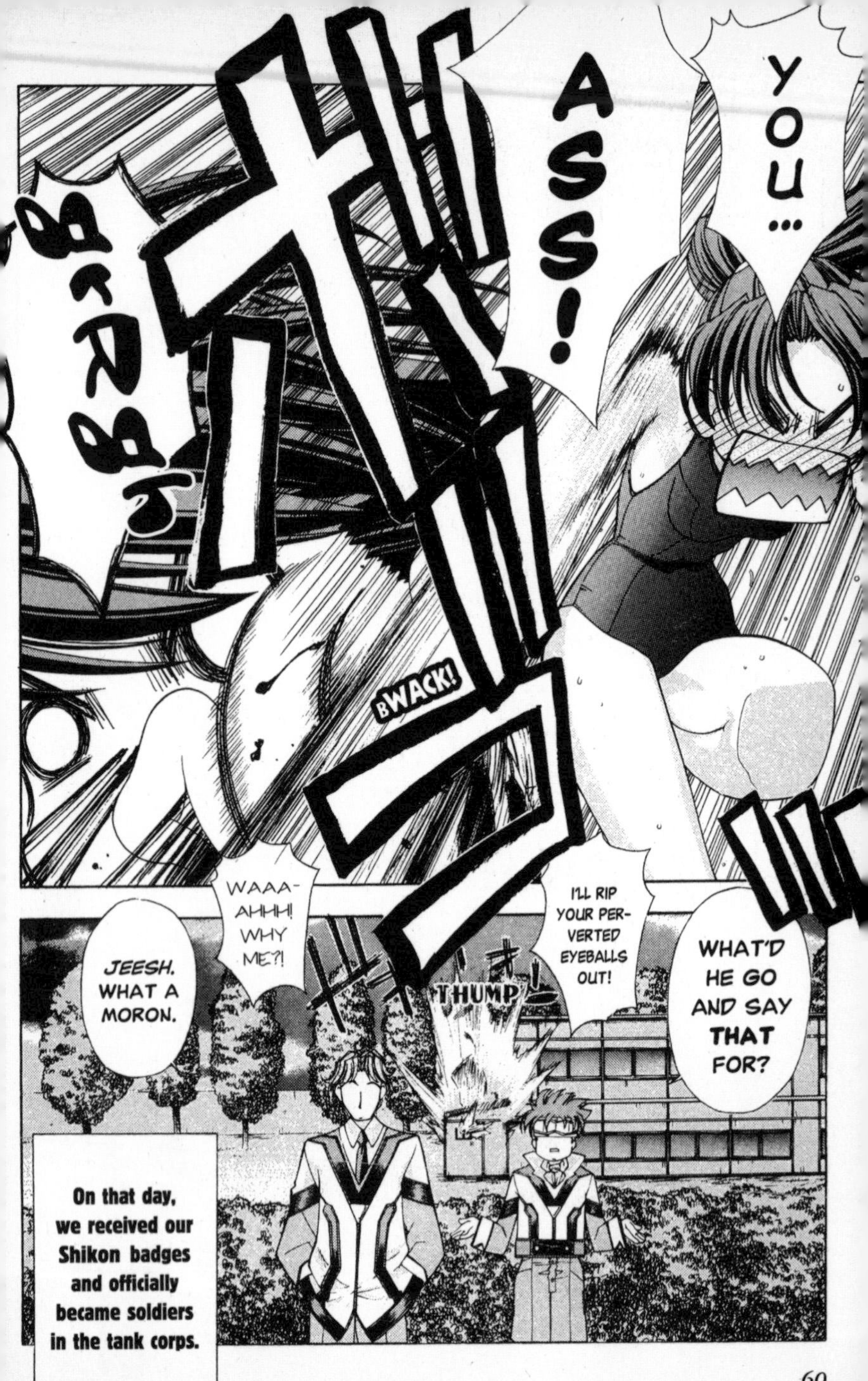
YOU...
ASS!
BWACK!
WHAT'D HE GO AND SAY THAT FOR?
I'LL RIP YOUR PER- VERTED EYEBALLS OUT!
THUMP
WAAA- AHHH! WHY ME?!
JEESH. WHAT A MORON.
On that day, we received our Shikon badges and officially became soldiers in the tank corps.

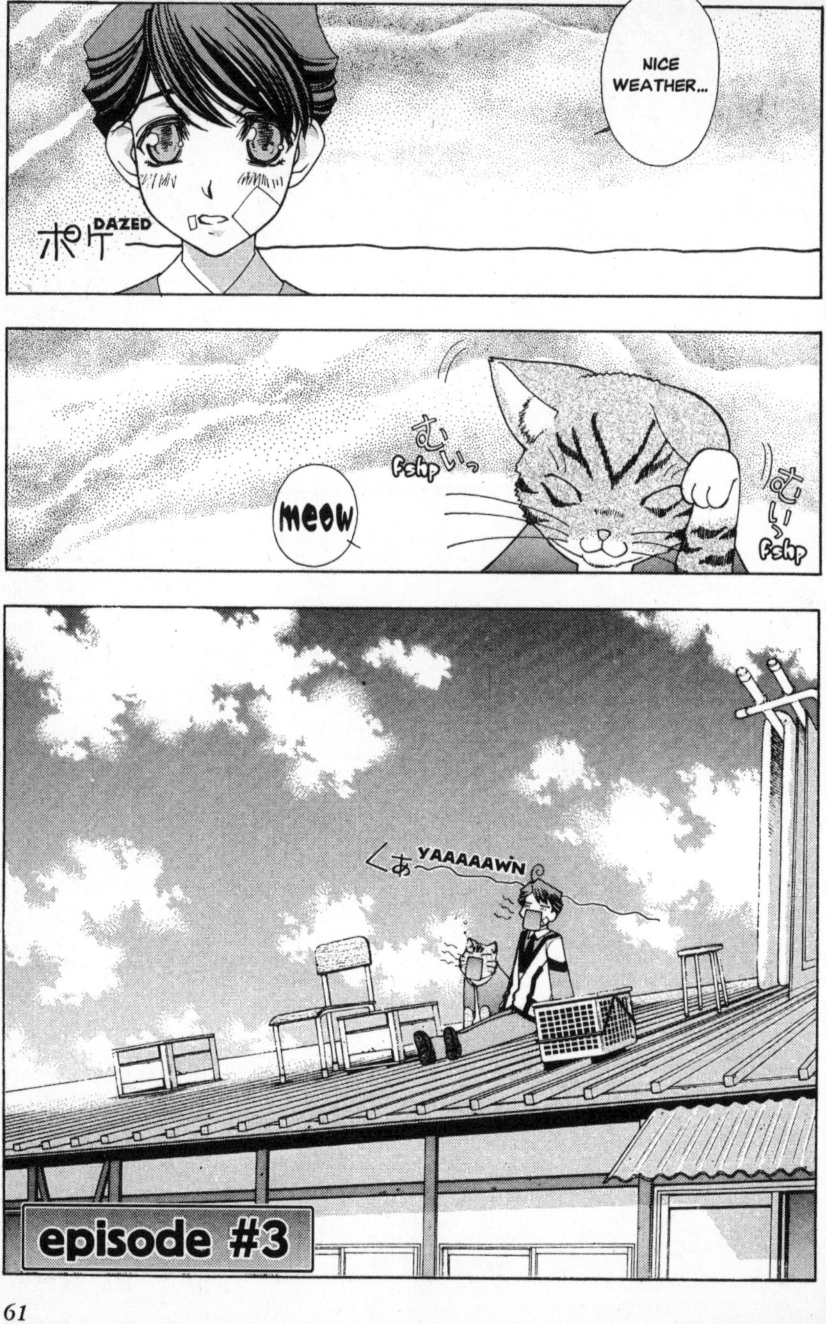
NICE WEATHER...
ポケ
DAZED
むいっ
FSHP
むいっ
FSHP
MEOW
くあ
YAAAAAWN
episode #3

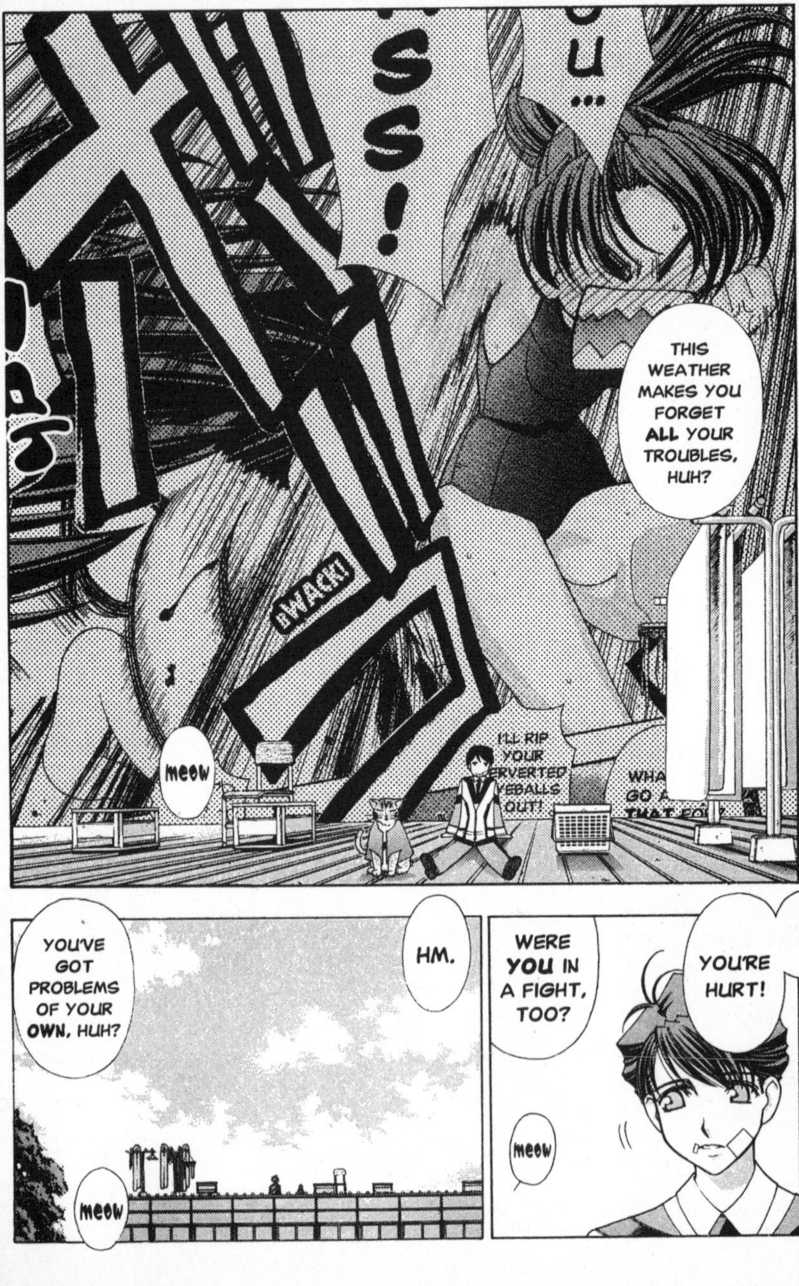
U...
SS!
THIS WEATHER MAKES YOU FORGET ALL YOUR TROUBLES, HUH?
WACK!
WHA GO A THAT FO
I'LL RIP YOUR ERVERTED YEBALLS OUT!
meow
HUH?
YOU'RE HURT!
WERE YOU IN A FIGHT, TOO?
meow
HM.
YOU'VE GOT PROBLEMS OF YOUR OWN, HUH?
meow

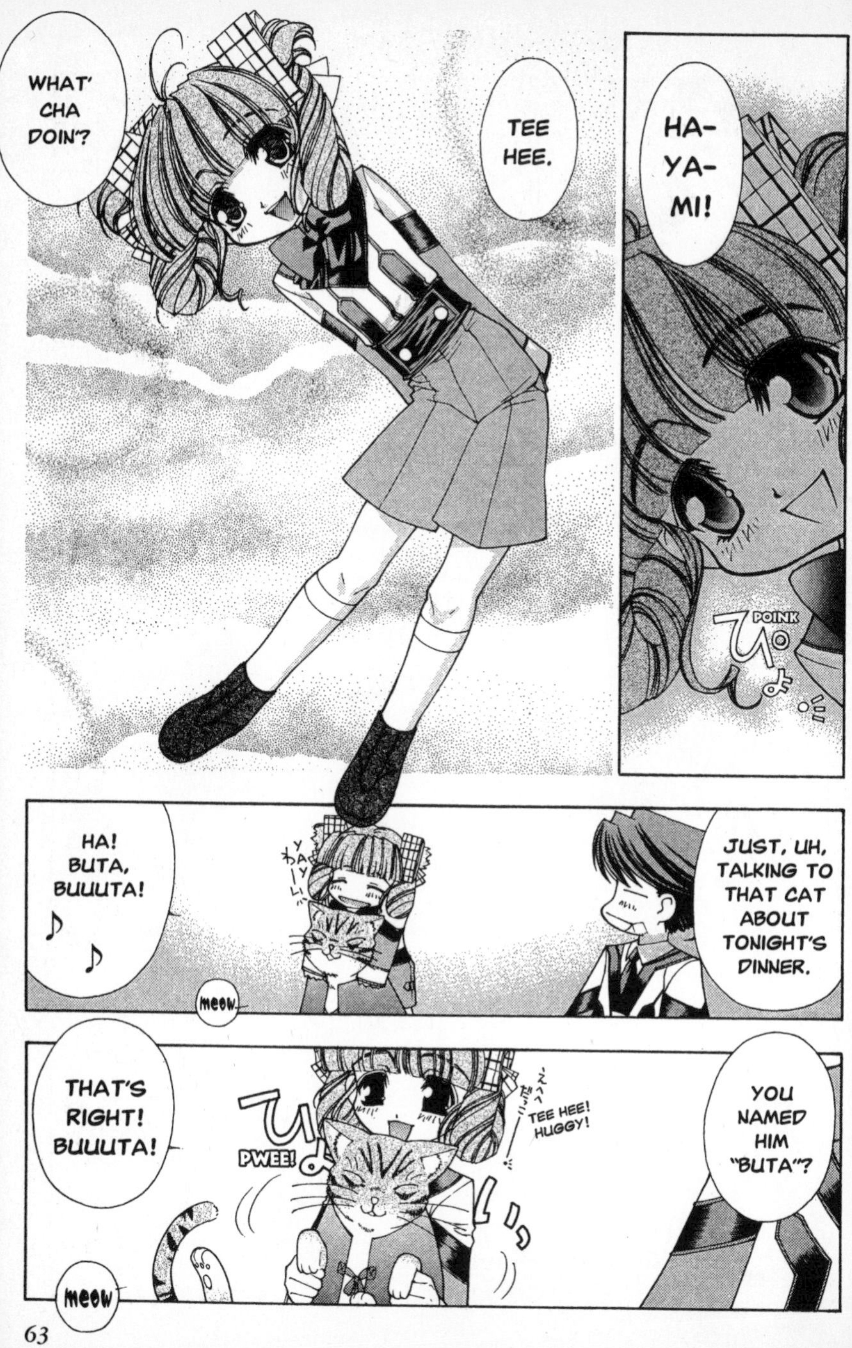
HA-YA-MI!
POINK
TEE HEE.
WHAT'CHA DOIN'?
JUST, UH, TALKING TO THAT CAT ABOUT TONIGHT'S DINNER.
HA! BUTA, BUUUTA! ♪ ♪
meow
YOU NAMED HIM "BUTA"?
TEE HEE! HUGGY!
PWEE!
THAT'S RIGHT! BUUUTA!
meow

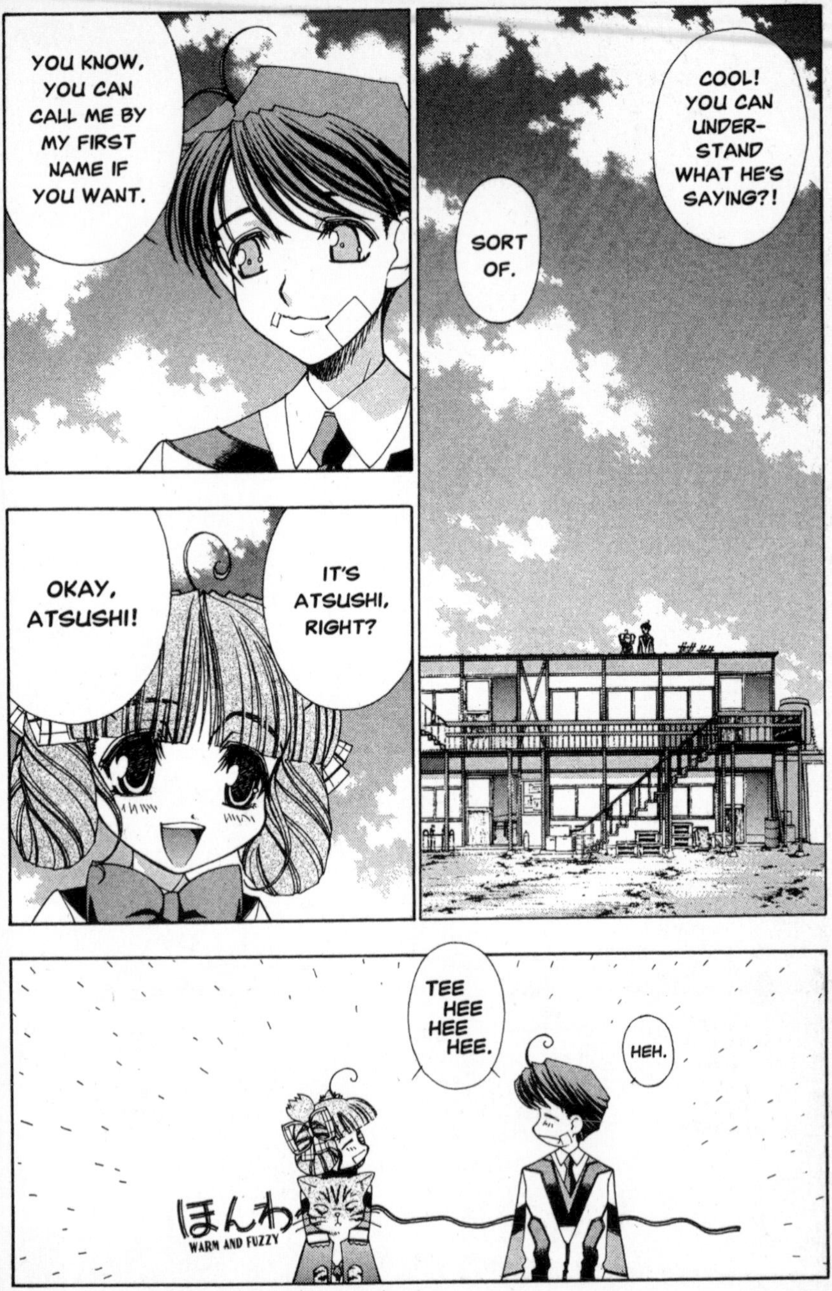
COOL! YOU CAN UNDER-STAND WHAT HE'S SAYING?!
SORT OF.
YOU KNOW, YOU CAN CALL ME BY MY FIRST NAME IF YOU WANT.
IT'S ATSUSHI, RIGHT?
OKAY, ATSUSHI!
HEH.
TEE HEE HEE HEE.
ほんわ
WARM AND FUZZY

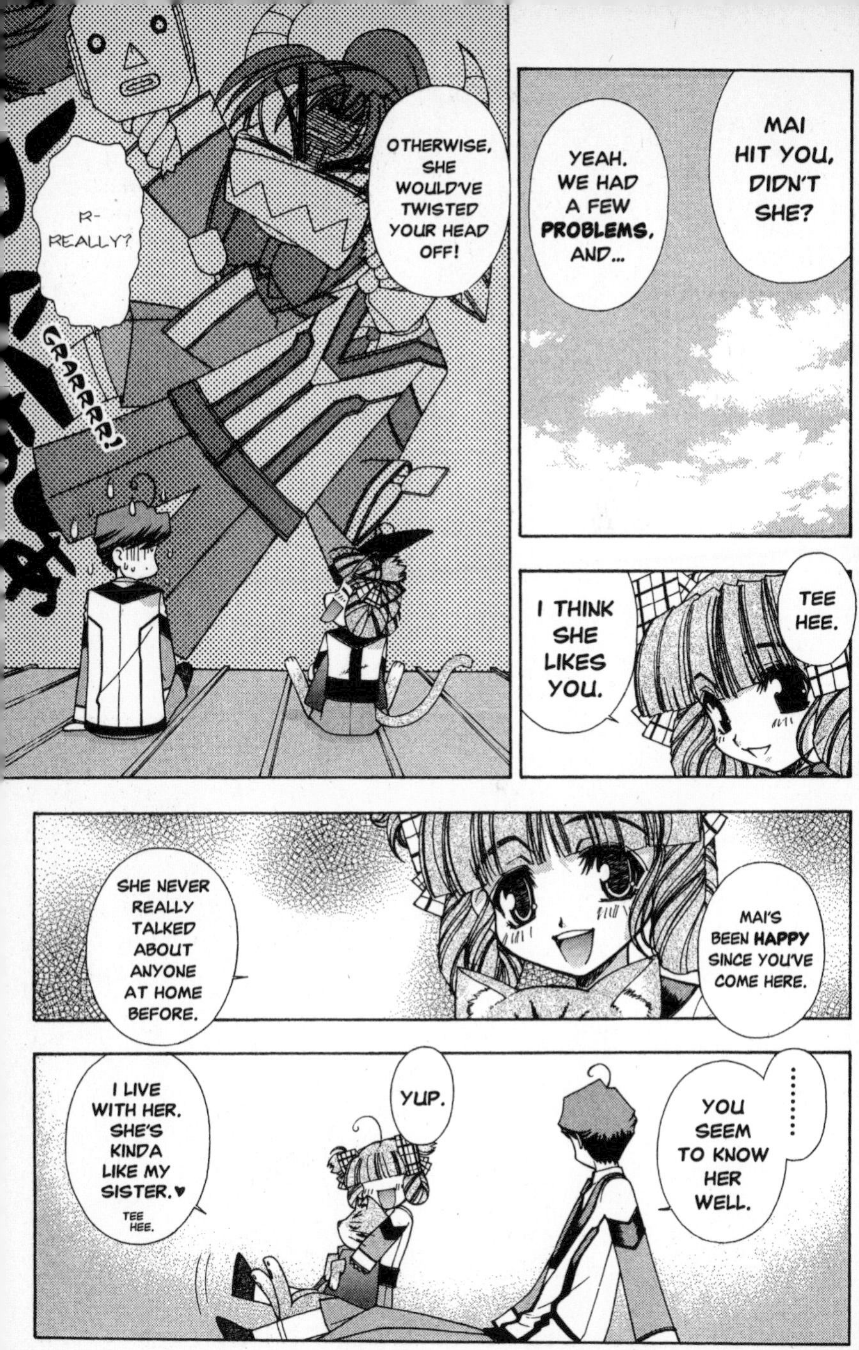

MAI HIT YOU, DIDN'T SHE?
YEAH. WE HAD A FEW PROBLEMS, AND...
TEE HEE.
I THINK SHE LIKES YOU.
OTHERWISE, SHE WOULD'VE TWISTED YOUR HEAD OFF!
R-REALLY?
GRARRRR!
MAI'S BEEN HAPPY SINCE YOU'VE COME HERE.
SHE NEVER REALLY TALKED ABOUT ANYONE AT HOME BEFORE.
......
YOU SEEM TO KNOW HER WELL.
YUP.
I LIVE WITH HER. SHE'S KINDA LIKE MY SISTER. ♥
TEE HEE.

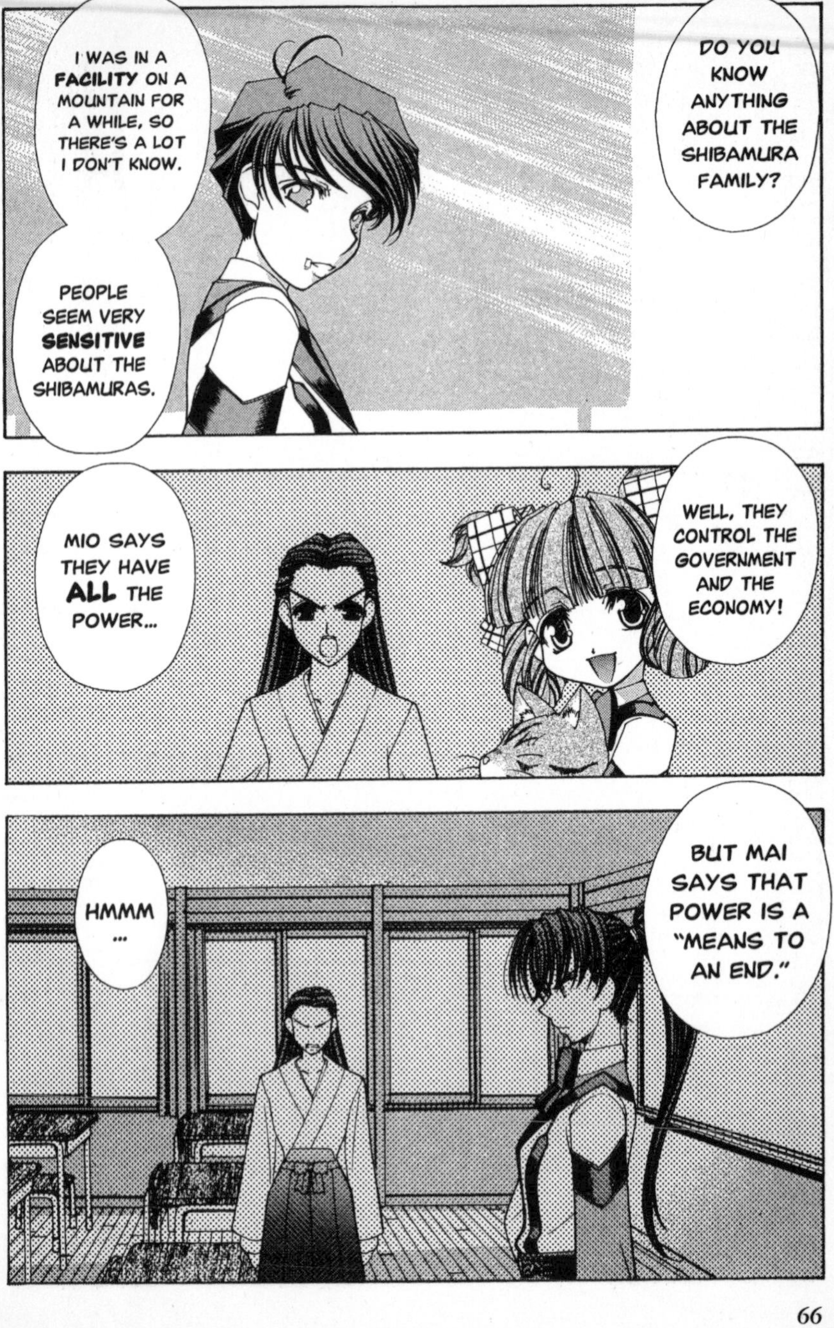
DO YOU KNOW ANYTHING ABOUT THE SHIBAMURA FAMILY?
I WAS IN A FACILITY ON A MOUNTAIN FOR A WHILE, SO THERE'S A LOT I DON'T KNOW.
PEOPLE SEEM VERY SENSITIVE ABOUT THE SHIBAMURAS.
WELL, THEY CONTROL THE GOVERNMENT AND THE ECONOMY!
MIO SAYS THEY HAVE ALL THE POWER...
BUT MAI SAYS THAT POWER IS A "MEANS TO AN END."
HMMM ...

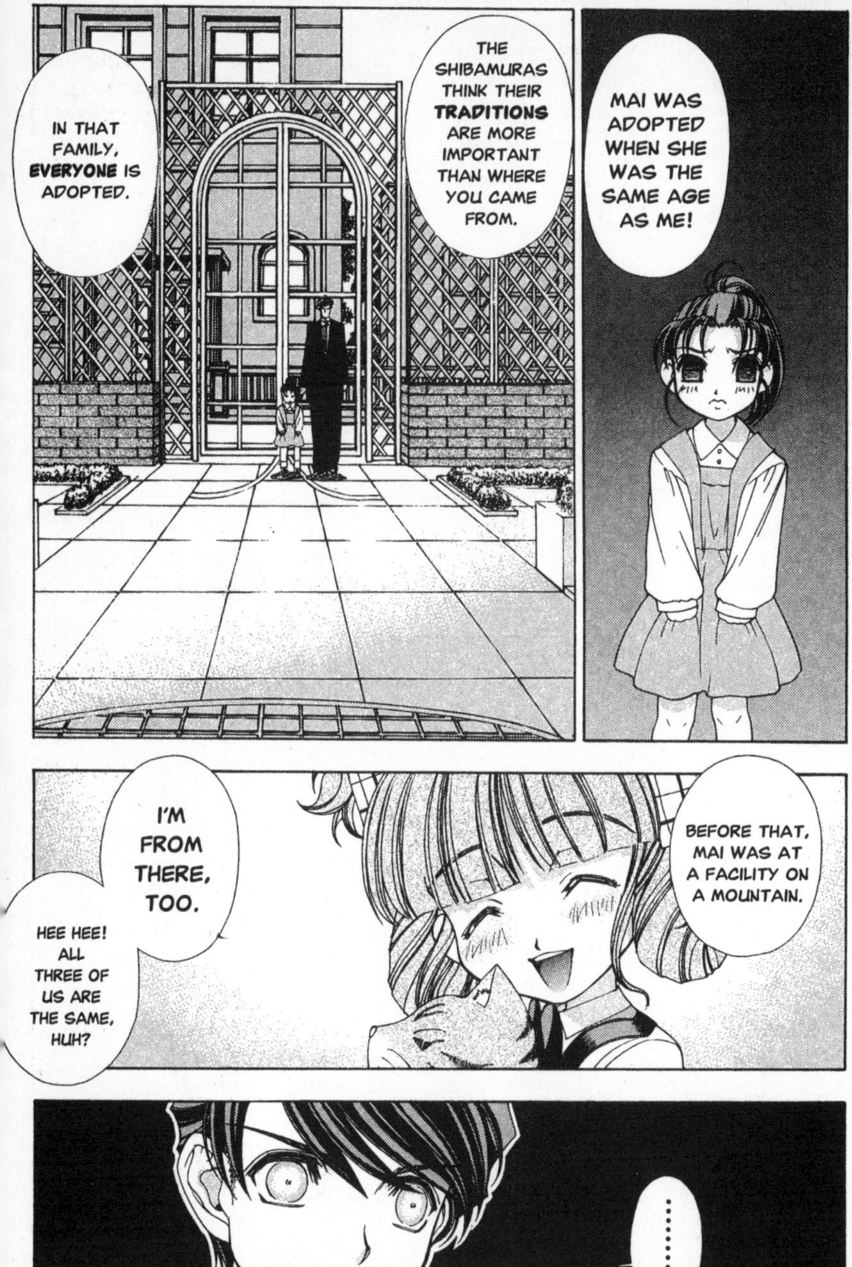
MAI WAS ADOPTED WHEN SHE WAS THE SAME AGE AS ME!
THE SHIBAMURAS THINK THEIR TRADITIONS ARE MORE IMPORTANT THAN WHERE YOU CAME FROM.
IN THAT FAMILY, EVERYONE IS ADOPTED.
BEFORE THAT, MAI WAS AT A FACILITY ON A MOUNTAIN.
I'M FROM THERE, TOO.
HEE HEE! ALL THREE OF US ARE THE SAME, HUH?
......

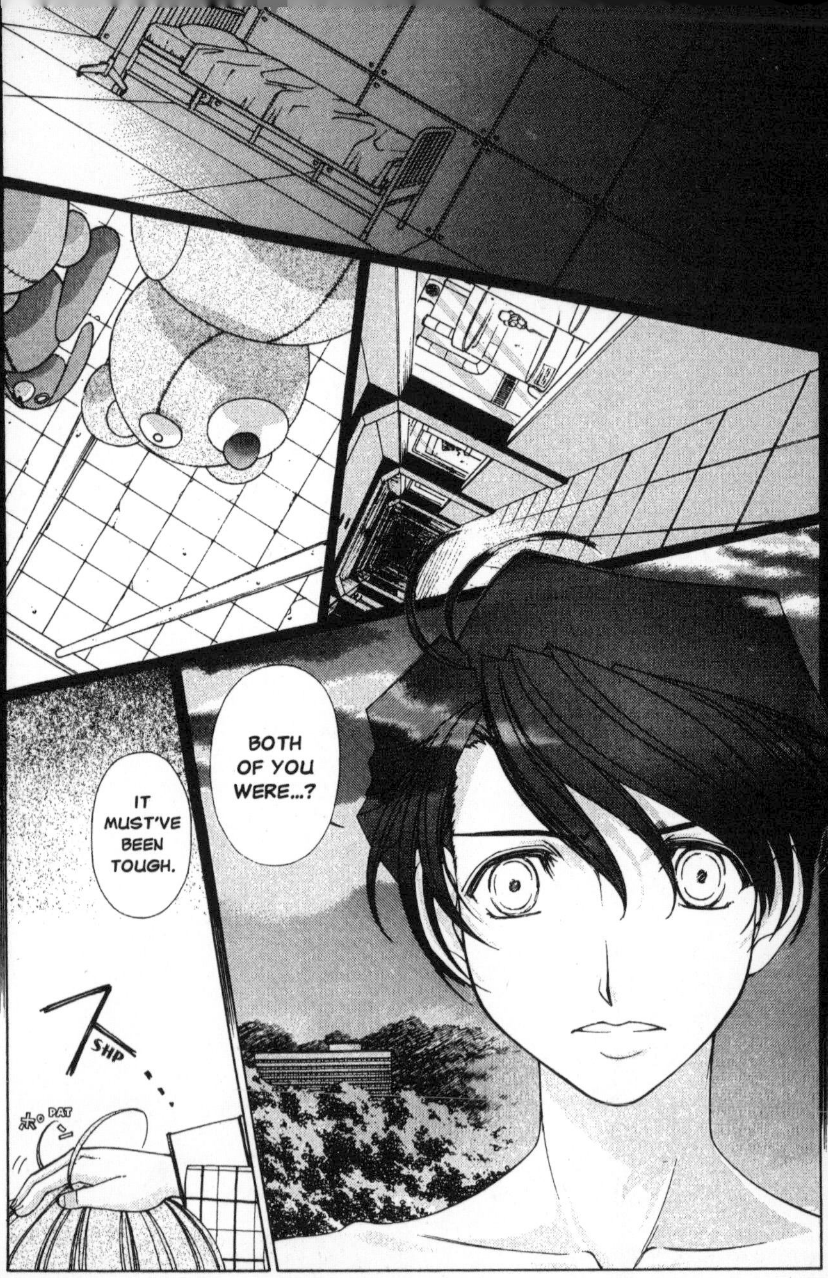
BOTH OF YOU WERE...?
IT MUST'VE BEEN TOUGH.
SHP
PAT

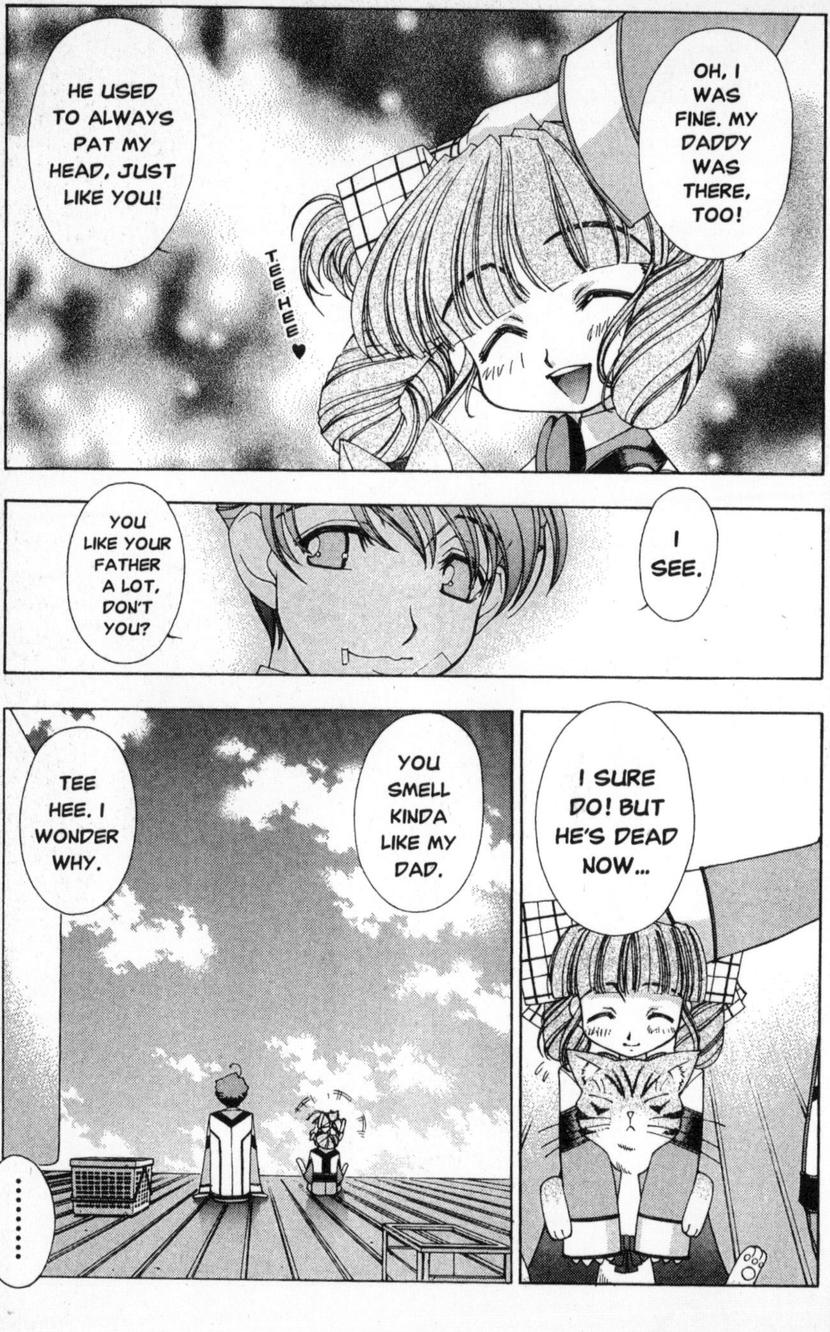
OH, I WAS FINE. MY DADDY WAS THERE, TOO!
HE USED TO ALWAYS PAT MY HEAD, JUST LIKE YOU!
TEE HEE ♥
I SEE.
YOU LIKE YOUR FATHER A LOT, DON'T YOU?
I SURE DO! BUT HE'S DEAD NOW...
YOU SMELL KINDA LIKE MY DAD.
TEE HEE. I WONDER WHY.
....

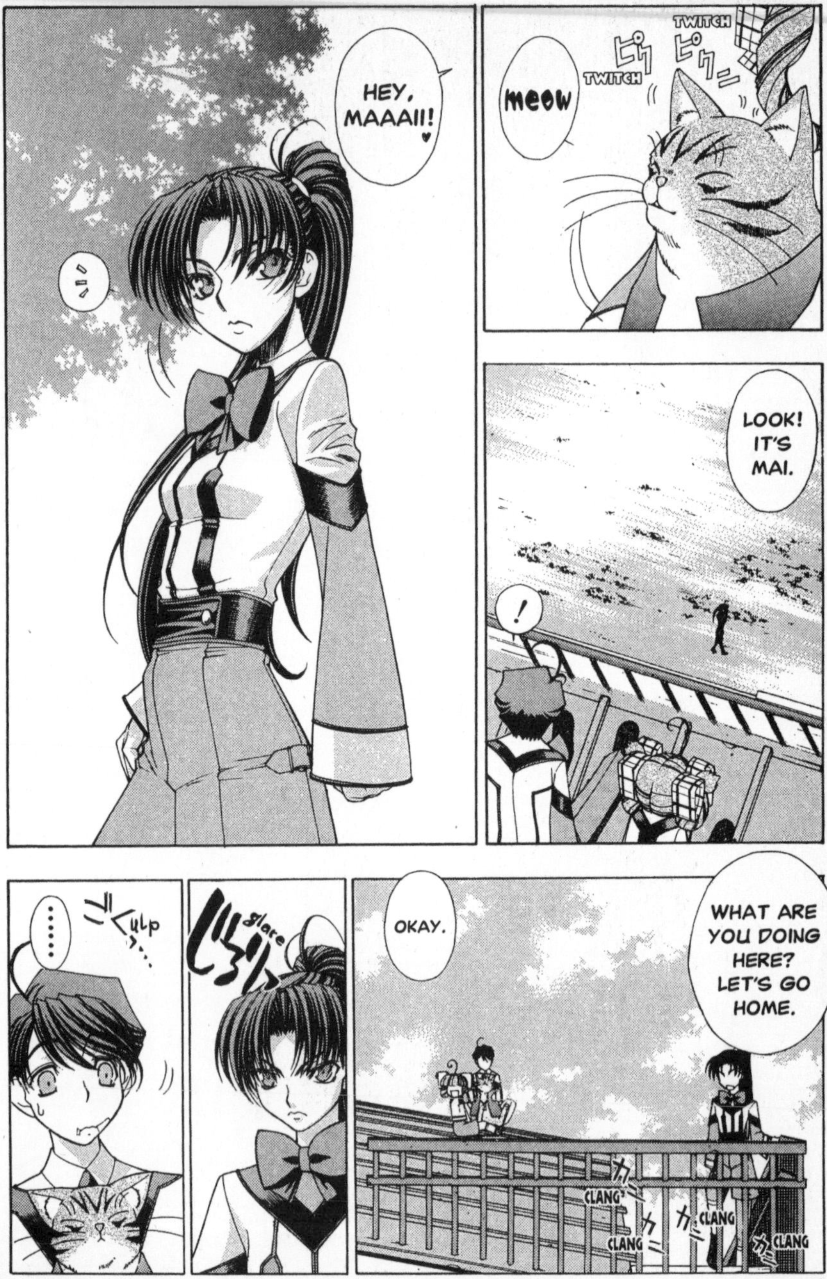
TWITCH
TWITCH
meow
LOOK! IT'S MAI.
!
HEY, MAAAII! ♥
WHAT ARE YOU DOING HERE? LET'S GO HOME.
OKAY.
CLANG
CLANG
CLANG
CLANG
glare
......
gulp

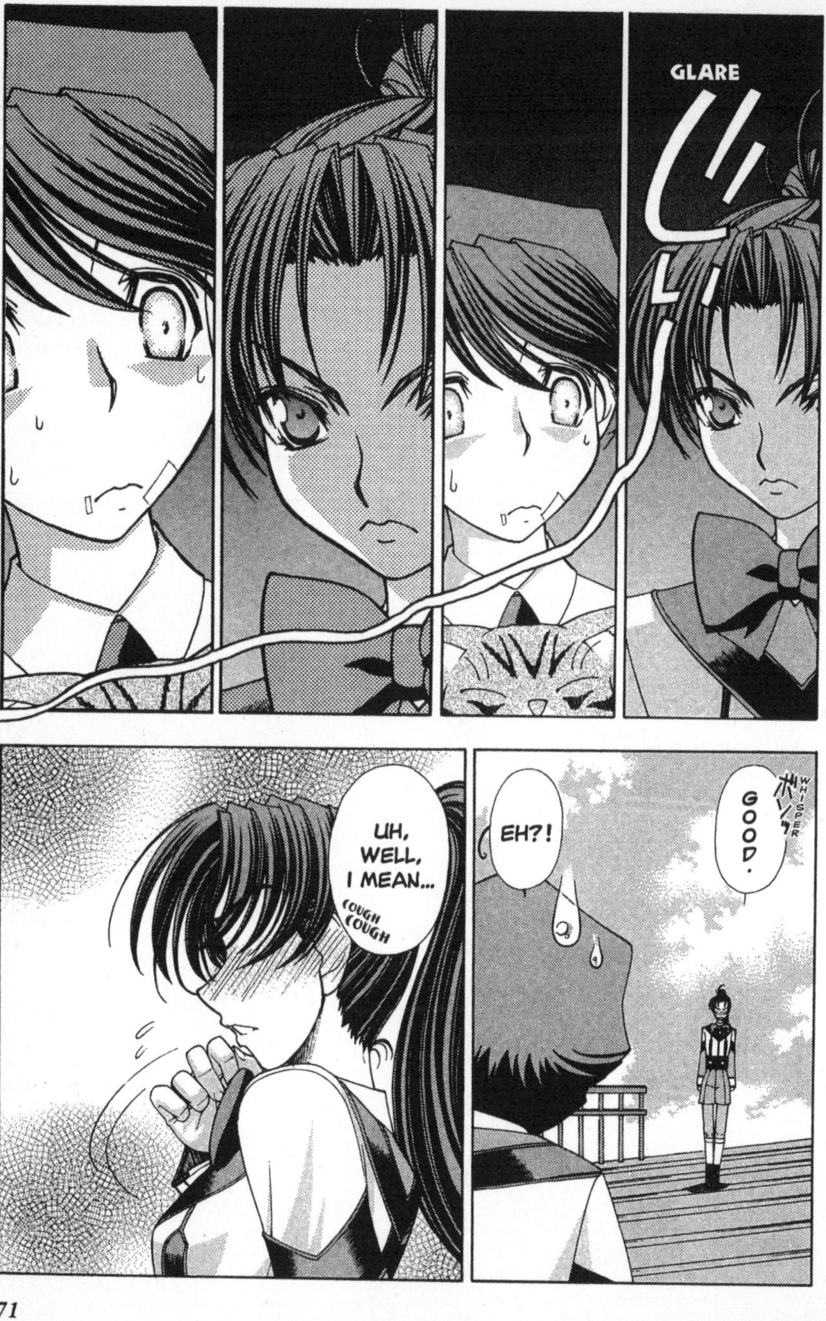
GLARE
WHISPER
GOOD.
EH?!
UH, WELL, I MEAN...
COUGH COUGH

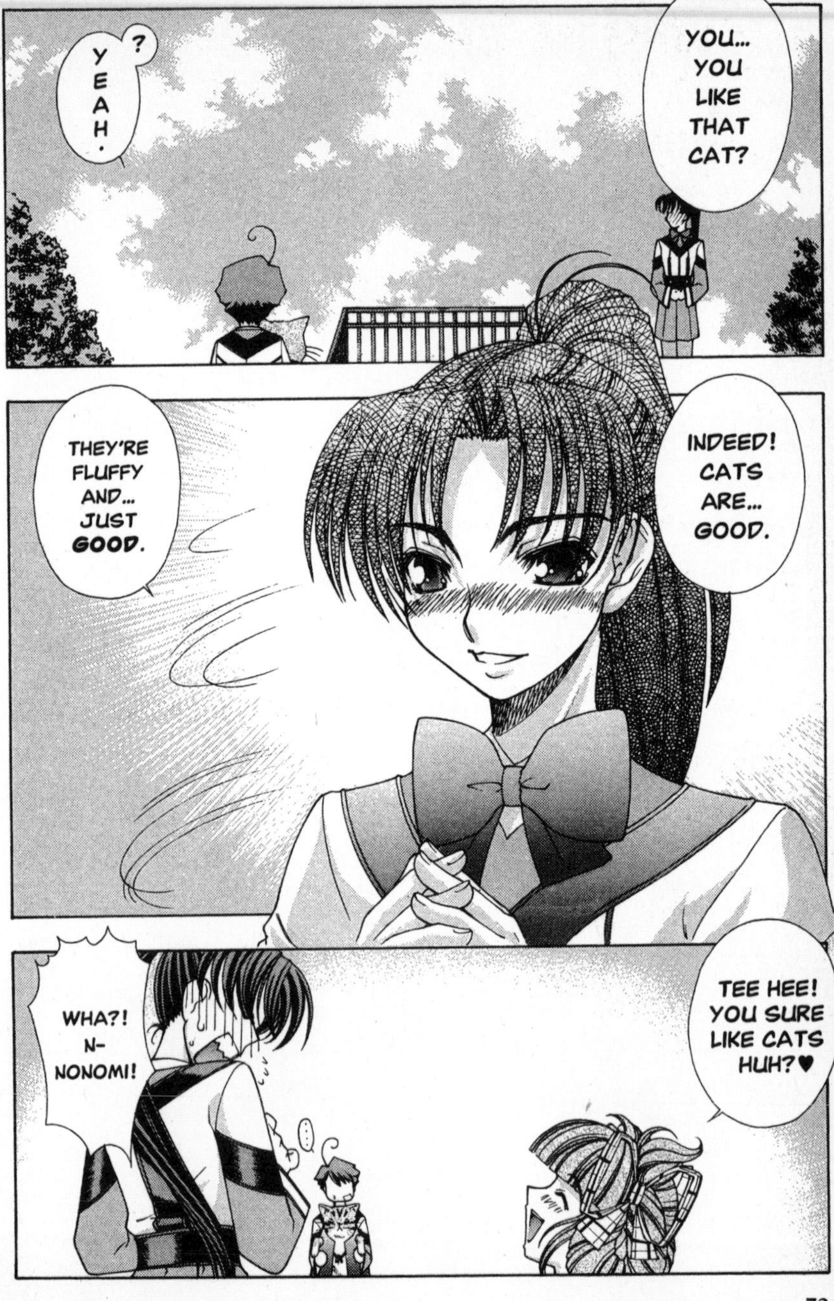
YOU... YOU LIKE THAT CAT?
? YEAH.
INDEED! CATS ARE... GOOD.
THEY'RE FLUFFY AND... JUST GOOD.
TEE HEE! YOU SURE LIKE CATS HUH?♥
...
WHA?! N- NONOMI!

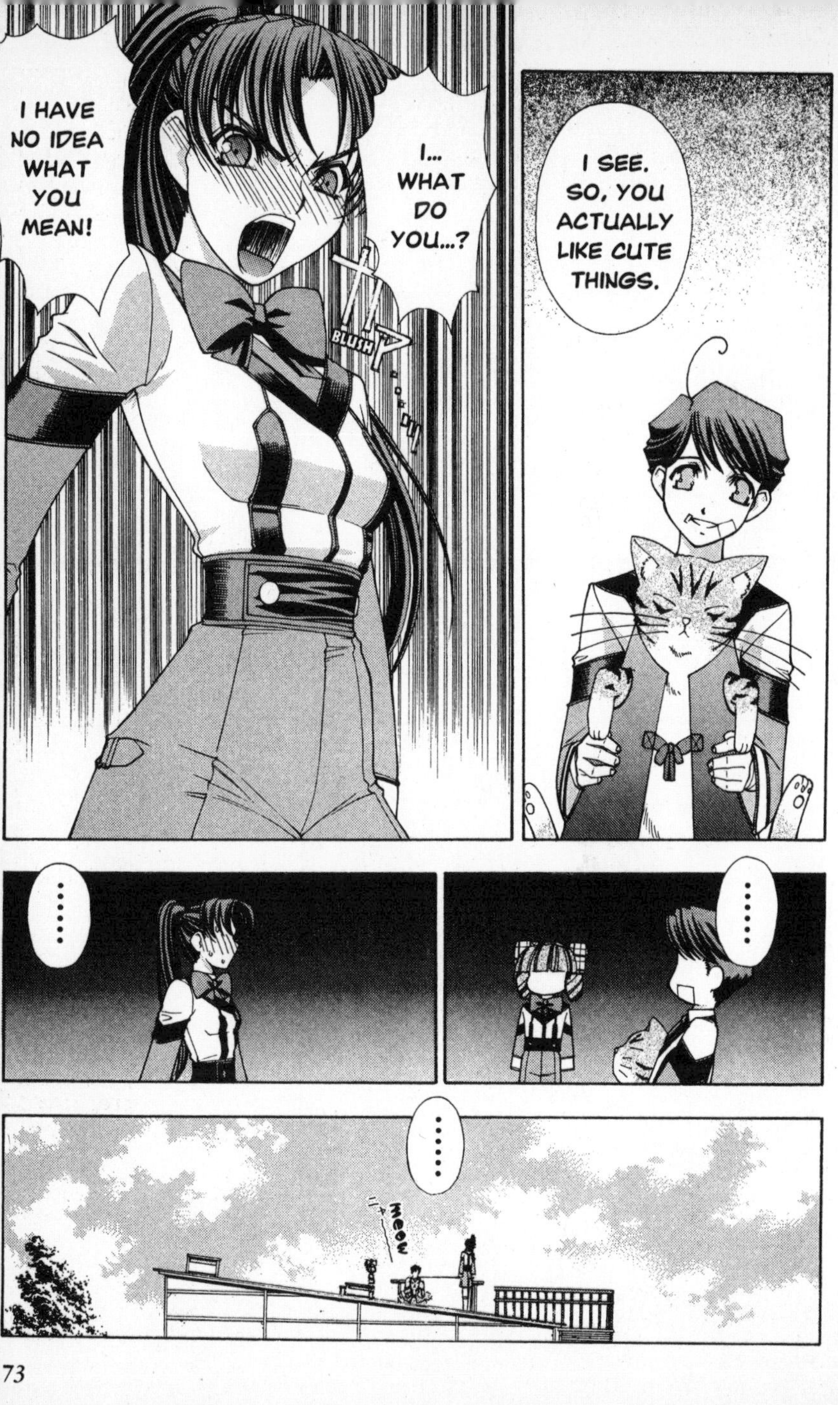
I SEE. SO, YOU ACTUALLY LIKE CUTE THINGS.
I... WHAT DO YOU...?
I HAVE NO IDEA WHAT YOU MEAN!
BLUSH
......
......
......
MEOW

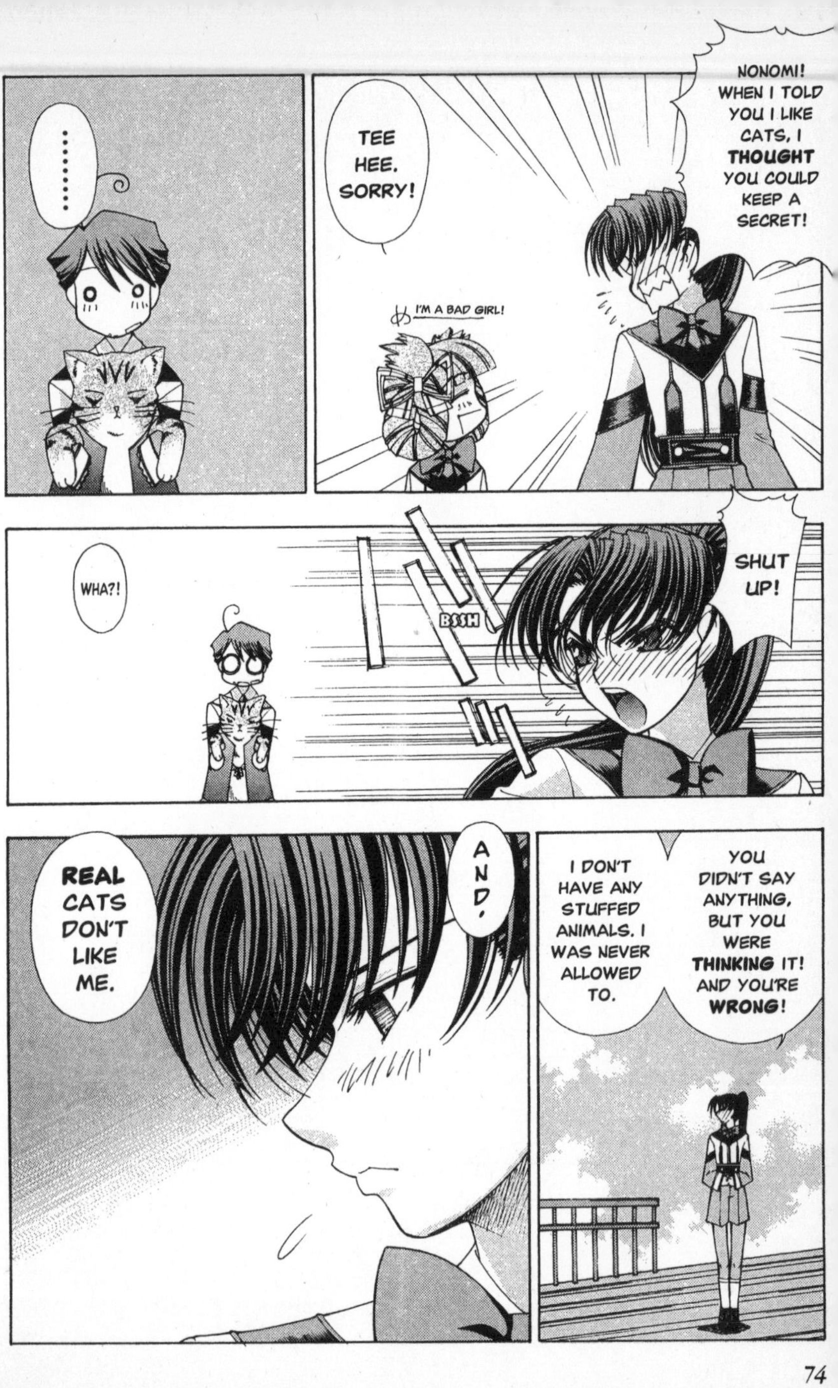
NONOMI! WHEN I TOLD YOU I LIKE CATS, I **THOUGHT** YOU COULD KEEP A SECRET!
TEE HEE. SORRY!
I'M A BAD GIRL!
......
SHUT UP!
BSSH
WHA?!
YOU DIDN'T SAY ANYTHING, BUT YOU WERE **THINKING** IT! AND YOU'RE **WRONG**!
I DON'T HAVE ANY STUFFED ANIMALS. I WAS NEVER ALLOWED TO.
AND.
REAL CATS DON'T LIKE ME.

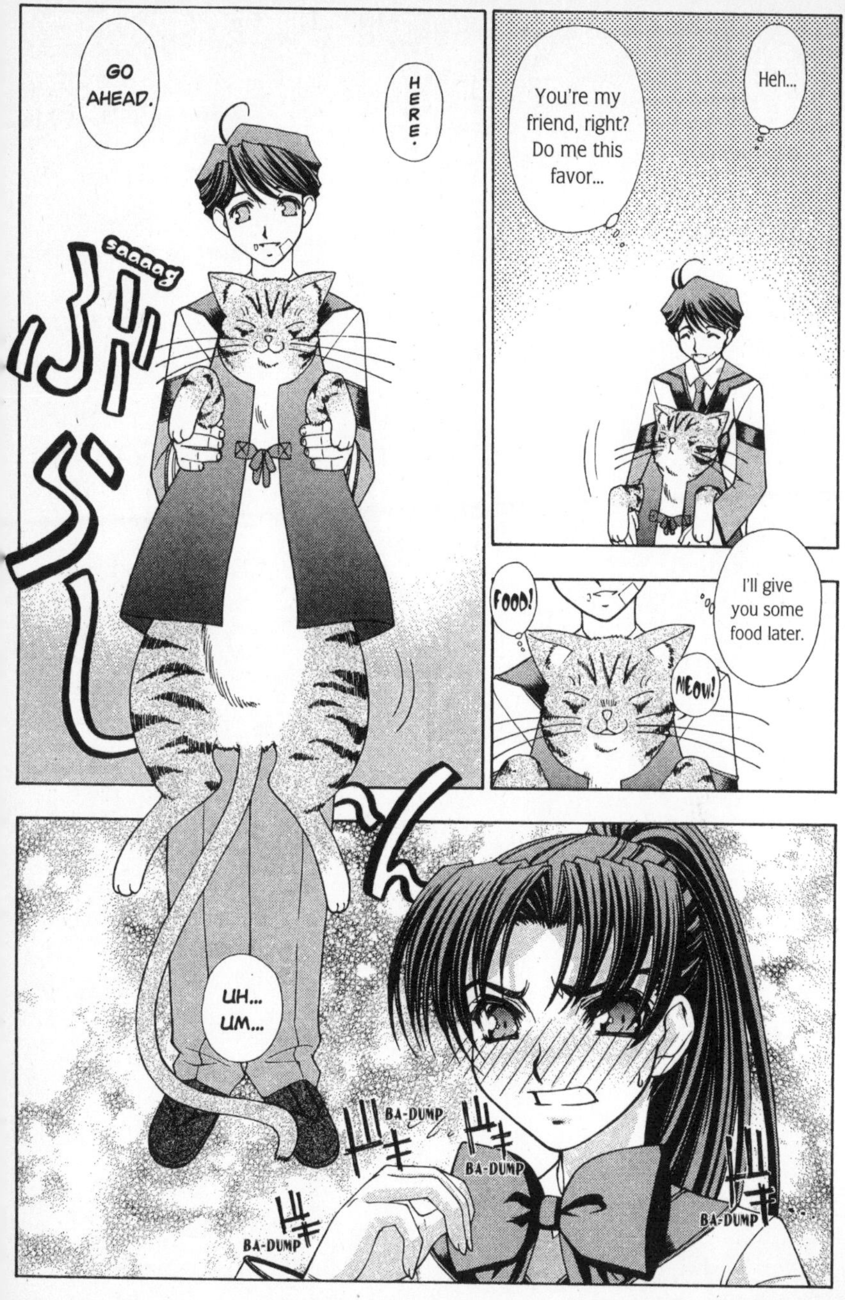
Heh...
You're my friend, right? Do me this favor...
I'll give you some food later.
MEOW!
FOOD!
HERE.
GO AHEAD.
saaaag
UH... UM...
BA-DUMP
BA-DUMP
BA-DUMP
BA-DUMP

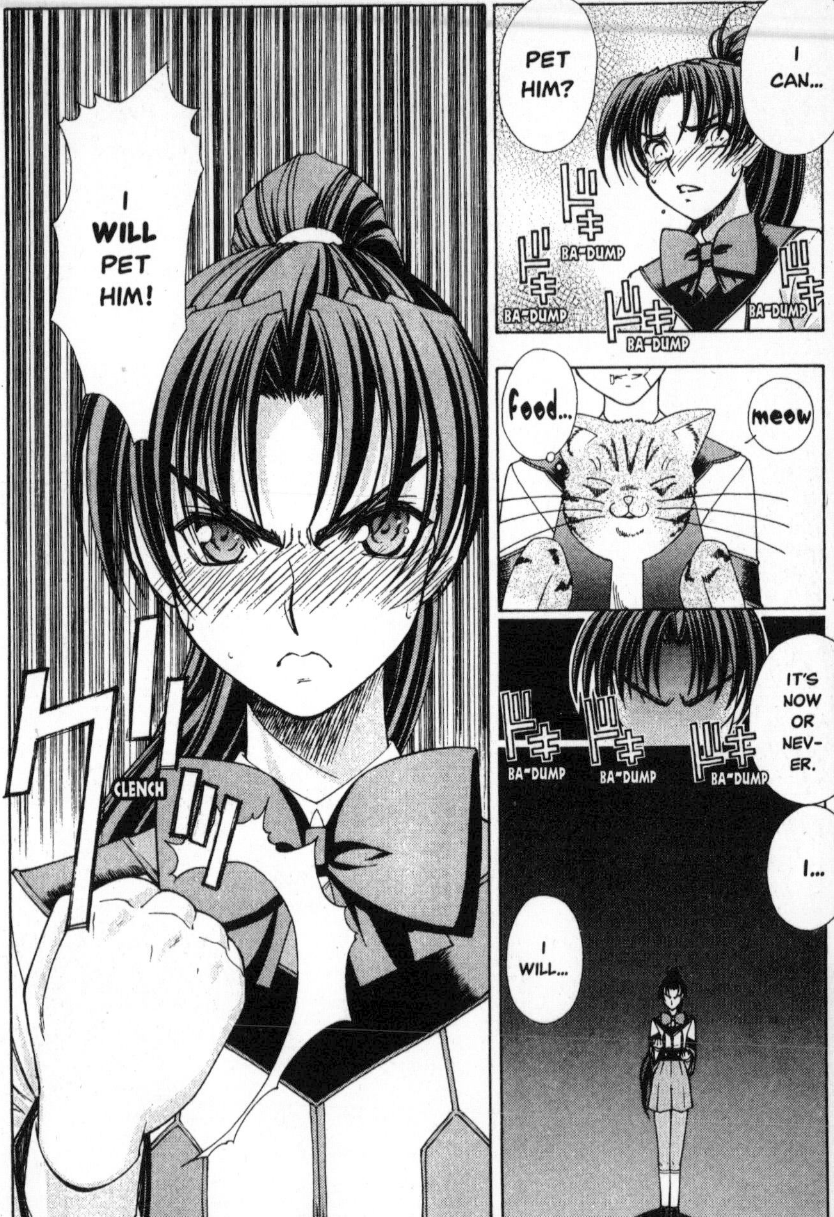
I CAN...
PET HIM?
ドキ
BA-DUMP
ドキ
BA-DUMP
ドキ
BA-DUMP
ドキ
BA-DUMP
meow
food...
IT'S NOW OR NEVER.
ドキ
BA-DUMP
ドキ
BA-DUMP
ドキ
BA-DUMP
I...
I WILL...
I WILL PET HIM!
CLENCH

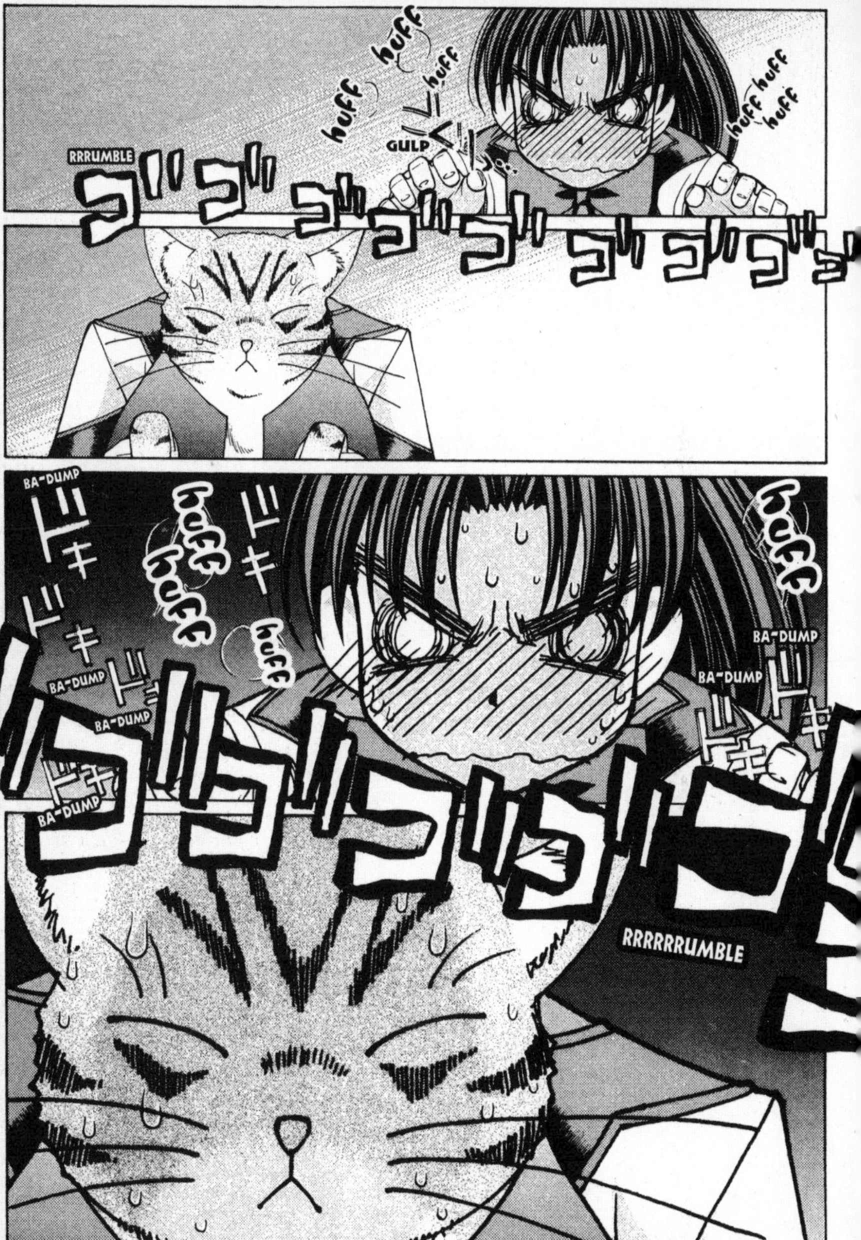
huff huff
huff
huff
huff
huff
huff
GULP
RRRUMBLE
huff
BA-DUMP
BA-DUMP
huff
huff
huff
BA-DUMP
BA-DUMP
BA-DUMP
BA-DUMP
RRRRRRUMBLE

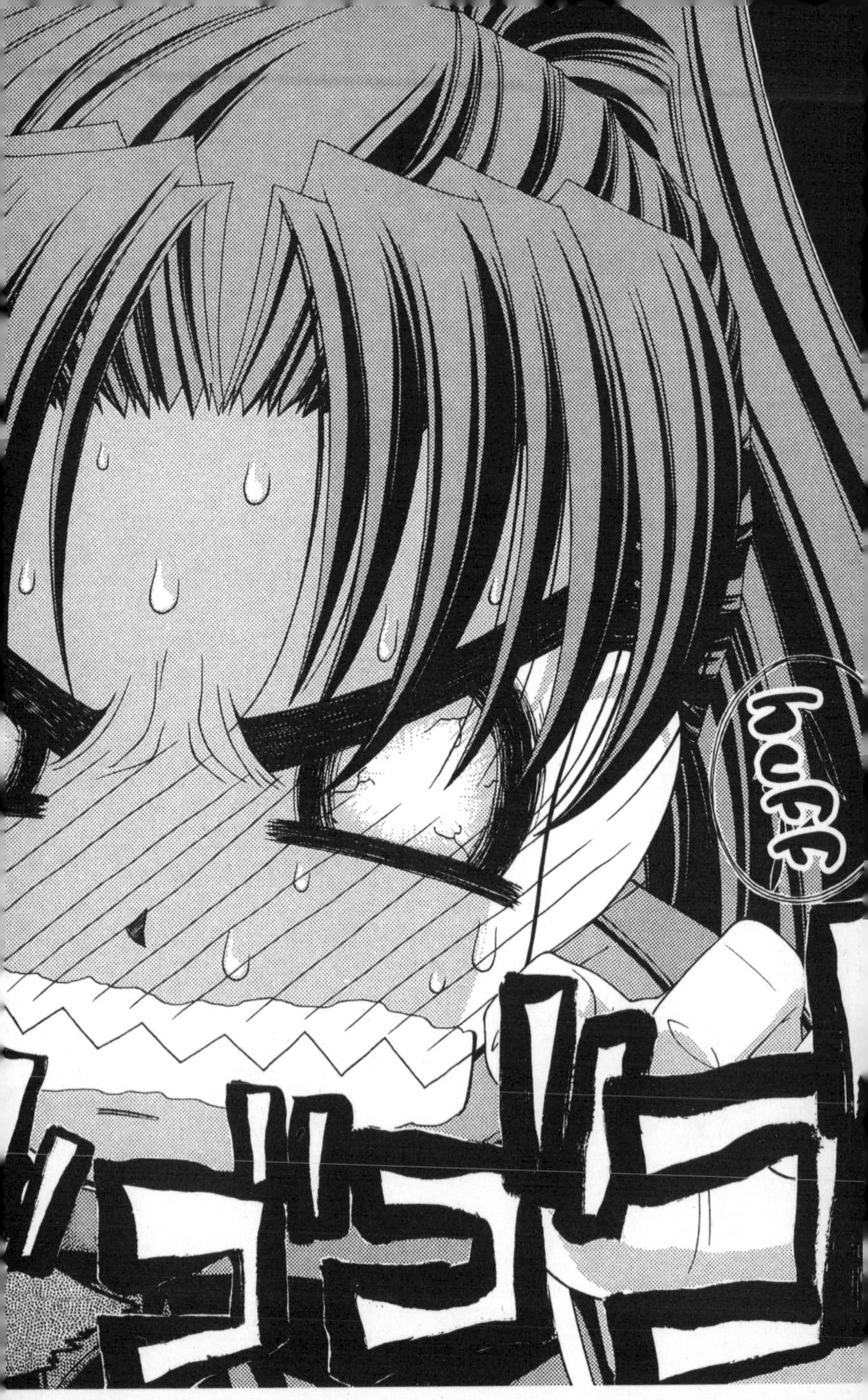
huff

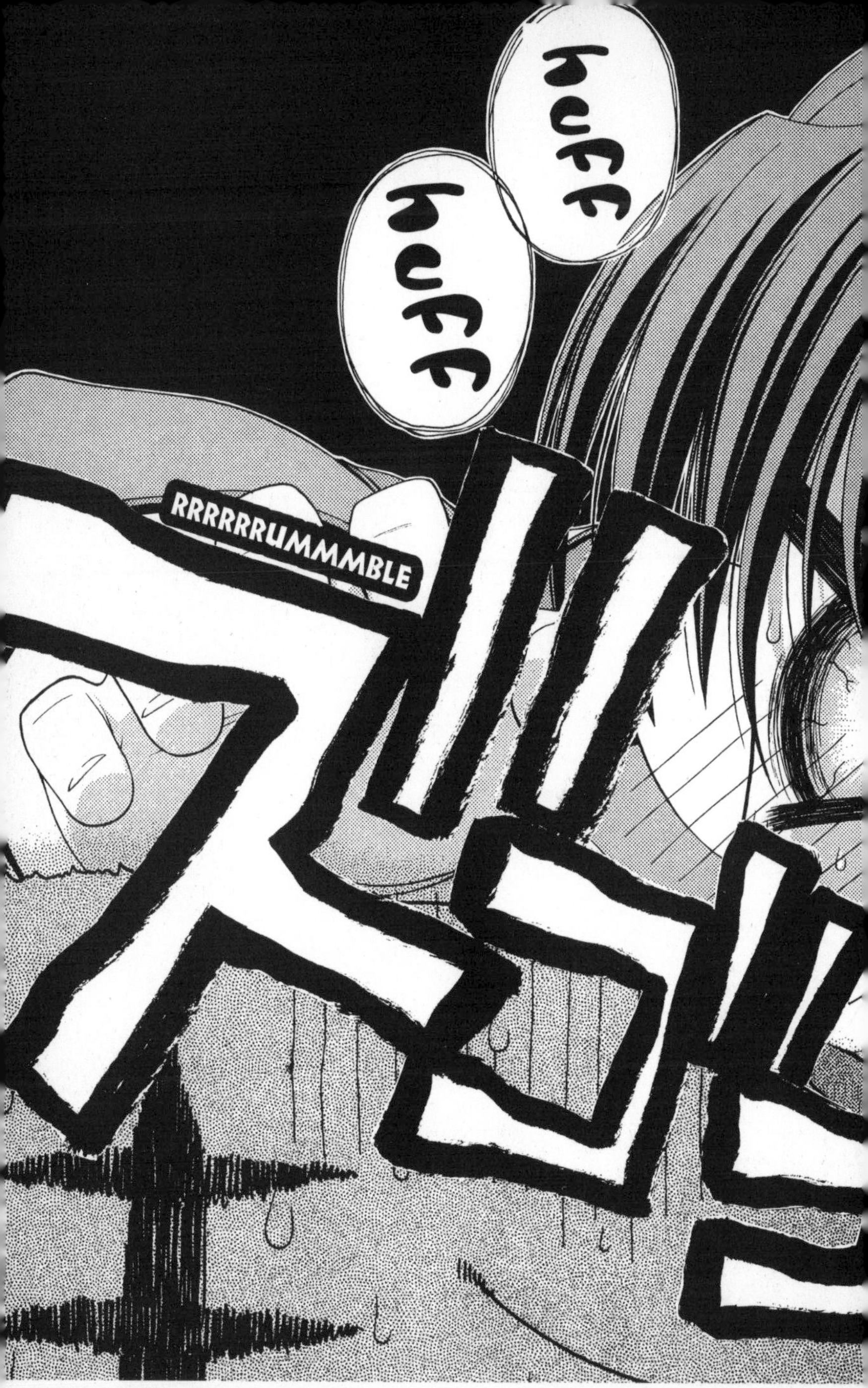
huff
huff
RRRRRRUMMMMBLE

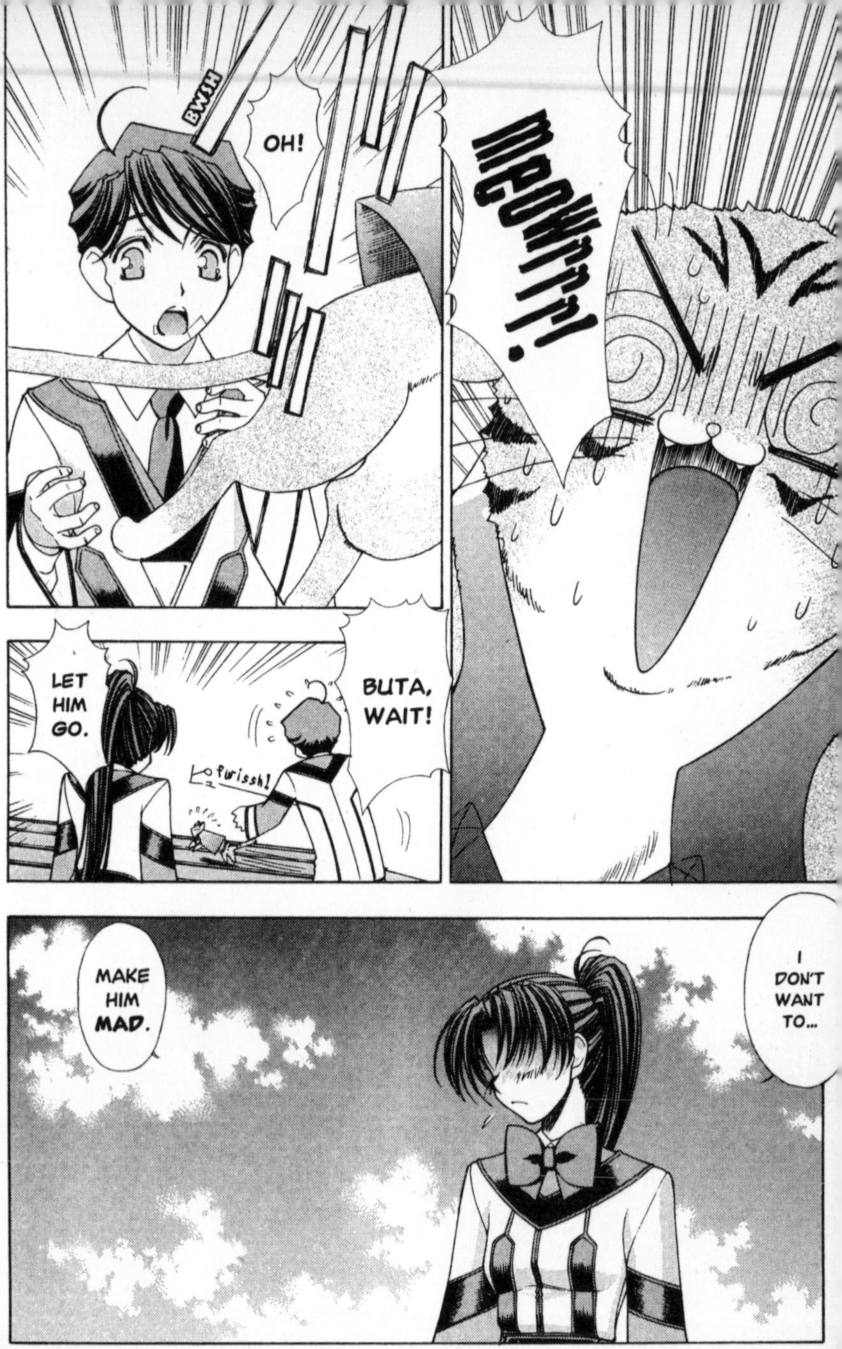
BWSH
OH!
MEOWWNNN!
BUTA, WAIT!
Fwissh!
LET HIM GO.
I DON'T WANT TO...
MAKE HIM MAD.

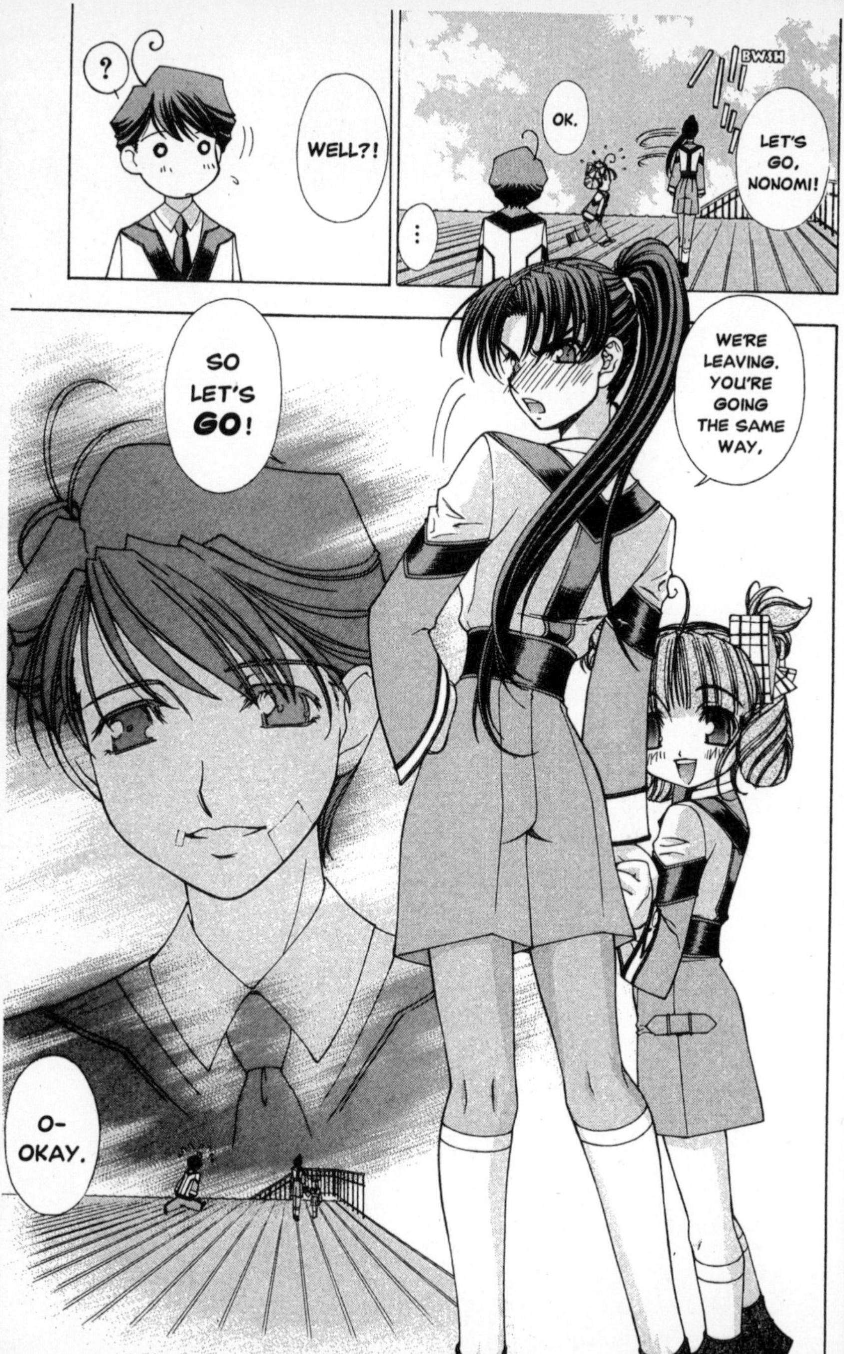

BWSH
LET'S GO, NONOMI!
OK.
...
WELL?!
?
WE'RE LEAVING. YOU'RE GOING THE SAME WAY,
SO LET'S GO!
O-OKAY.

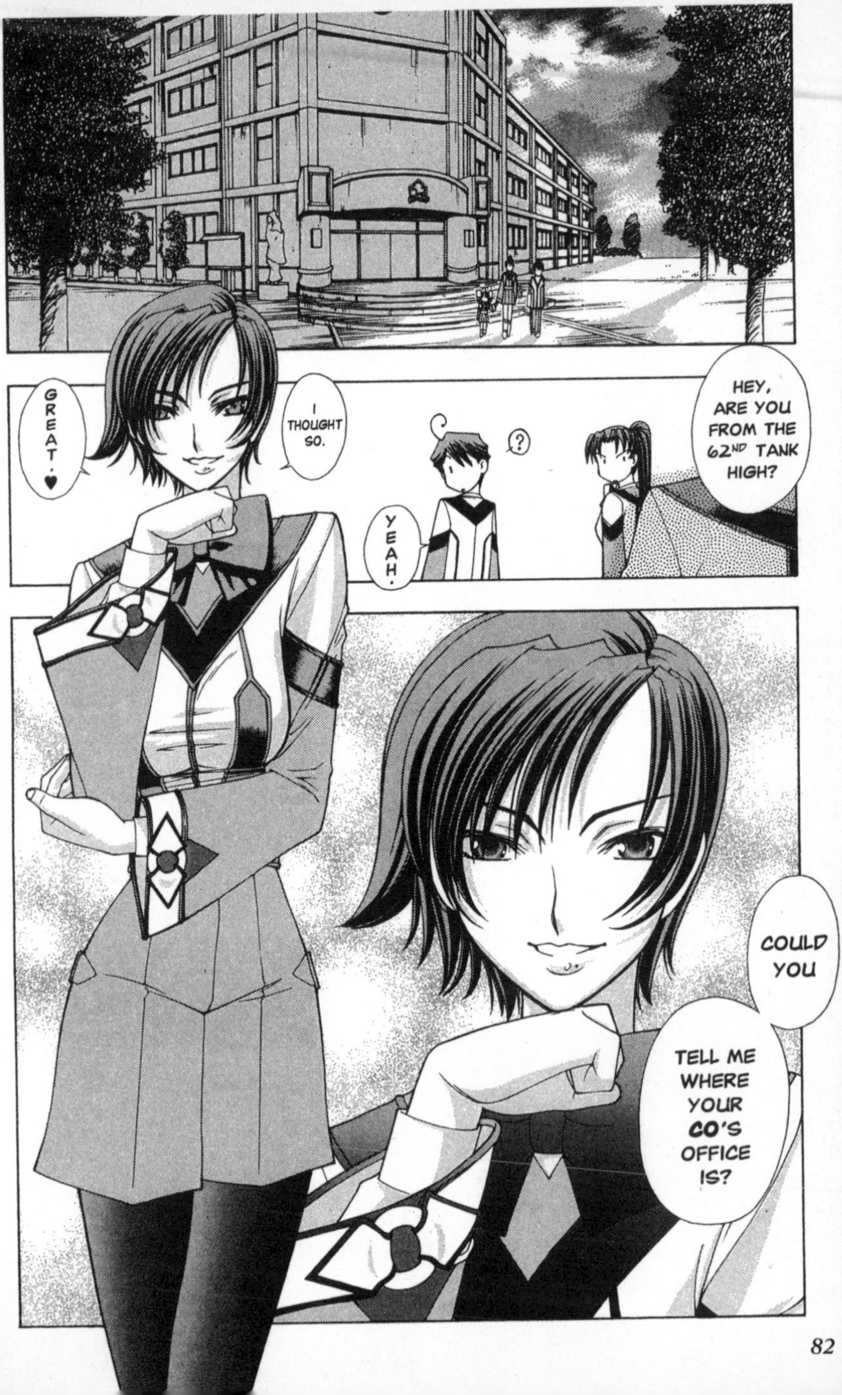
HEY, ARE YOU FROM THE 62ND TANK HIGH?
?
YEAH.
I THOUGHT SO.
GREAT. ♥
COULD YOU
TELL ME WHERE YOUR CO'S OFFICE IS?

episode #4

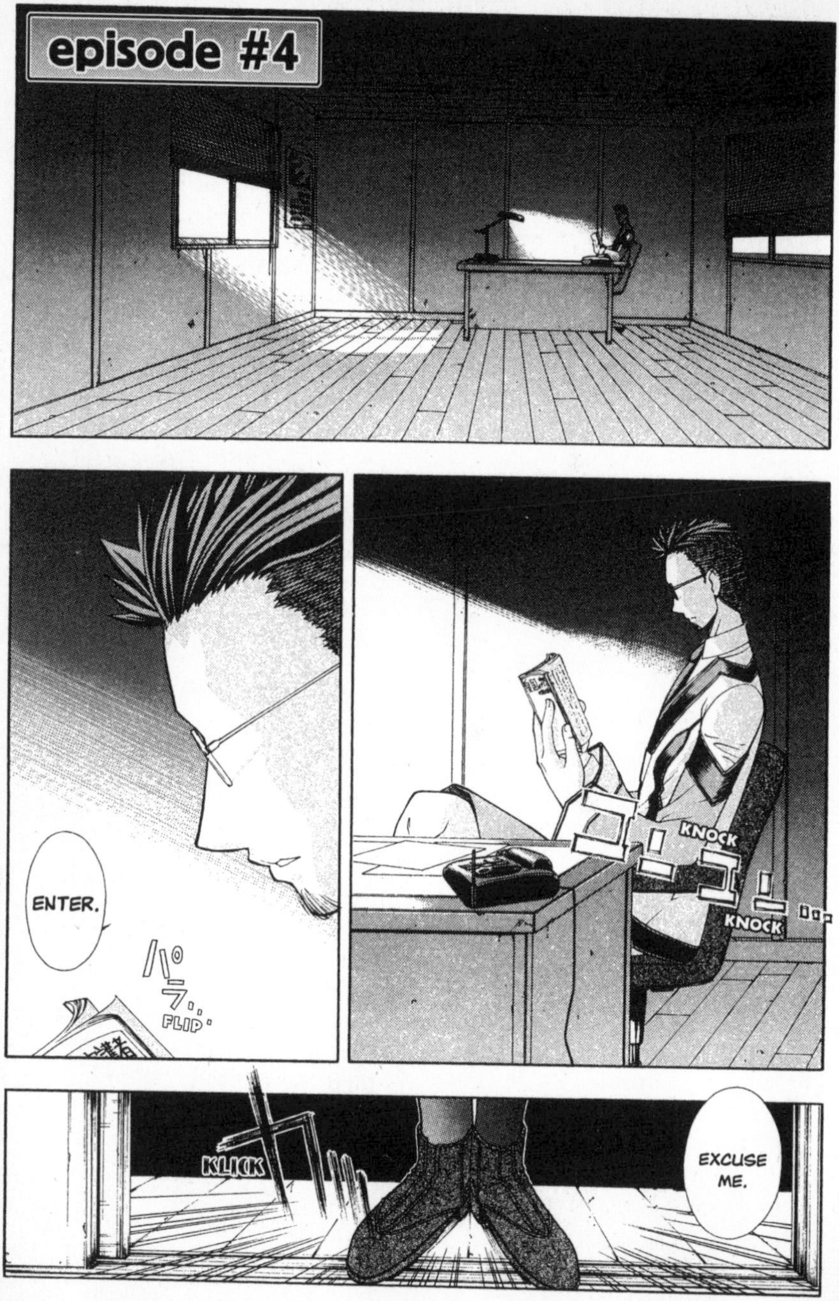

KNOCK
KNOCK
ENTER.
パラ
FLIP
EXCUSE ME.
KLICK

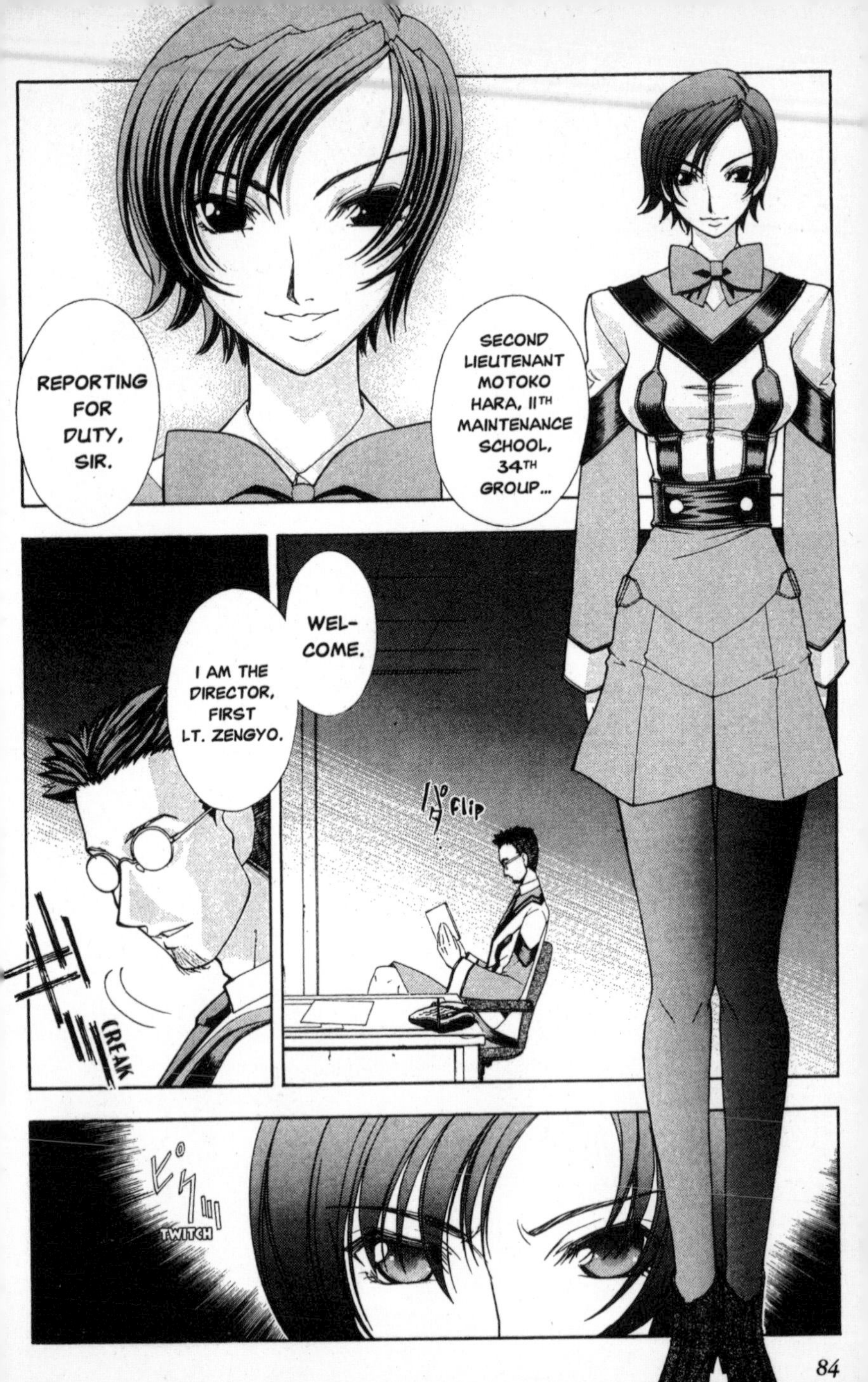
SECOND LIEUTENANT MOTOKO HARA, 11TH MAINTENANCE SCHOOL, 34TH GROUP...
REPORTING FOR DUTY, SIR.
WEL-COME.
FLIP
I AM THE DIRECTOR, FIRST LT. ZENGYO.
CREAK
TWITCH

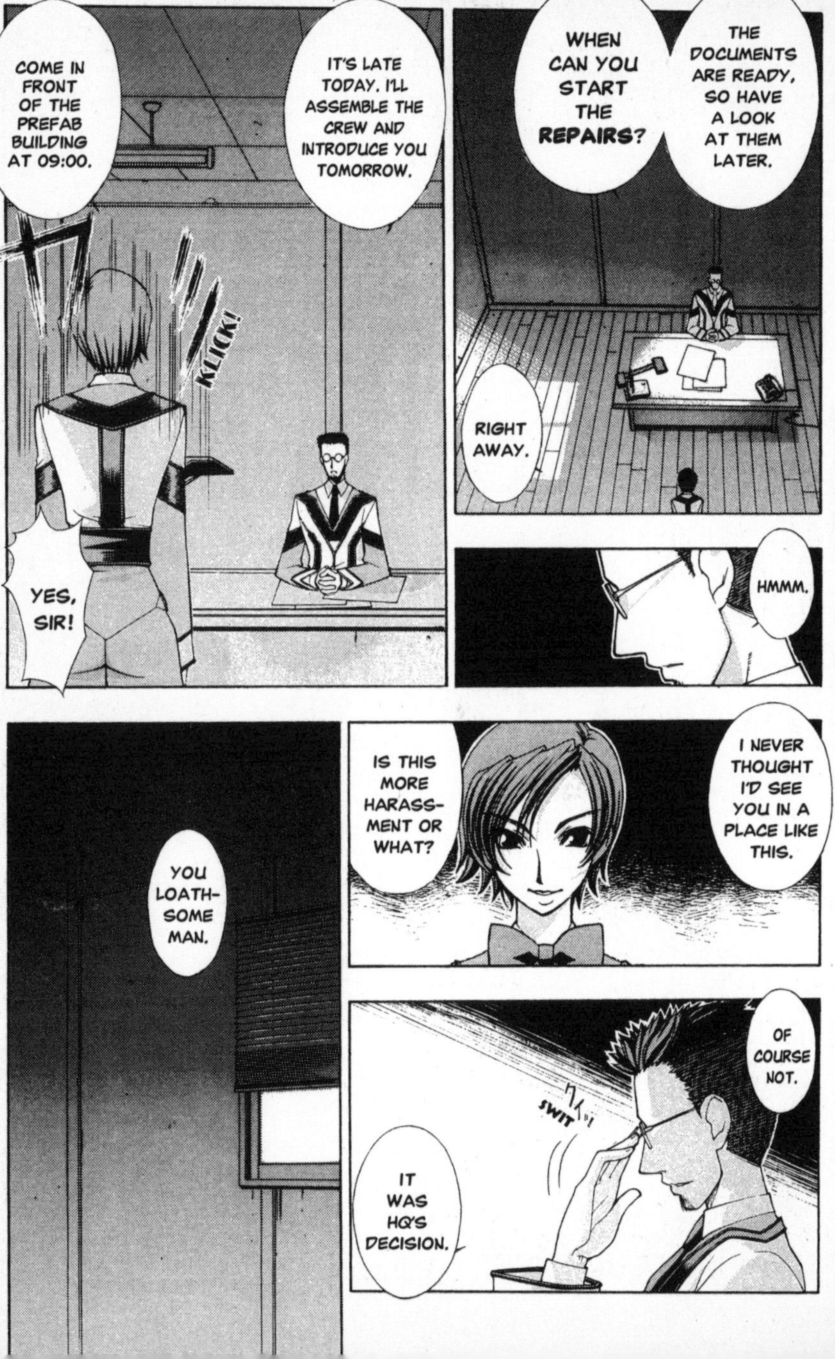
THE DOCUMENTS ARE READY, SO HAVE A LOOK AT THEM LATER.
WHEN CAN YOU START THE REPAIRS?
RIGHT AWAY.
HMMM.
IT'S LATE TODAY. I'LL ASSEMBLE THE CREW AND INTRODUCE YOU TOMORROW.
COME IN FRONT OF THE PREFAB BUILDING AT 09:00.
KLICK!
YES, SIR!
I NEVER THOUGHT I'D SEE YOU IN A PLACE LIKE THIS.
IS THIS MORE HARASS-MENT OR WHAT?
OF COURSE NOT.
SWIT
IT WAS HQ'S DECISION.
YOU LOATH-SOME MAN.

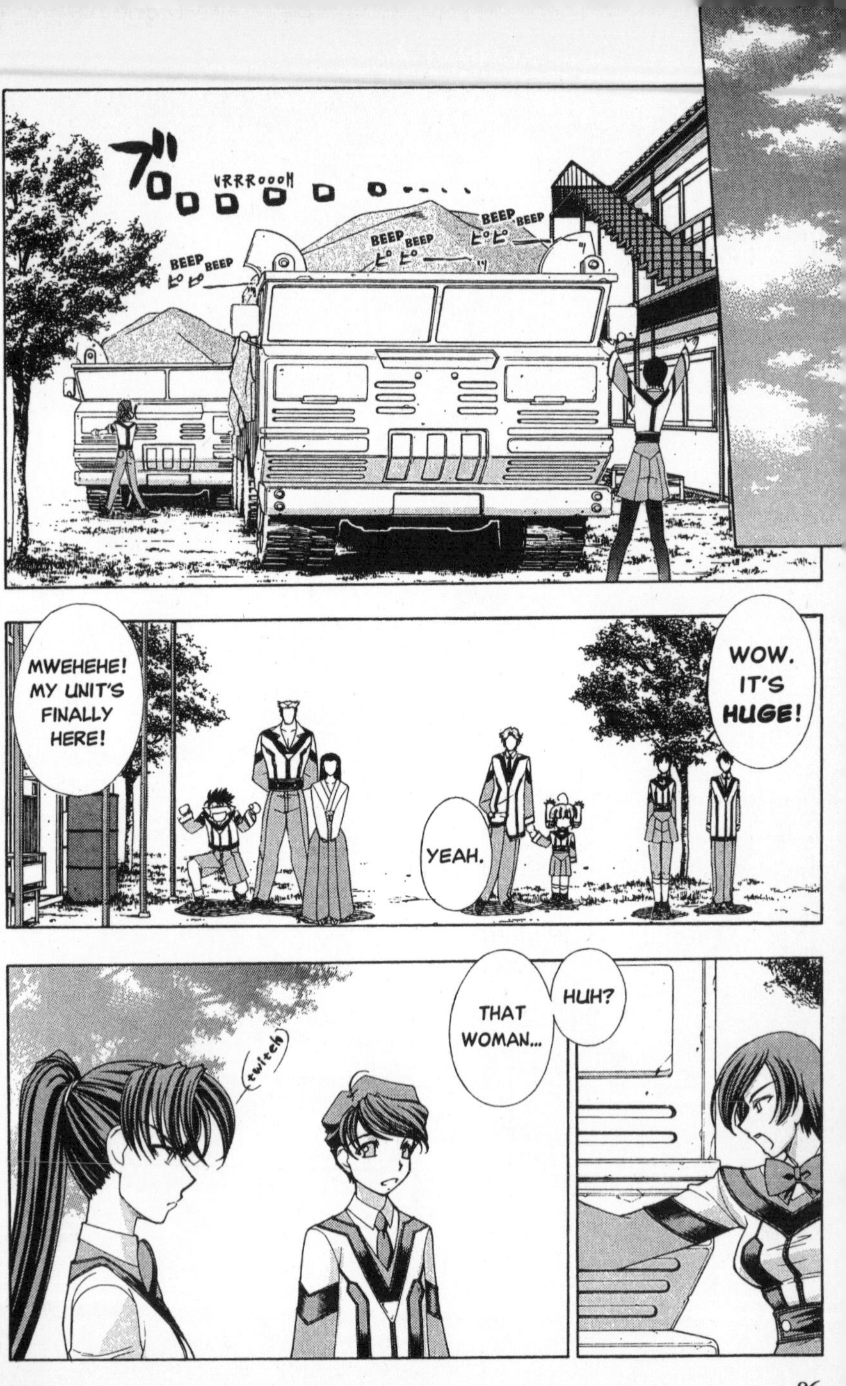
ブロロロロロ……
VRRROOOM
BEEP BEEP
ピピ
BEEP BEEP
ピピーー
BEEP BEEP
ピピーー
WOW. IT'S HUGE!
YEAH.
MWEHEHE! MY UNIT'S FINALLY HERE!
HUH?
THAT WOMAN...
twitch

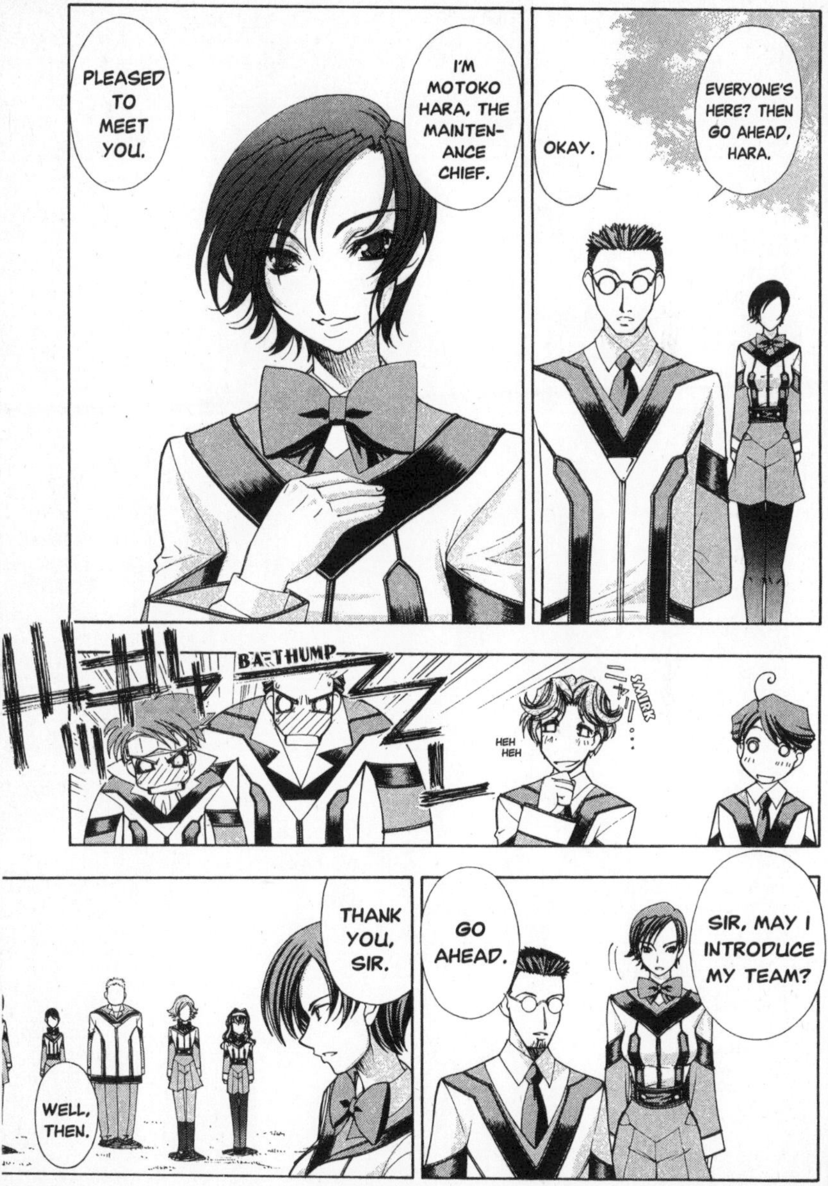
EVERYONE'S HERE? THEN GO AHEAD, HARA.
OKAY.
I'M MOTOKO HARA, THE MAINTEN- ANCE CHIEF.
PLEASED TO MEET YOU.
SMIRK
HEH HEH
BA-THUMP
SIR, MAY I INTRODUCE MY TEAM?
GO AHEAD.
THANK YOU, SIR.
WELL, THEN.

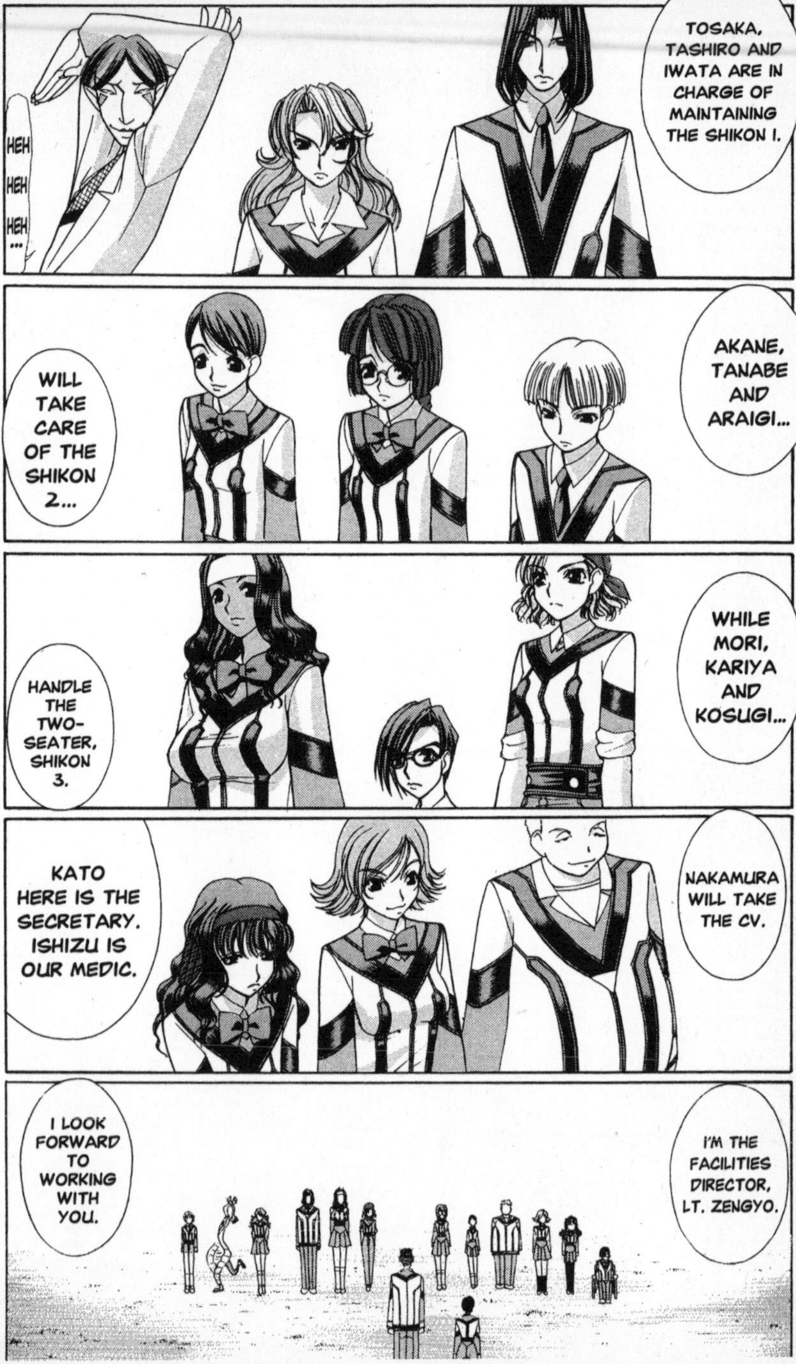
TOSAKA, TASHIRO AND IWATA ARE IN CHARGE OF MAINTAINING THE SHIKON 1.
HEH HEH HEH...
AKANE, TANABE AND ARAIGI...
WILL TAKE CARE OF THE SHIKON 2...
WHILE MORI, KARIYA AND KOSUGI...
HANDLE THE TWO-SEATER, SHIKON 3.
NAKAMURA WILL TAKE THE CV.
KATO HERE IS THE SECRETARY. ISHIZU IS OUR MEDIC.
I'M THE FACILITIES DIRECTOR, LT. ZENGYO.
I LOOK FORWARD TO WORKING WITH YOU.

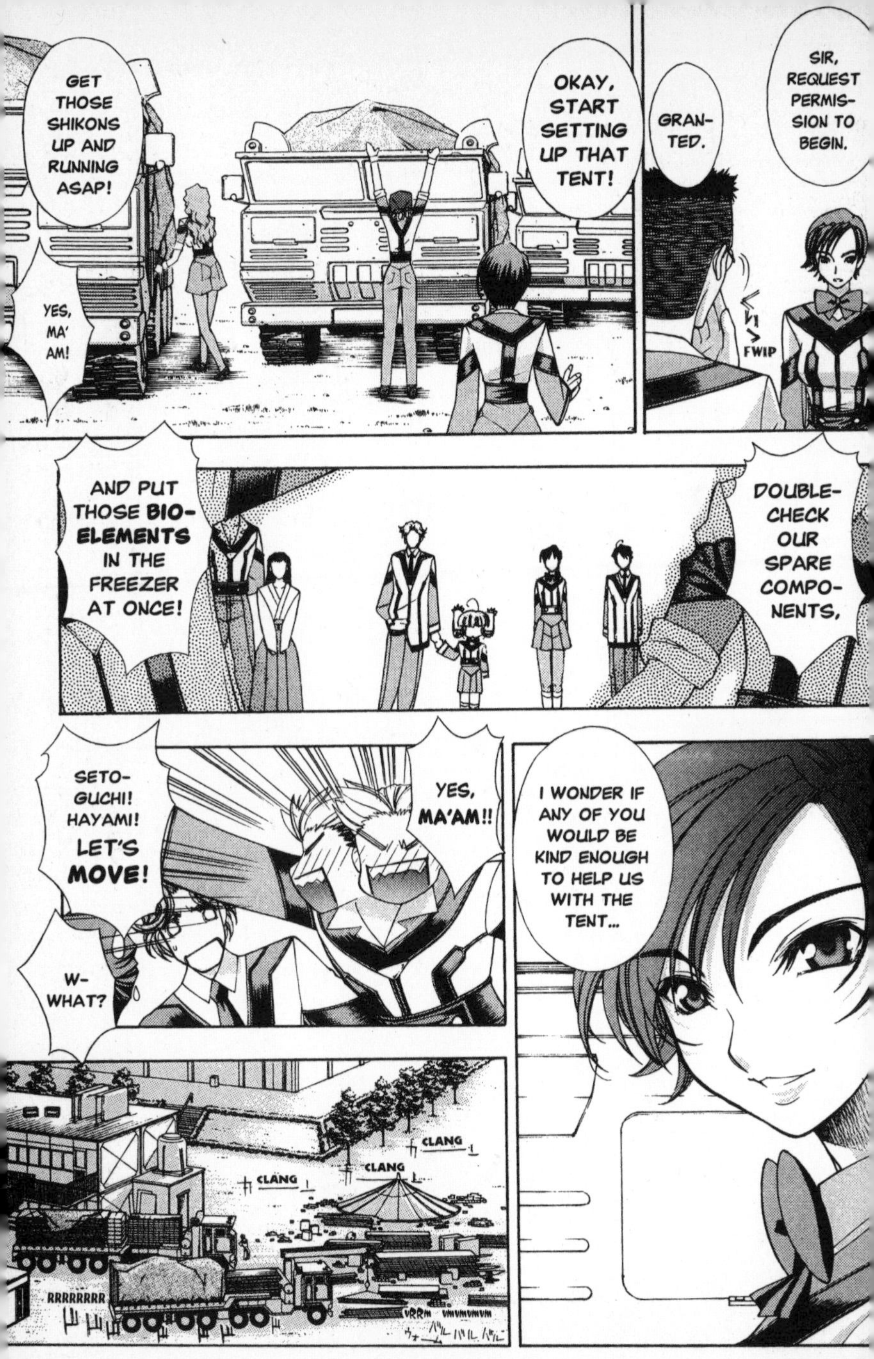
SIR, REQUEST PERMISSION TO BEGIN.
GRANTED.
FWIP
OKAY, START SETTING UP THAT TENT!
GET THOSE SHIKONS UP AND RUNNING ASAP!
YES, MA'AM!
DOUBLE-CHECK OUR SPARE COMPONENTS,
AND PUT THOSE BIO-ELEMENTS IN THE FREEZER AT ONCE!
I WONDER IF ANY OF YOU WOULD BE KIND ENOUGH TO HELP US WITH THE TENT...
YES, MA'AM!!
SETOGUCHI! HAYAMI! LET'S MOVE!
W-WHAT?
CLANG
CLANG
CLANG
RRRRRRRR
VRRM
VMVMVMVM

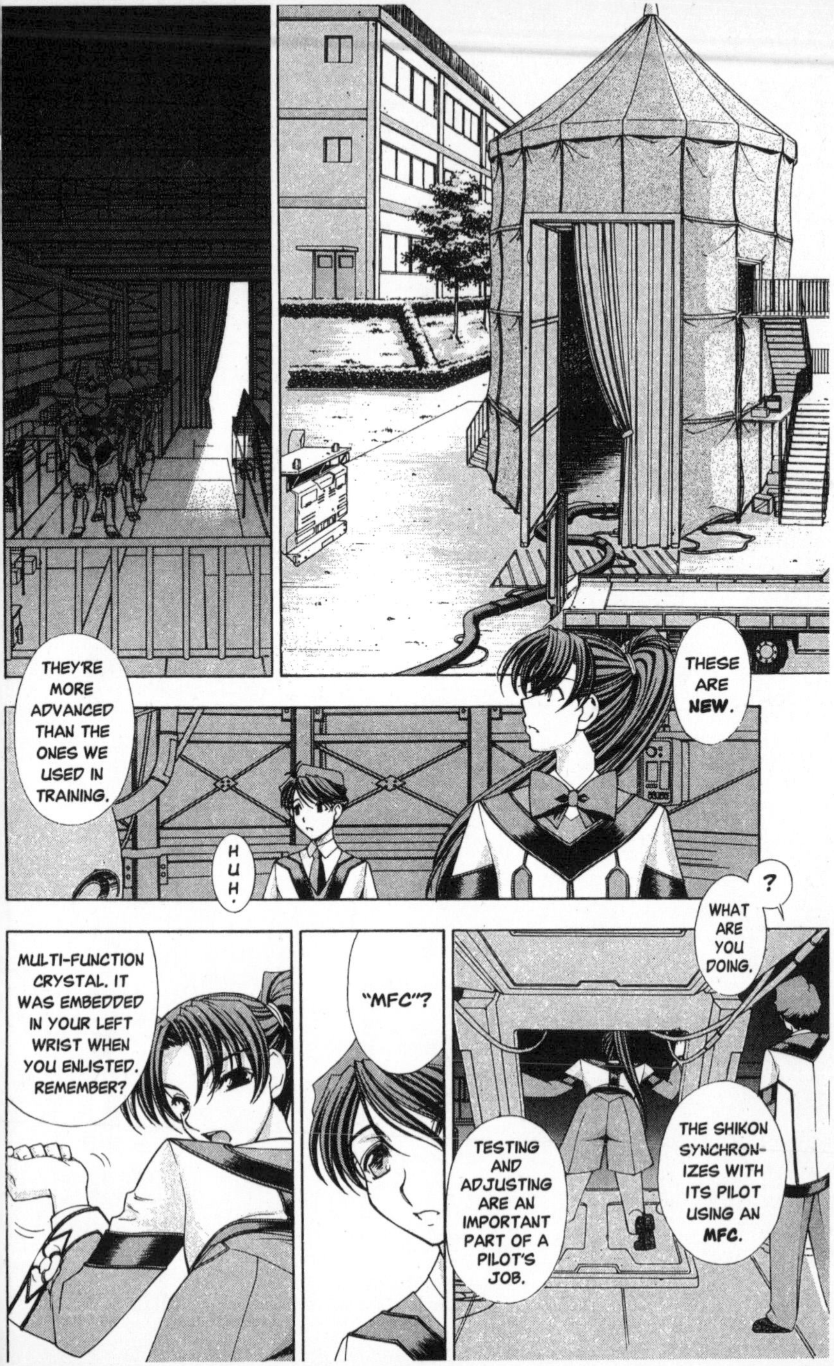
THESE ARE NEW.
THEY'RE MORE ADVANCED THAN THE ONES WE USED IN TRAINING.
HUH.
?
WHAT ARE YOU DOING.
THE SHIKON SYNCHRON-IZES WITH ITS PILOT USING AN MFC.
TESTING AND ADJUSTING ARE AN IMPORTANT PART OF A PILOT'S JOB.
"MFC"?
MULTI-FUNCTION CRYSTAL. IT WAS EMBEDDED IN YOUR LEFT WRIST WHEN YOU ENLISTED. REMEMBER?

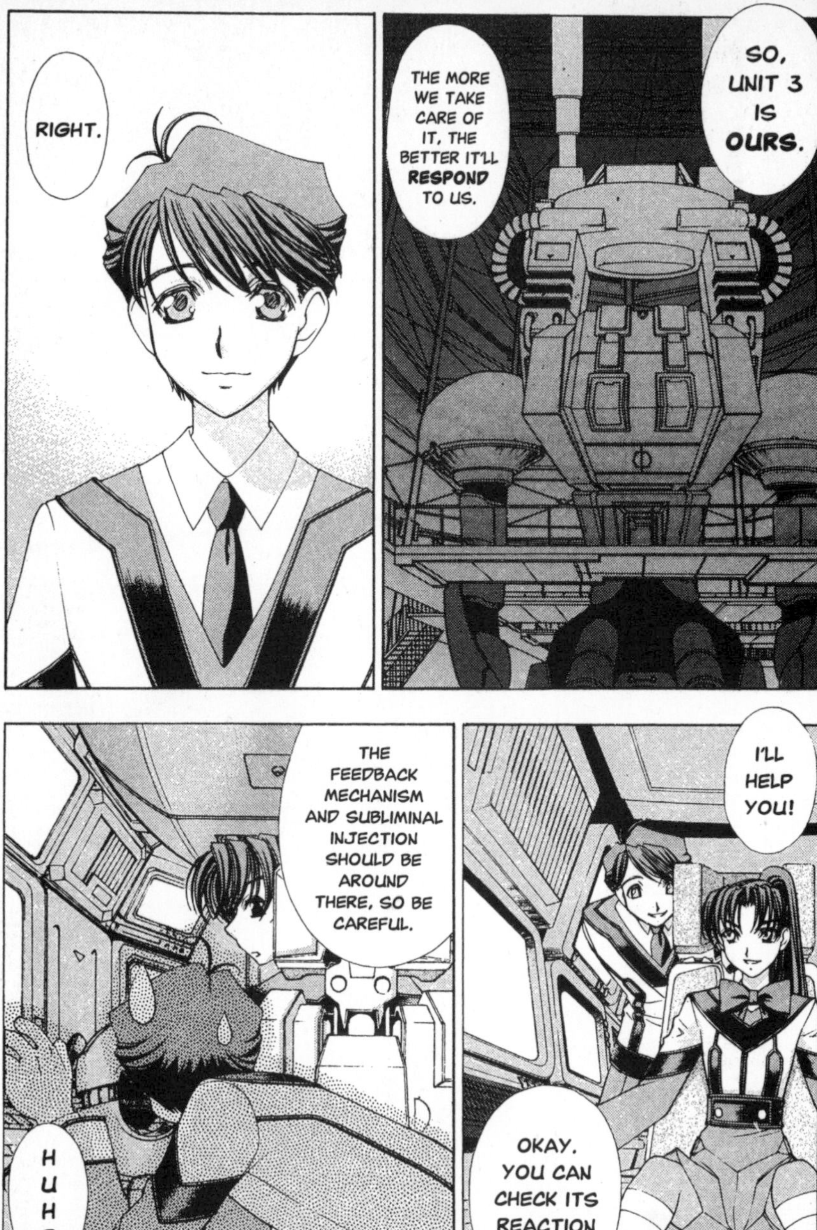
SO, UNIT 3 IS OURS.
THE MORE WE TAKE CARE OF IT, THE BETTER IT'LL RESPOND TO US.
RIGHT.
I'LL HELP YOU!
OKAY. YOU CAN CHECK ITS REACTION TIME.
THE FEEDBACK MECHANISM AND SUBLIMINAL INJECTION SHOULD BE AROUND THERE, SO BE CAREFUL.
HUH?

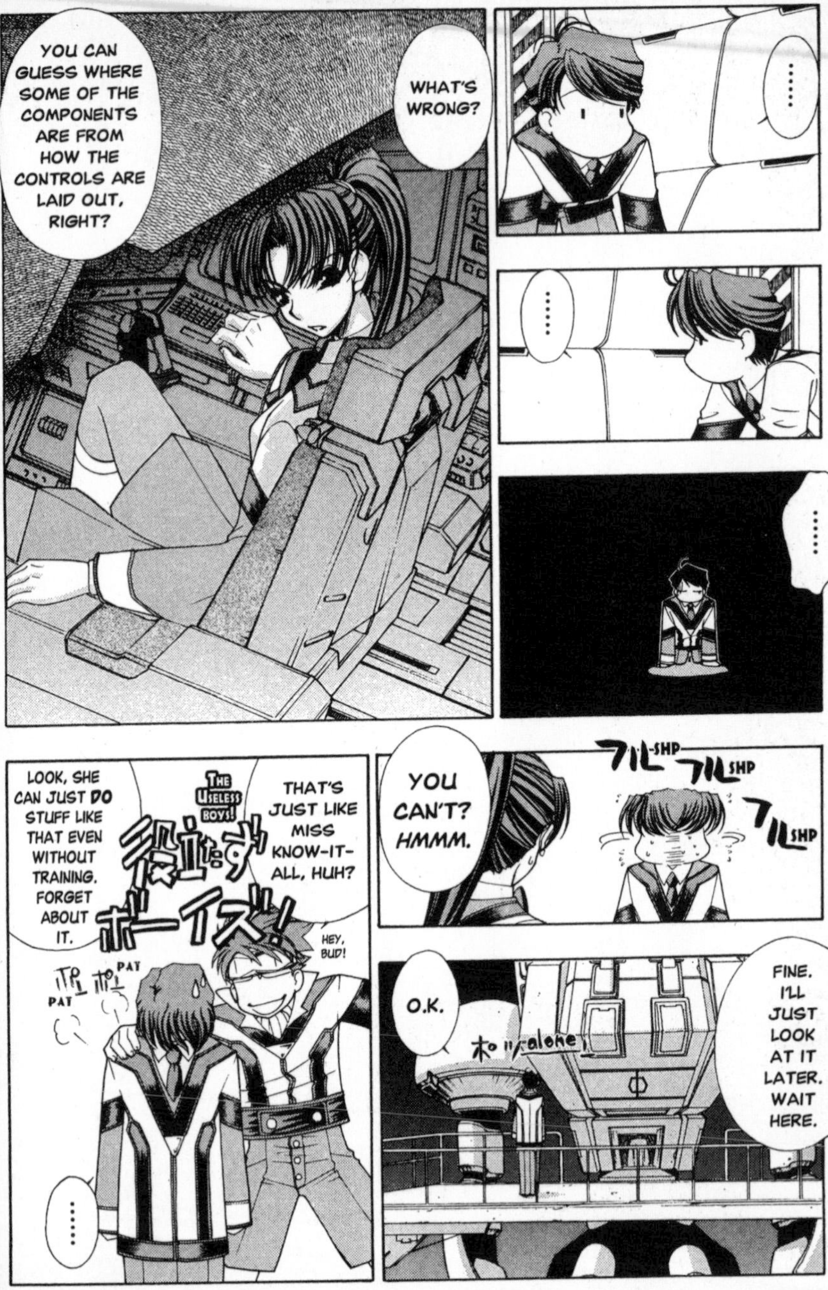
......
WHAT'S WRONG?
YOU CAN GUESS WHERE SOME OF THE COMPONENTS ARE FROM HOW THE CONTROLS ARE LAID OUT, RIGHT?
......
......
SHP SHP SHP
YOU CAN'T? HMMM.
FINE. I'LL JUST LOOK AT IT LATER. WAIT HERE.
O.K.
alone
THAT'S JUST LIKE MISS KNOW-IT-ALL, HUH?
THE USELESS BOYS!
LOOK, SHE CAN JUST DO STUFF LIKE THAT EVEN WITHOUT TRAINING. FORGET ABOUT IT.
HEY, BUD!
PAT PAT
......

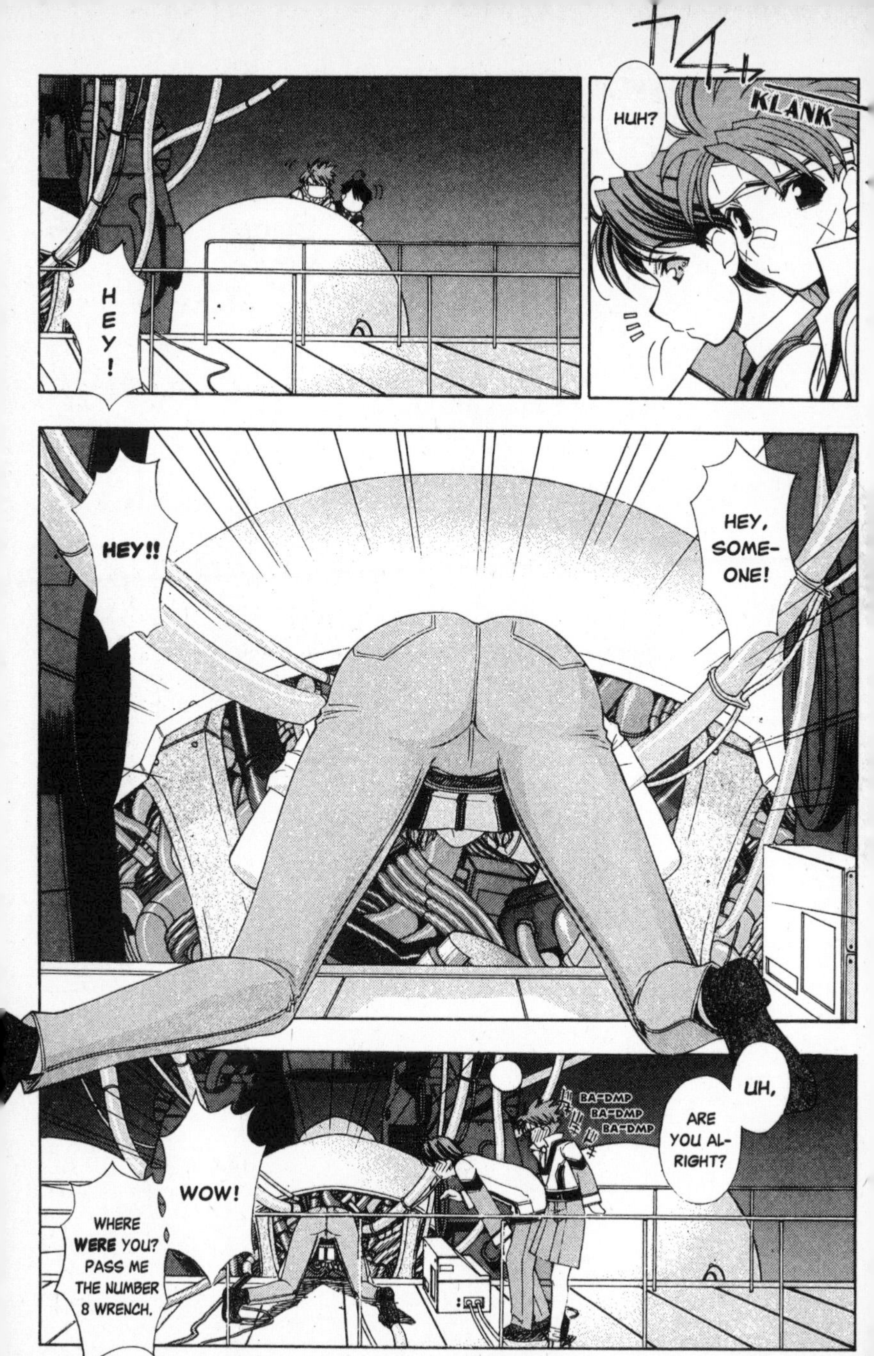
KLANK
HUH?
HEY!
HEY, SOME-ONE!
HEY!!
UH, ARE YOU AL-RIGHT?
BA-DMP BA-DMP BA-DMP
WOW!
WHERE WERE YOU? PASS ME THE NUMBER 8 WRENCH.

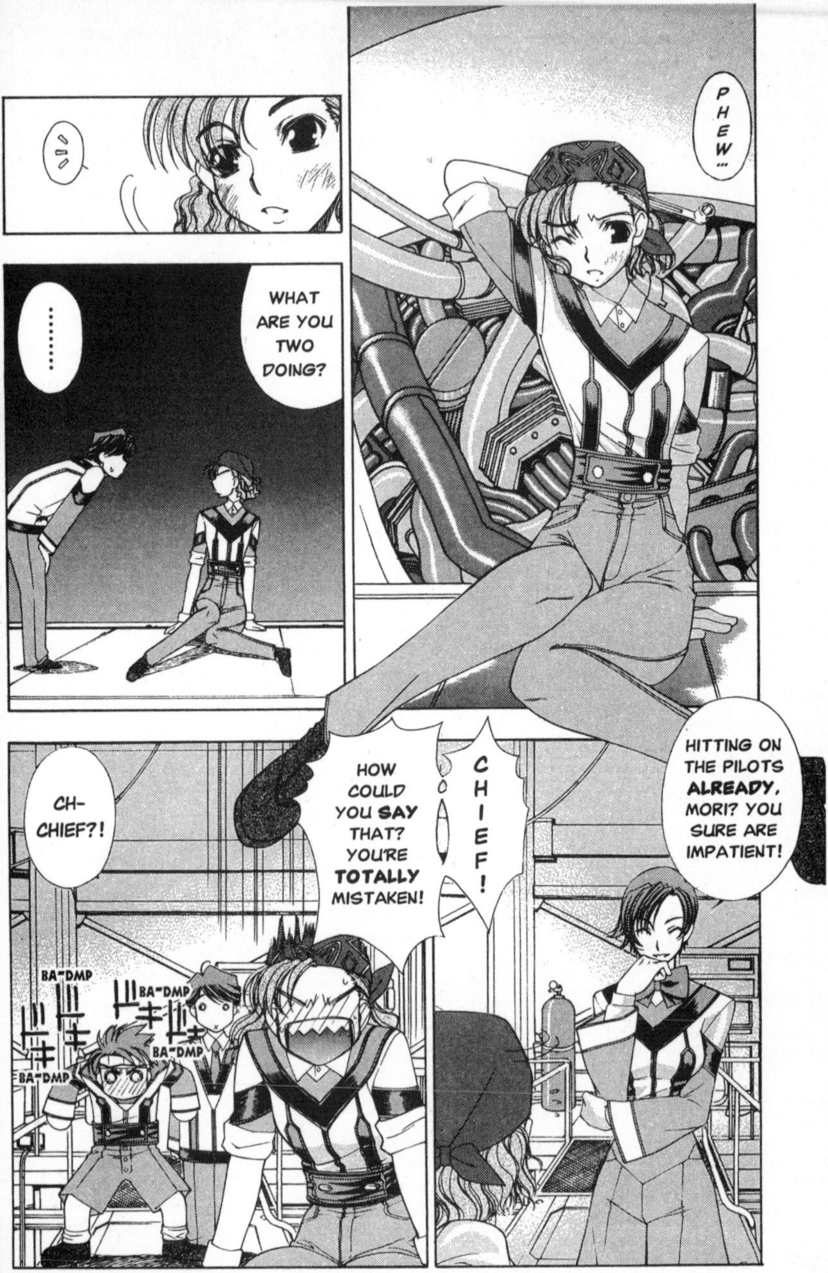
PHEW...
WHAT ARE YOU TWO DOING?
....
!
HITTING ON THE PILOTS **ALREADY**, MORI? YOU SURE ARE IMPATIENT!
CHIEF!
HOW COULD YOU **SAY** THAT? YOU'RE **TOTALLY** MISTAKEN!
CH-CHIEF?!
BA-DMP
BA-DMP
BA-DMP
BA-DMP

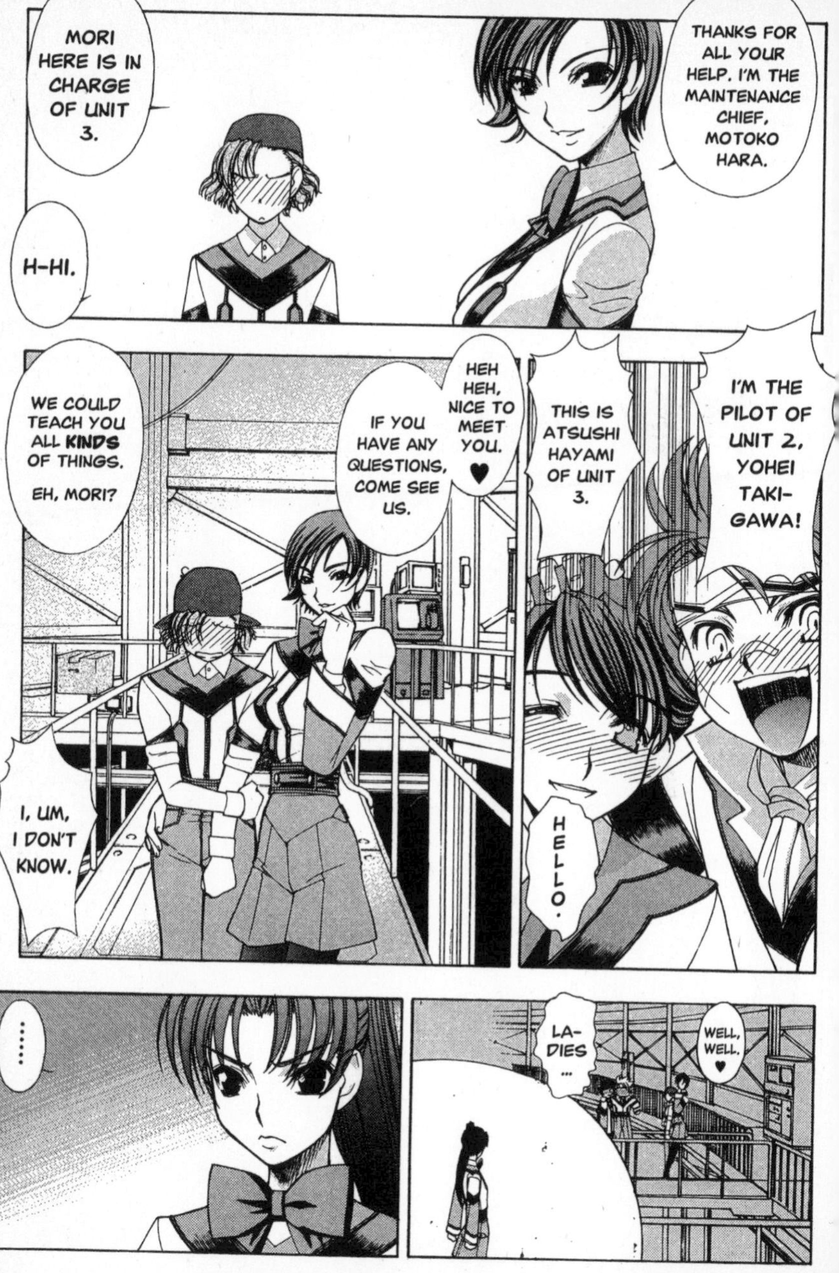
THANKS FOR ALL YOUR HELP. I'M THE MAINTENANCE CHIEF, MOTOKO HARA.
MORI HERE IS IN CHARGE OF UNIT 3.
H-HI.
I'M THE PILOT OF UNIT 2, YOHEI TAKI-GAWA!
THIS IS ATSUSHI HAYAMI OF UNIT 3.
HELLO.
HEH HEH, NICE TO MEET YOU. ♥
IF YOU HAVE ANY QUESTIONS, COME SEE US.
WE COULD TEACH YOU ALL **KINDS** OF THINGS. EH, MORI?
I, UM, I DON'T KNOW.
WELL, WELL. ♥
LA-DIES ...
......

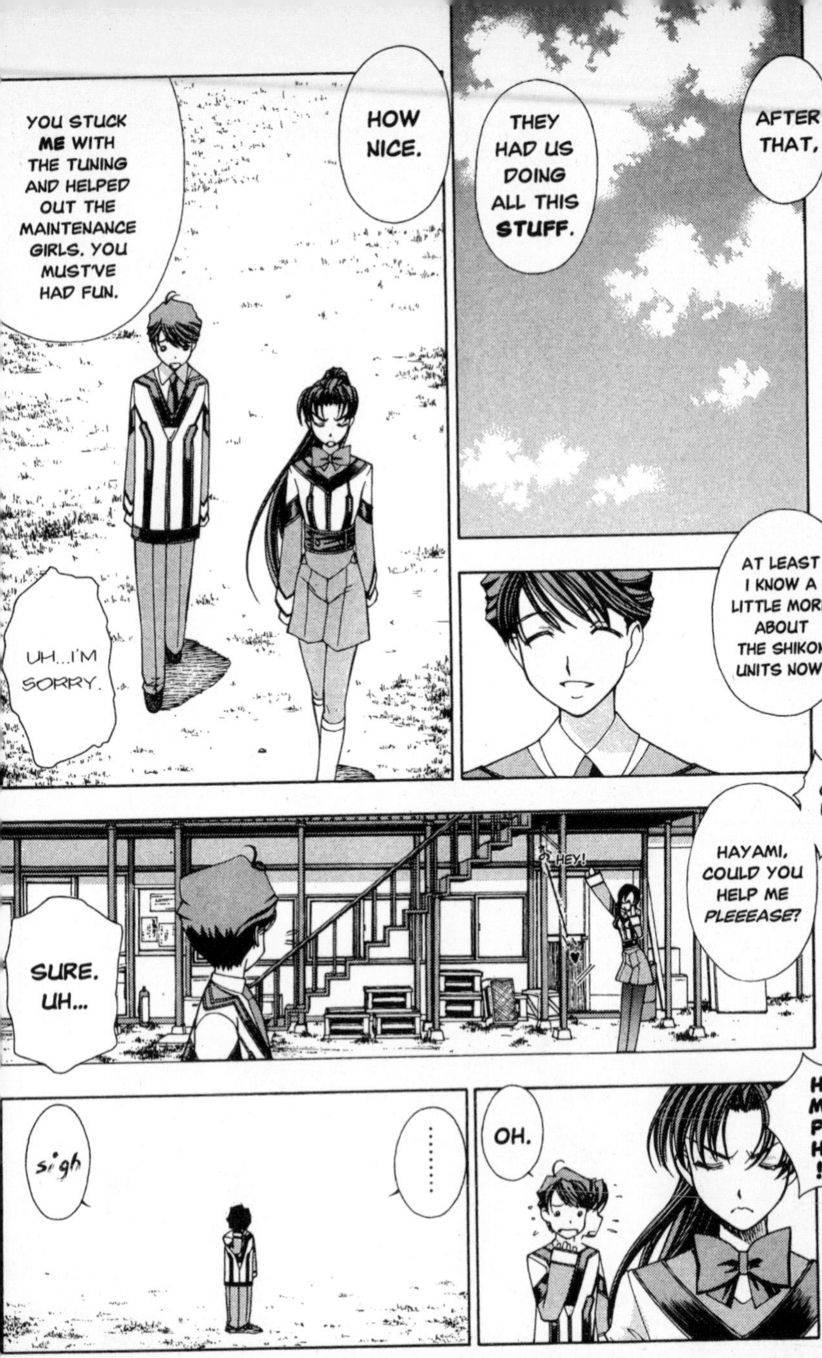
AFTER THAT,
THEY HAD US DOING ALL THIS STUFF.
HOW NICE.
YOU STUCK ME WITH THE TUNING AND HELPED OUT THE MAINTENANCE GIRLS. YOU MUST'VE HAD FUN.
AT LEAST I KNOW A LITTLE MORE ABOUT THE SHIKON UNITS NOW!
UH...I'M SORRY.
OH!
HAYAMI, COULD YOU HELP ME PLEEEASE?
HEY!
SURE. UH...
HMPH!
OH.
....
sigh

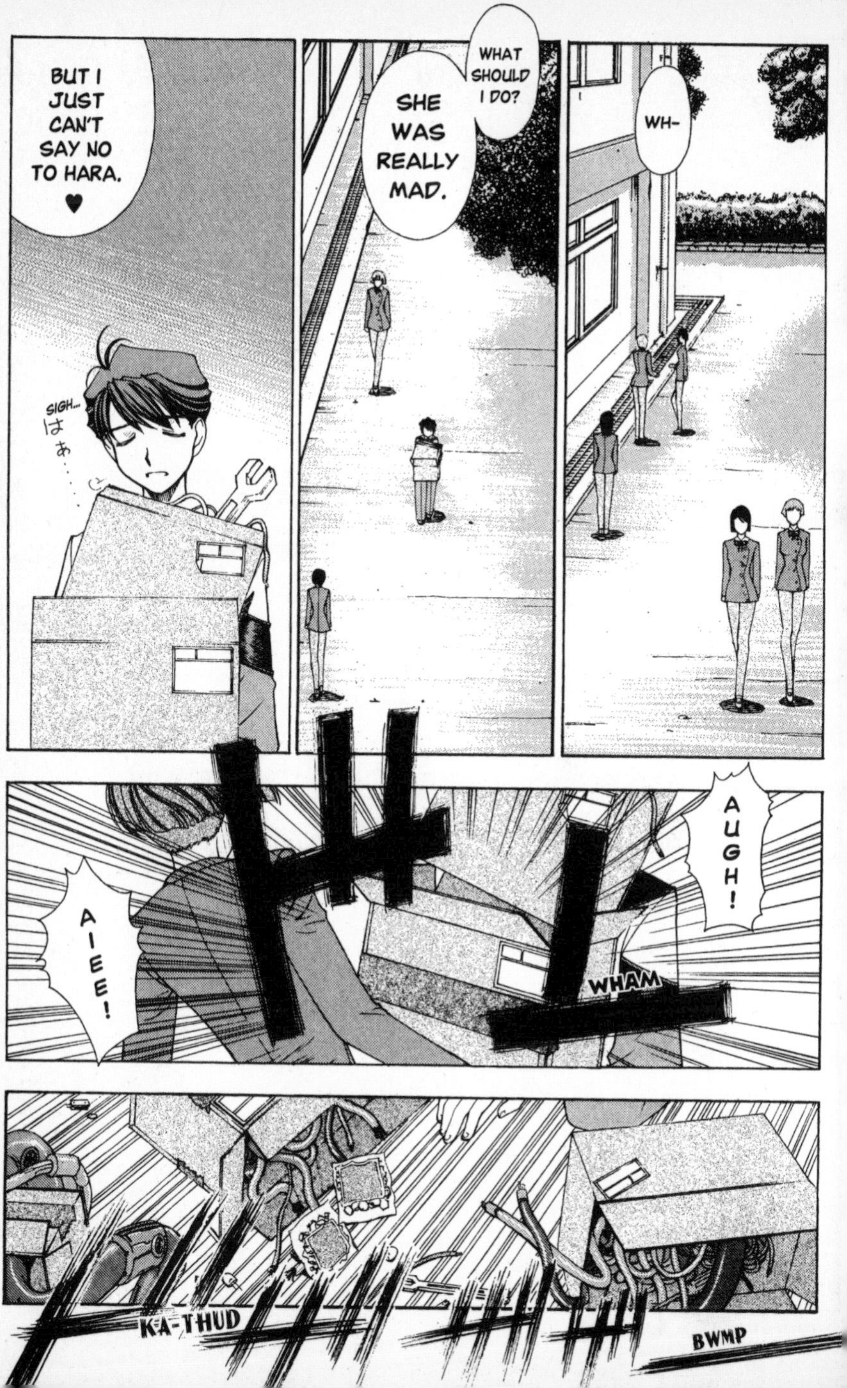
WH-
WHAT SHOULD I DO?
SHE WAS REALLY MAD.
BUT I JUST CAN'T SAY NO TO HARA. ♥
SIGH... はぁ…
AUGH!
AIEE!
WHAM
BWMP
KA-THUD

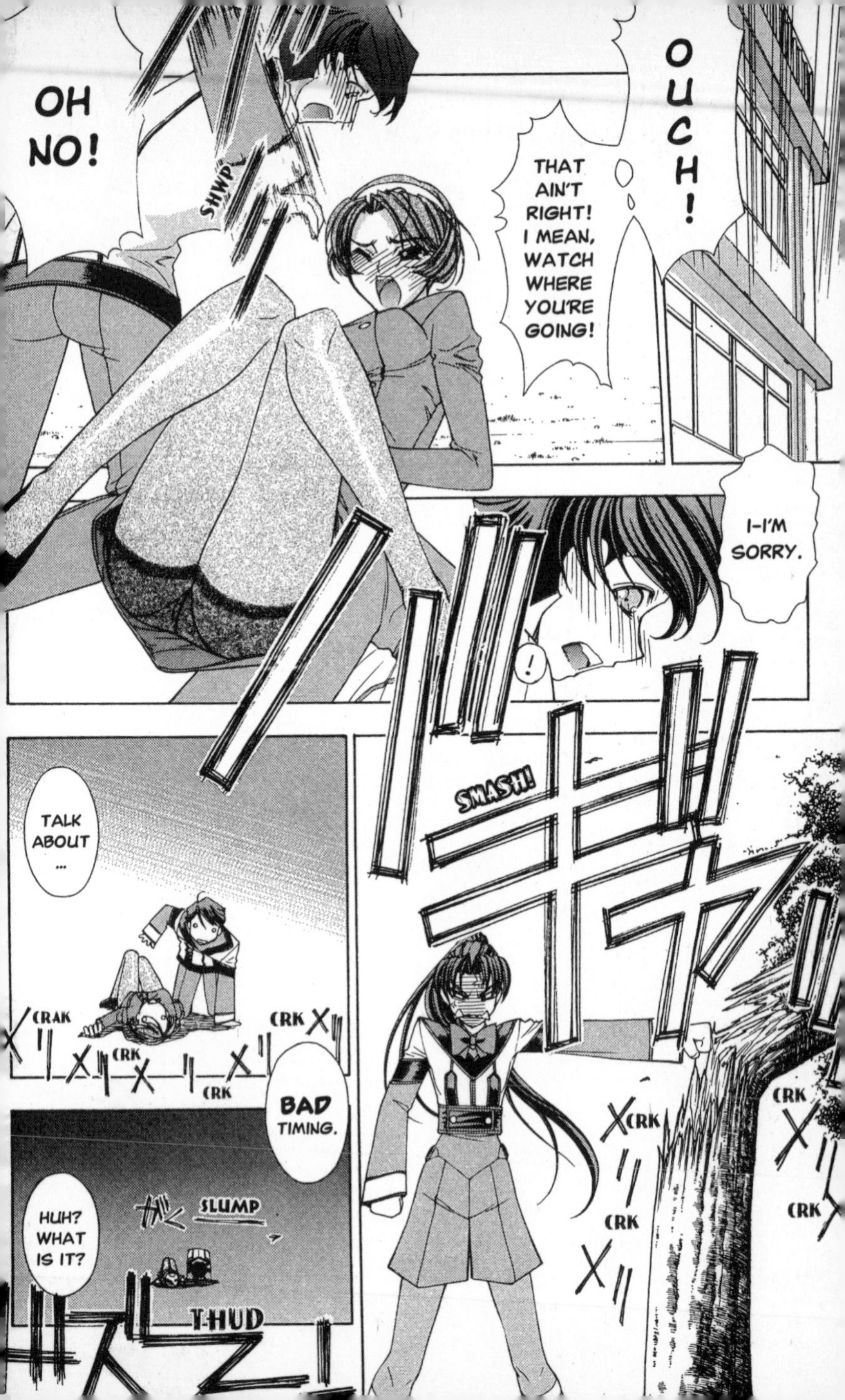
OUCH!
THAT AIN'T RIGHT! I MEAN, WATCH WHERE YOU'RE GOING!
SHWP
OH NO!
I-I'M SORRY.
!
SMASH!
CRK
CRK
CRK
CRK
TALK ABOUT ...
CRAK
CRK
CRK
CRK
BAD TIMING.
HUH? WHAT IS IT?
SLUMP
THUD

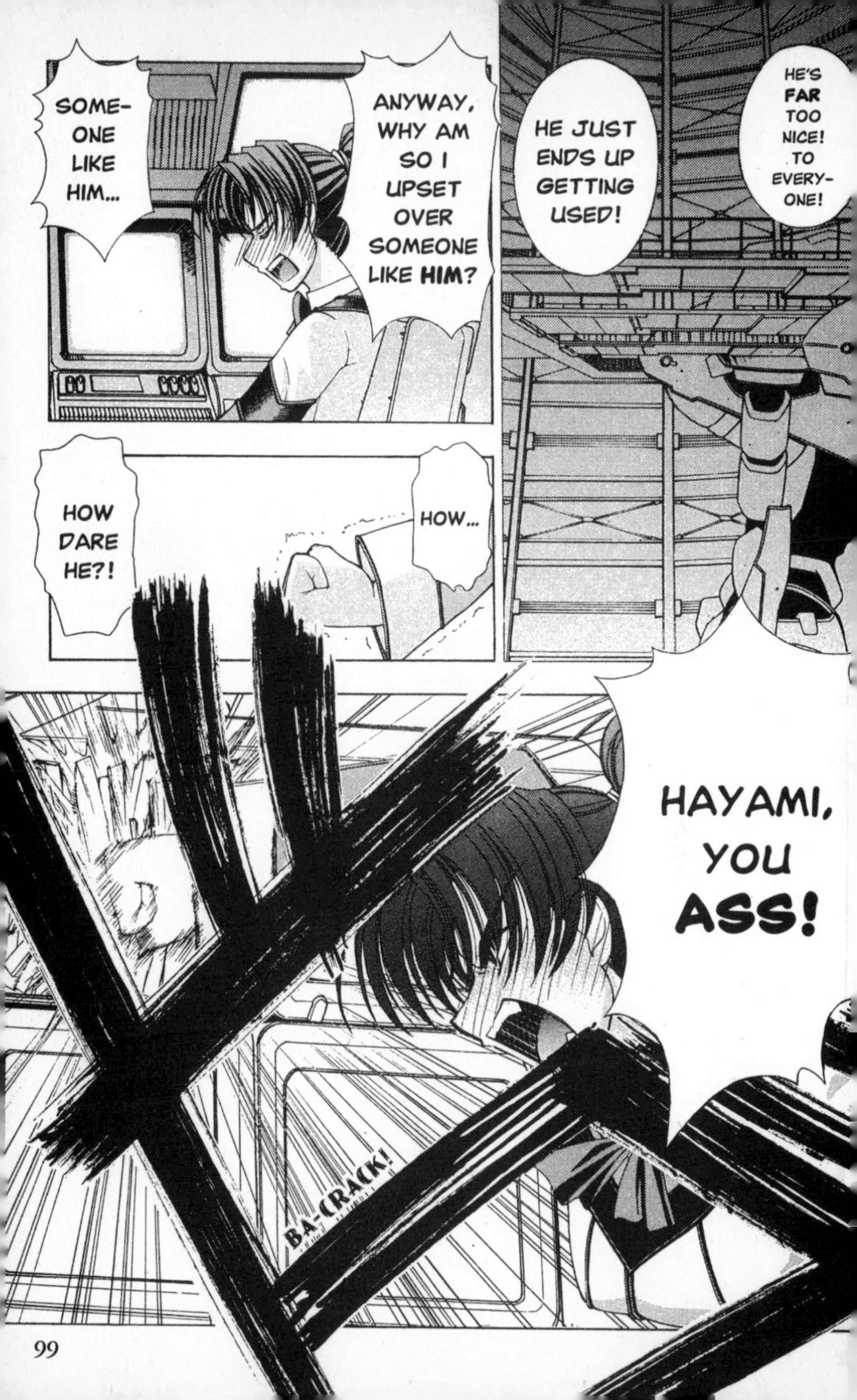
HE'S FAR TOO NICE! TO EVERYONE!
HE JUST ENDS UP GETTING USED!
ANYWAY, WHY AM SO I UPSET OVER SOMEONE LIKE HIM?
SOME-ONE LIKE HIM...
HOW...
HOW DARE HE?!
HAYAMI, YOU ASS!
BA-CRACK!

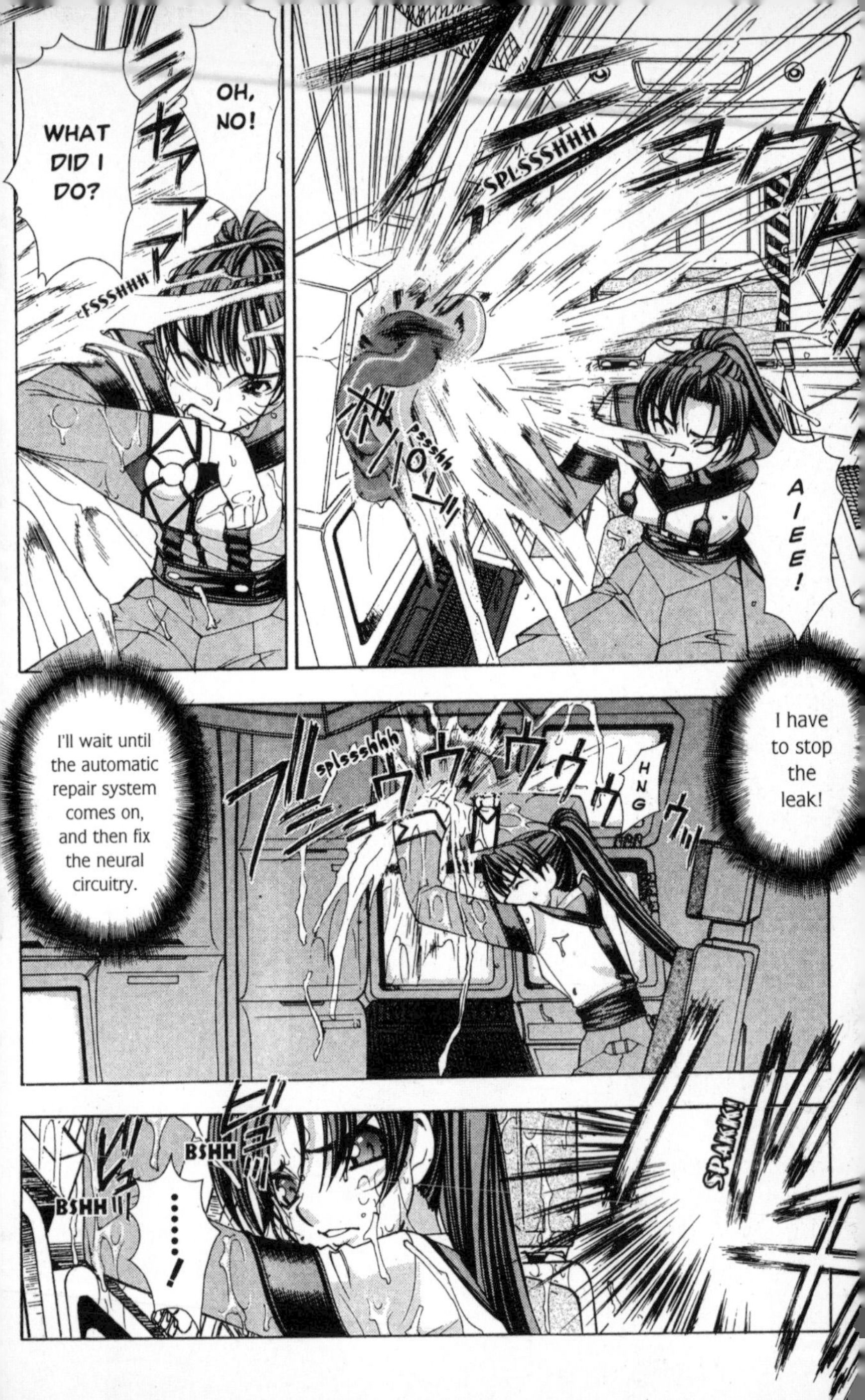
SPLSSSHHH
pssshh
AIEEE!
OH, NO!
WHAT DID I DO?
FSSSHHH
I have to stop the leak!
HNG
splsssshhh
I'll wait until the automatic repair system comes on, and then fix the neural circuitry.
SPARK!
BSHH
BSHH
......!

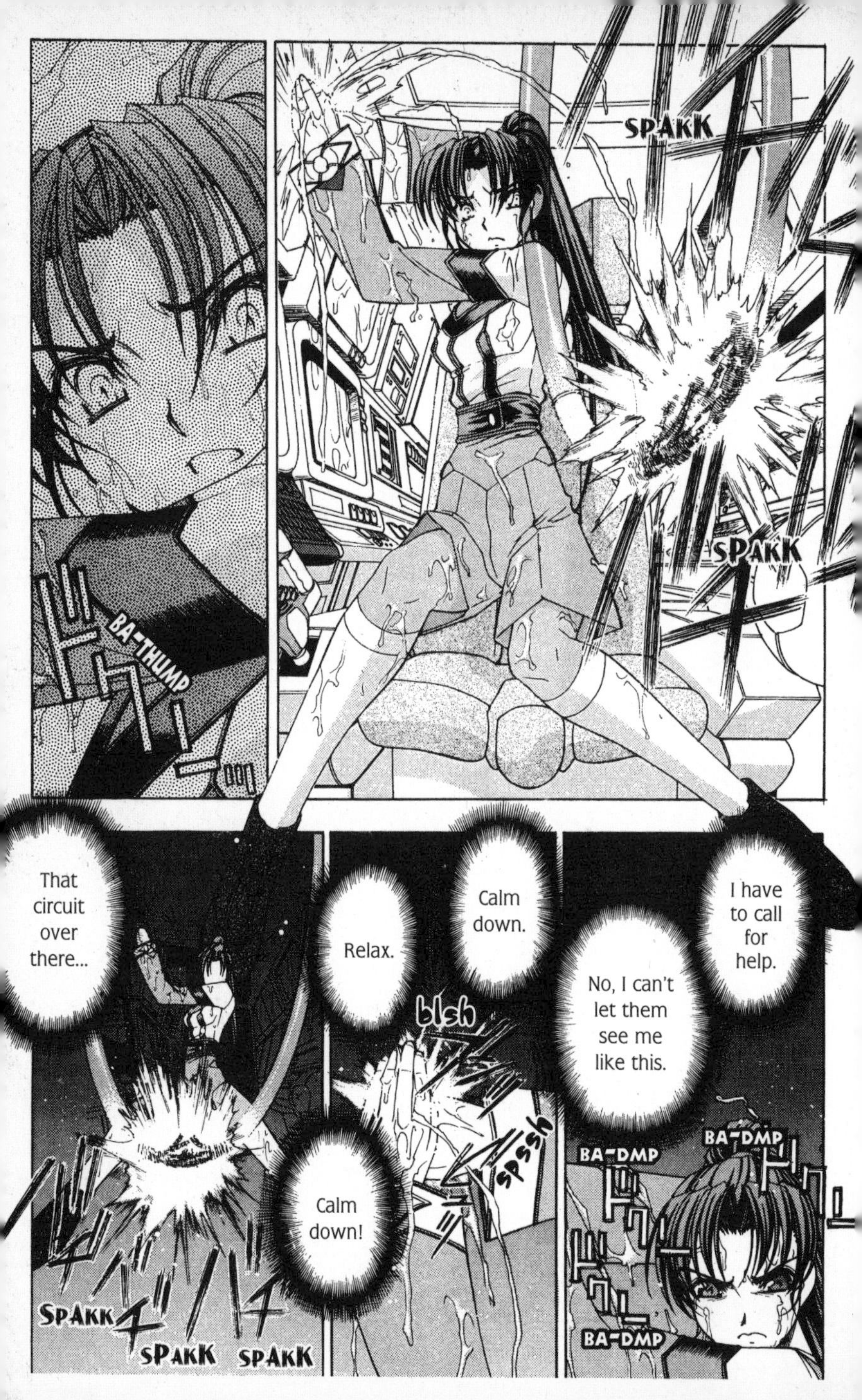

SPAKK
SPAKK
BA-THUMP
That circuit over there...
Calm down.
Relax.
blsh
Calm down!
spssh
SPAKK
SPAKK
SPAKK
I have to call for help.
No, I can't let them see me like this.
BA-DMP
BA-DMP
BA-DMP

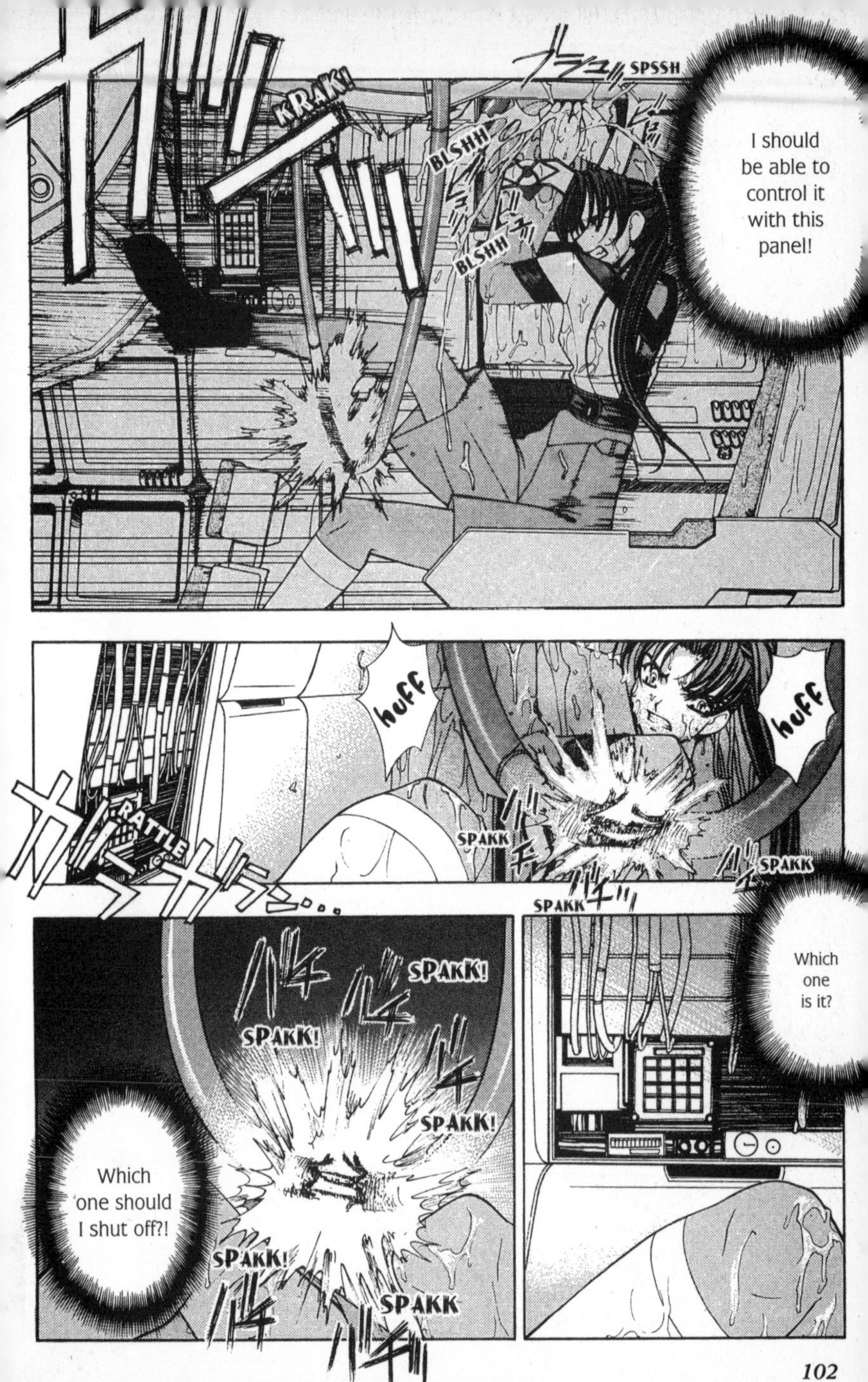
SPSSH
I should be able to control it with this panel!
KRAK!
BLSHH
BLSHH
huff
huff
RATTLE
SPAKK
SPAKK
SPAKK
Which one is it?
SPAKK!
SPAKK!
SPAKK!
Which one should I shut off?!
SPAKK!
SPAKK

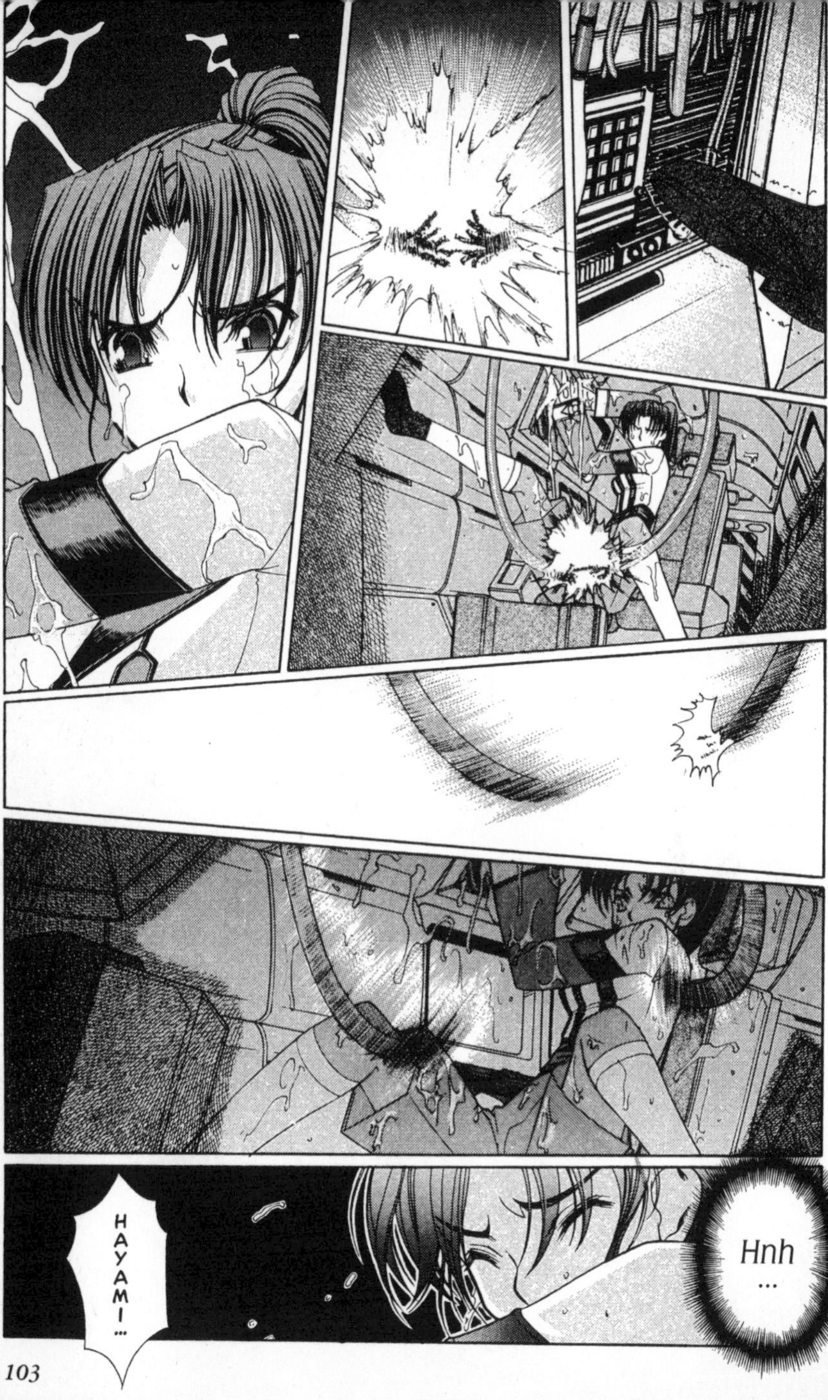
Hnh ...
HAYAMI...

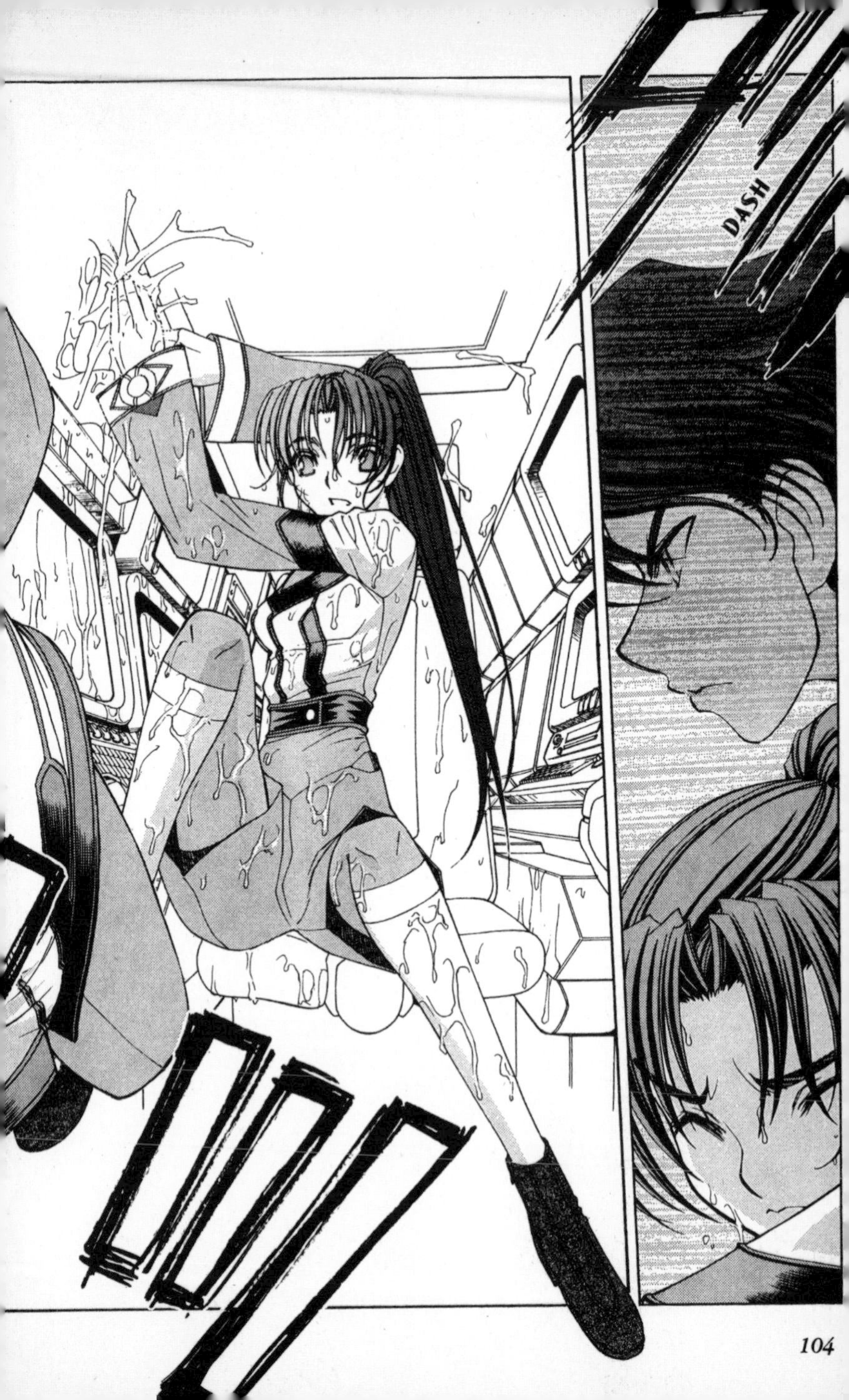
DASH

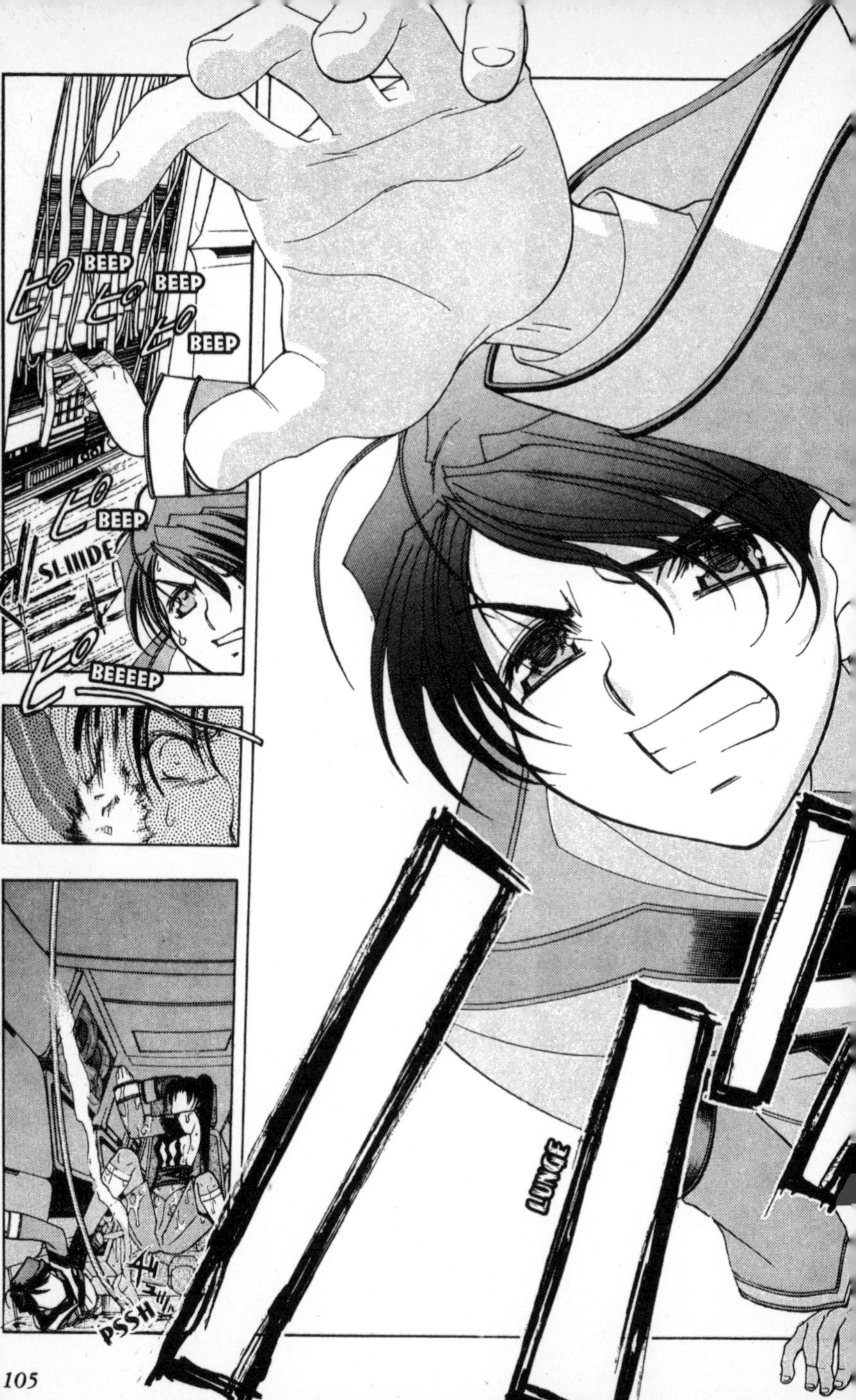
LUNGE
BEEP
BEEP
BEEP
BEEP
SLIIIDE
BEEEEP
PSSH

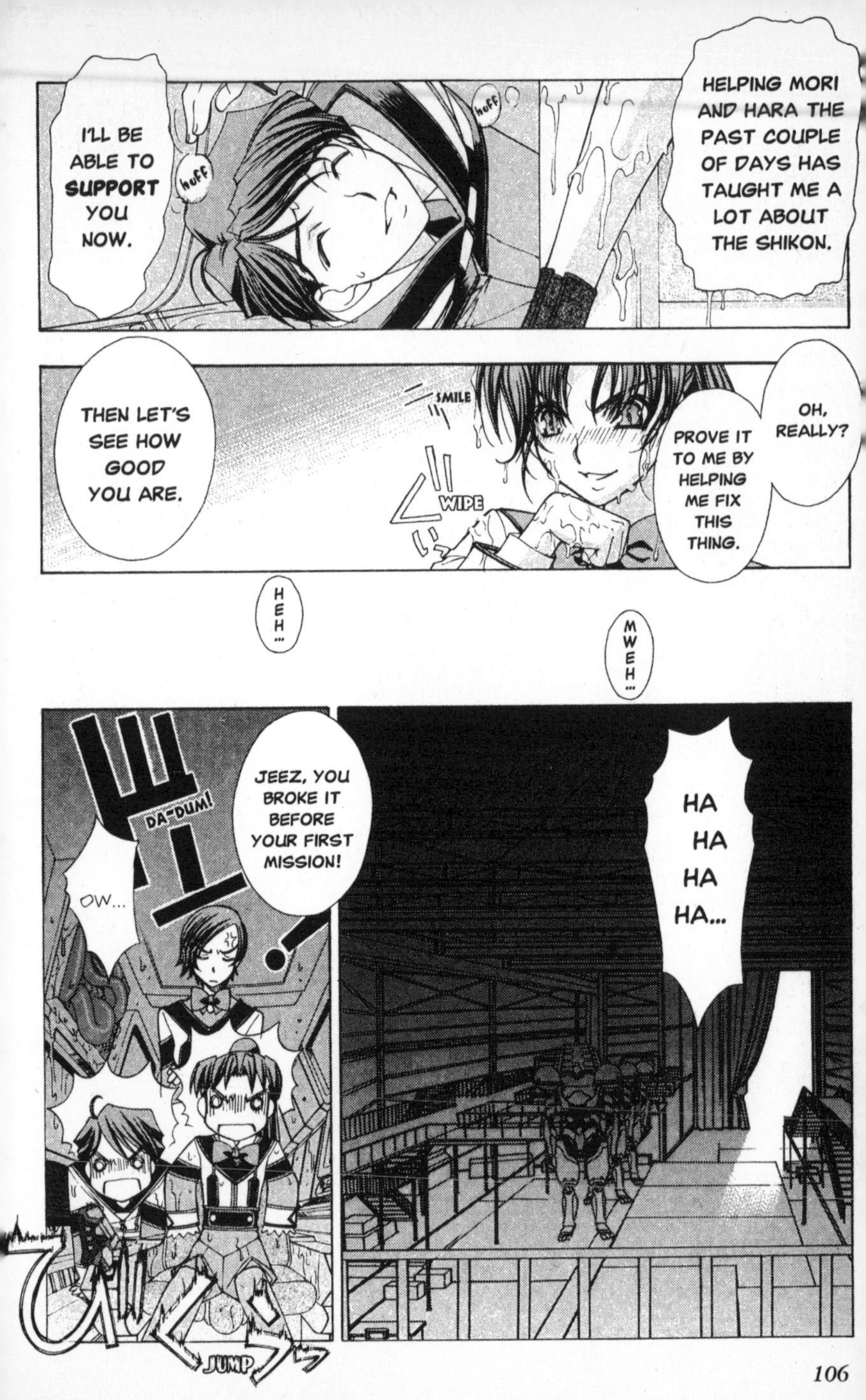
HELPING MORI AND HARA THE PAST COUPLE OF DAYS HAS TAUGHT ME A LOT ABOUT THE SHIKON.
huff
huff
I'LL BE ABLE TO SUPPORT YOU NOW.
OH, REALLY?
PROVE IT TO ME BY HELPING ME FIX THIS THING.
SMILE
WIPE
THEN LET'S SEE HOW GOOD YOU ARE.
MWEH...
HEH...
HA HA HA HA...
JEEZ, YOU BROKE IT BEFORE YOUR FIRST MISSION!
DA-DUM!
OW...
JUMP

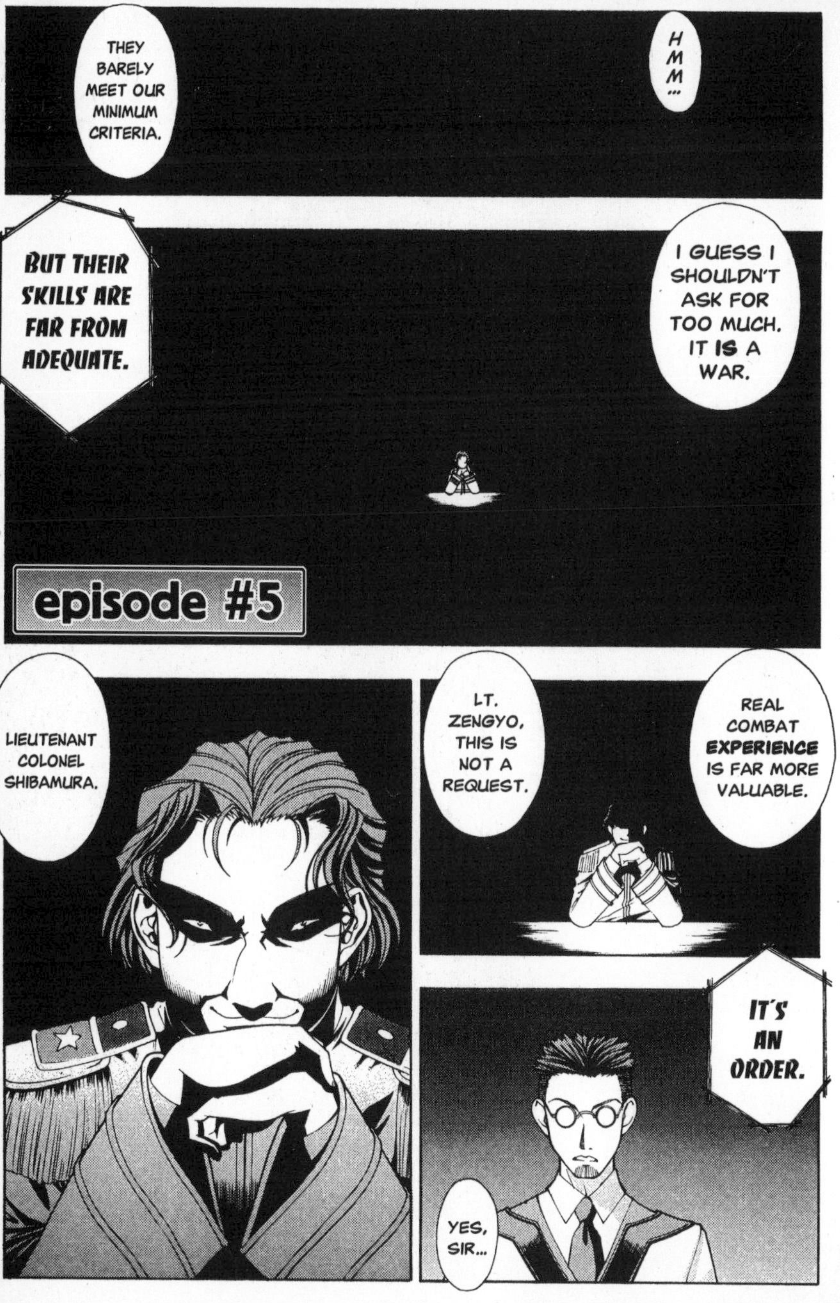

THEY BARELY MEET OUR MINIMUM CRITERIA.
HMM...
BUT THEIR SKILLS ARE FAR FROM ADEQUATE.
I GUESS I SHOULDN'T ASK FOR TOO MUCH. IT IS A WAR.
episode #5
LIEUTENANT COLONEL SHIBAMURA.
LT. ZENGYO, THIS IS NOT A REQUEST.
REAL COMBAT EXPERIENCE IS FAR MORE VALUABLE.
IT'S AN ORDER.
YES, SIR...

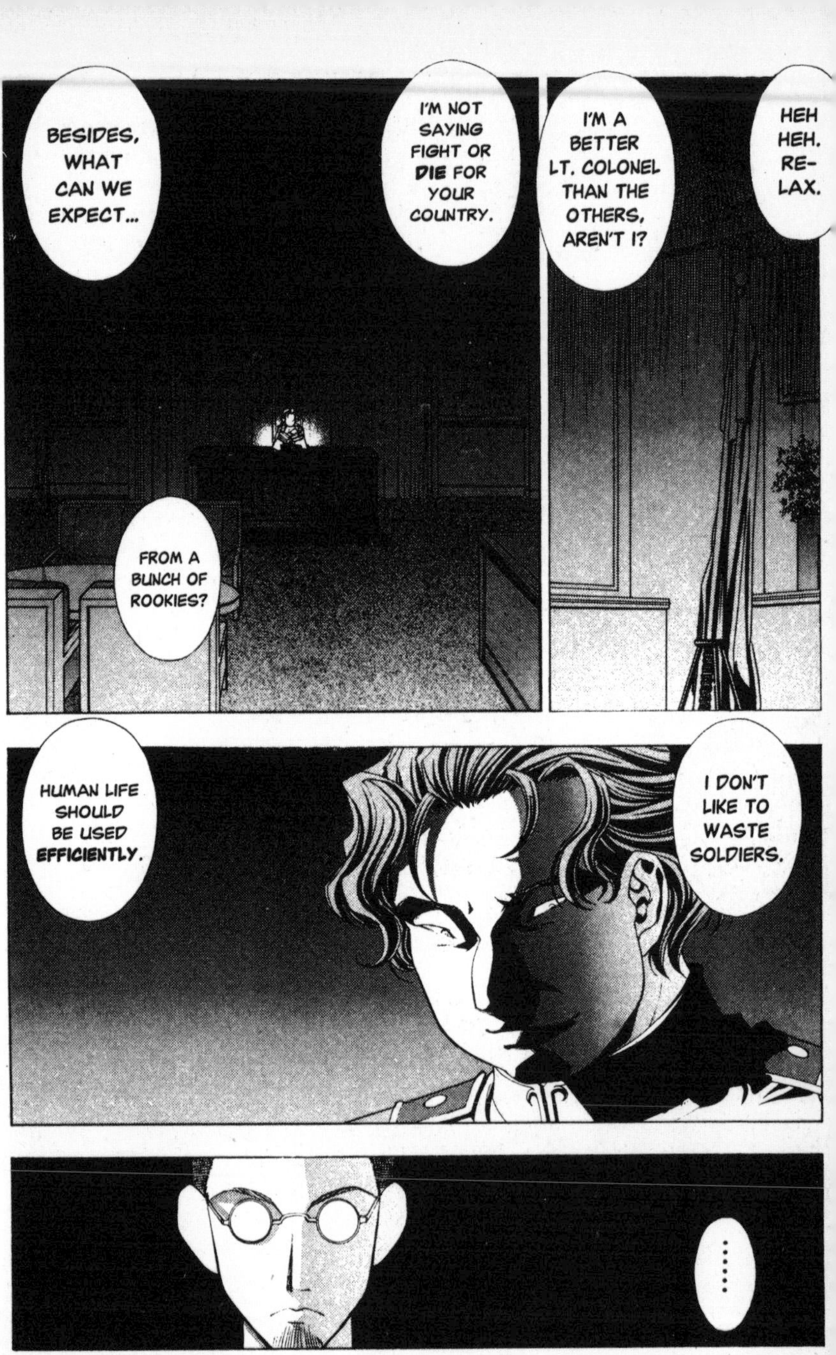
HEH HEH. RE-LAX.
I'M A BETTER LT. COLONEL THAN THE OTHERS, AREN'T I?
I'M NOT SAYING FIGHT OR DIE FOR YOUR COUNTRY.
BESIDES, WHAT CAN WE EXPECT...
FROM A BUNCH OF ROOKIES?
I DON'T LIKE TO WASTE SOLDIERS.
HUMAN LIFE SHOULD BE USED EFFICIENTLY.
......

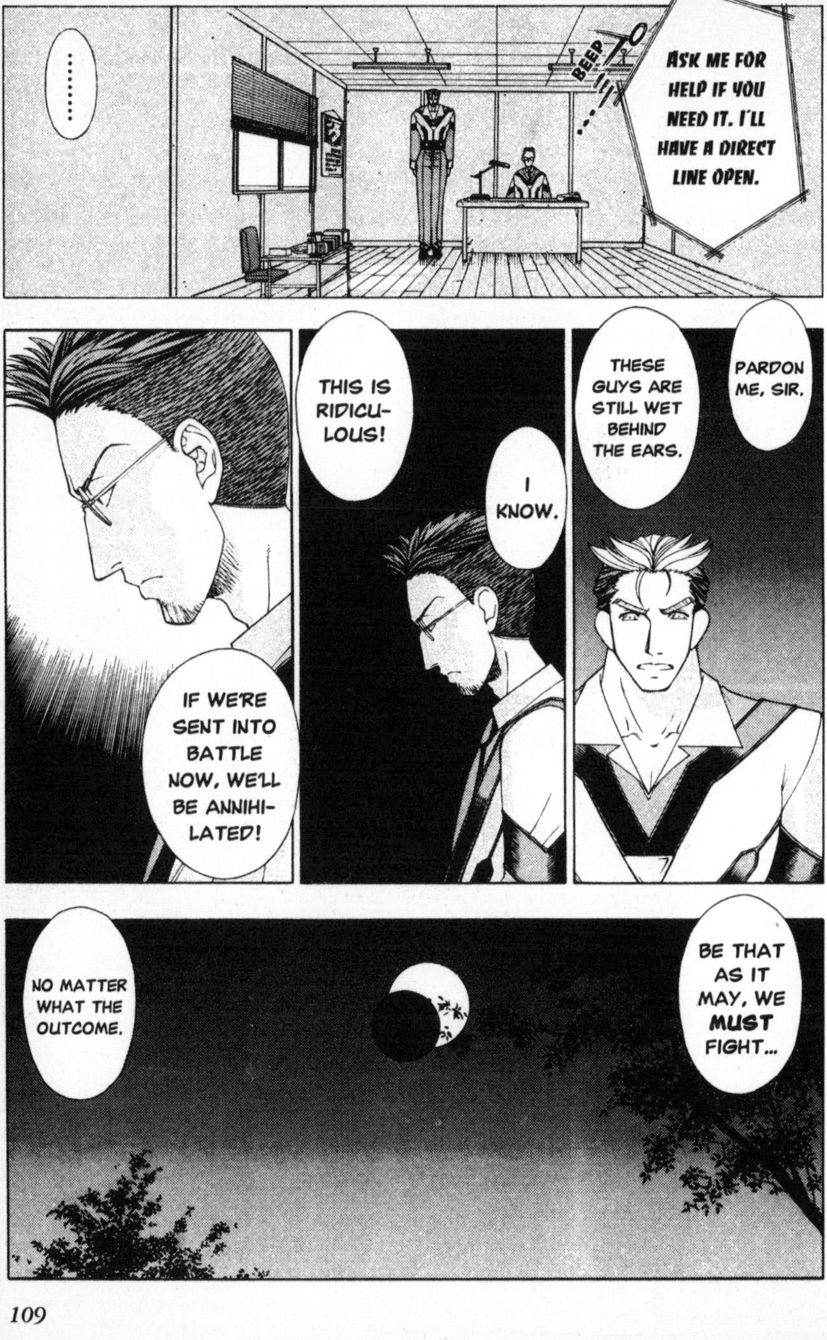
ASK ME FOR HELP IF YOU NEED IT. I'LL HAVE A DIRECT LINE OPEN.
BEEP
......
PARDON ME, SIR.
THESE GUYS ARE STILL WET BEHIND THE EARS.
I KNOW.
THIS IS RIDICULOUS!
IF WE'RE SENT INTO BATTLE NOW, WE'LL BE ANNIHILATED!
BE THAT AS IT MAY, WE **MUST** FIGHT...
NO MATTER WHAT THE OUTCOME.

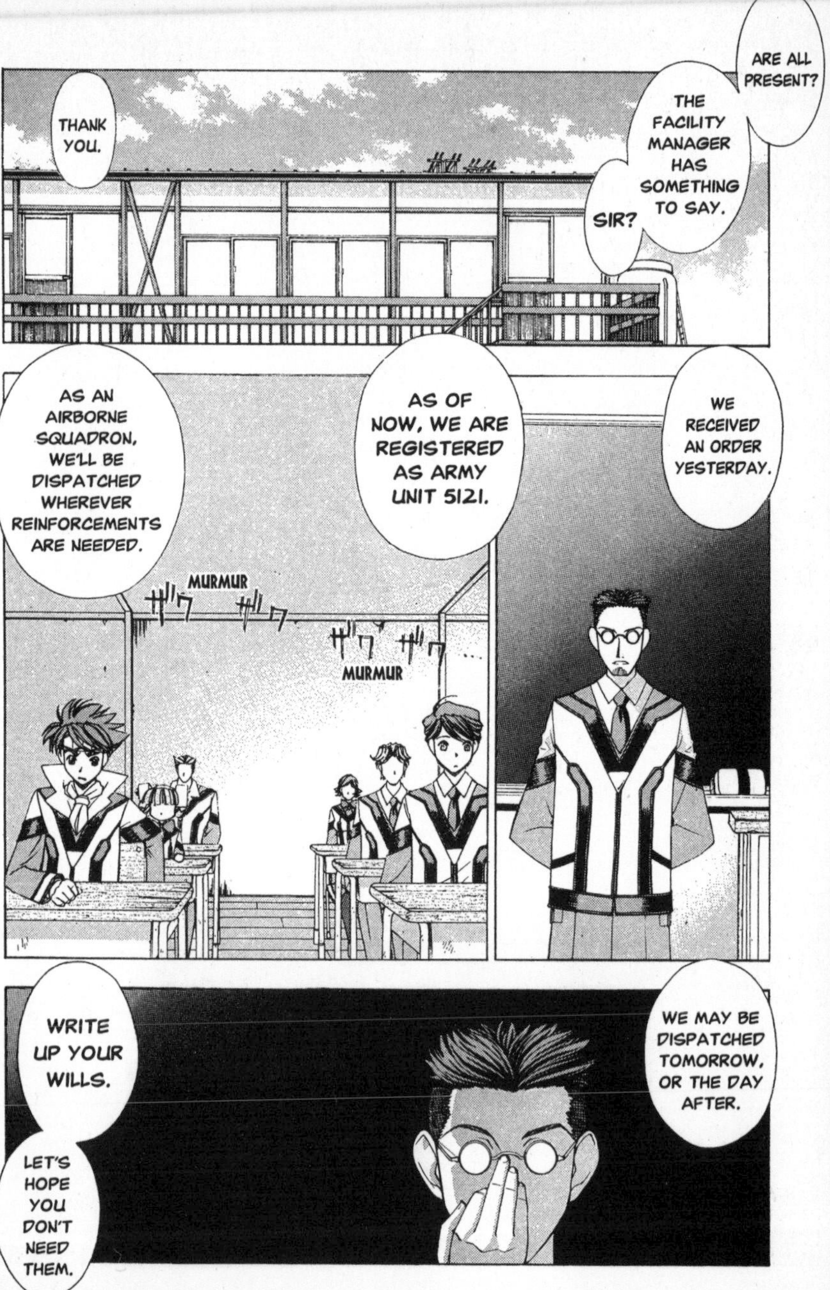
ARE ALL PRESENT?
THE FACILITY MANAGER HAS SOMETHING TO SAY.
SIR?
THANK YOU.
WE RECEIVED AN ORDER YESTERDAY.
AS OF NOW, WE ARE REGISTERED AS ARMY UNIT 5121.
AS AN AIRBORNE SQUADRON, WE'LL BE DISPATCHED WHEREVER REINFORCEMENTS ARE NEEDED.
MURMUR
MURMUR
WE MAY BE DISPATCHED TOMORROW, OR THE DAY AFTER.
WRITE UP YOUR WILLS.
LET'S HOPE YOU DON'T NEED THEM.

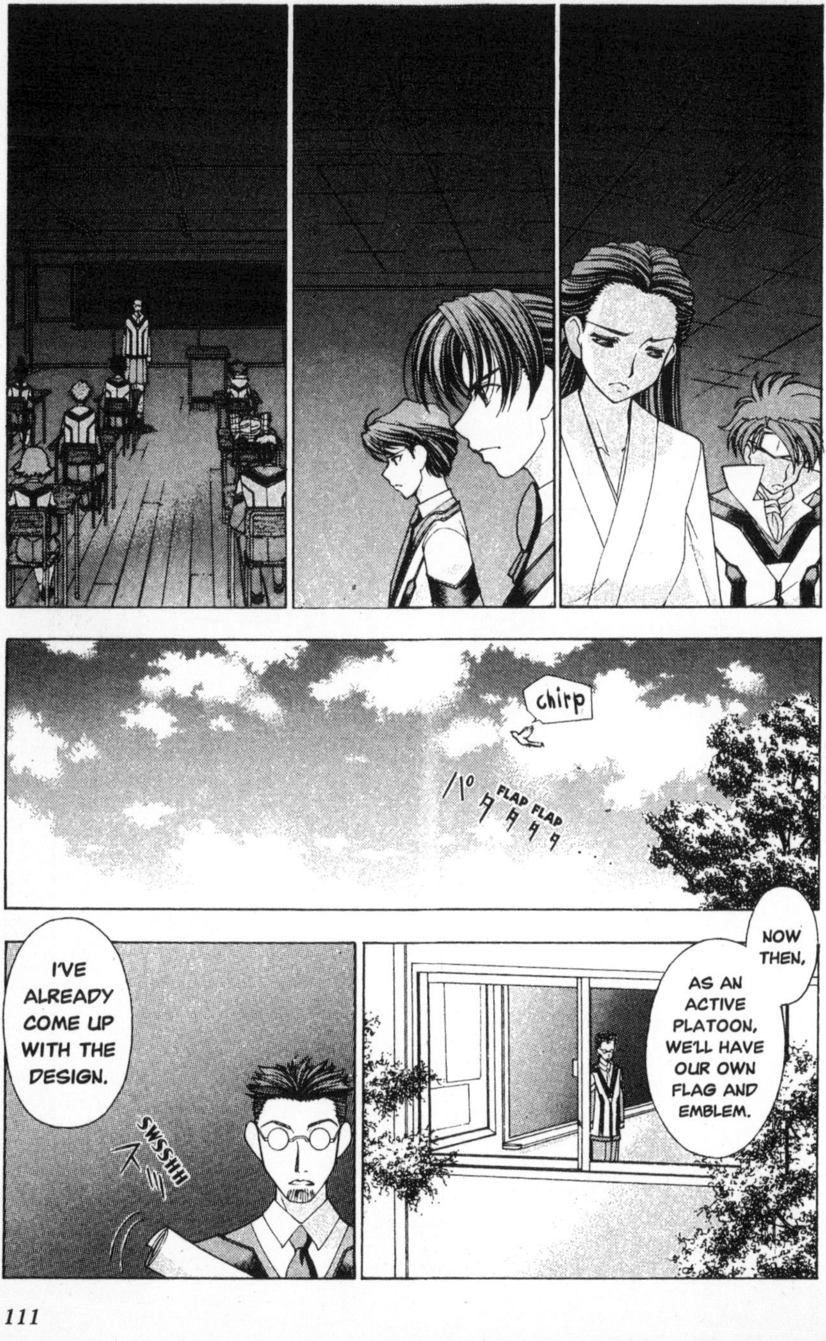
chirp
パタタタ
FLAP FLAP
NOW THEN, AS AN ACTIVE PLATOON, WE'LL HAVE OUR OWN FLAG AND EMBLEM.
I'VE ALREADY COME UP WITH THE DESIGN.
SWSSHH

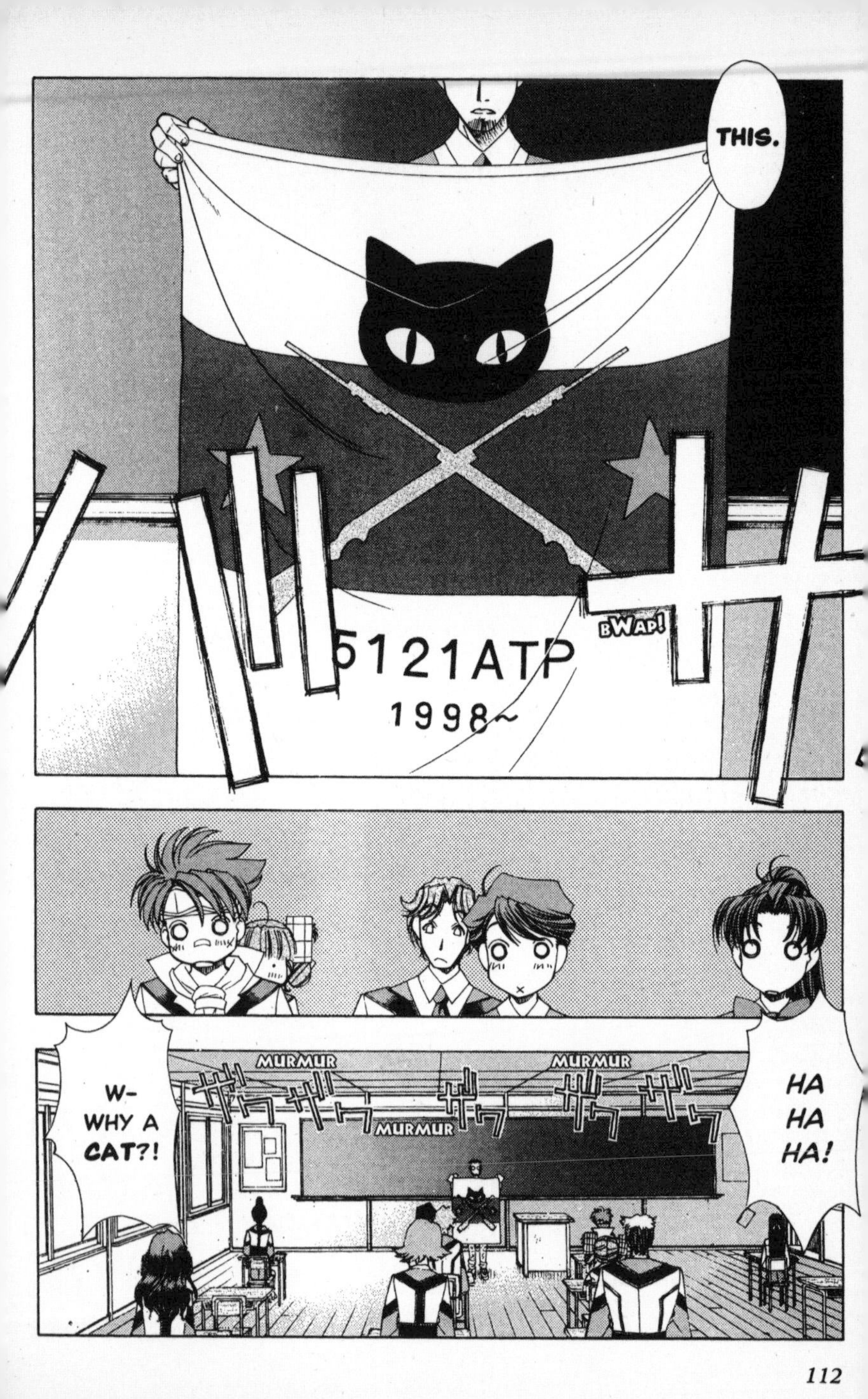
THIS.
5121ATP
1998~
BWAP!
HA HA HA!
MURMUR
MURMUR
MURMUR
W- WHY A CAT?!

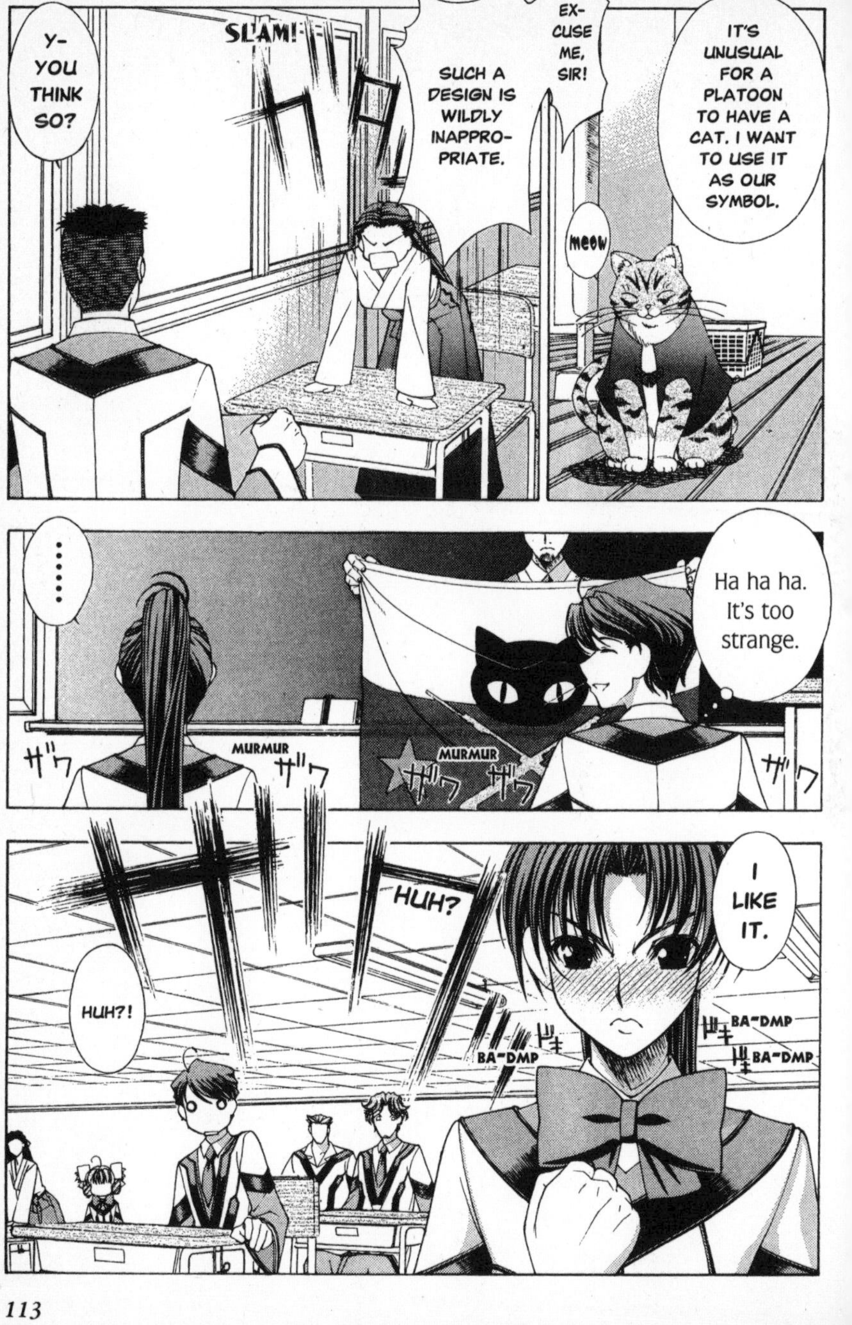
IT'S UNUSUAL FOR A PLATOON TO HAVE A CAT. I WANT TO USE IT AS OUR SYMBOL.
meow
EX-CUSE ME, SIR!
SUCH A DESIGN IS WILDLY INAPPRO-PRIATE.
SLAM!
Y-YOU THINK SO?
Ha ha ha. It's too strange.
......
MURMUR
MURMUR
I LIKE IT.
BA-DMP
BA-DMP
BA-DMP
HUH?
HUH?!

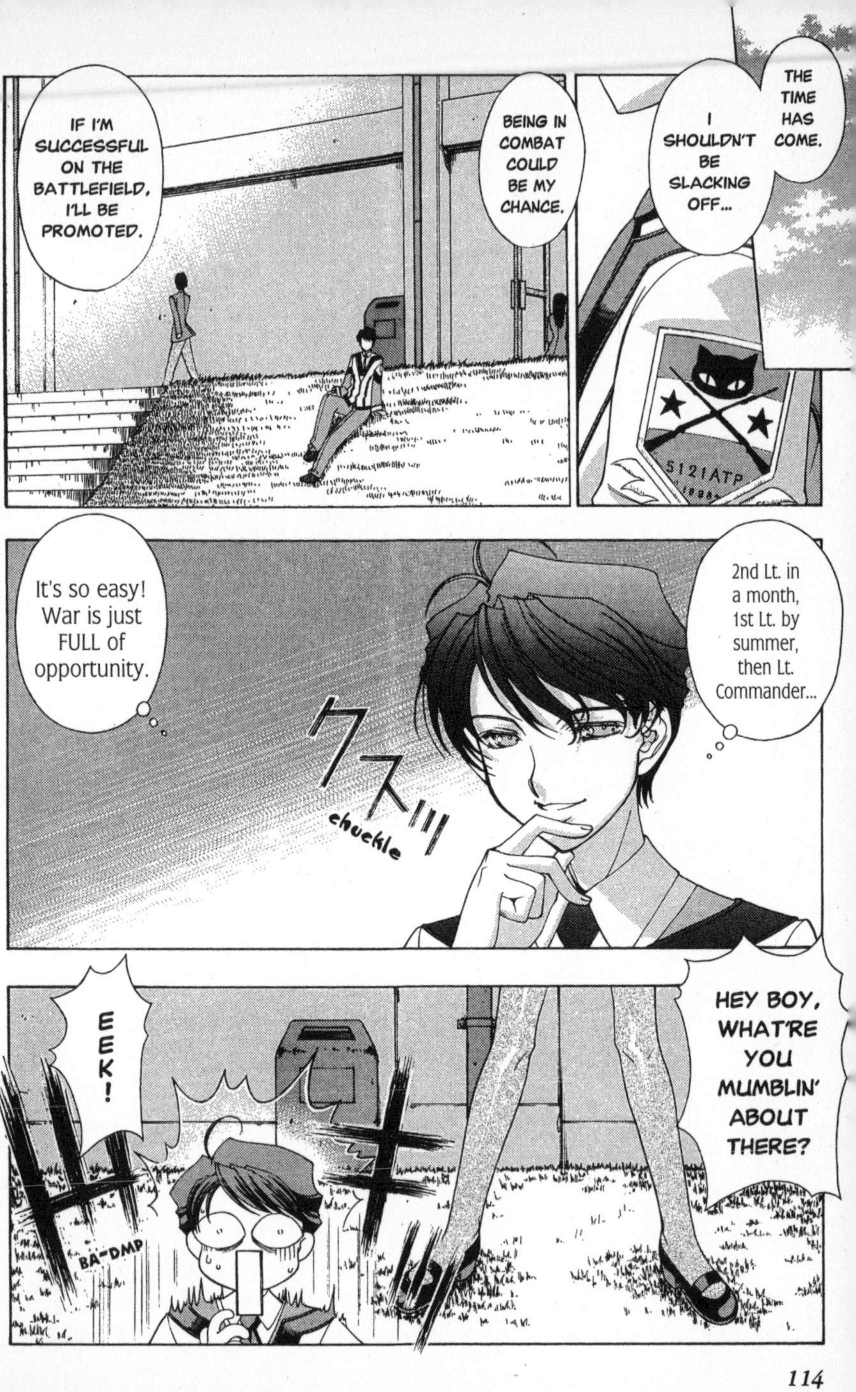
THE TIME HAS COME.
I SHOULDN'T BE SLACKING OFF...
BEING IN COMBAT COULD BE MY CHANCE.
IF I'M SUCCESSFUL ON THE BATTLEFIELD, I'LL BE PROMOTED.
5121ATP
2nd Lt. in a month, 1st Lt. by summer, then Lt. Commander...
It's so easy! War is just FULL of opportunity.
chuckle
HEY BOY, WHAT'RE YOU MUMBLIN' ABOUT THERE?
EEK!
BA-DMP

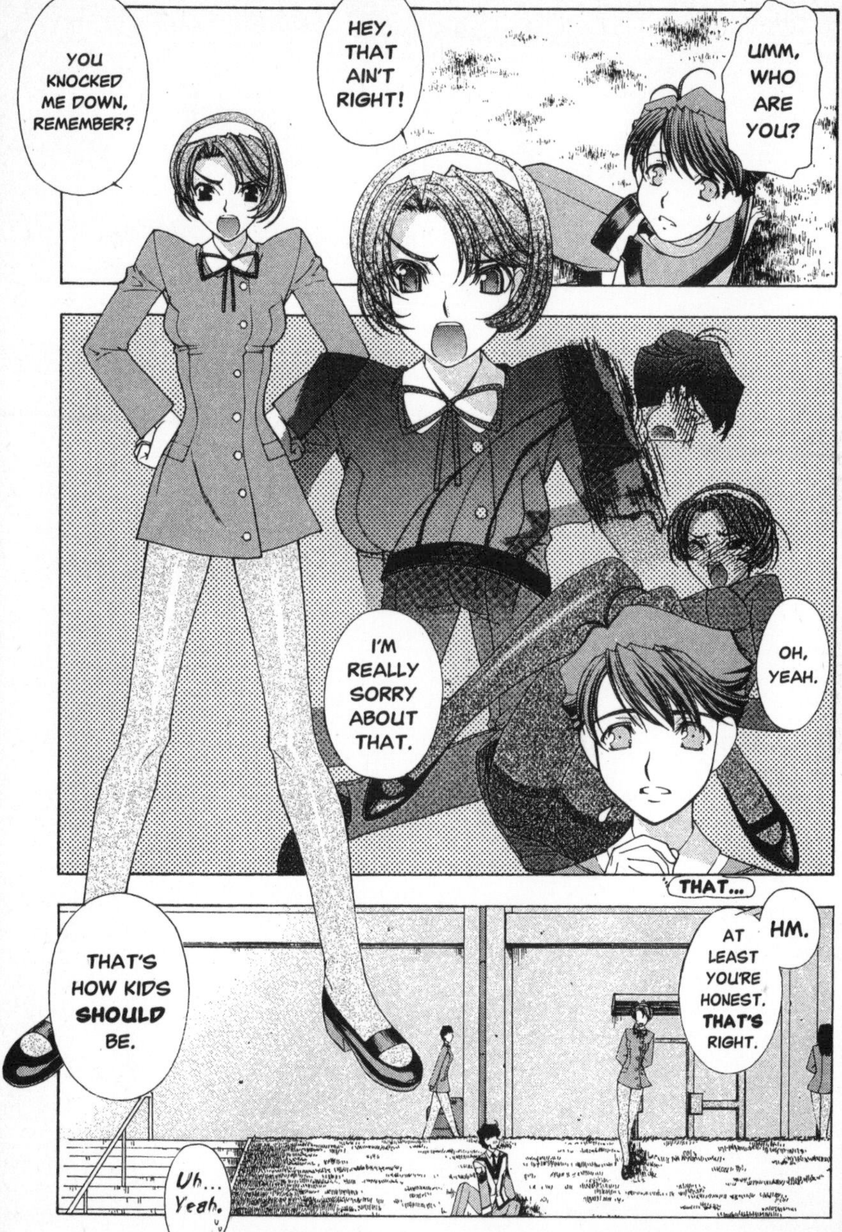

UMM, WHO ARE YOU?
HEY, THAT AIN'T RIGHT!
YOU KNOCKED ME DOWN, REMEMBER?
OH, YEAH.
I'M REALLY SORRY ABOUT THAT.
THAT...
HM.
AT LEAST YOU'RE HONEST. THAT'S RIGHT.
THAT'S HOW KIDS SHOULD BE.
Uh... Yeah.

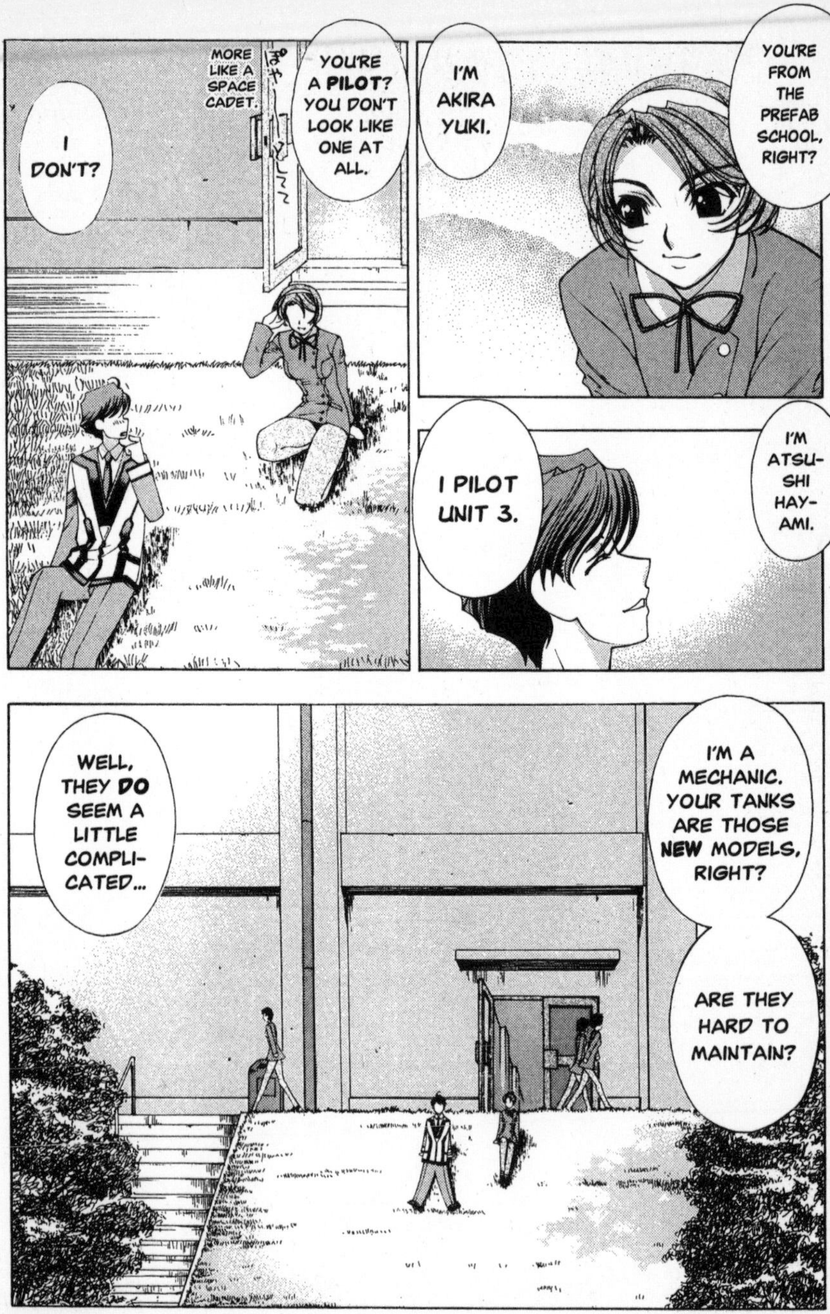
YOU'RE FROM THE PREFAB SCHOOL, RIGHT?
I'M AKIRA YUKI.
I'M ATSUSHI HAYAMI.
I PILOT UNIT 3.
YOU'RE A PILOT? YOU DON'T LOOK LIKE ONE AT ALL.
MORE LIKE A SPACE CADET.
I DON'T?
I'M A MECHANIC. YOUR TANKS ARE THOSE NEW MODELS, RIGHT?
ARE THEY HARD TO MAINTAIN?
WELL, THEY DO SEEM A LITTLE COMPLICATED...

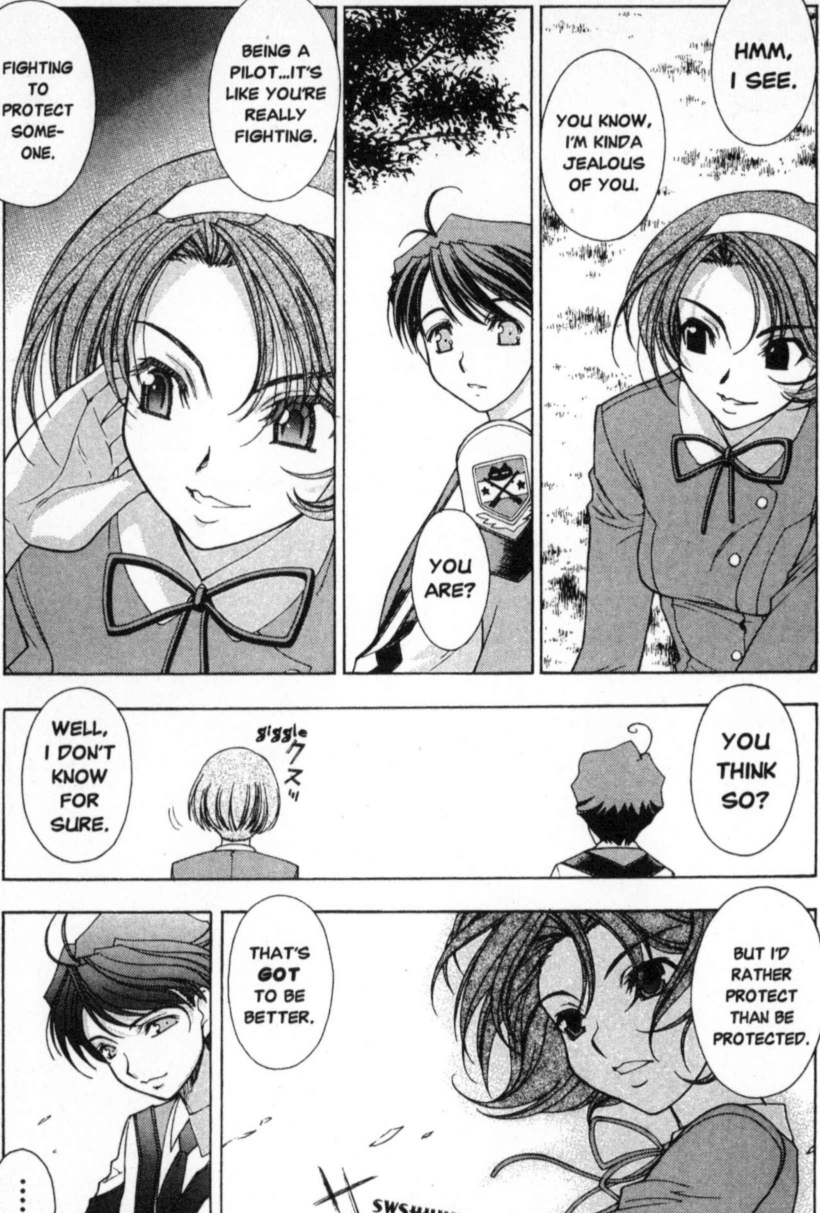
HMM, I SEE.
YOU KNOW, I'M KINDA JEALOUS OF YOU.
YOU ARE?
BEING A PILOT...IT'S LIKE YOU'RE REALLY FIGHTING.
FIGHTING TO PROTECT SOME-ONE.
YOU THINK SO?
giggle クスッ
WELL, I DON'T KNOW FOR SURE.
BUT I'D RATHER PROTECT THAN BE PROTECTED.
THAT'S GOT TO BE BETTER.
SWSHHHHH
......

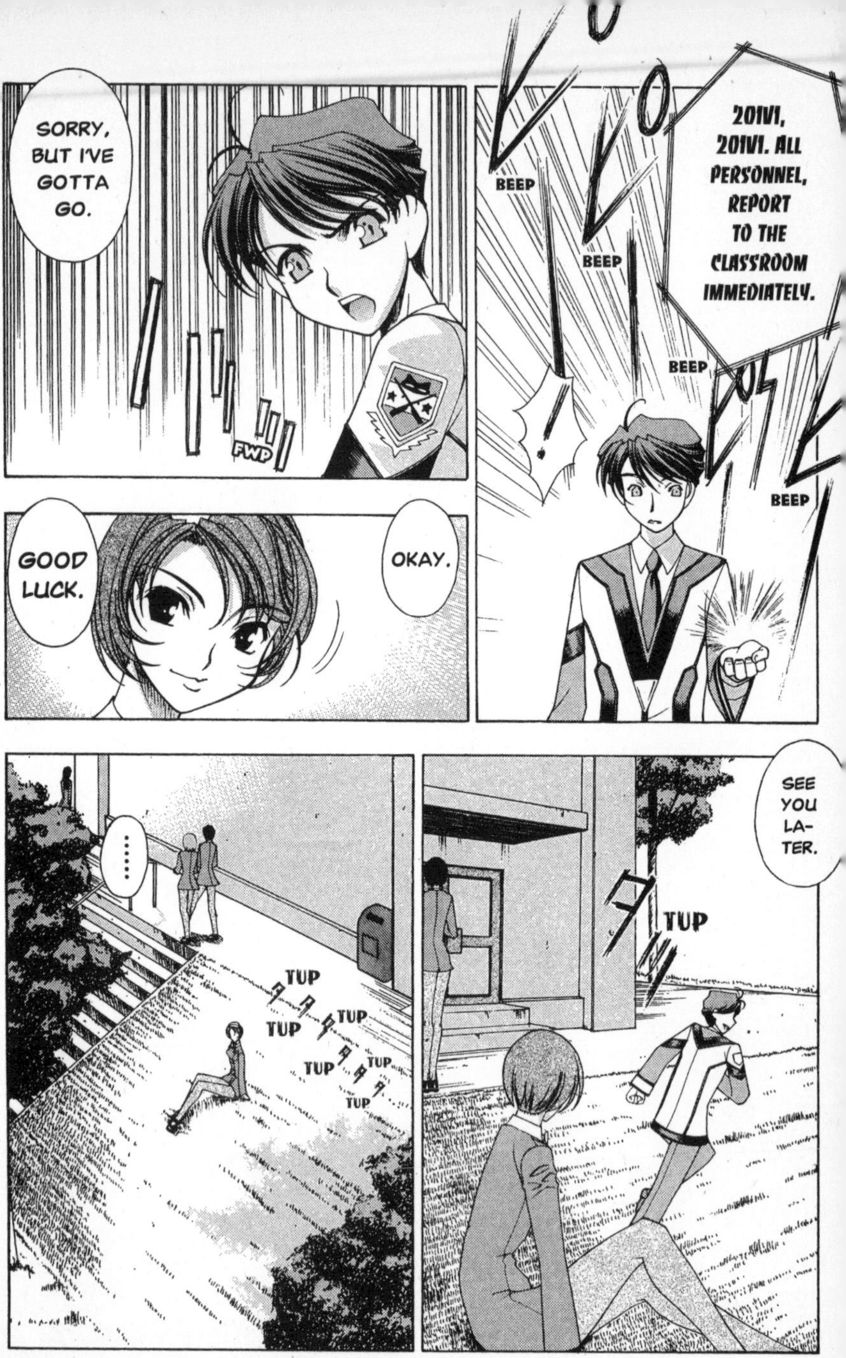
BEEP
BEEP
BEEP
BEEP
201V1, 201V1. ALL PERSONNEL, REPORT TO THE CLASSROOM IMMEDIATELY.
!
SORRY, BUT I'VE GOTTA GO.
FWP
OKAY.
GOOD LUCK.
SEE YOU LA-TER.
TUP
......
TUP
TUP
TUP
TUP
TUP
TUP

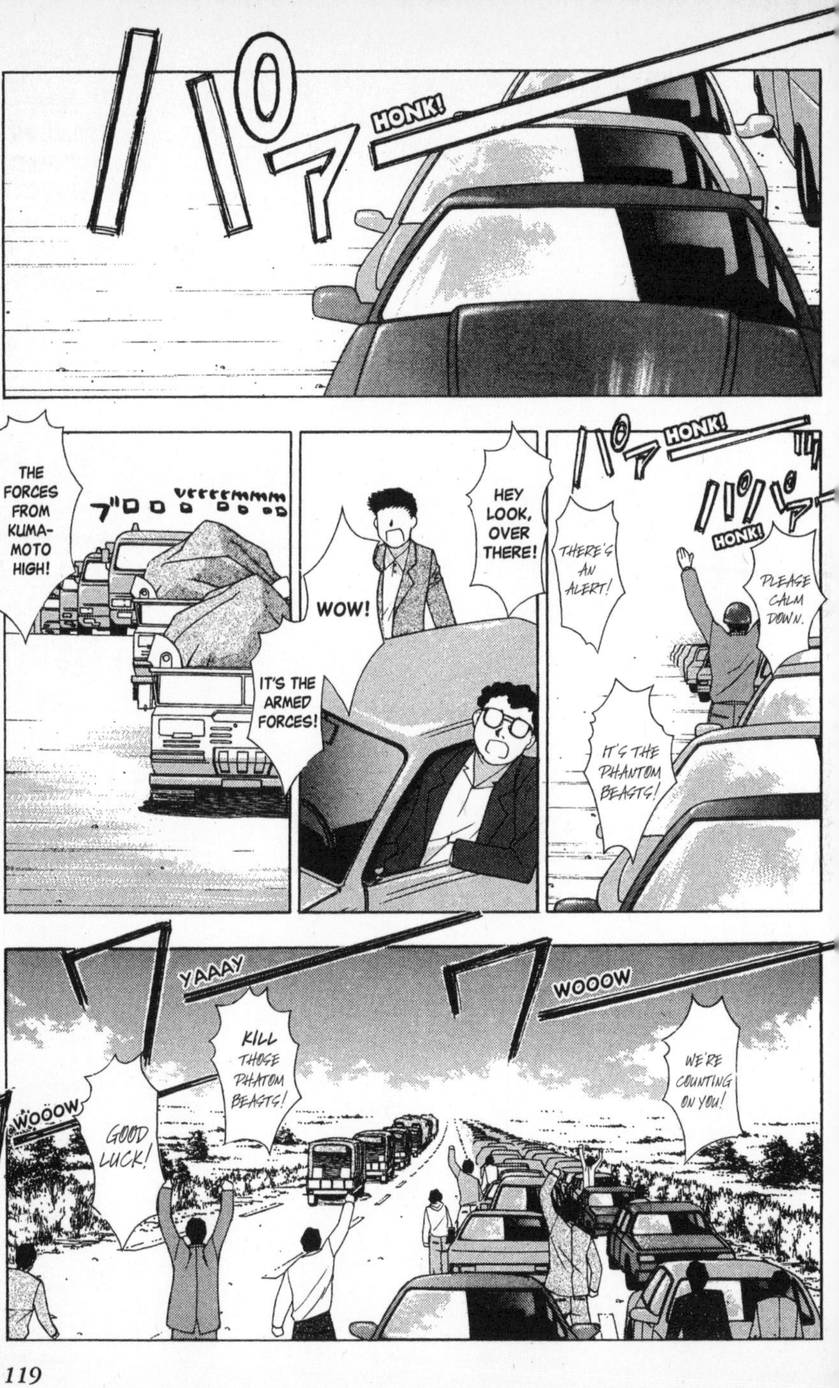

HONK!
HONK!
HONK!
PLEASE CALM DOWN.
THERE'S AN ALERT!
IT'S THE PHANTOM BEASTS!
HEY LOOK, OVER THERE!
WOW!
IT'S THE ARMED FORCES!
VRRRRMMMM
THE FORCES FROM KUMAMOTO HIGH!
WOOOW
WE'RE COUNTING ON YOU!
YAAAY
KILL THOSE PHATOM BEASTS!
WOOOW
GOOD LUCK!

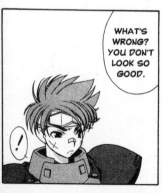

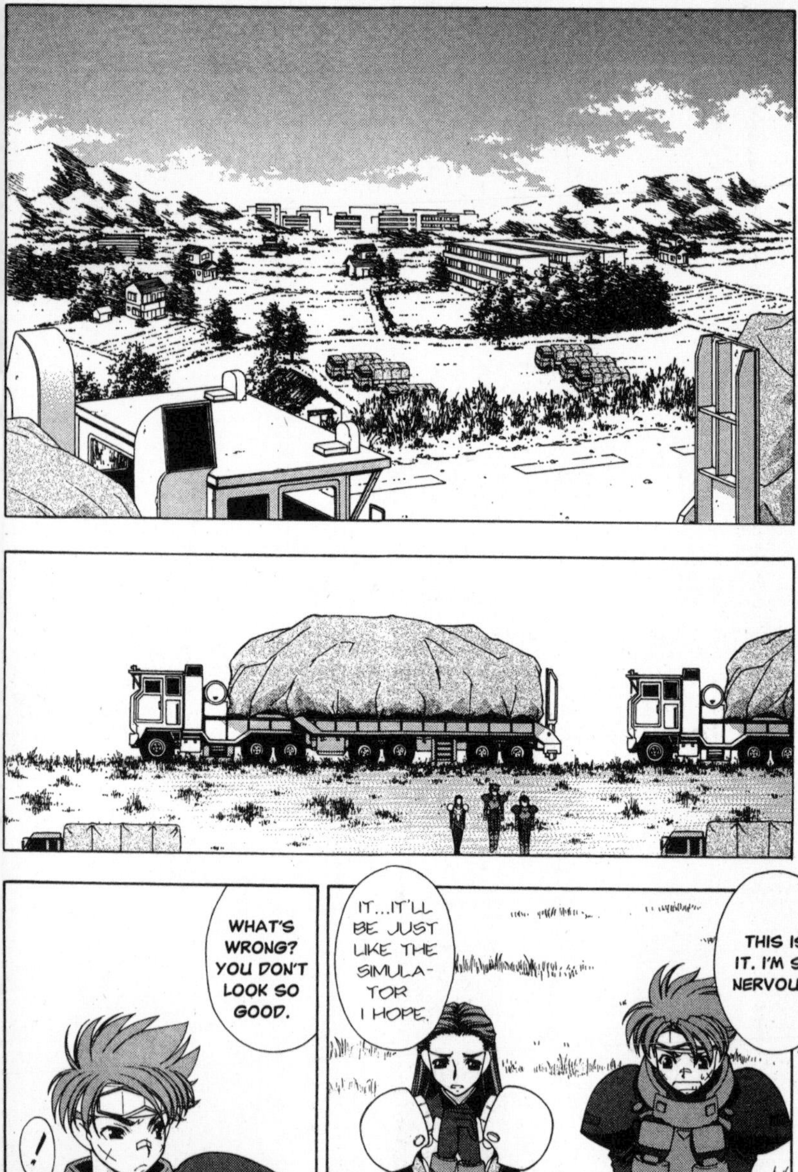
THIS IS IT. I'M SO NERVOUS!
IT...IT'LL BE JUST LIKE THE SIMULA-TOR I HOPE.
WHAT'S WRONG? YOU DON'T LOOK SO GOOD.
!

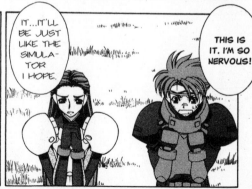

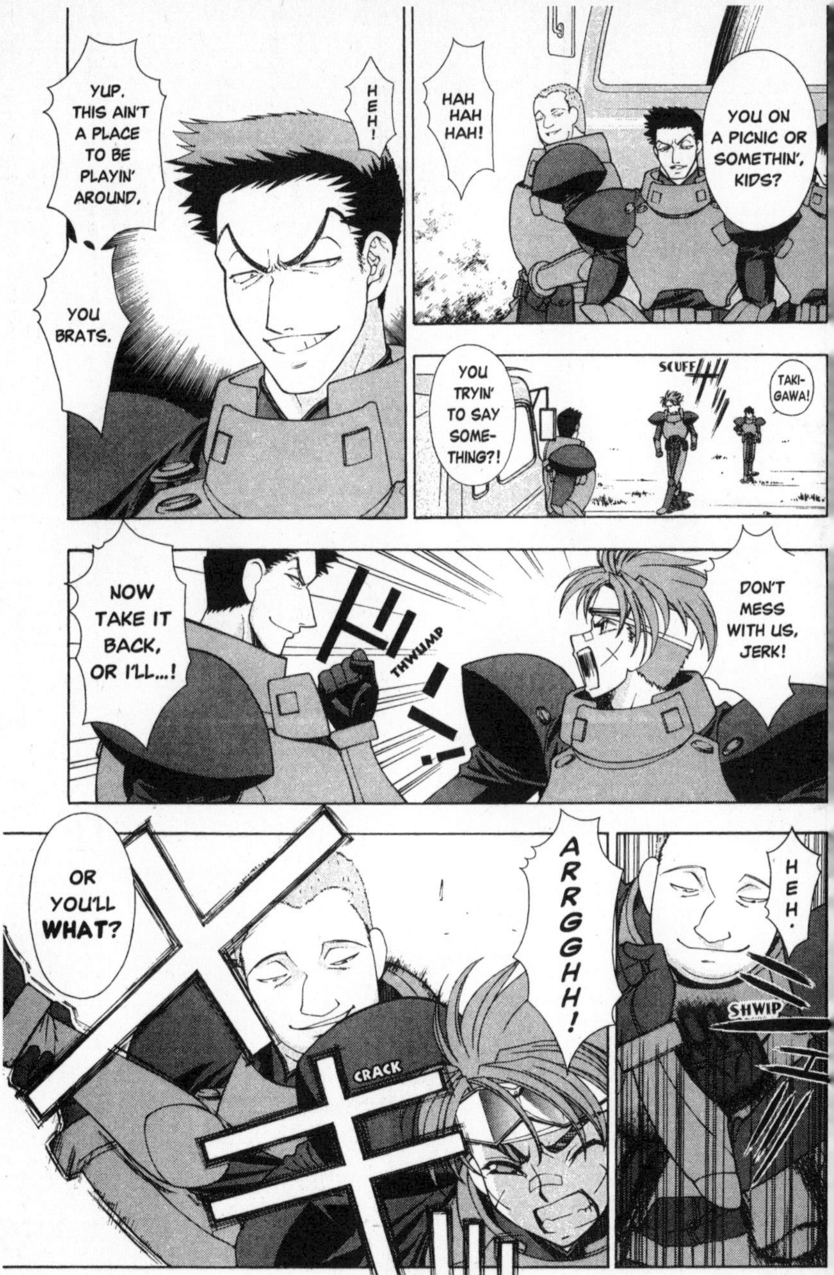
YOU ON A PICNIC OR SOMETHIN', KIDS?
HAH HAH HAH!
HEH!
YUP. THIS AIN'T A PLACE TO BE PLAYIN' AROUND,
...
YOU BRATS.
TAKI-GAWA!
SCUFF
YOU TRYIN' TO SAY SOME-THING?!
DON'T MESS WITH US, JERK!
THWUMP
NOW TAKE IT BACK, OR I'LL...!
HEH.
SHWIP
ARRGGHH!
CRACK
OR YOU'LL **WHAT?**

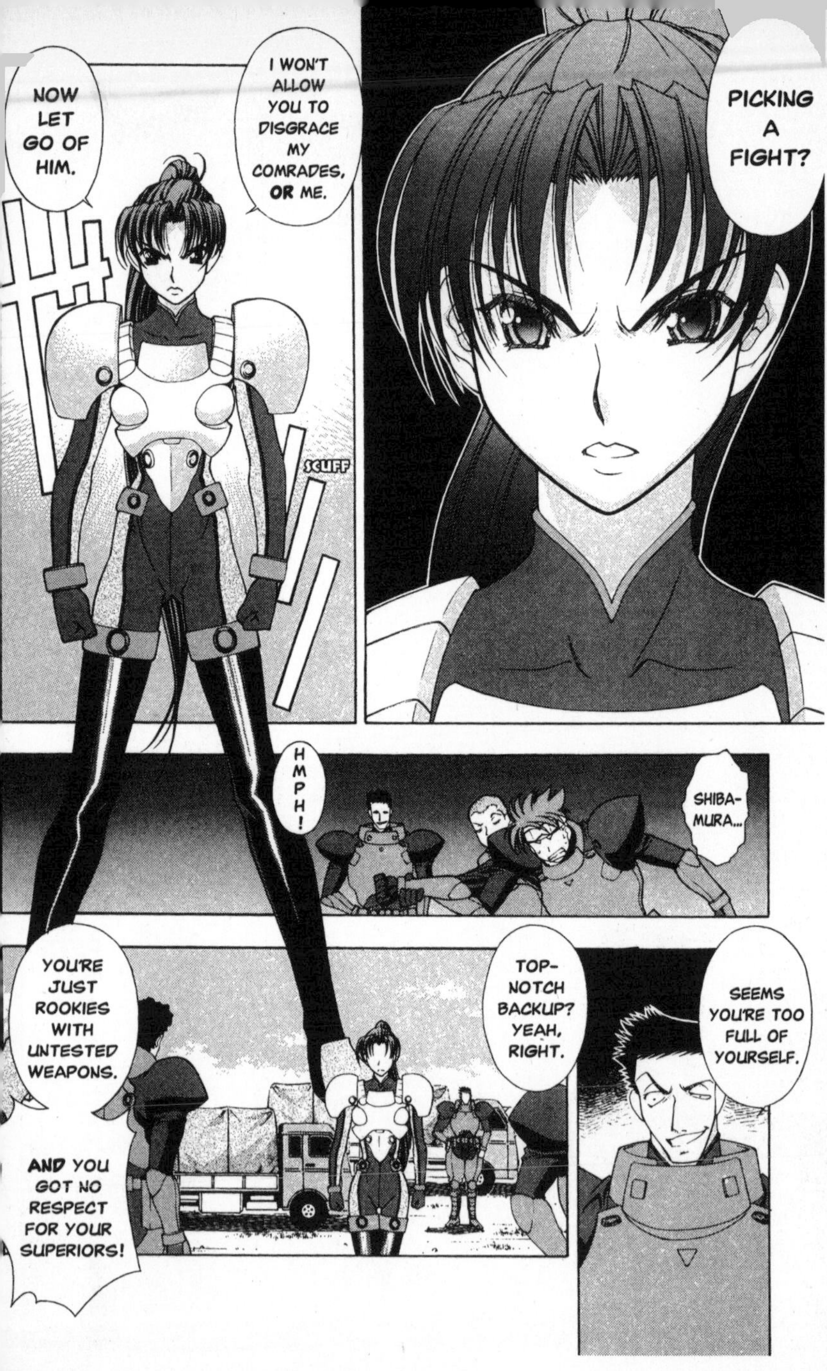

PICKING A FIGHT?
I WON'T ALLOW YOU TO DISGRACE MY COMRADES, OR ME.
NOW LET GO OF HIM.
SCUFF
SHIBA-MURA...
HMPH!
SEEMS YOU'RE TOO FULL OF YOURSELF.
TOP-NOTCH BACKUP? YEAH, RIGHT.
YOU'RE JUST ROOKIES WITH UNTESTED WEAPONS.
AND YOU GOT NO RESPECT FOR YOUR SUPERIORS!

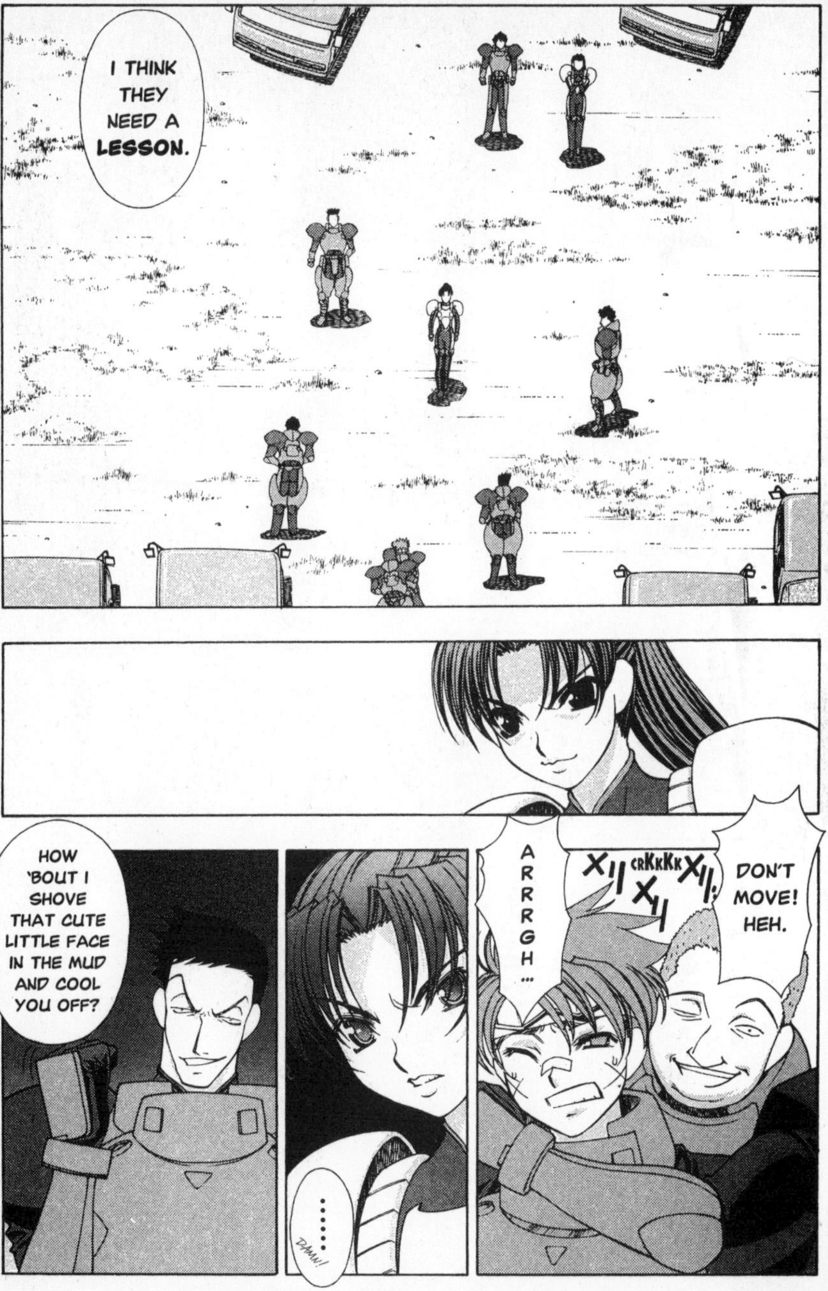
I THINK THEY NEED A LESSON.
HOW 'BOUT I SHOVE THAT CUTE LITTLE FACE IN THE MUD AND COOL YOU OFF?
......
DAMN!
ARRRGH...
CRKKKK
DON'T MOVE! HEH.

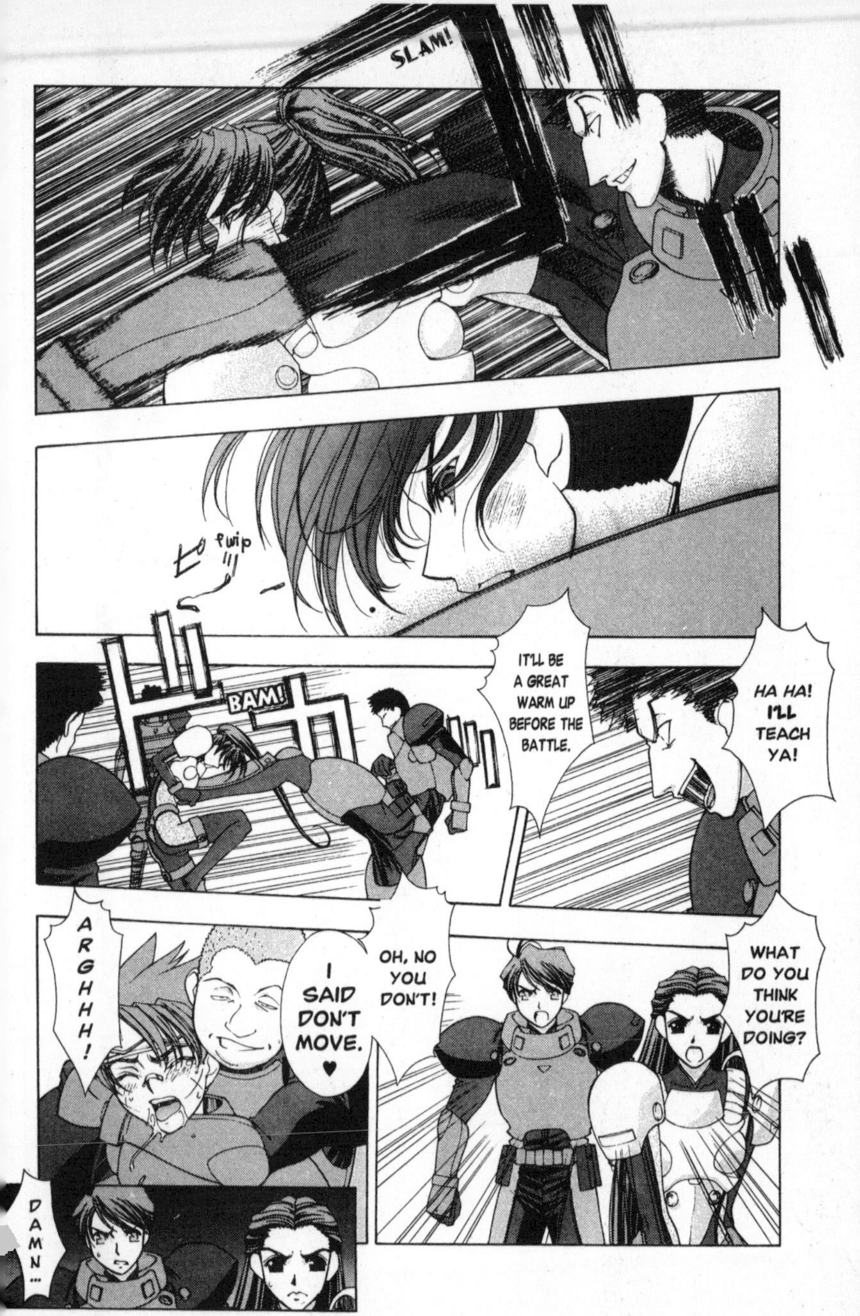
SLAM!
fwip
HA HA! I'LL TEACH YA!
IT'LL BE A GREAT WARM UP BEFORE THE BATTLE.
BAM!
WHAT DO YOU THINK YOU'RE DOING?
OH, NO YOU DON'T!
I SAID DON'T MOVE. ♥
ARGHHH!
DAMN...

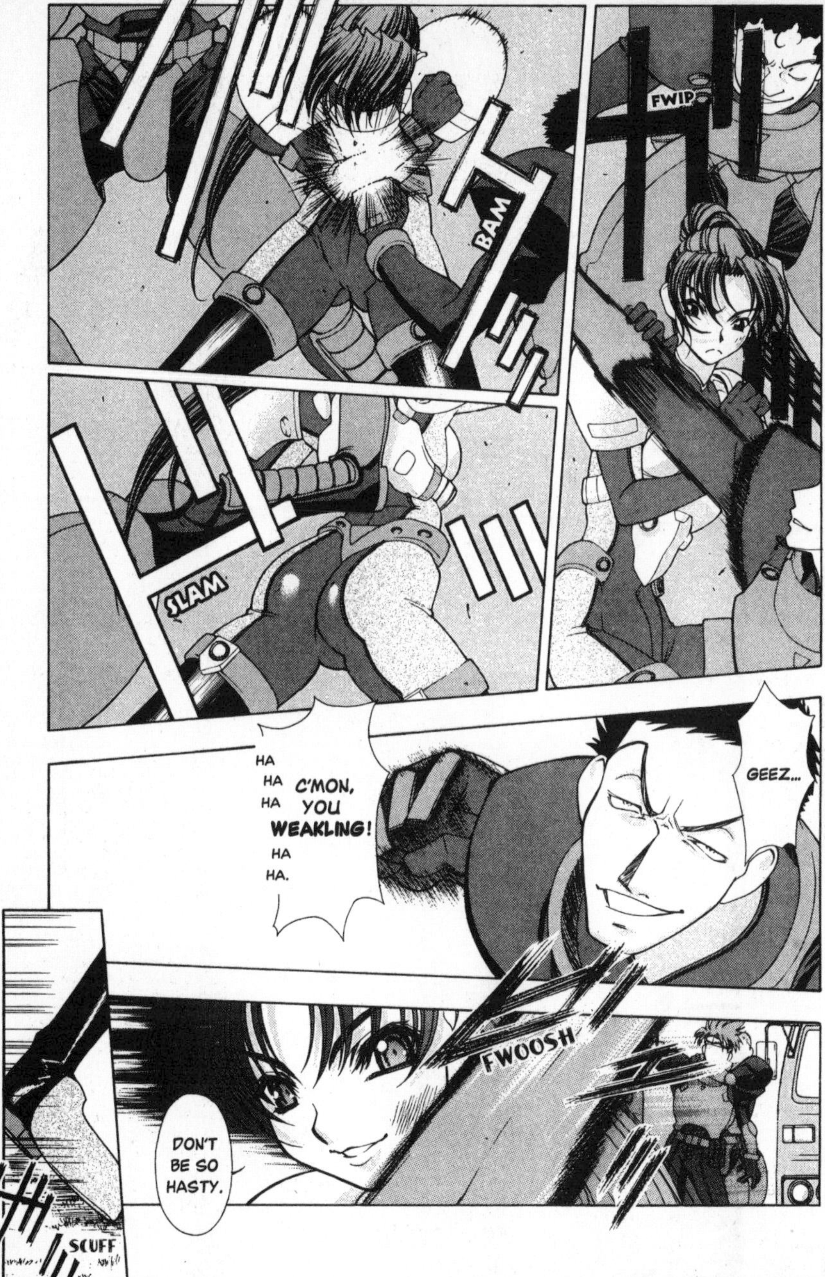
FWIP
BAM
SLAM
GEEZ...
HA HA HA
C'MON, YOU WEAKLING!
HA HA.
FWOOSH
DON'T BE SO HASTY.
SCUFF

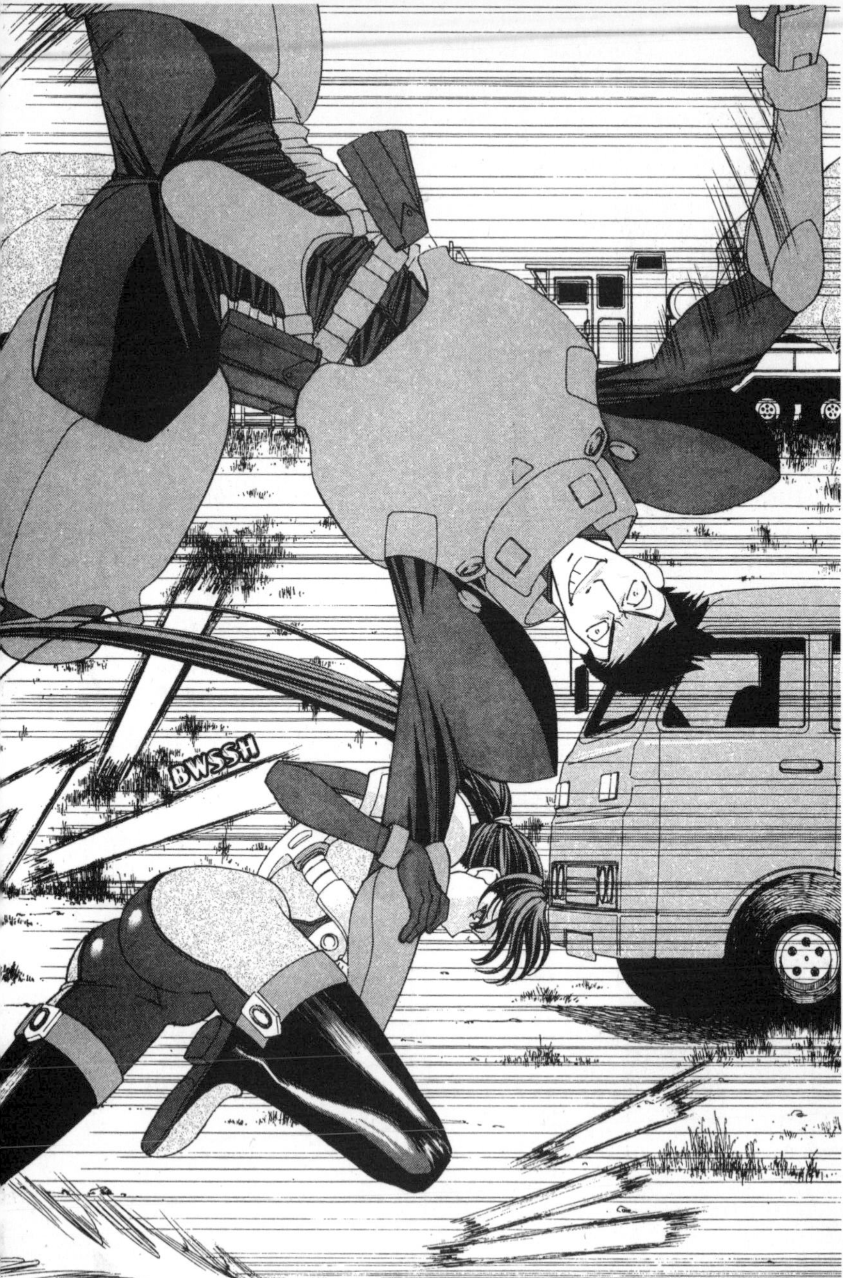
BWSSH

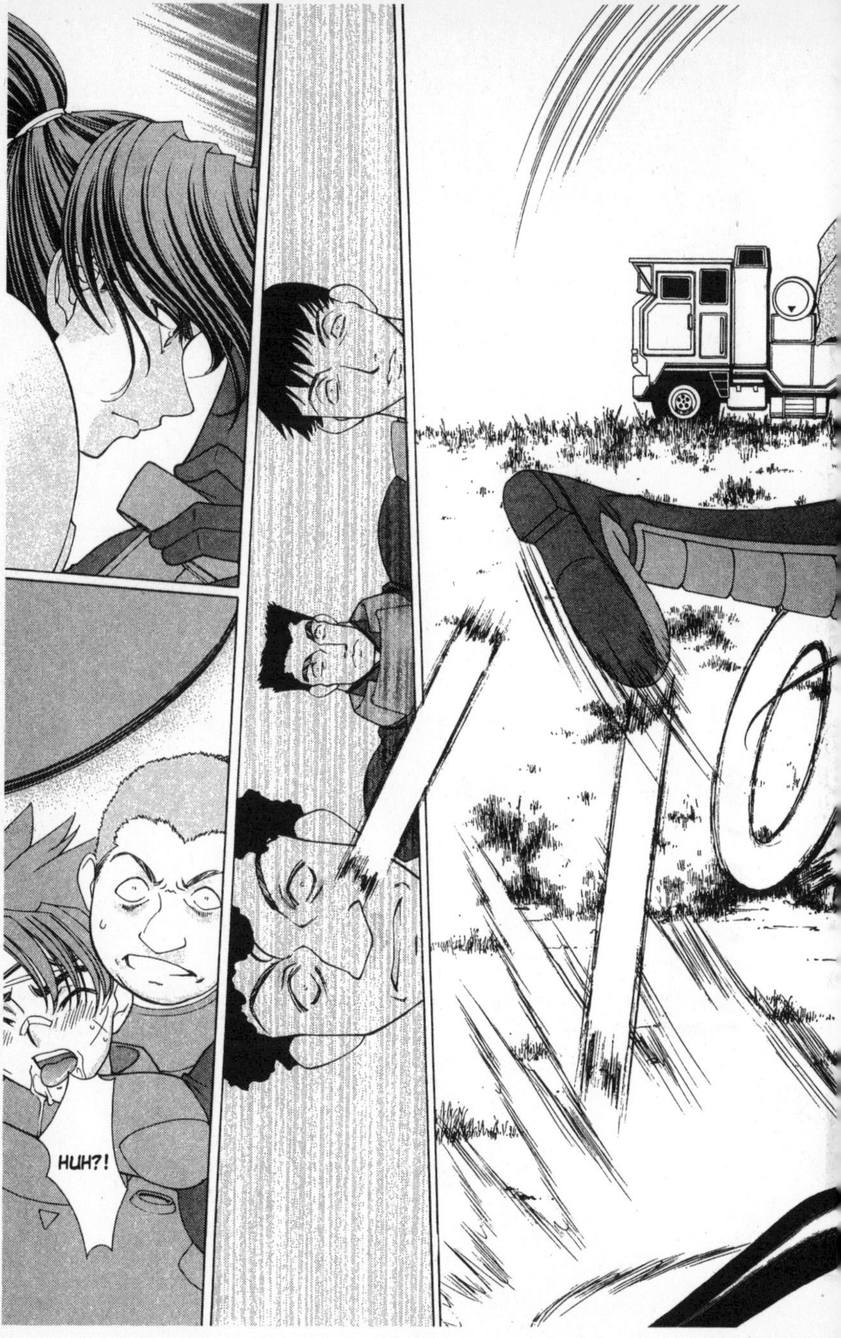
HUH?!

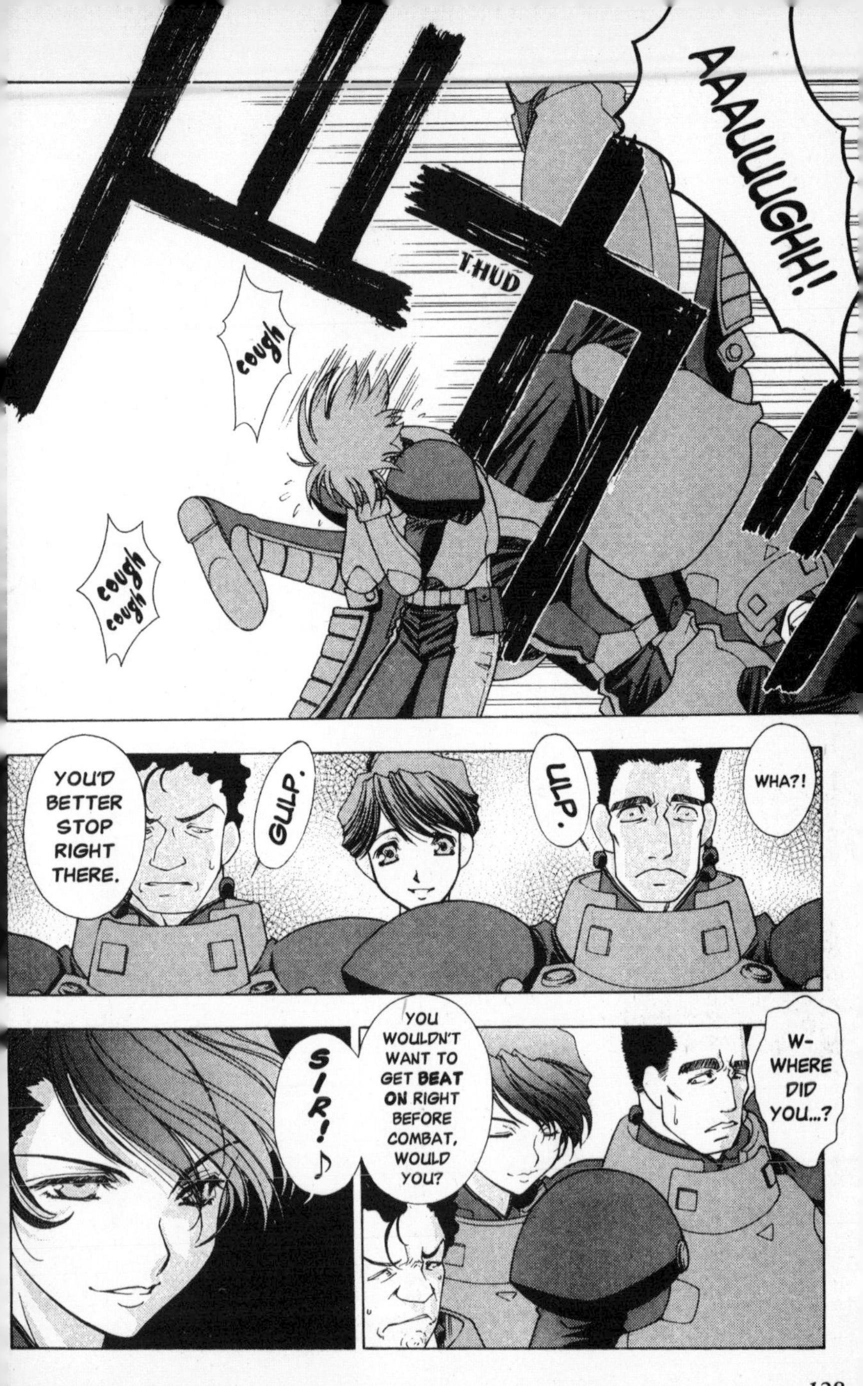
AAAUUUGHH!
THUD
cough
cough cough
WHA?!
ULP.
GULP.
YOU'D BETTER STOP RIGHT THERE.
W-WHERE DID YOU...?
YOU WOULDN'T WANT TO GET BEAT ON RIGHT BEFORE COMBAT, WOULD YOU?
SIR!♪

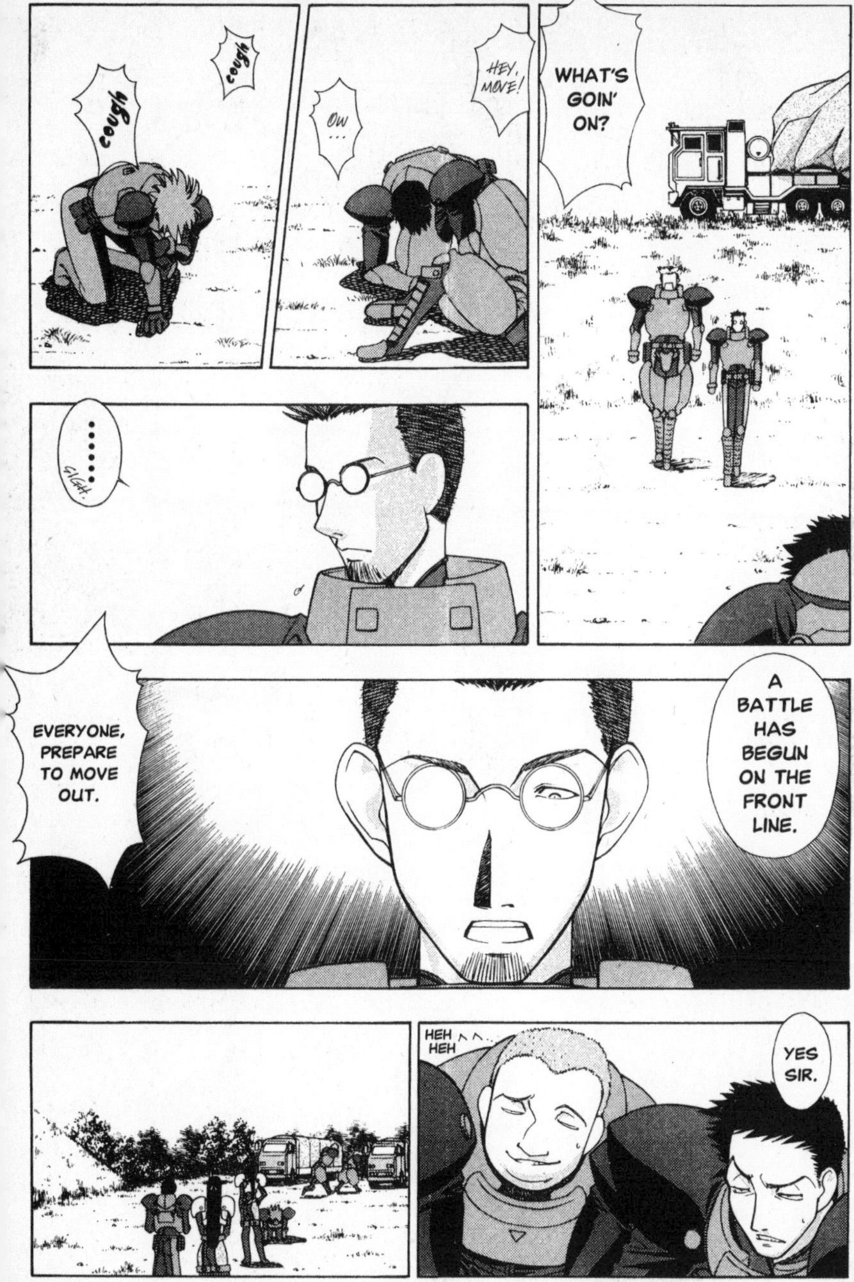
cough
cough
HEY, MOVE!
OW ...
WHAT'S GOIN' ON?
......
SIGH.
A BATTLE HAS BEGUN ON THE FRONT LINE.
EVERYONE, PREPARE TO MOVE OUT.
YES SIR.
HEH HEH

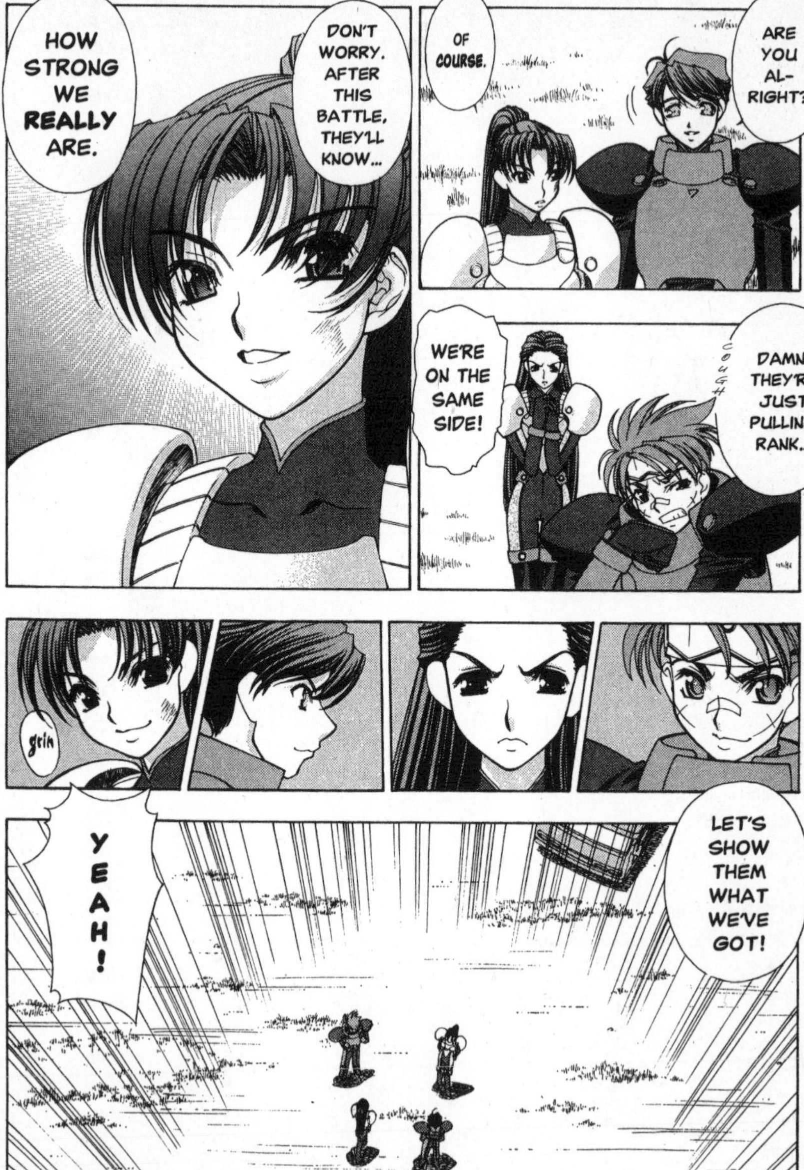
ARE YOU AL- RIGHT?
OF COURSE.
COUGH
DAMN, THEY'RE JUST PULLING RANK...
WE'RE ON THE SAME SIDE!
DON'T WORRY. AFTER THIS BATTLE, THEY'LL KNOW...
HOW STRONG WE REALLY ARE.
grin
LET'S SHOW THEM WHAT WE'VE GOT!
YEAH!

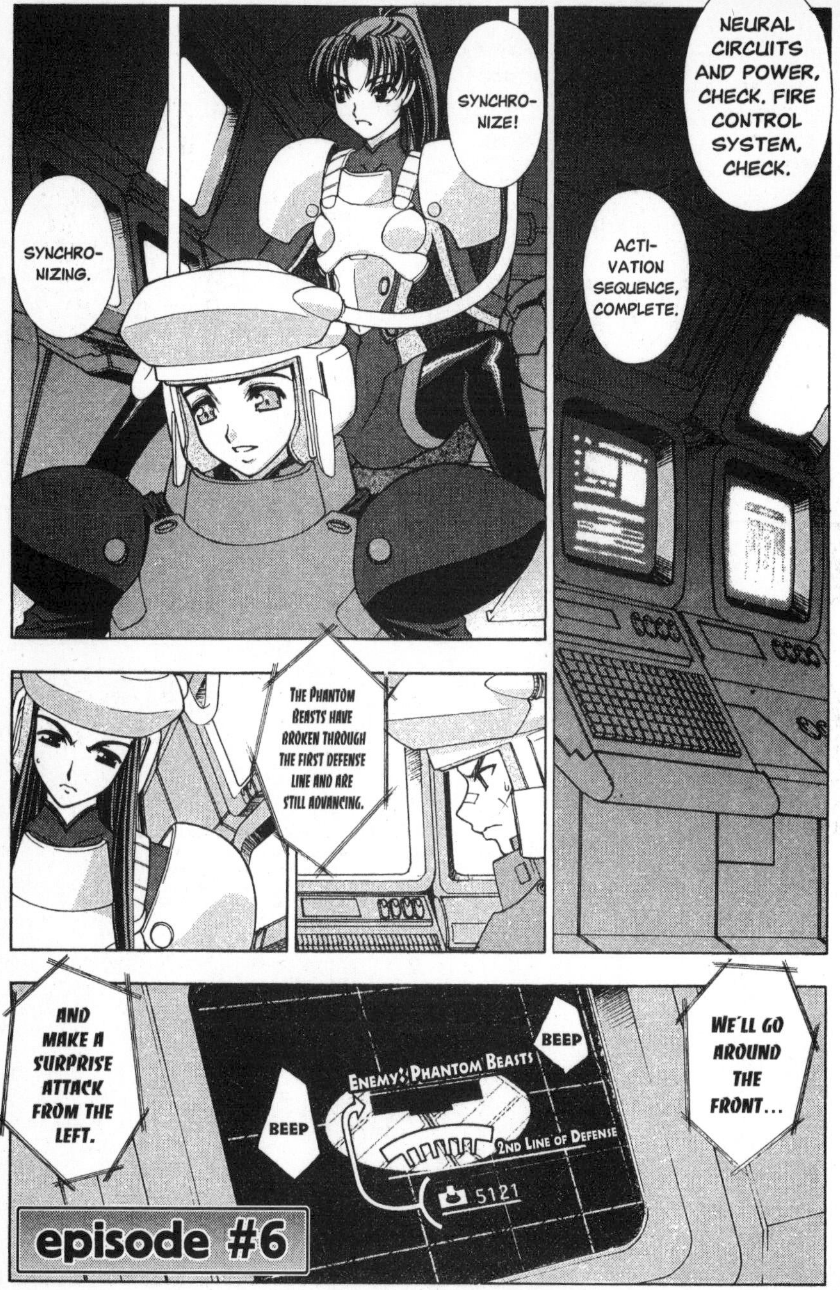
NEURAL CIRCUITS AND POWER, CHECK. FIRE CONTROL SYSTEM, CHECK.
ACTI-VATION SEQUENCE, COMPLETE.
SYNCHRO-NIZE!
SYNCHRO-NIZING.
THE PHANTOM BEASTS HAVE BROKEN THROUGH THE FIRST DEFENSE LINE AND ARE STILL ADVANCING.
WE'LL GO AROUND THE FRONT...
AND MAKE A SURPRISE ATTACK FROM THE LEFT.
BEEP
BEEP
ENEMY: PHANTOM BEASTS
2ND LINE OF DEFENSE
5121
episode #6

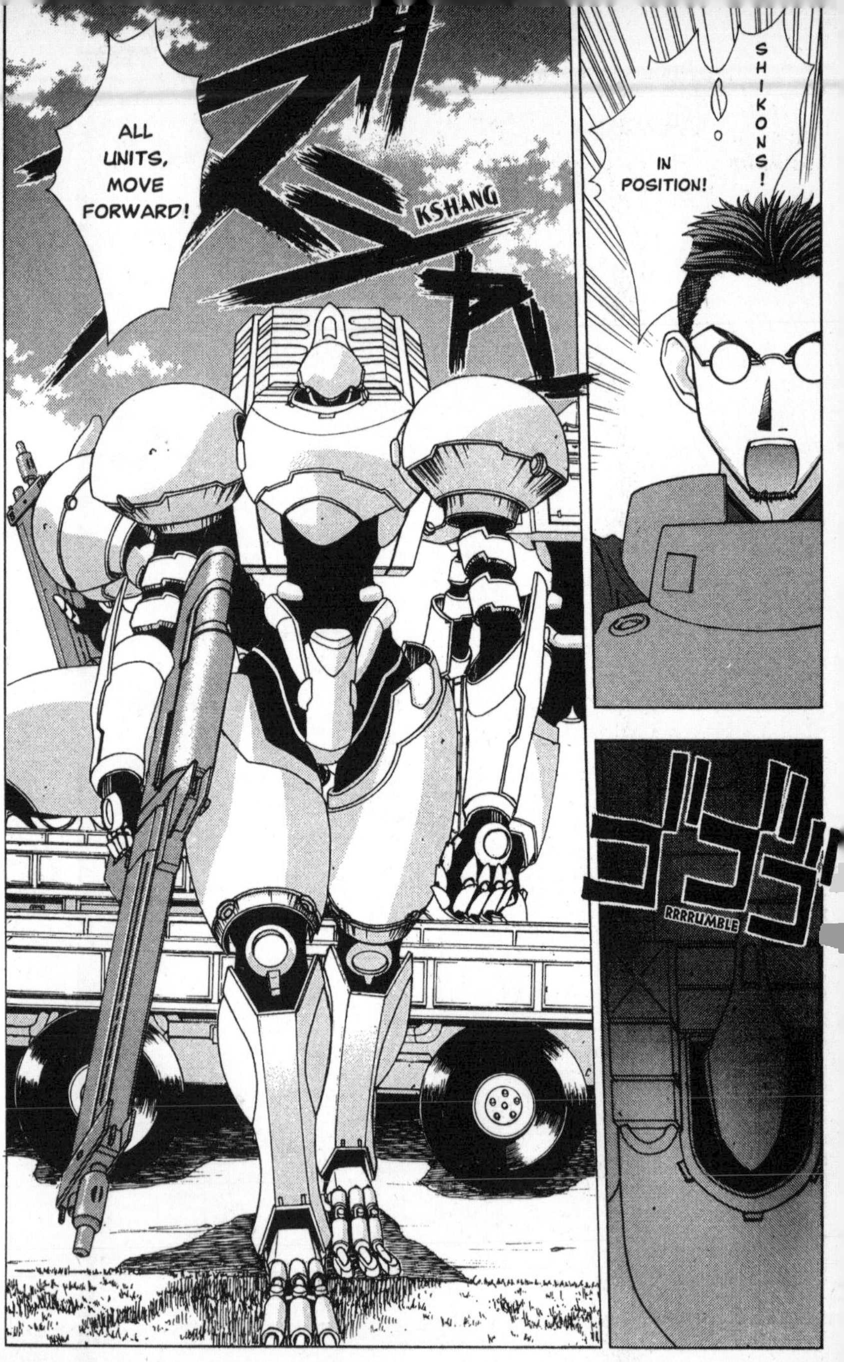

SHIKONS!
IN POSITION!
ALL UNITS, MOVE FORWARD!
KSHANG
RRRRUMBLE

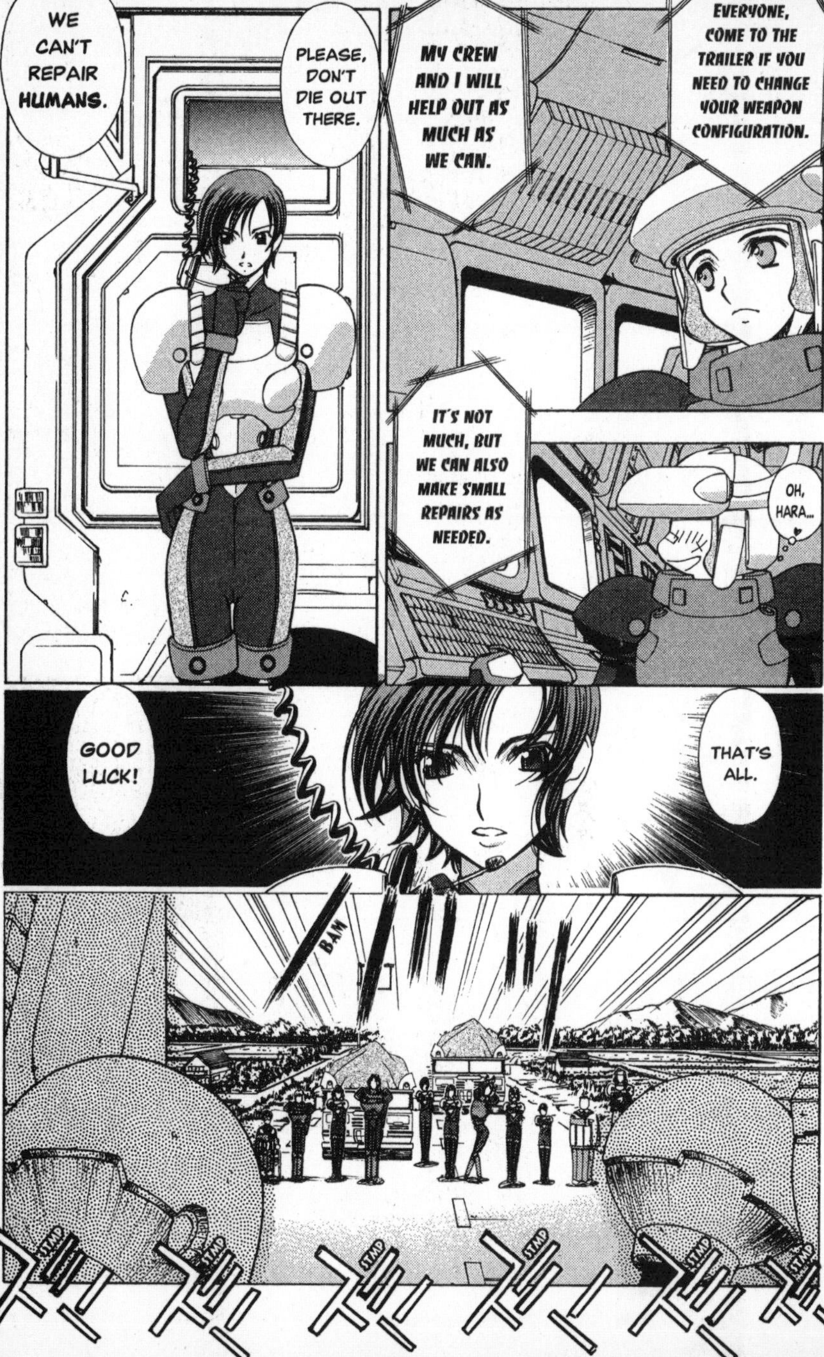
EVERYONE, COME TO THE TRAILER IF YOU NEED TO CHANGE YOUR WEAPON CONFIGURATION.
MY CREW AND I WILL HELP OUT AS MUCH AS WE CAN.
IT'S NOT MUCH, BUT WE CAN ALSO MAKE SMALL REPAIRS AS NEEDED.
OH, HARA...
PLEASE, DON'T DIE OUT THERE.
WE CAN'T REPAIR HUMANS.
THAT'S ALL.
GOOD LUCK!
BAM
STMP
STMP
STMP
STMP
STMP
STMP

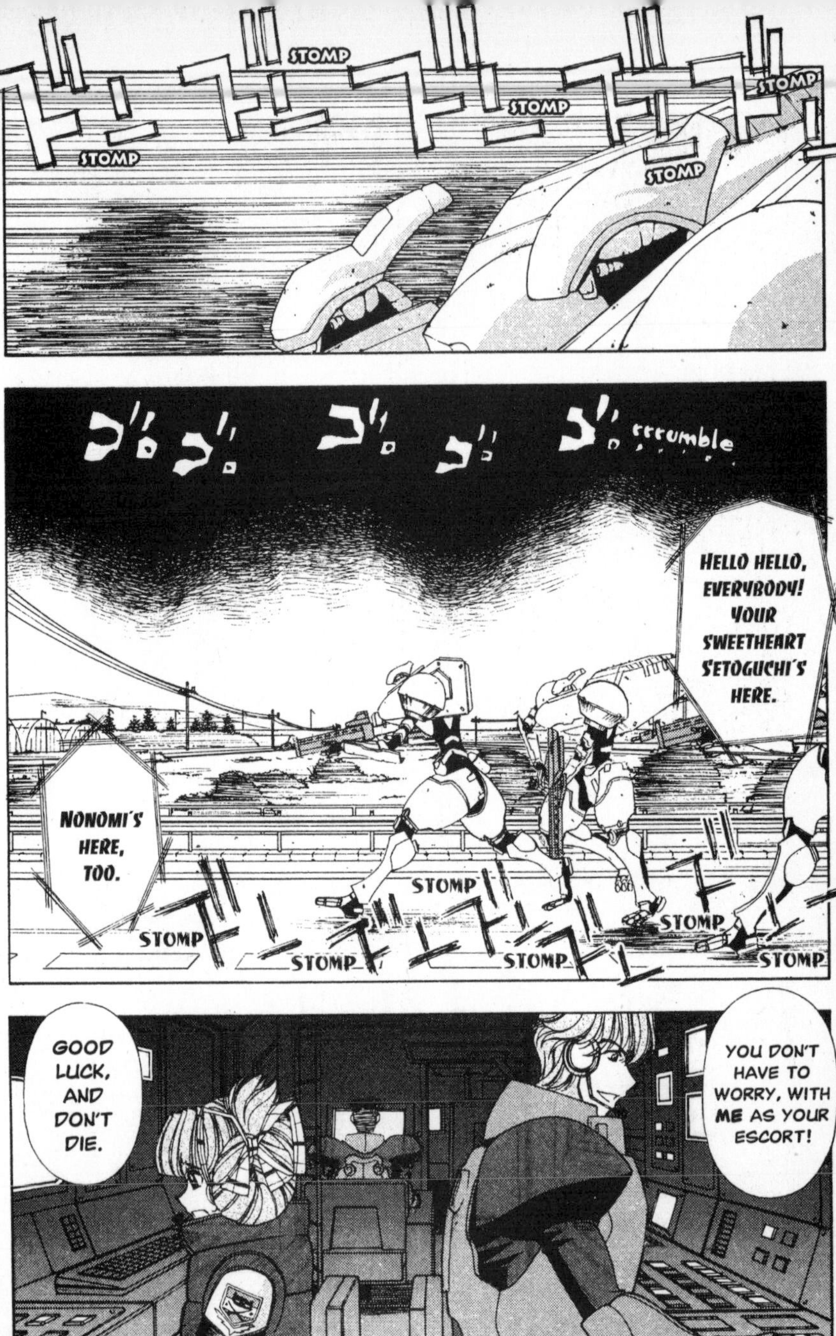
STOMP
STOMP
STOMP
STOMP
STOMP
rrrumble
HELLO HELLO, EVERYBODY! YOUR SWEETHEART SETOGUCHI'S HERE.
NONOMI'S HERE, TOO.
STOMP
STOMP
STOMP
STOMP
STOMP
STOMP
YOU DON'T HAVE TO WORRY, WITH ME AS YOUR ESCORT!
GOOD LUCK, AND DON'T DIE.

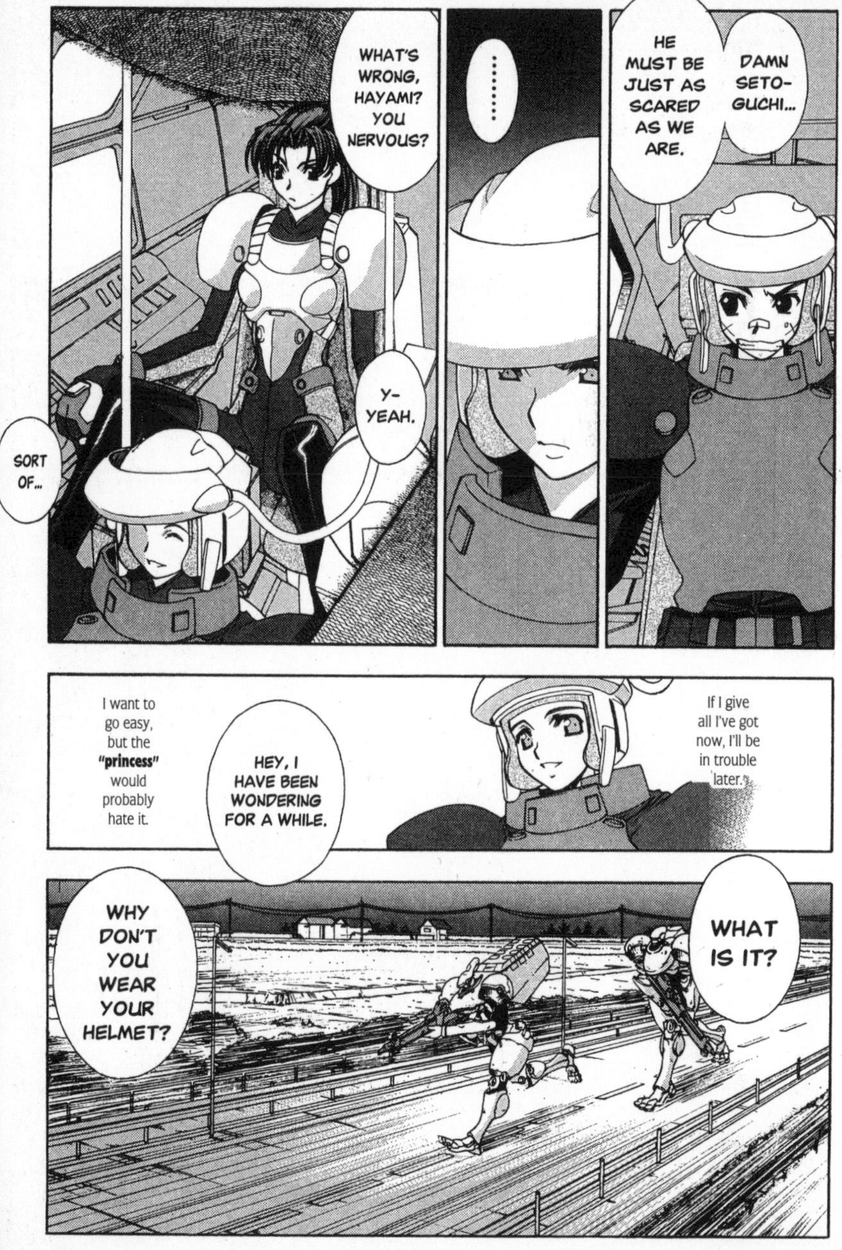
DAMN SETO-GUCHI...
HE MUST BE JUST AS SCARED AS WE ARE.
....
WHAT'S WRONG, HAYAMI? YOU NERVOUS?
Y-YEAH.
SORT OF...
If I give all I've got now, I'll be in trouble later.
HEY, I HAVE BEEN WONDERING FOR A WHILE.
I want to go easy, but the **"princess"** would probably hate it.
WHAT IS IT?
WHY DON'T YOU WEAR YOUR HELMET?

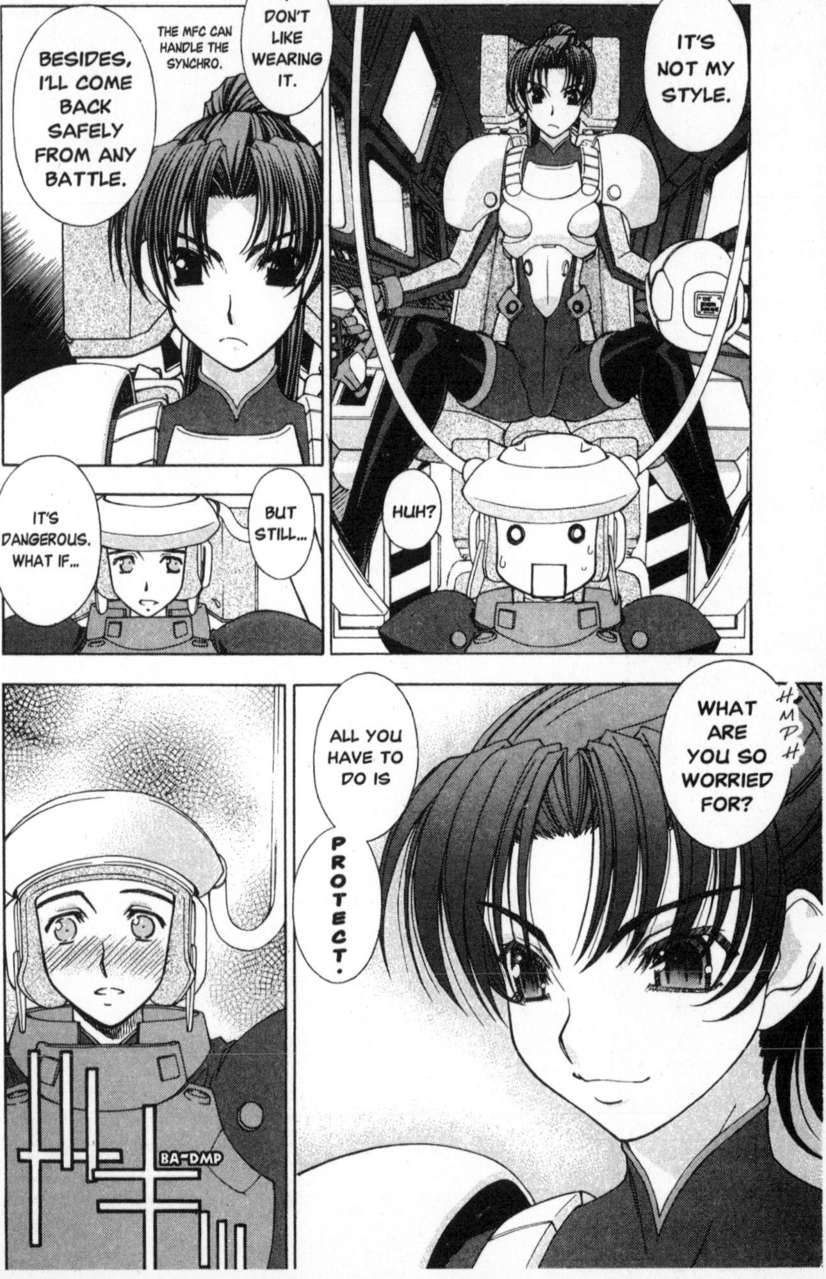

IT'S NOT MY STYLE.
I DON'T LIKE WEARING IT.
THE MFC CAN HANDLE THE SYNCHRO.
BESIDES, I'LL COME BACK SAFELY FROM ANY BATTLE.
HUH?
BUT STILL...
IT'S DANGEROUS. WHAT IF...
HMPH
WHAT ARE YOU SO WORRIED FOR?
ALL YOU HAVE TO DO IS
PROTECT.
BA-DMP

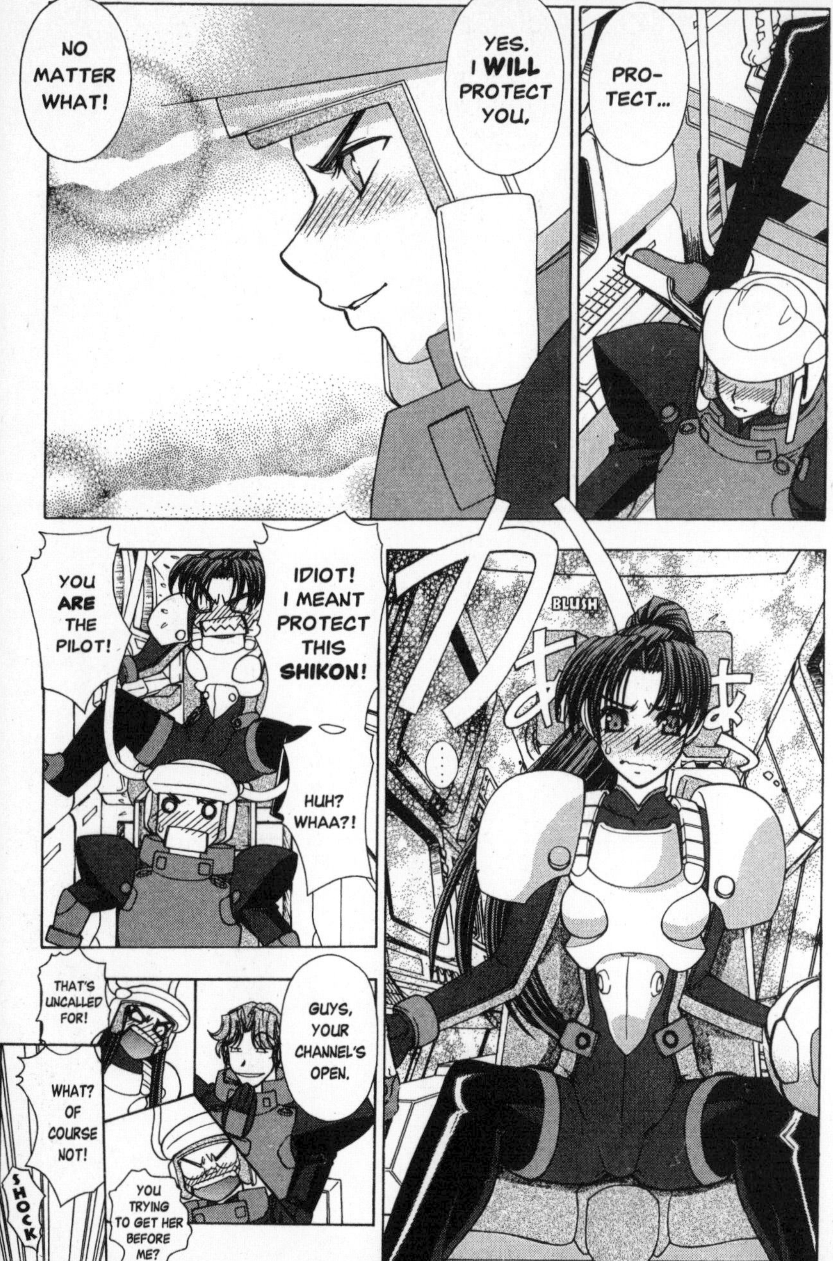
PRO-TECT...
YES. I WILL PROTECT YOU,
NO MATTER WHAT!
BLUSH
IDIOT! I MEANT PROTECT THIS SHIKON!
YOU ARE THE PILOT!
HUH? WHAA?!
GUYS, YOUR CHANNEL'S OPEN.
THAT'S UNCALLED FOR!
WHAT? OF COURSE NOT!
SHOCK
YOU TRYING TO GET HER BEFORE ME?

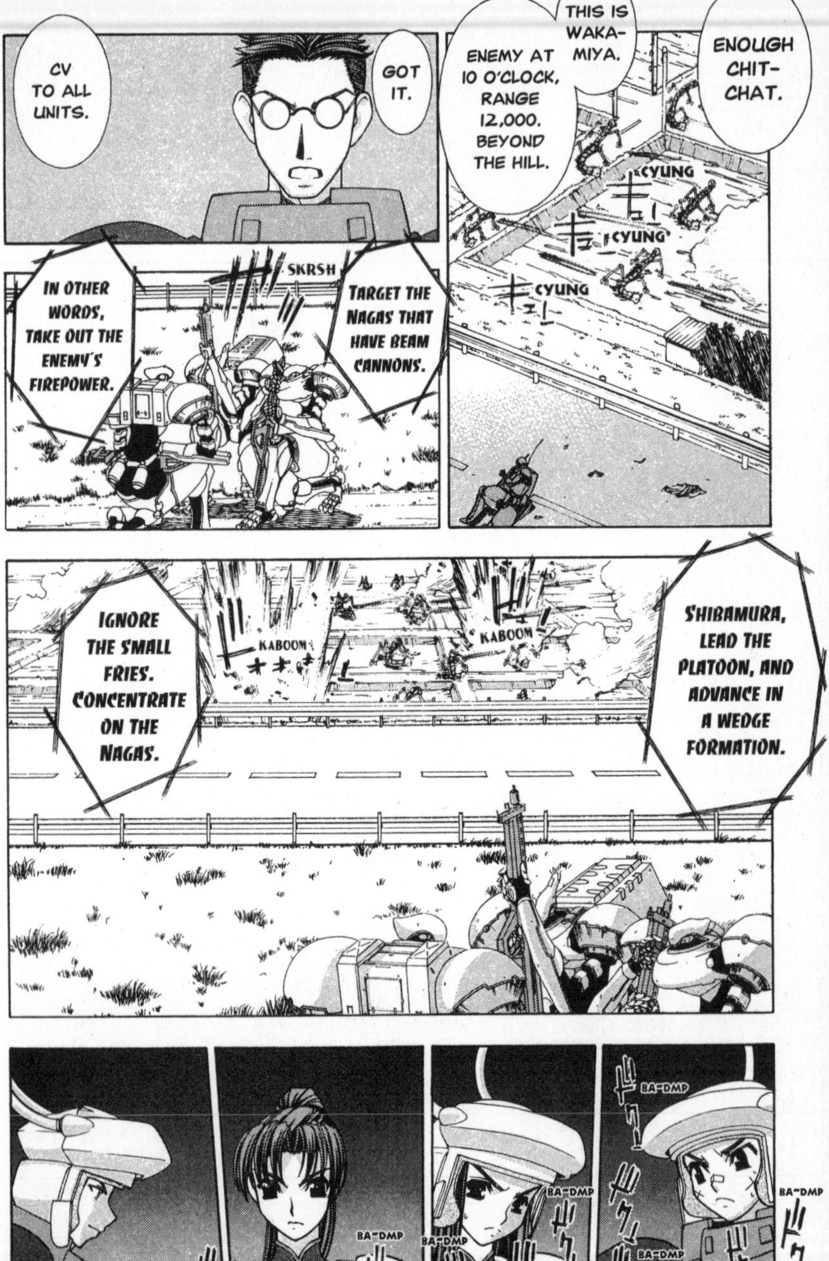
ENOUGH CHIT-CHAT.
THIS IS WAKAMIYA.
ENEMY AT 10 O'CLOCK, RANGE 12,000. BEYOND THE HILL.
CYUNG
CYUNG
CYUNG
GOT IT.
CV TO ALL UNITS.
TARGET THE NAGAS THAT HAVE BEAM CANNONS.
SKRSH
IN OTHER WORDS, TAKE OUT THE ENEMY'S FIREPOWER.
SHIBAMURA, LEAD THE PLATOON, AND ADVANCE IN A WEDGE FORMATION.
KABOOM
KABOOM
IGNORE THE SMALL FRIES. CONCENTRATE ON THE NAGAS.
BA-DMP
BA-DMP
BA-DMP
BA-DMP
BA-DMP
BA-DMP
BA-DMP
BA-DMP
BA-DMP

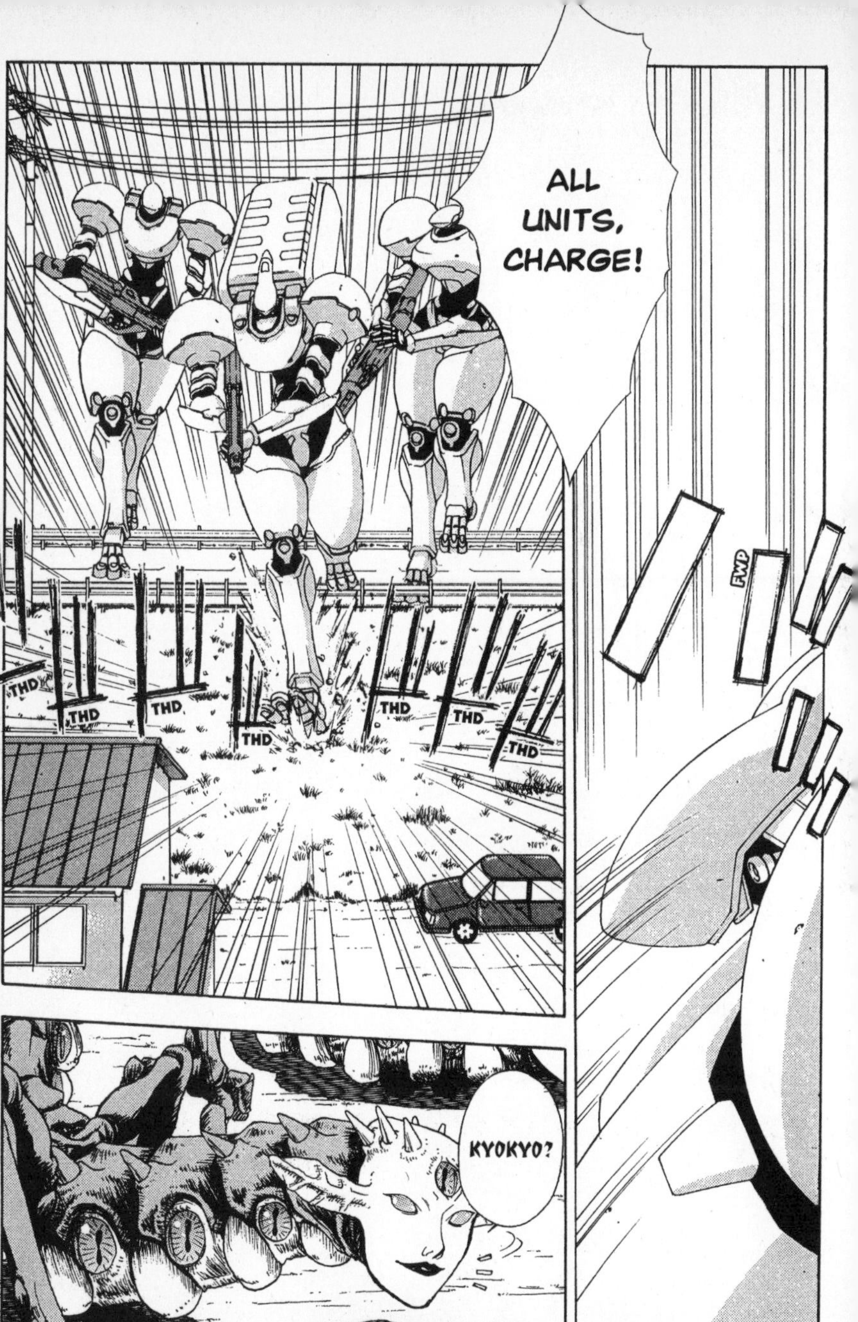
ALL UNITS, CHARGE!
FWP
THD
THD
THD
THD
THD
THD
THD
KYOKYO?

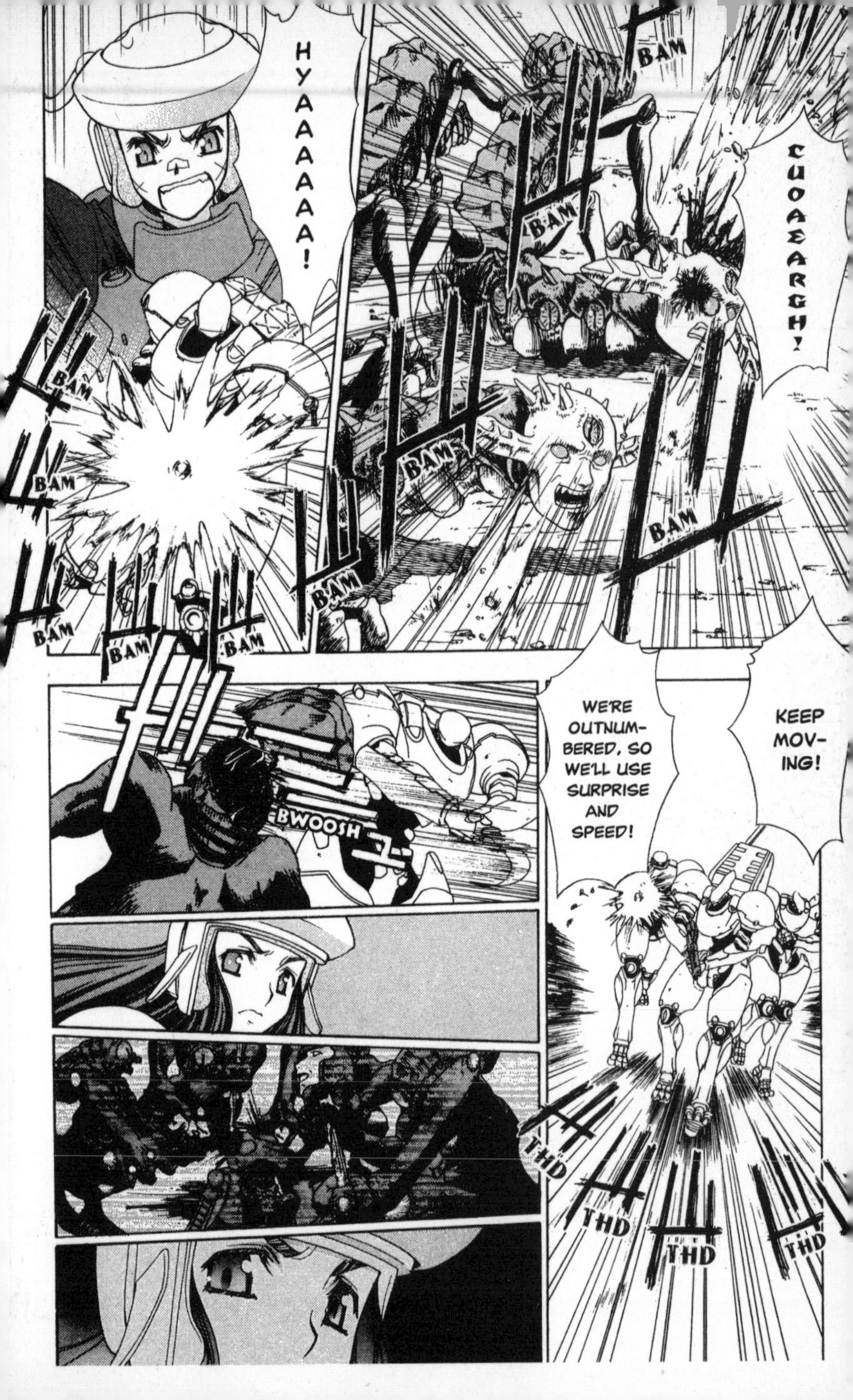
BAM
CUOAEARGH!
BAM
BAM
BAM
BAM
HYAAAAAAA!
BAM
BAM
BAM
BAM
BAM
KEEP MOV-ING!
WE'RE OUTNUM-BERED, SO WE'LL USE SURPRISE AND SPEED!
THD
THD
THD
THD
BWOOSH

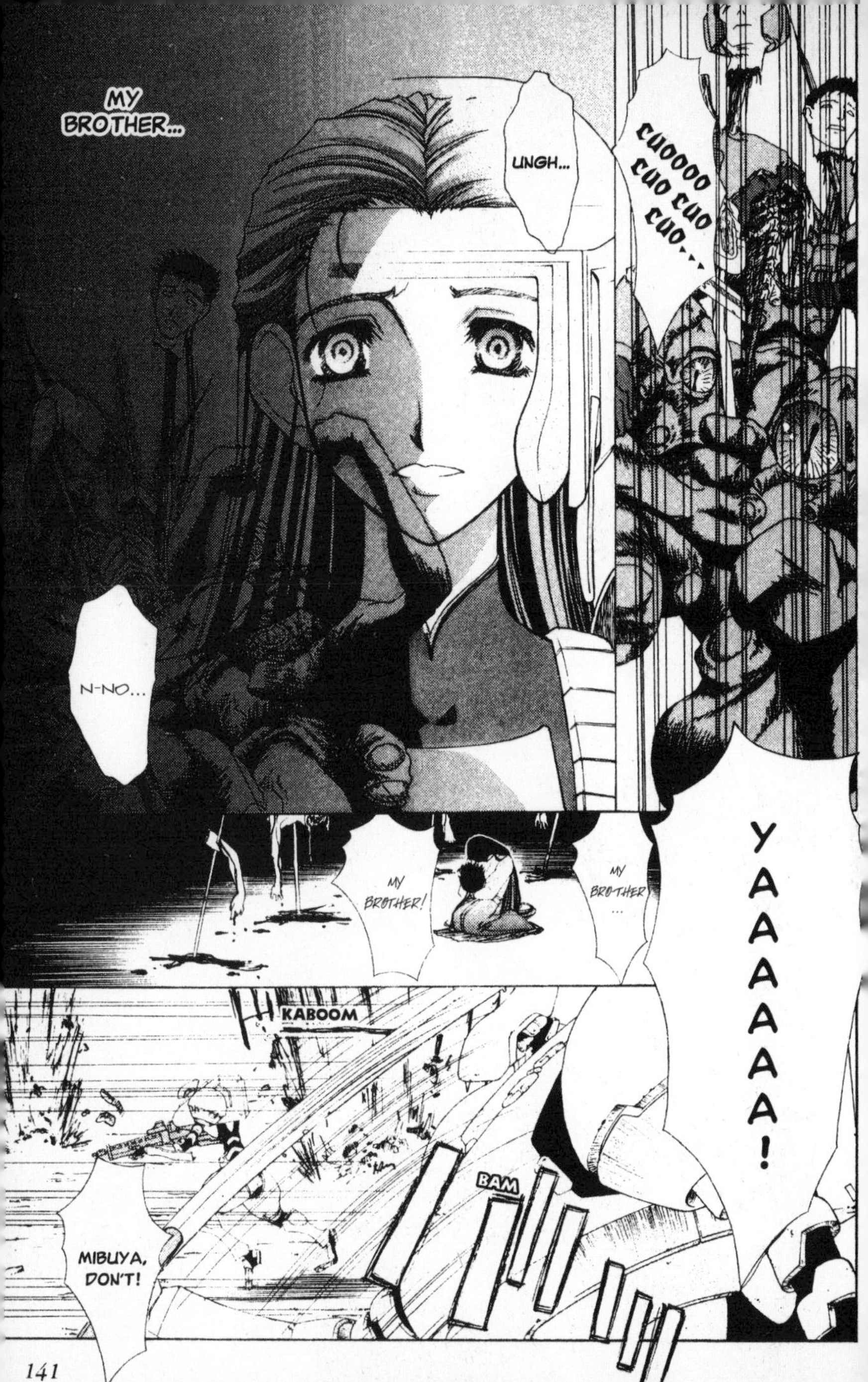
GUOOOO GUO GUO GUO...
UNGH...
MY BROTHER...
N-NO...
YAAAAAAA!
MY BROTHER...
MY BROTHER!
KABOOM
BAM
MIBUYA, DON'T!

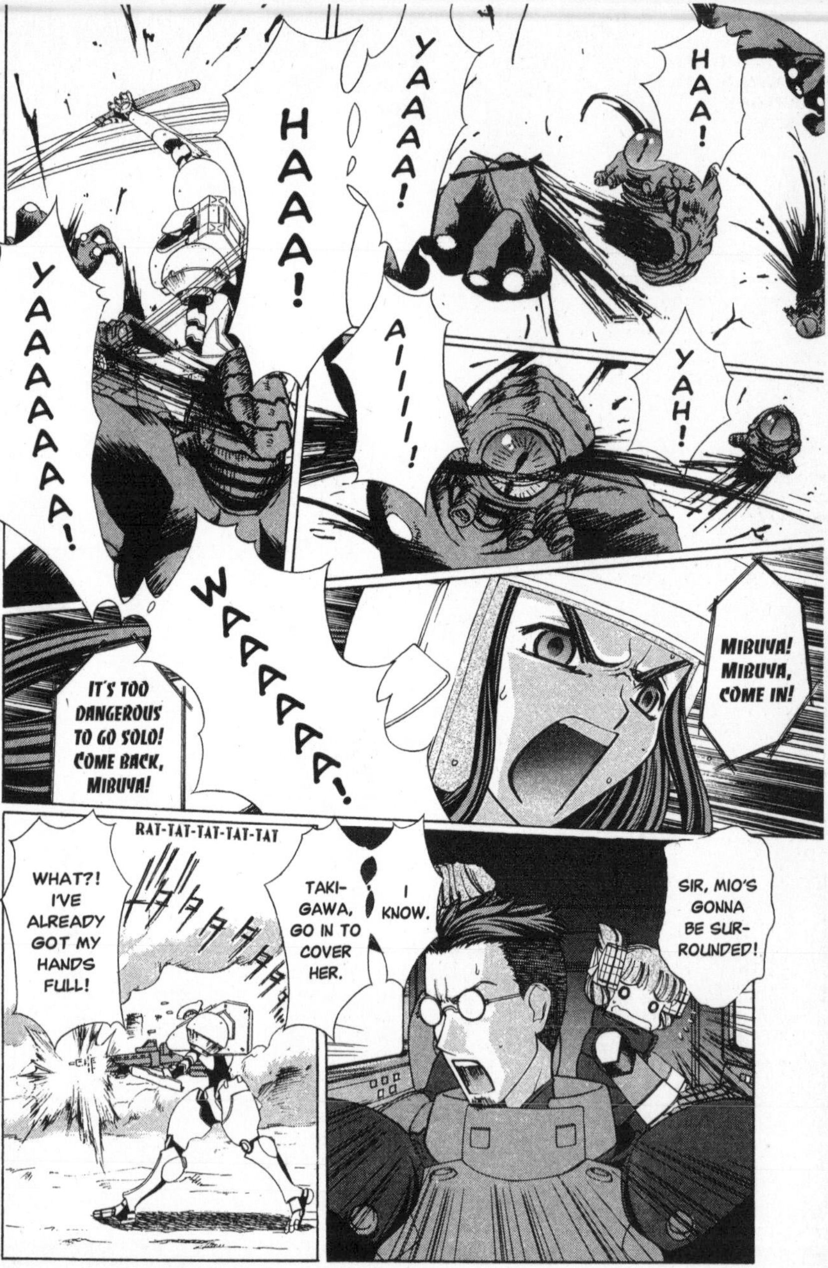
HAA!
YAAAA!
HAAAA!
YAAAAAAA!
YAH!
AIIII!
MIBUYA! MIBUYA, COME IN!
WAAAAAA!
IT'S TOO DANGEROUS TO GO SOLO! COME BACK, MIBUYA!
SIR, MIO'S GONNA BE SUR-ROUNDED!
I KNOW.
TAKI-GAWA, GO IN TO COVER HER.
RAT-TAT-TAT-TAT-TAT
WHAT?! I'VE ALREADY GOT MY HANDS FULL!

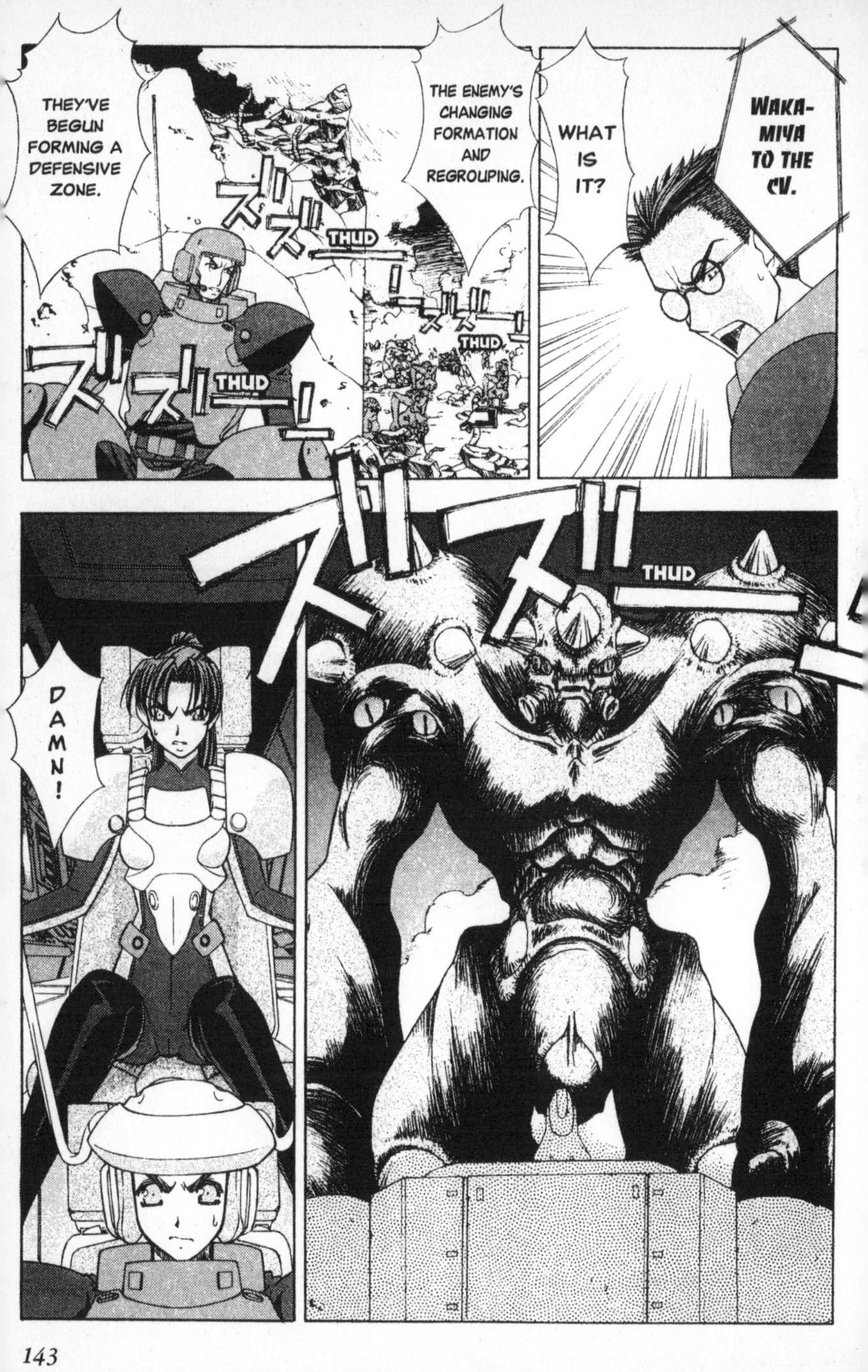
WAKA-MIYA TO THE CV.
WHAT IS IT?
THE ENEMY'S CHANGING FORMATION AND REGROUPING.
THUD
THUD
THEY'VE BEGUN FORMING A DEFENSIVE ZONE.
THUD
THUD
DAMN!

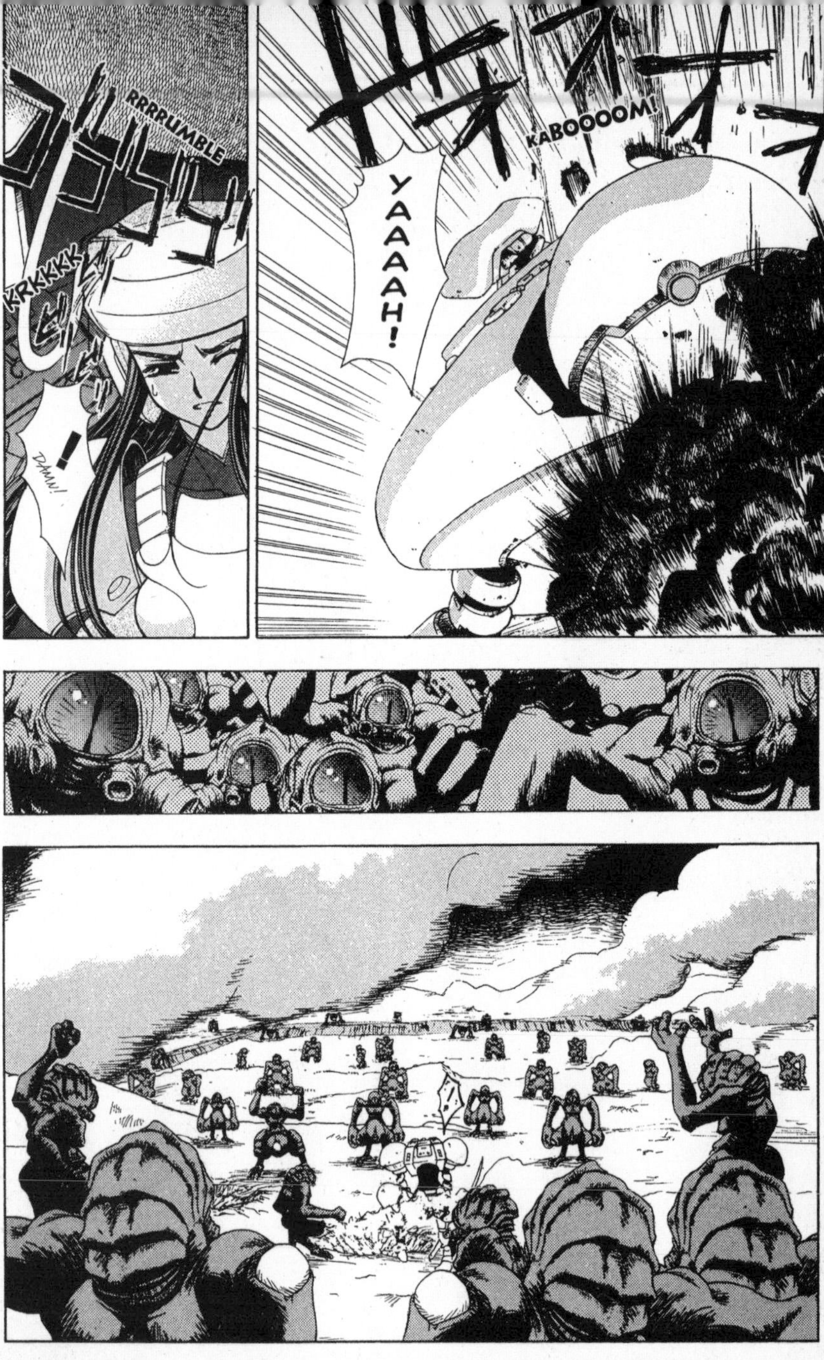
KABOOOOM!
YAAAAAH!
RRRRUMBLE
KRKKKK
!
DAMN!

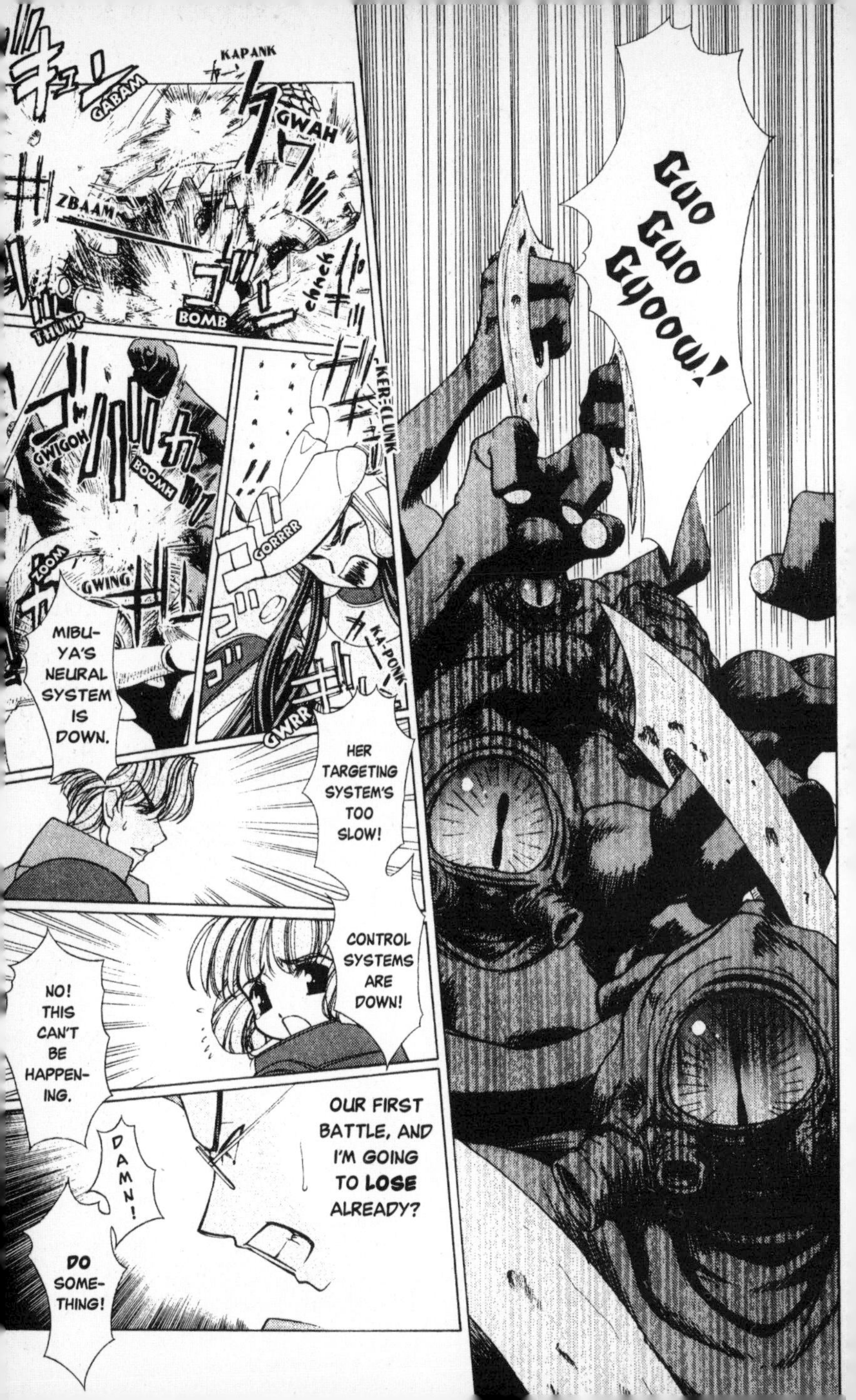
GUO GUO GYOOOW!
KAPANK
GABAM
GWAH
ZBAAM
chnck
BOMB
THUMP
KER-CLUNK
GORRRR
KA-PONK
GWRR
GWIGOH
BOOMH
ZOOM
GWING
MIBU-YA'S NEURAL SYSTEM IS DOWN.
HER TARGETING SYSTEM'S TOO SLOW!
CONTROL SYSTEMS ARE DOWN!
NO! THIS CAN'T BE HAPPEN-ING.
OUR FIRST BATTLE, AND I'M GOING TO **LOSE** ALREADY?
DAMN!
DO SOME-THING!

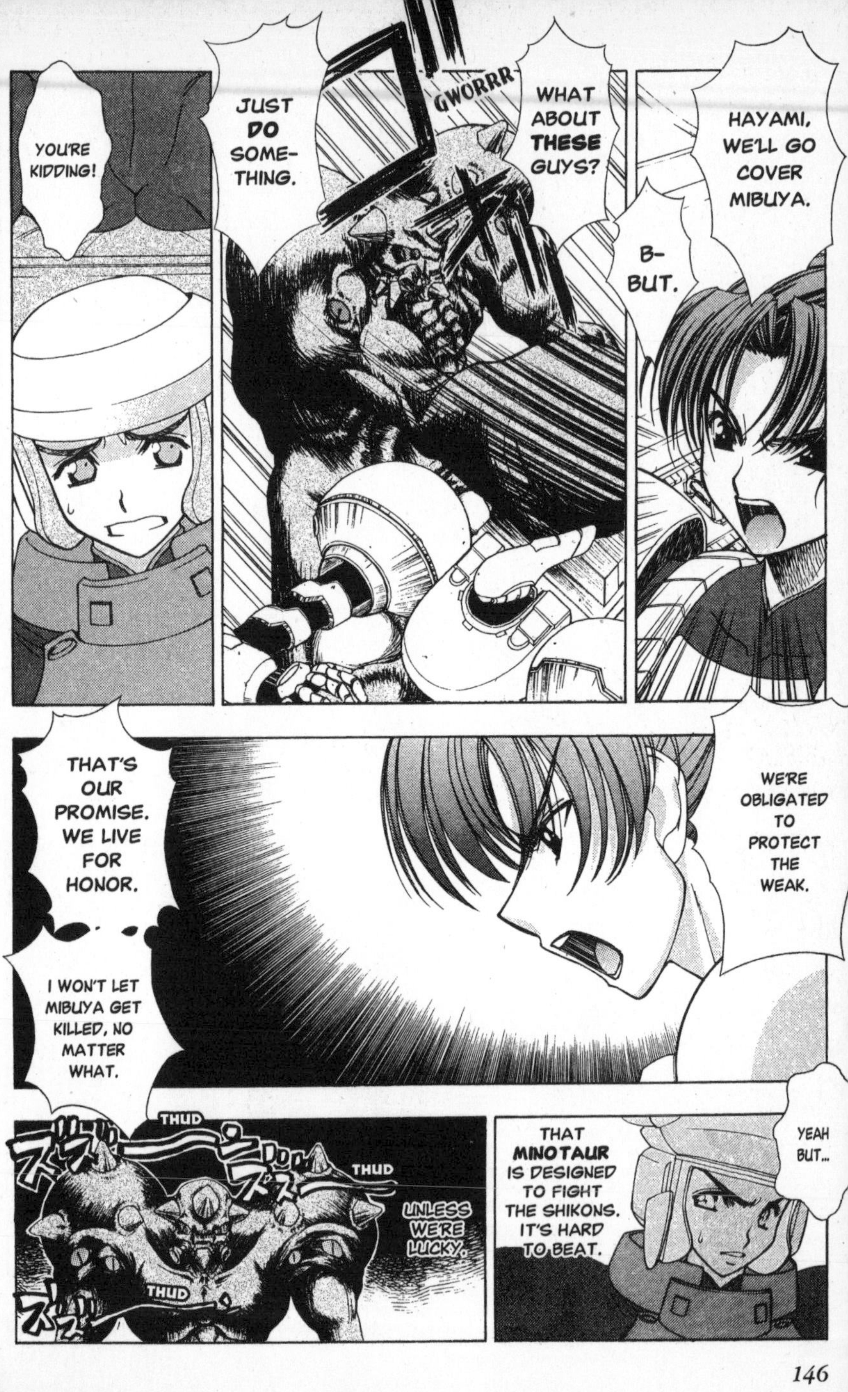
HAYAMI, WE'LL GO COVER MIBUYA.
B-BUT.
WHAT ABOUT THESE GUYS?
GWORRR
JUST DO SOME-THING.
YOU'RE KIDDING!
WE'RE OBLIGATED TO PROTECT THE WEAK.
THAT'S OUR PROMISE. WE LIVE FOR HONOR.
...
I WON'T LET MIBUYA GET KILLED, NO MATTER WHAT.
YEAH BUT...
THAT MINOTAUR IS DESIGNED TO FIGHT THE SHIKONS. IT'S HARD TO BEAT.
UNLESS WE'RE LUCKY.
THUD
THUD
THUD

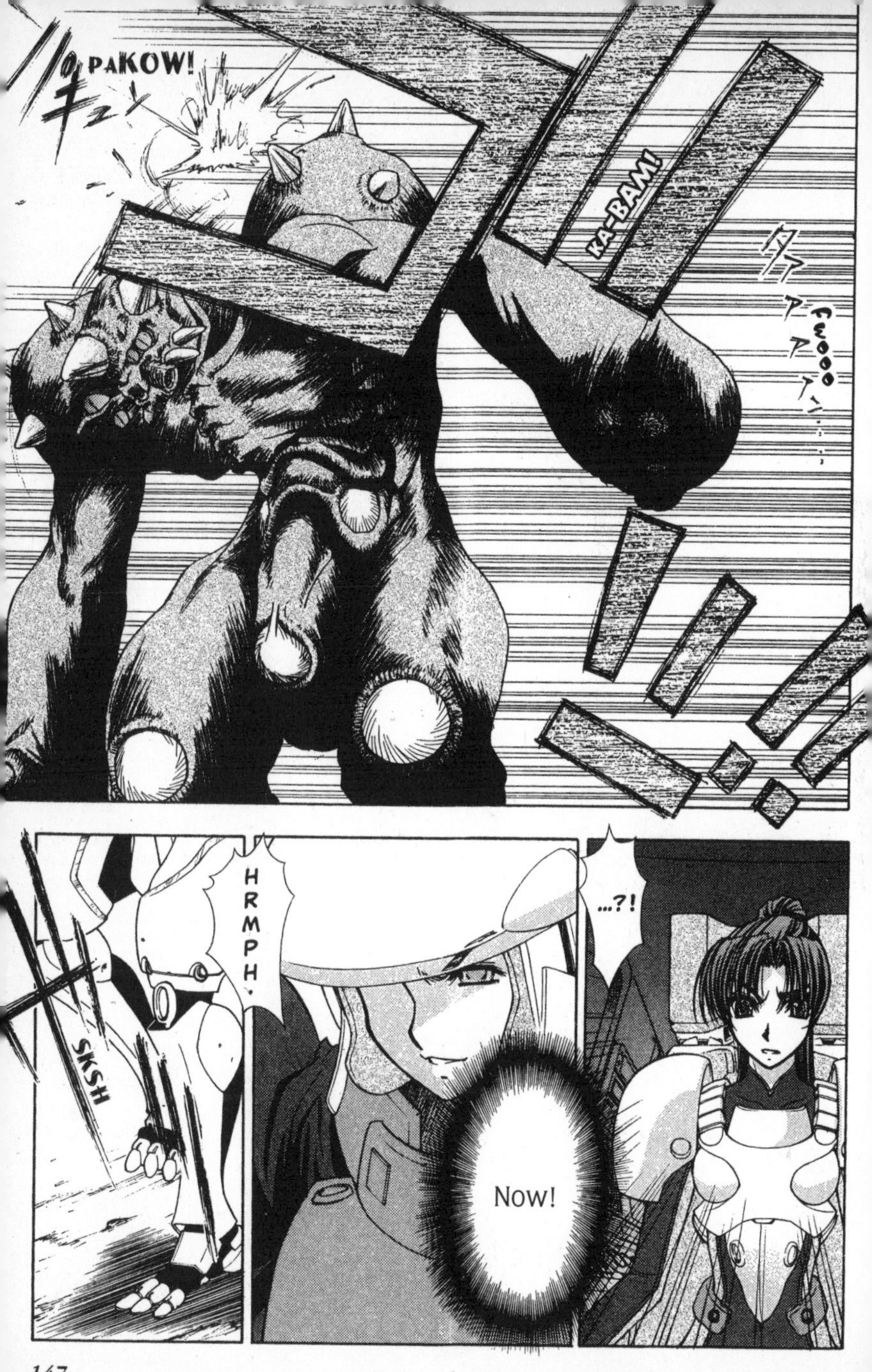
PAKOW!
キュン
KA-BAM!
FWOOO
ダァァァ
...?!
HRMPH.
SKSH
Now!

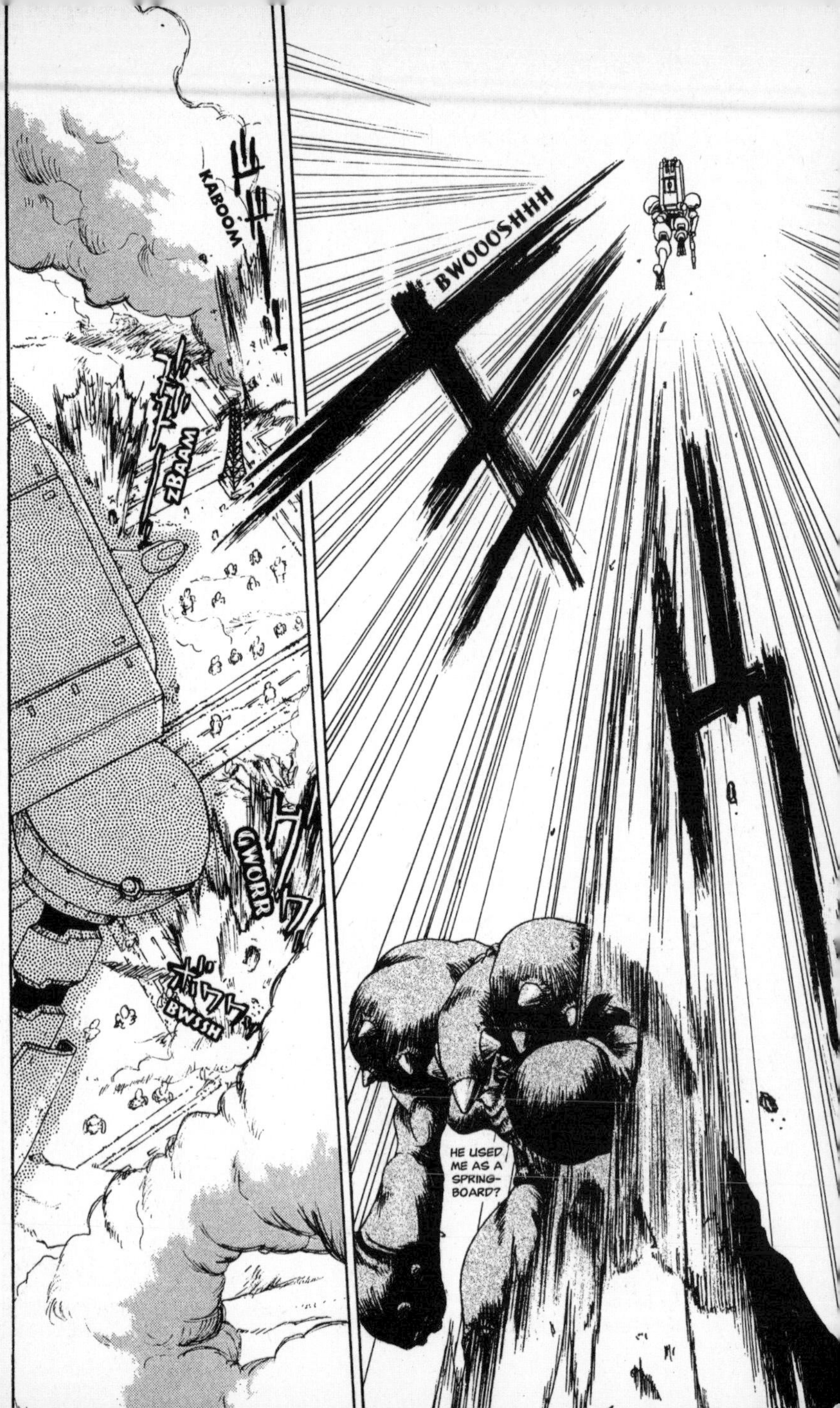
BWOOOSHHH
HE USED ME AS A SPRING-BOARD?
KABOOM
ZBAAM
GWORR
BWSH

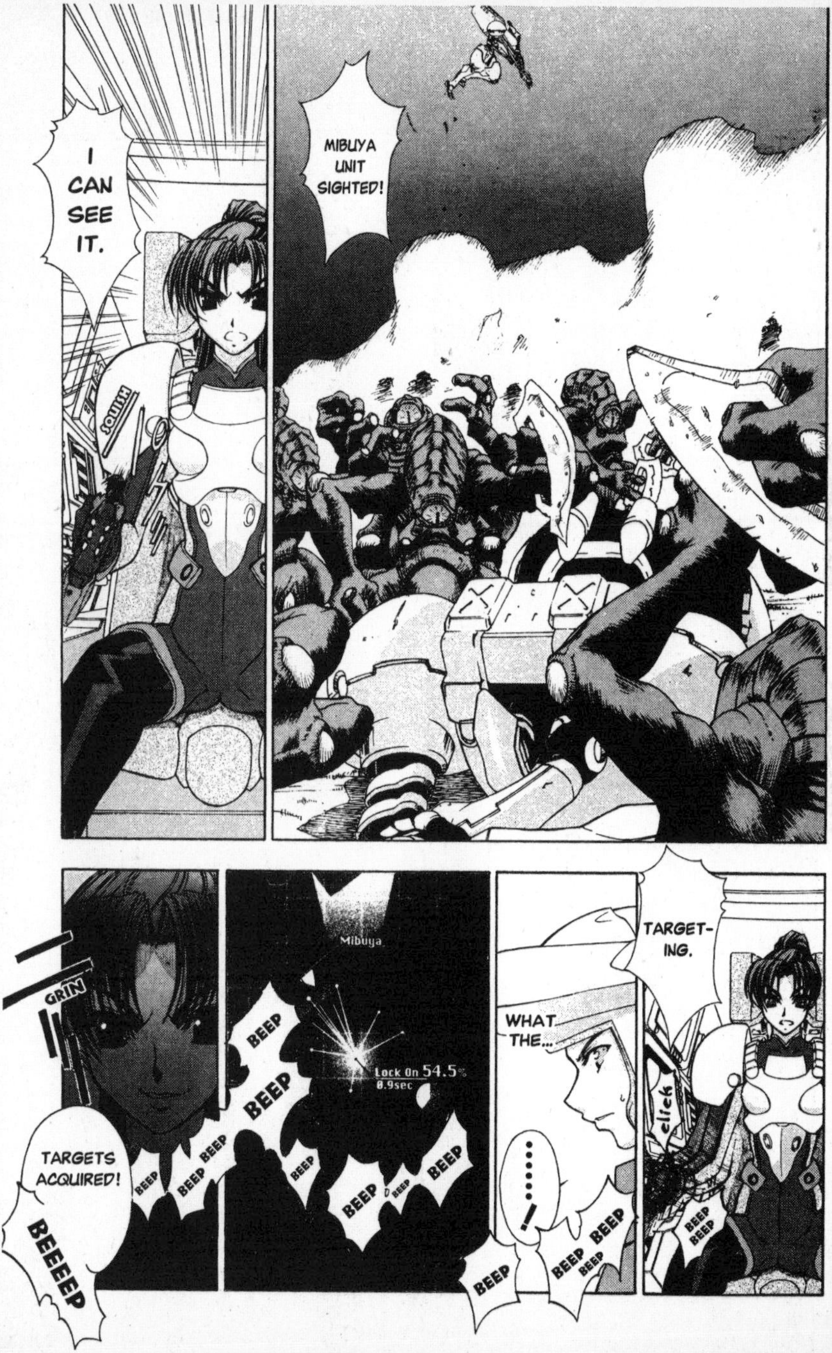
MIBUYA UNIT SIGHTED!
I CAN SEE IT.
SQUISH
TARGET-ING.
WHAT THE...
......!
click
BEEP BEEP
BEEP BEEP BEEP
BEEP
Mibuya
Lock On 54.5%
0.9sec
BEEP
BEEP
BEEP BEEP
BEEP
BEEP BEEP BEEP
GRIN
TARGETS ACQUIRED!
BEEEEP

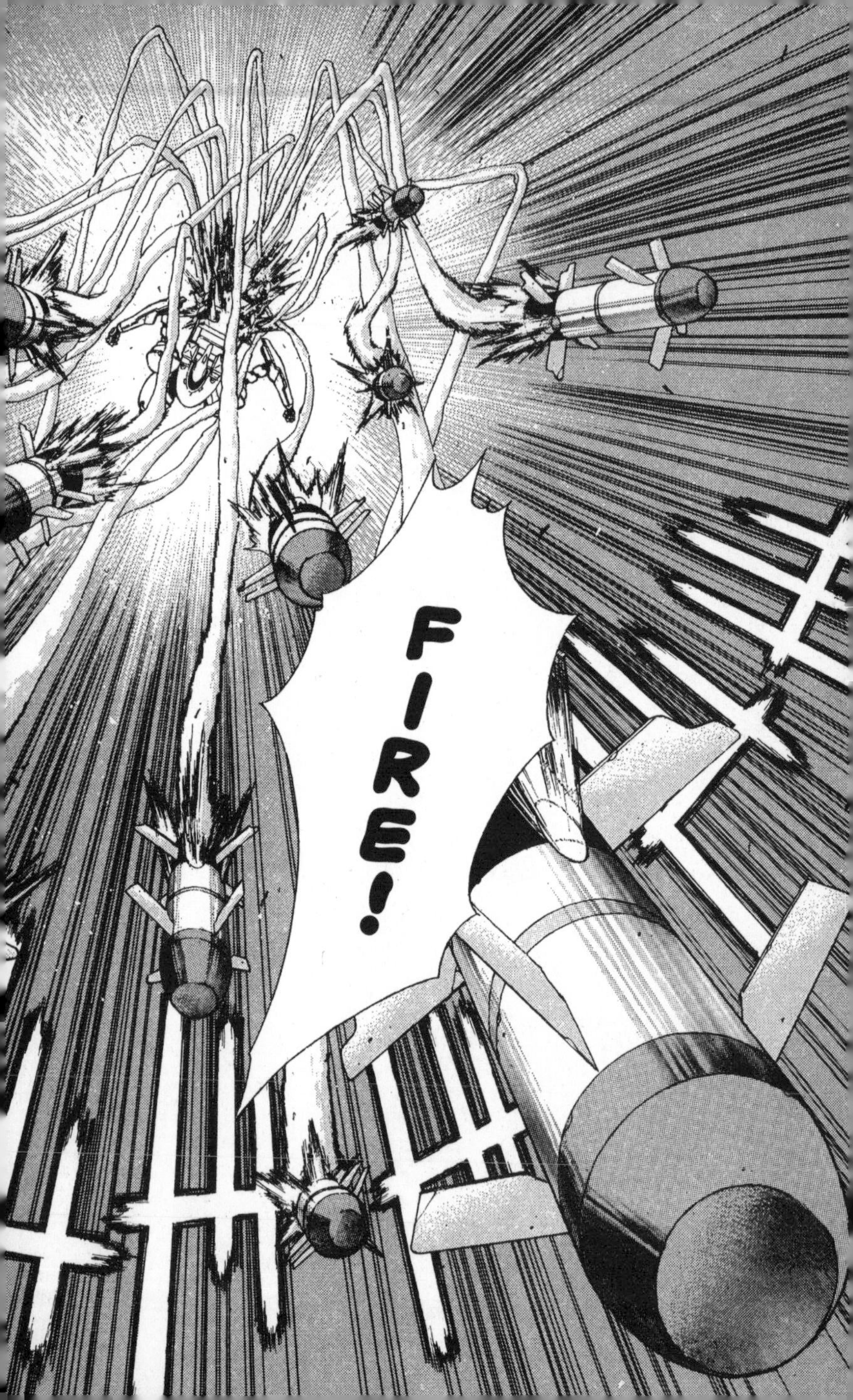
FIRE!

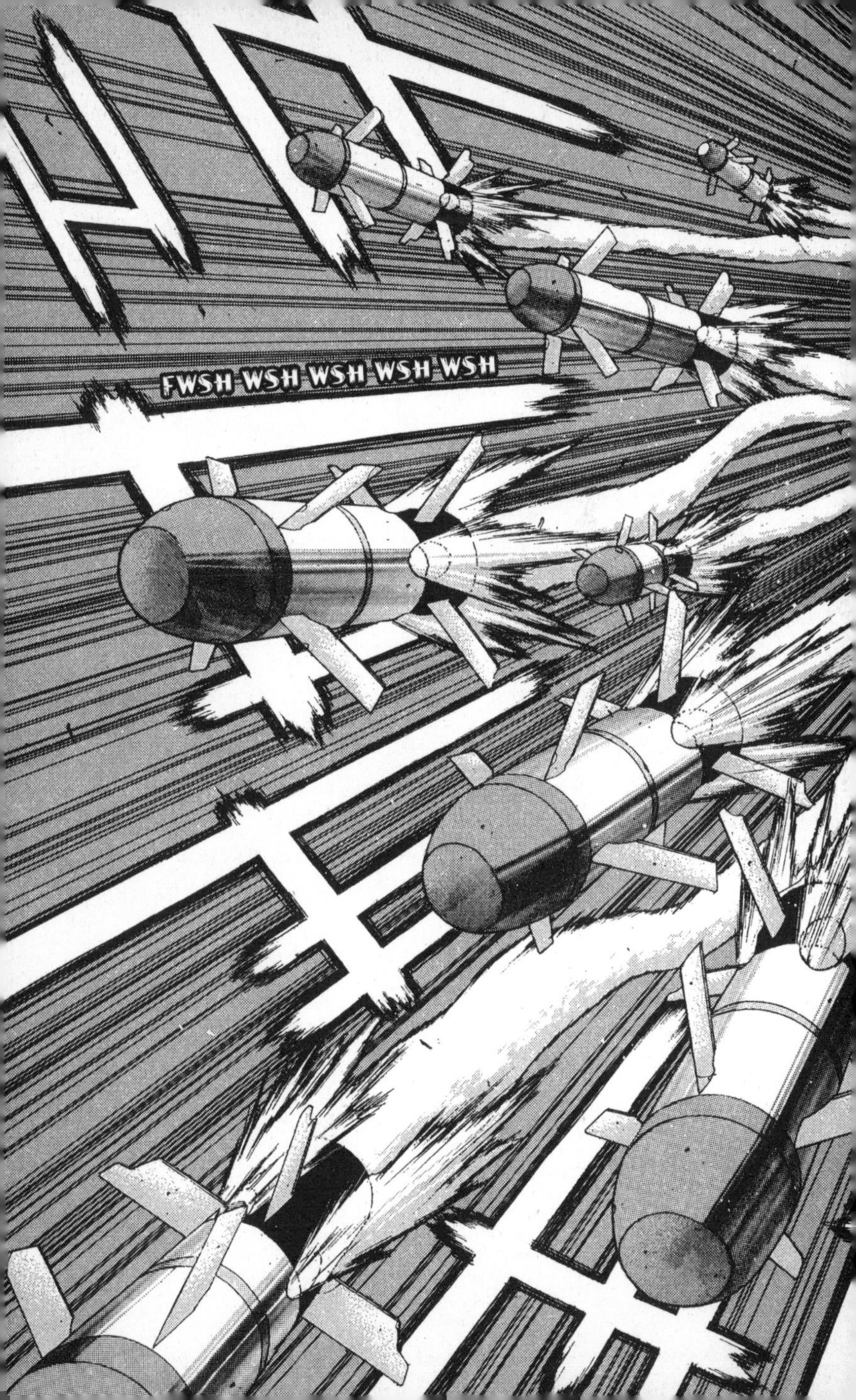
FWSH WSH WSH WSH WSH

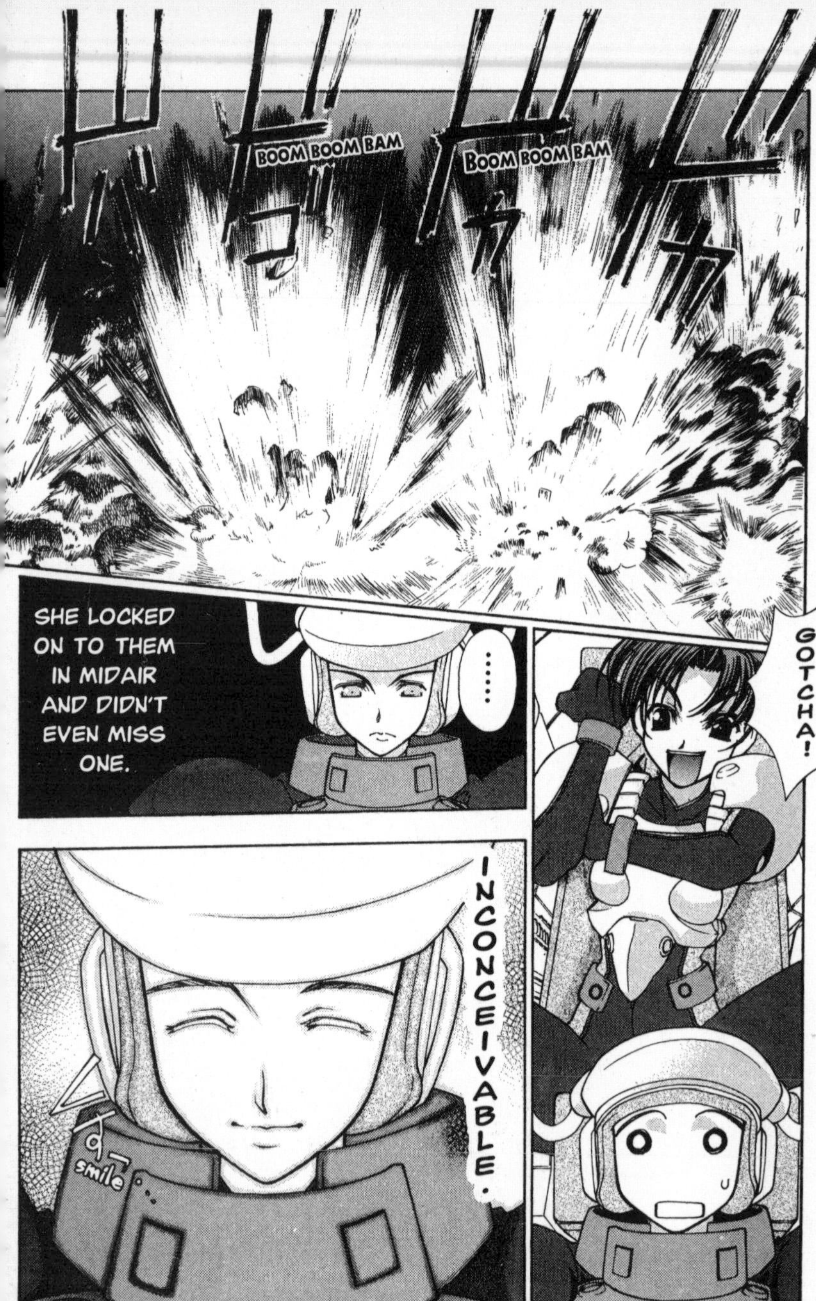
BOOM BOOM BAM
BOOM BOOM BAM
GOTCHA!
SHE LOCKED ON TO THEM IN MIDAIR AND DIDN'T EVEN MISS ONE.
......
INCONCEIVABLE.
smile
I LIKE HER EVEN MORE.

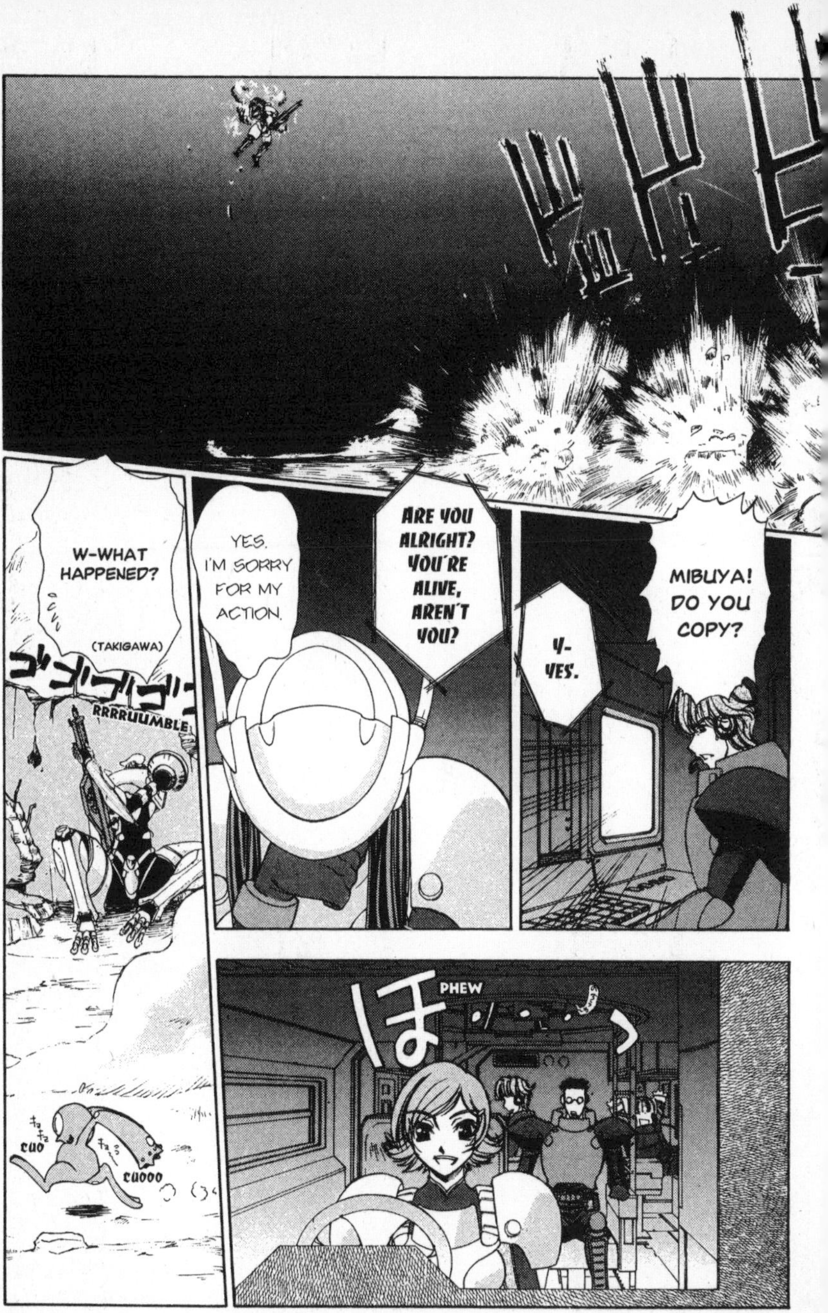
MIBUYA! DO YOU COPY?
Y- YES.
ARE YOU ALRIGHT? YOU'RE ALIVE, AREN'T YOU?
YES. I'M SORRY FOR MY ACTION.
W-WHAT HAPPENED?
(TAKIGAWA)
RRRRUUMBLE
ほ
PHEW
CUO
CUOOO

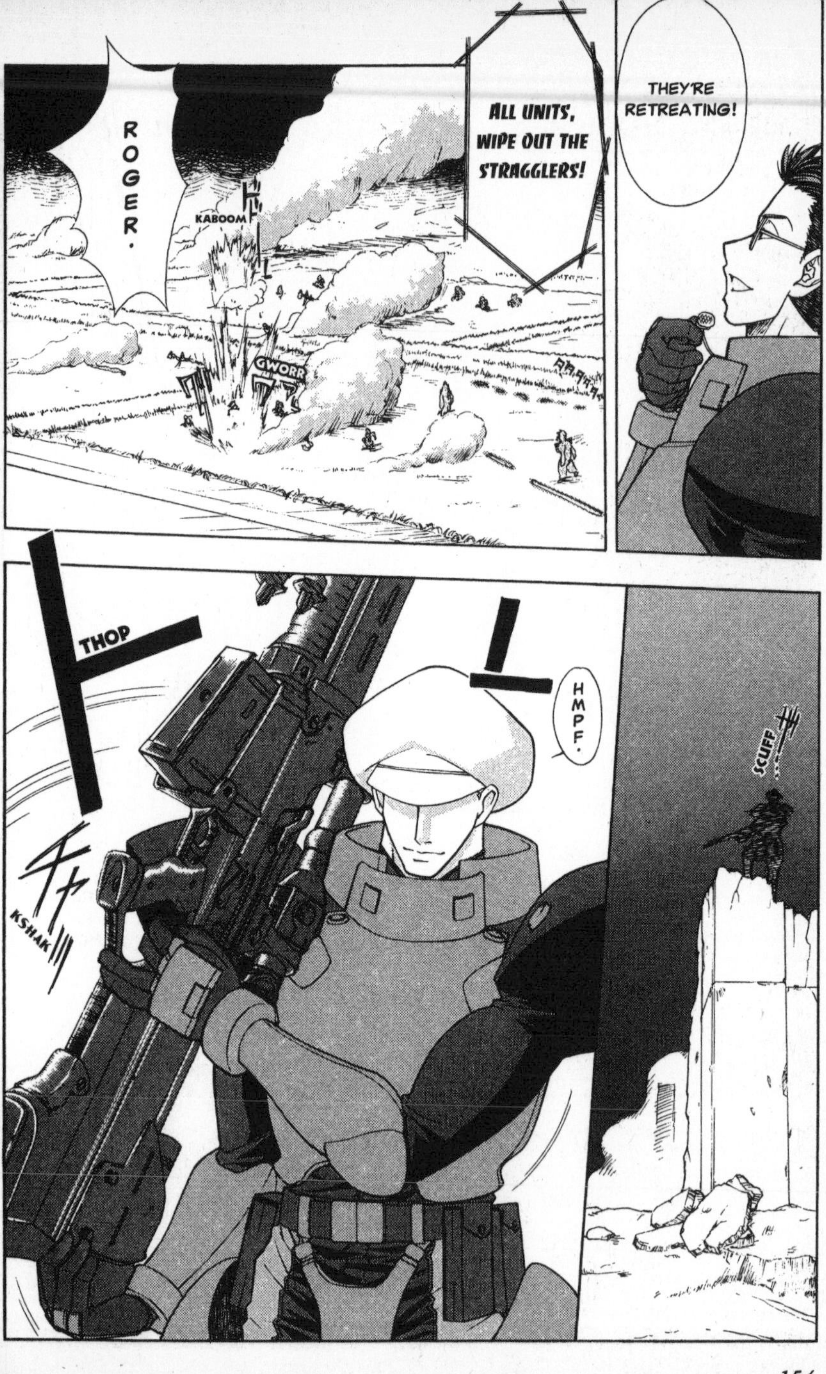
THEY'RE RETREATING!
ALL UNITS, WIPE OUT THE STRAGGLERS!
ROGER.
KABOOM
GWORR
THOP
HMPF.
SCUFF
KSHAK

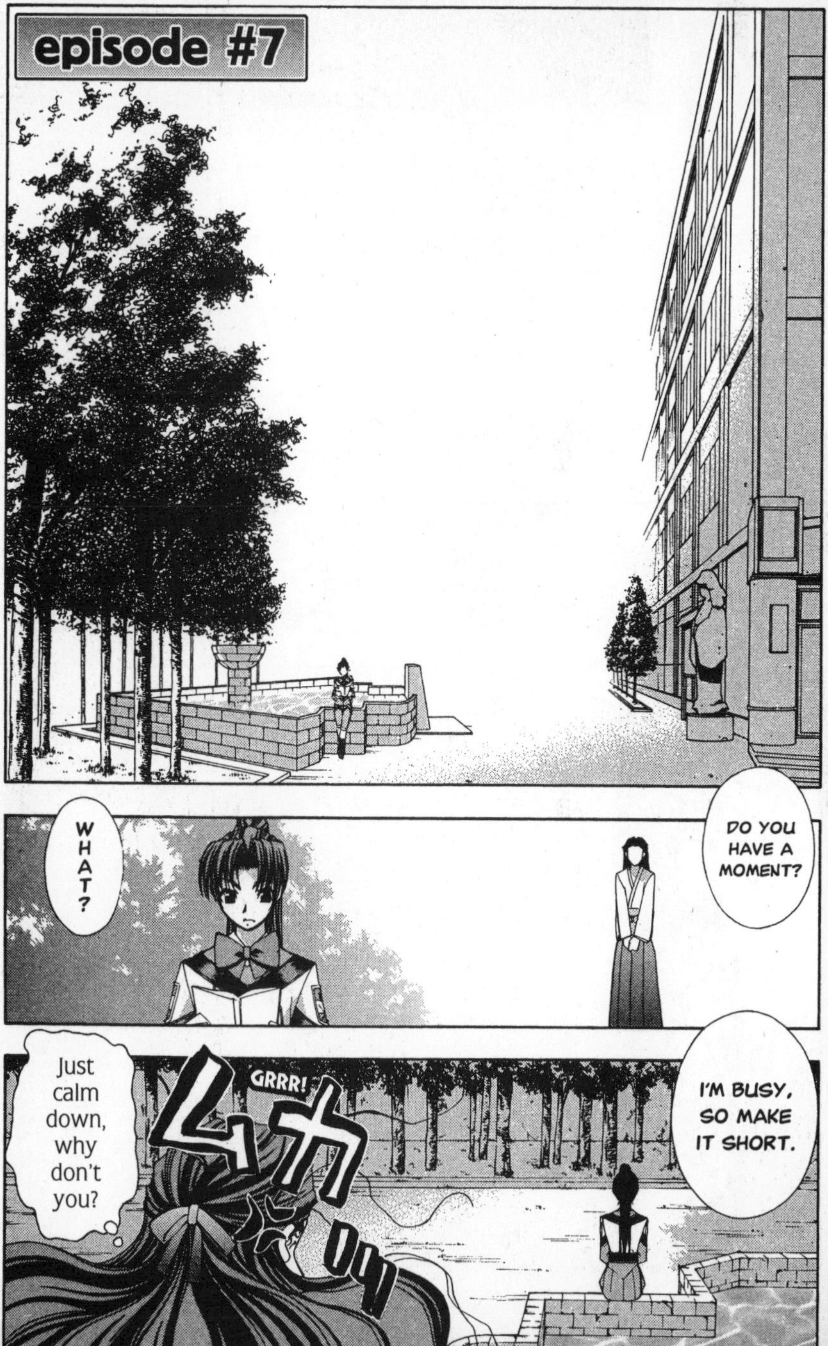
episode #7
DO YOU HAVE A MOMENT?
WHAT?
I'M BUSY, SO MAKE IT SHORT.
GRRR!
Just calm down, why don't you?

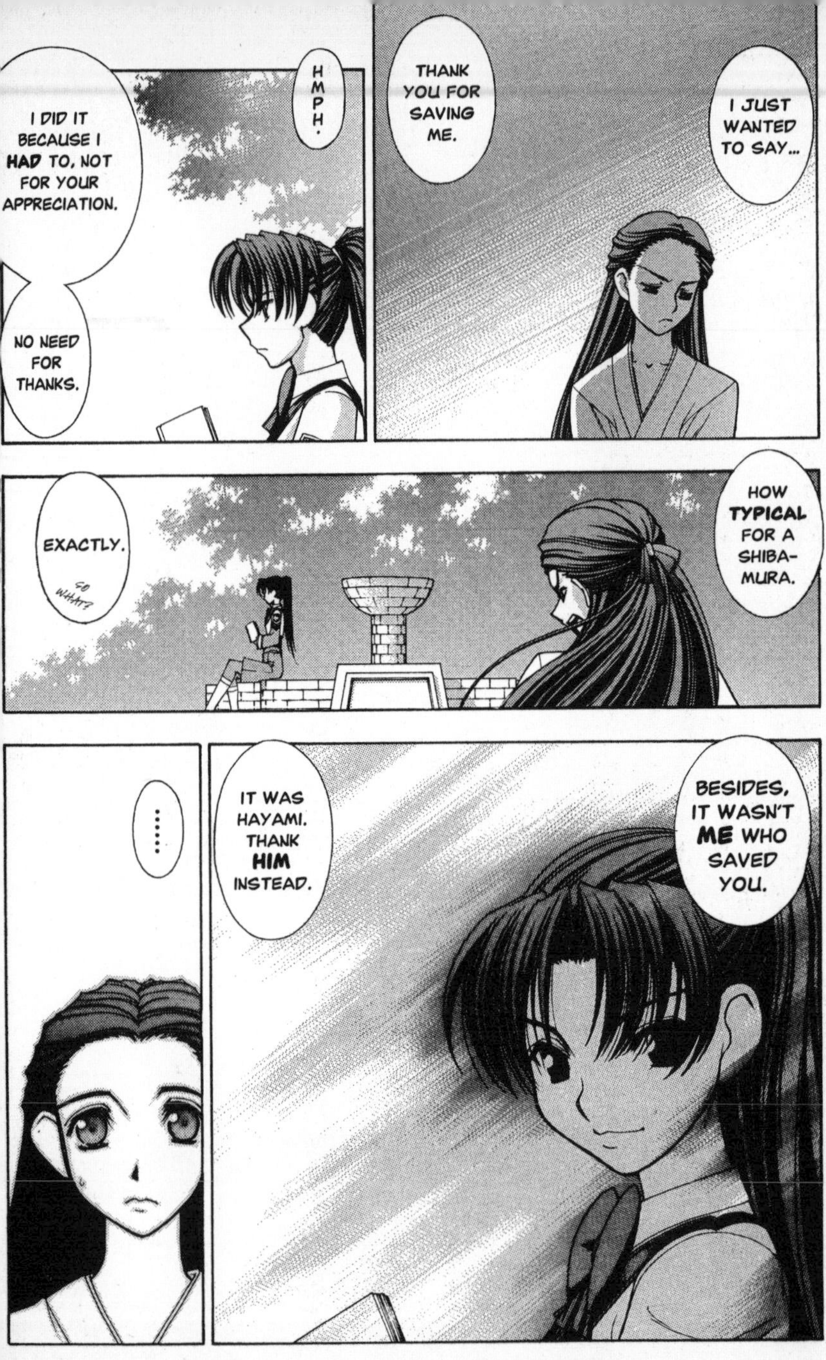
I JUST WANTED TO SAY...
THANK YOU FOR SAVING ME.
HMPH.
I DID IT BECAUSE I HAD TO, NOT FOR YOUR APPRECIATION.
NO NEED FOR THANKS.
HOW TYPICAL FOR A SHIBA-MURA.
EXACTLY.
SO WHAT?
BESIDES, IT WASN'T ME WHO SAVED YOU.
IT WAS HAYAMI. THANK HIM INSTEAD.
......

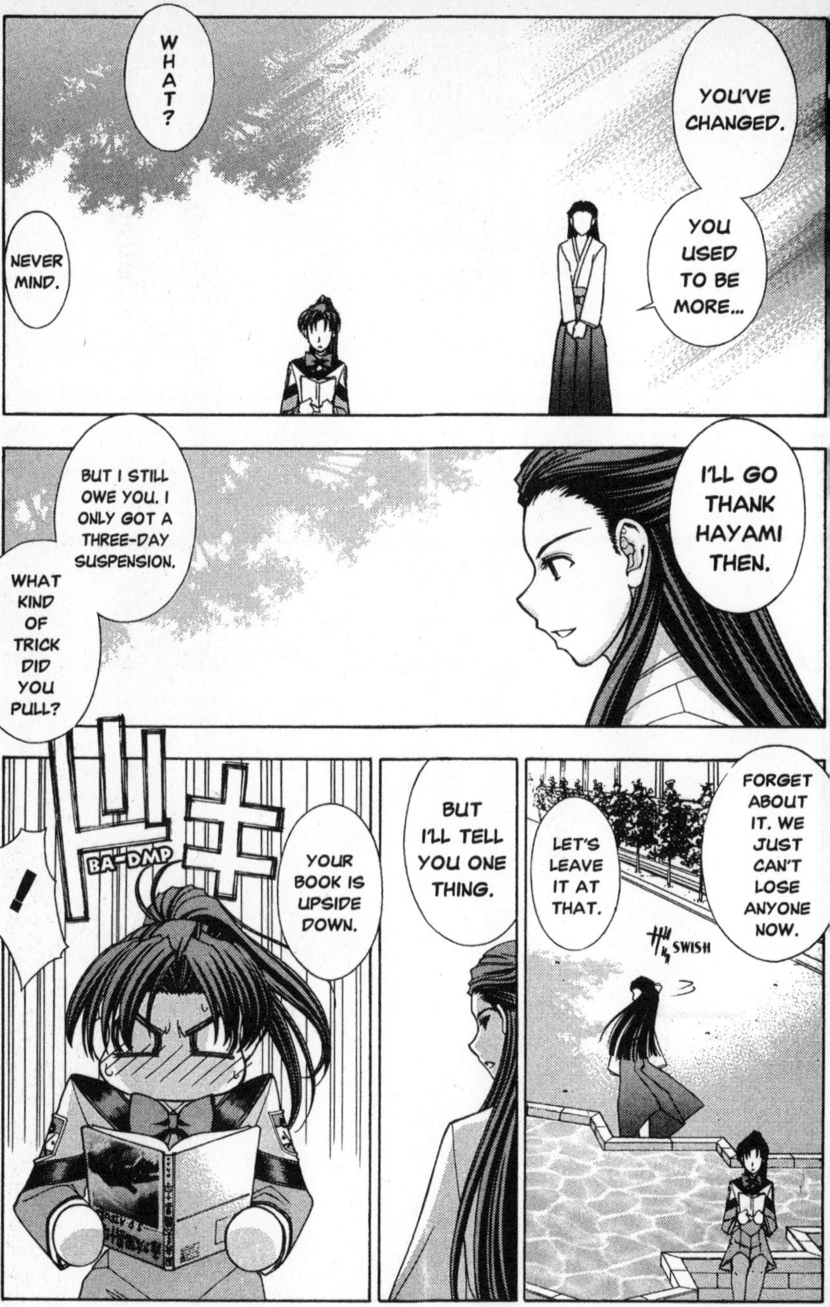
YOU'VE CHANGED.
YOU USED TO BE MORE...
WHAT?
NEVER MIND.
I'LL GO THANK HAYAMI THEN.
BUT I STILL OWE YOU. I ONLY GOT A THREE-DAY SUSPENSION.
WHAT KIND OF TRICK DID YOU PULL?
FORGET ABOUT IT. WE JUST CAN'T LOSE ANYONE NOW.
LET'S LEAVE IT AT THAT.
SWISH
BUT I'LL TELL YOU ONE THING.
YOUR BOOK IS UPSIDE DOWN.
BA-DMP
!

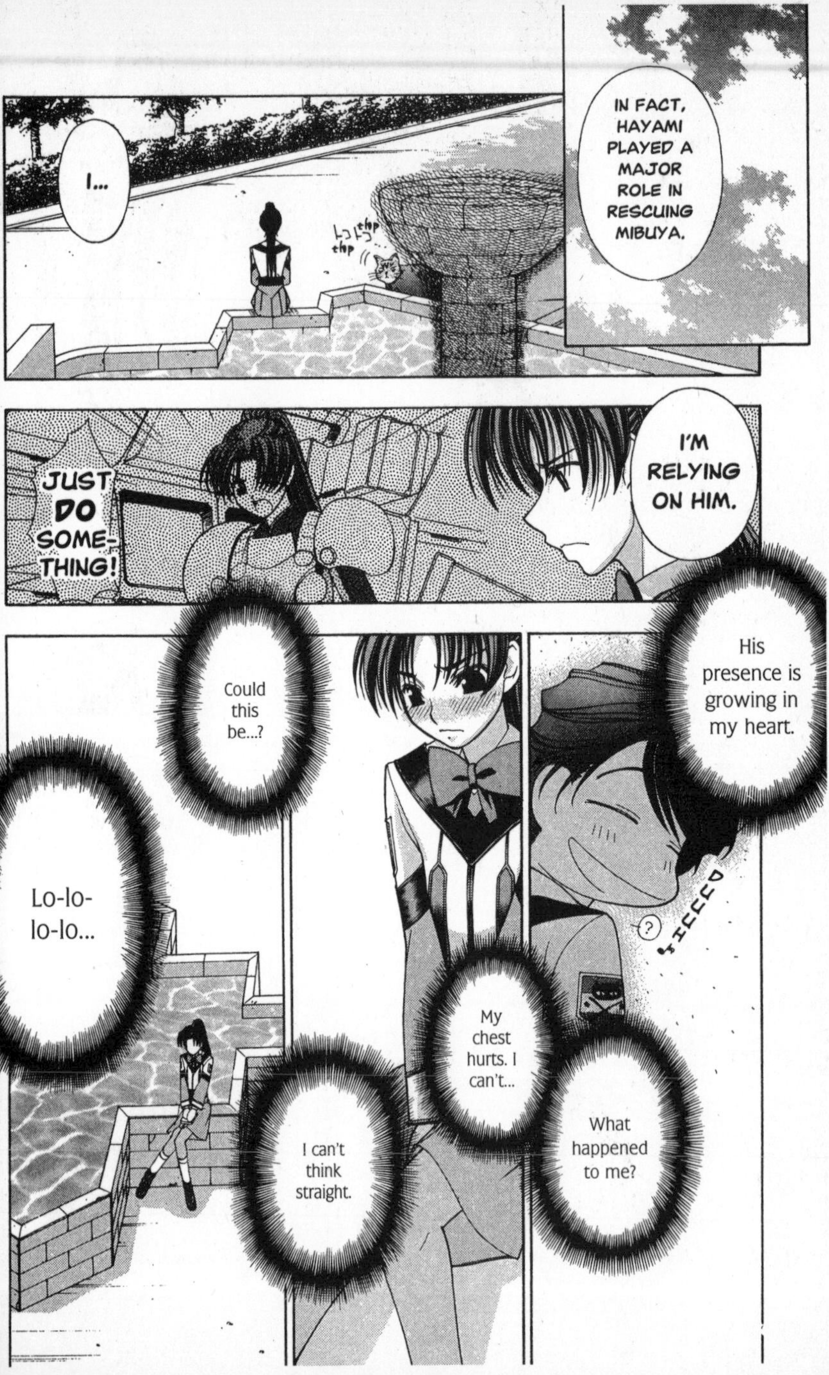
IN FACT, HAYAMI PLAYED A MAJOR ROLE IN RESCUING MIBUYA.
I...
thop thop
I'M RELYING ON HIM.
JUST DO SOME-THING!
His presence is growing in my heart.
?
Could this be...?
My chest hurts. I can't...
What happened to me?
I can't think straight.
Lo-lo-lo-lo...

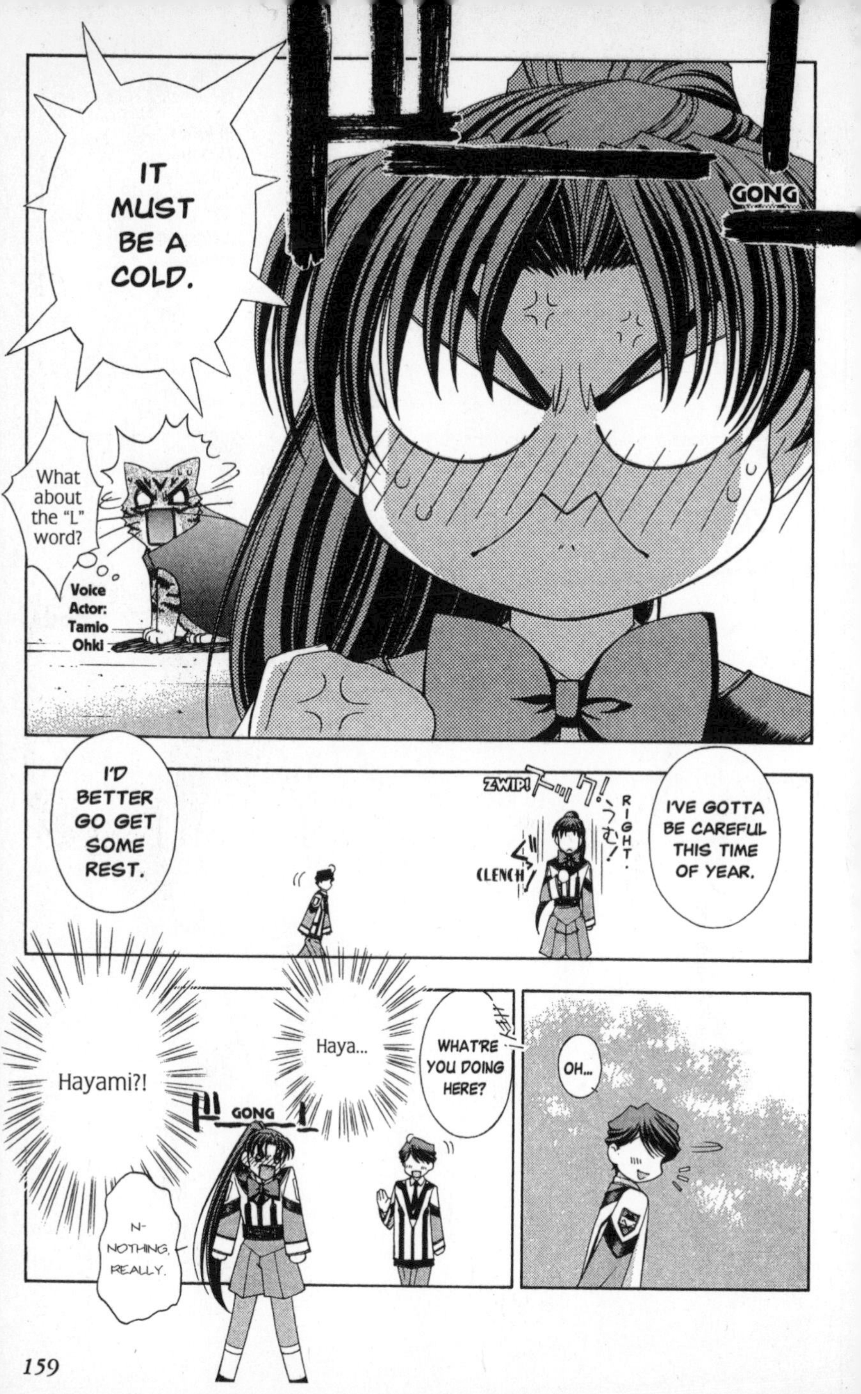
IT MUST BE A COLD.
GONG
What about the "L" word?
Voice Actor: Tamio Ohki
I'VE GOTTA BE CAREFUL THIS TIME OF YEAR.
ZWIP!
RIGHT.
CLENCH
I'D BETTER GO GET SOME REST.
OH...
WHAT'RE YOU DOING HERE?
Haya...
Hayami?!
GONG
N-NOTHING, REALLY.

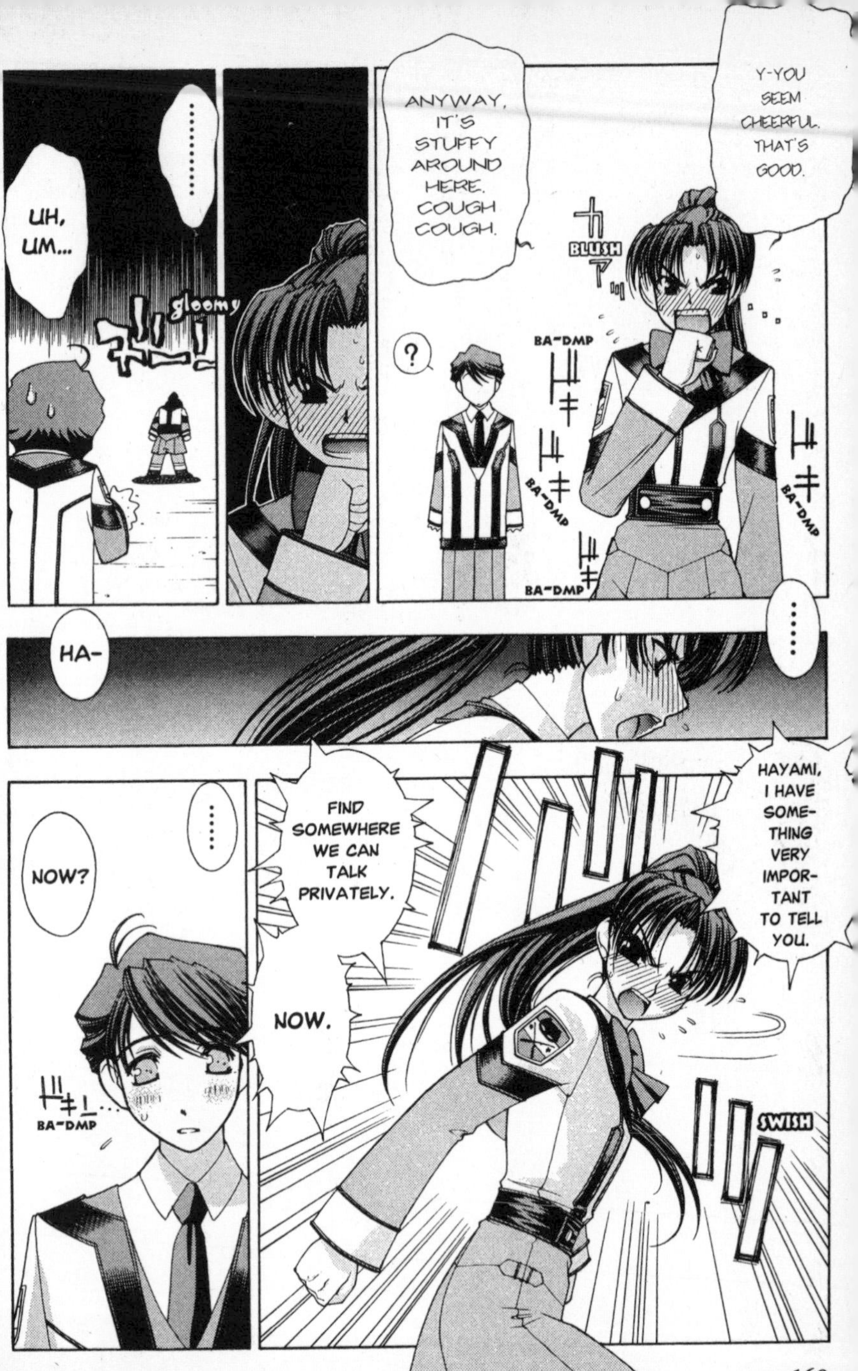
Y-YOU SEEM CHEERFUL. THAT'S GOOD.
BLUSH
BA-DMP
BA-DMP
BA-DMP
BA-DMP
ANYWAY, IT'S STUFFY AROUND HERE. COUGH COUGH.
?
......
UH, UM...
gloomy
......
HA-
HAYAMI, I HAVE SOMETHING VERY IMPORTANT TO TELL YOU.
SWISH
FIND SOMEWHERE WE CAN TALK PRIVATELY.
NOW.
......
NOW?
BA-DMP

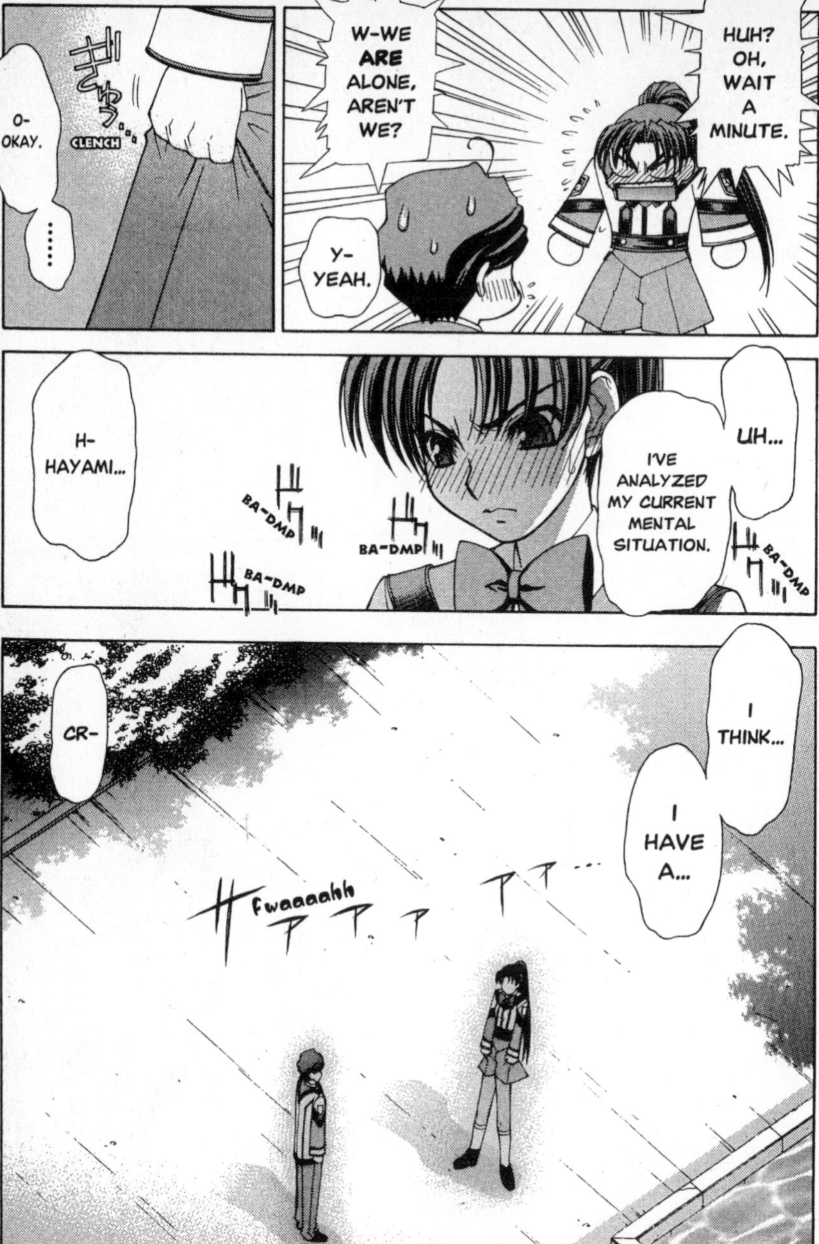
HUH? OH, WAIT A MINUTE.
W-WE ARE ALONE, AREN'T WE?
Y-YEAH.
O-OKAY.
CLENCH
......
UH...
I'VE ANALYZED MY CURRENT MENTAL SITUATION.
BA-DMP
BA-DMP
BA-DMP
BA-DMP
H-HAYAMI...
I THINK...
I HAVE A...
fwaaaahh
CR-

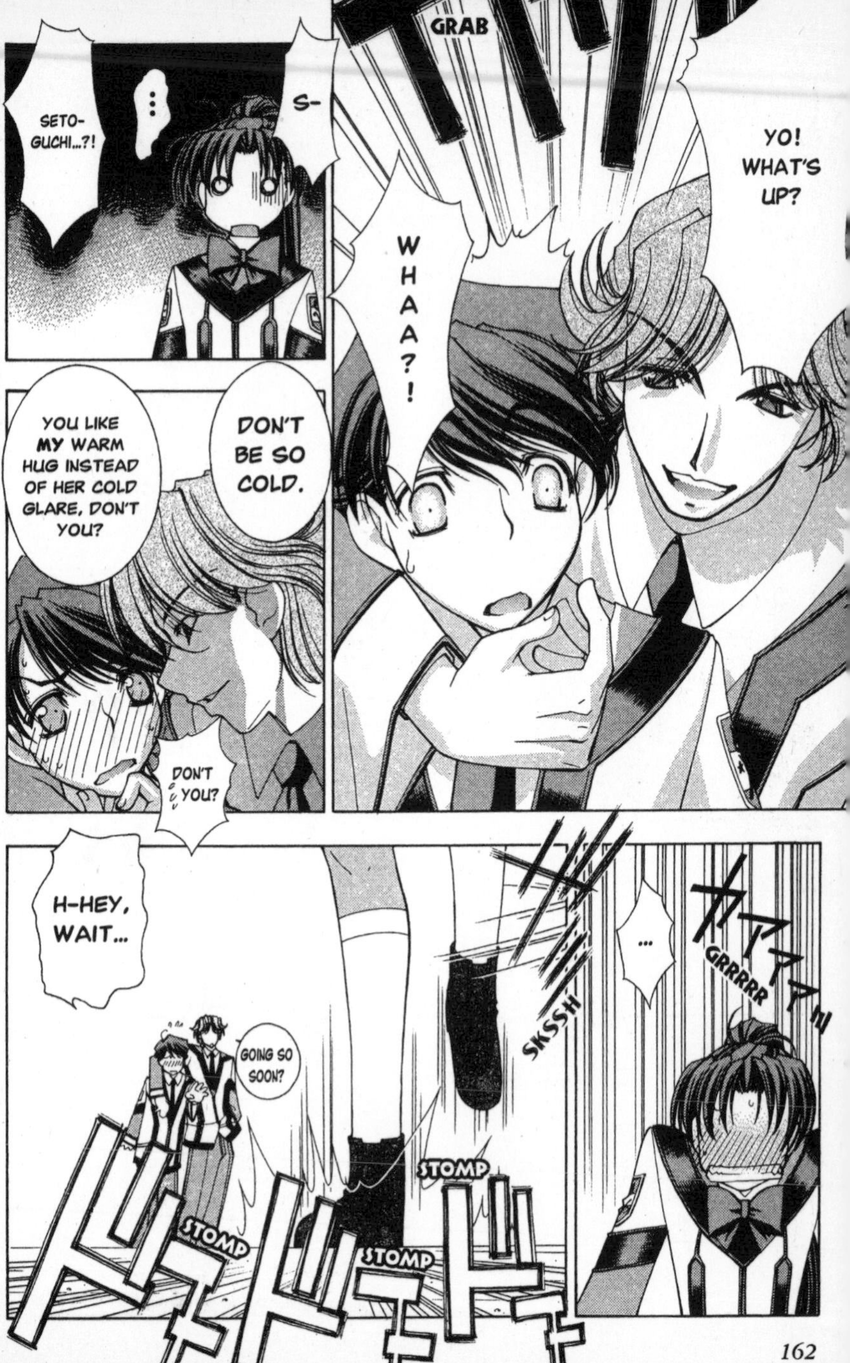
GRAB
YO! WHAT'S UP?
WHAA?!
S-
...
SETO-GUCHI...?!
DON'T BE SO COLD.
YOU LIKE MY WARM HUG INSTEAD OF HER COLD GLARE, DON'T YOU?
DON'T YOU?
...
GRRRRR
SKSSH
H-HEY, WAIT...
GOING SO SOON?
STOMP
STOMP
STOMP

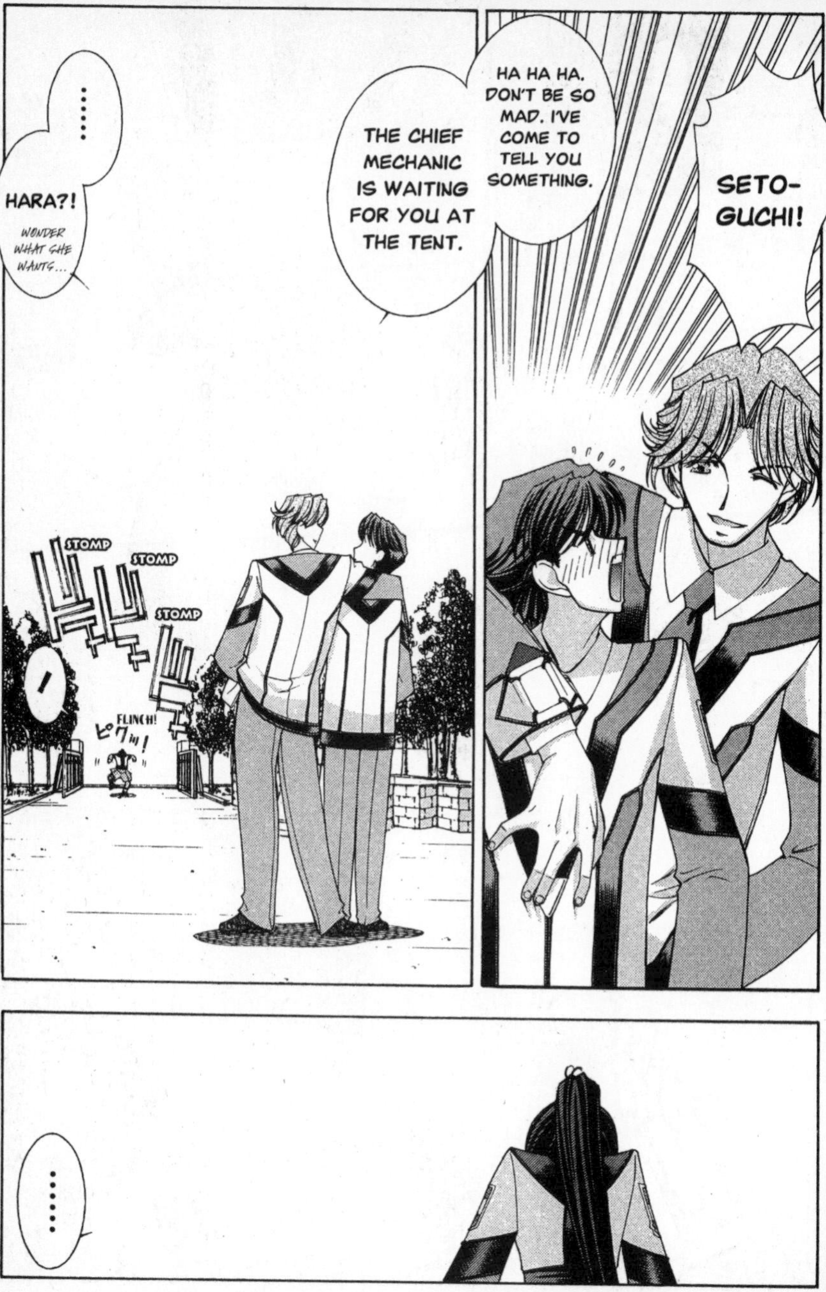
SETO-GUCHI!
HA HA HA. DON'T BE SO MAD. I'VE COME TO TELL YOU SOMETHING.
THE CHIEF MECHANIC IS WAITING FOR YOU AT THE TENT.
......
HARA?!
WONDER WHAT SHE WANTS...
STOMP
STOMP
STOMP
!
FLINCH!
ピクッ!
......

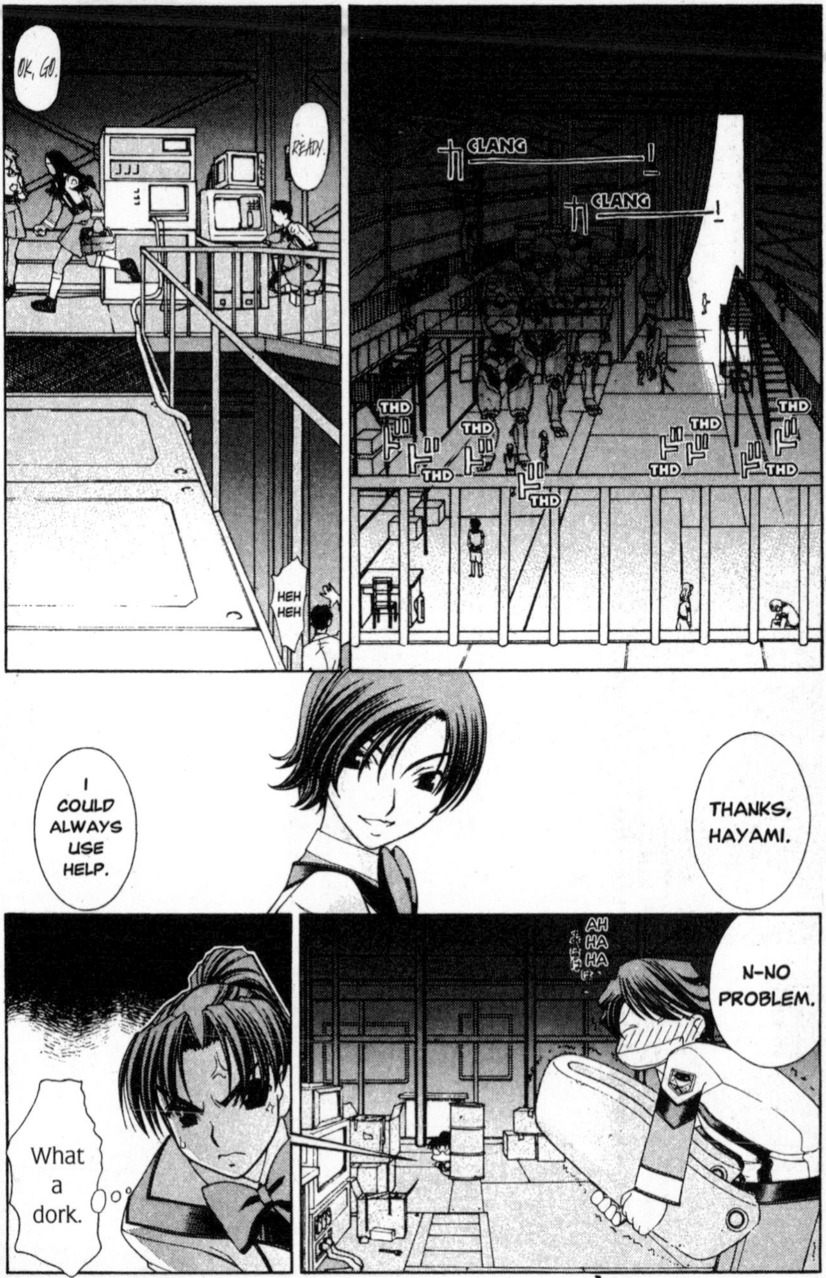
CLANG
CLANG
THD
THD
THD
THD
THD
THD
THD
THD
OK, GO.
READY.
HEH HEH
THANKS, HAYAMI.
I COULD ALWAYS USE HELP.
N-NO PROBLEM.
AH HA HA
What a dork.

110 lb Armor plate for the small finger

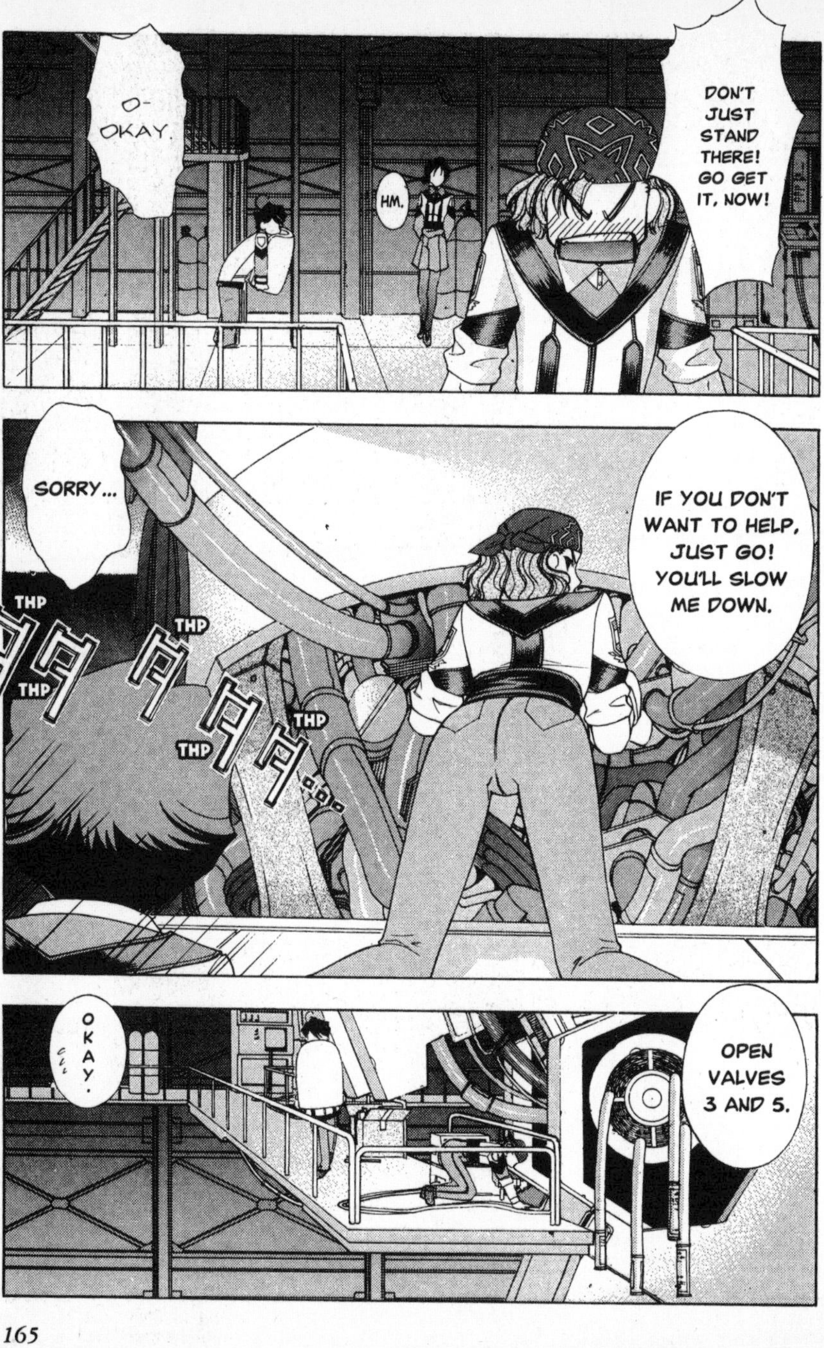
DON'T JUST STAND THERE! GO GET IT, NOW!
HM.
O-OKAY.
IF YOU DON'T WANT TO HELP, JUST GO! YOU'LL SLOW ME DOWN.
SORRY...
THP
THP
THP
THP
THP
OPEN VALVES 3 AND 5.
OKAY.

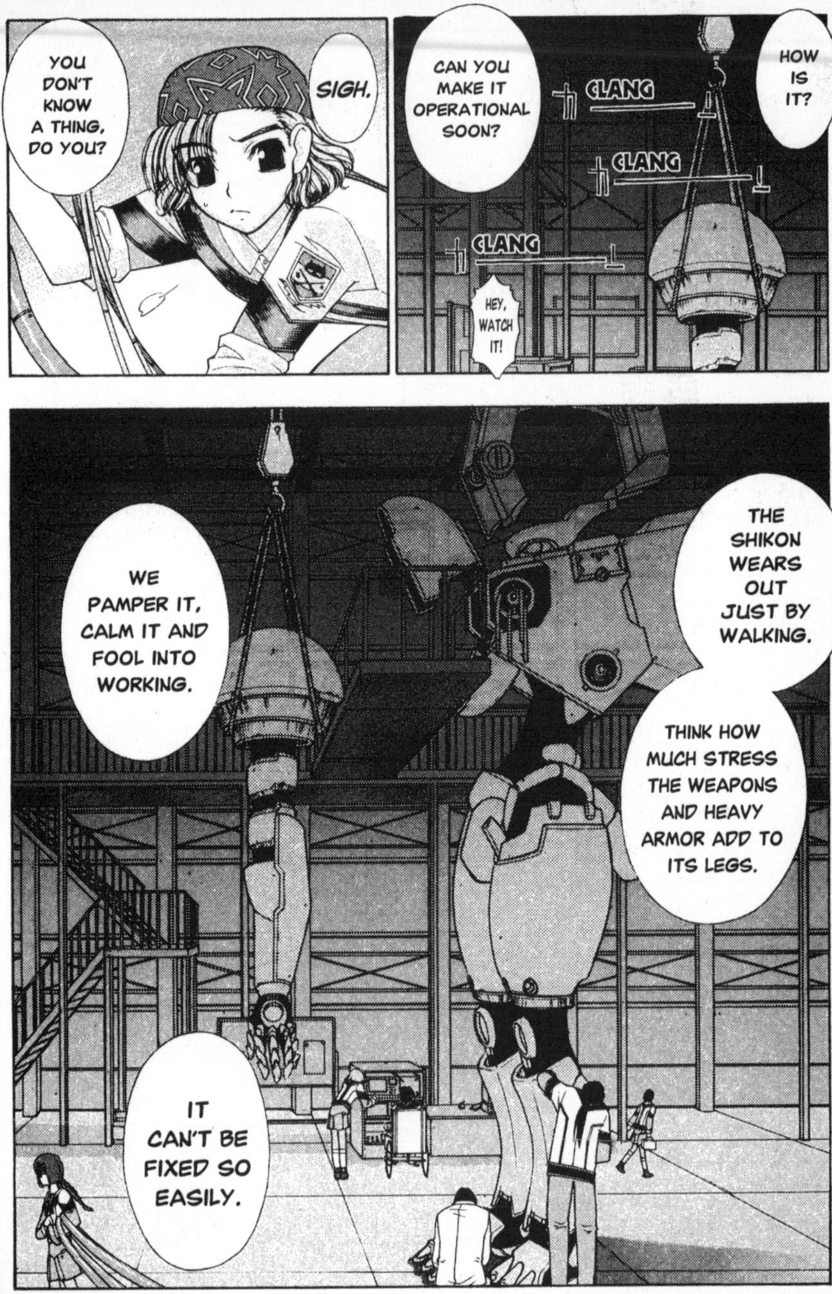
HOW IS IT?
CLANG
CLANG
CLANG
HEY, WATCH IT!
CAN YOU MAKE IT OPERATIONAL SOON?
SIGH.
YOU DON'T KNOW A THING, DO YOU?
THE SHIKON WEARS OUT JUST BY WALKING.
THINK HOW MUCH STRESS THE WEAPONS AND HEAVY ARMOR ADD TO ITS LEGS.
WE PAMPER IT, CALM IT AND FOOL INTO WORKING.
IT CAN'T BE FIXED SO EASILY.

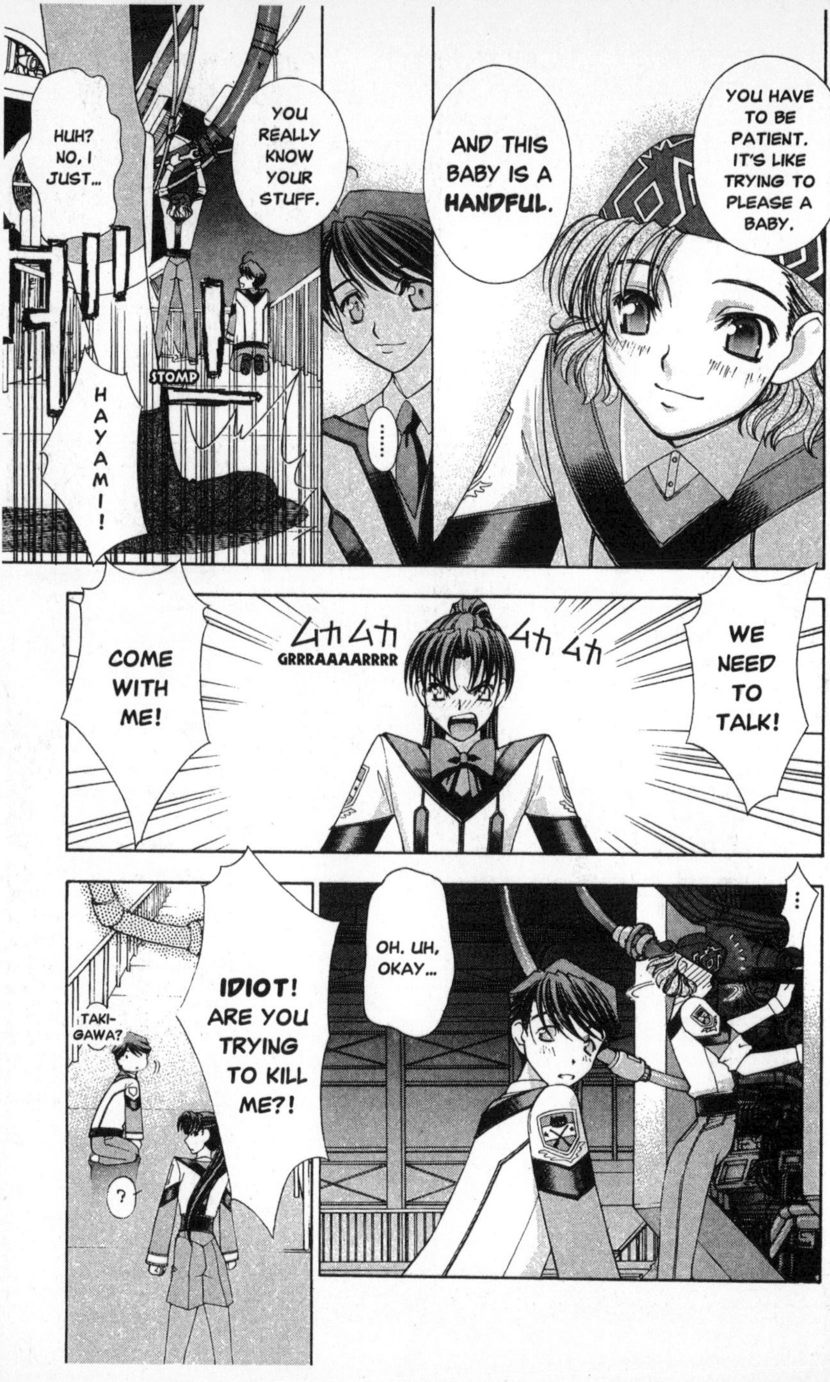
YOU HAVE TO BE PATIENT. IT'S LIKE TRYING TO PLEASE A BABY.
AND THIS BABY IS A HANDFUL.
YOU REALLY KNOW YOUR STUFF.
HUH? NO, I JUST...
......
STOMP
HAYAMI!
WE NEED TO TALK!
ムカムカ
ムカムカ
GRRRAAAARRRR
COME WITH ME!
...
OH. UH, OKAY...
IDIOT! ARE YOU TRYING TO KILL ME?!
TAKI-GAWA?
?

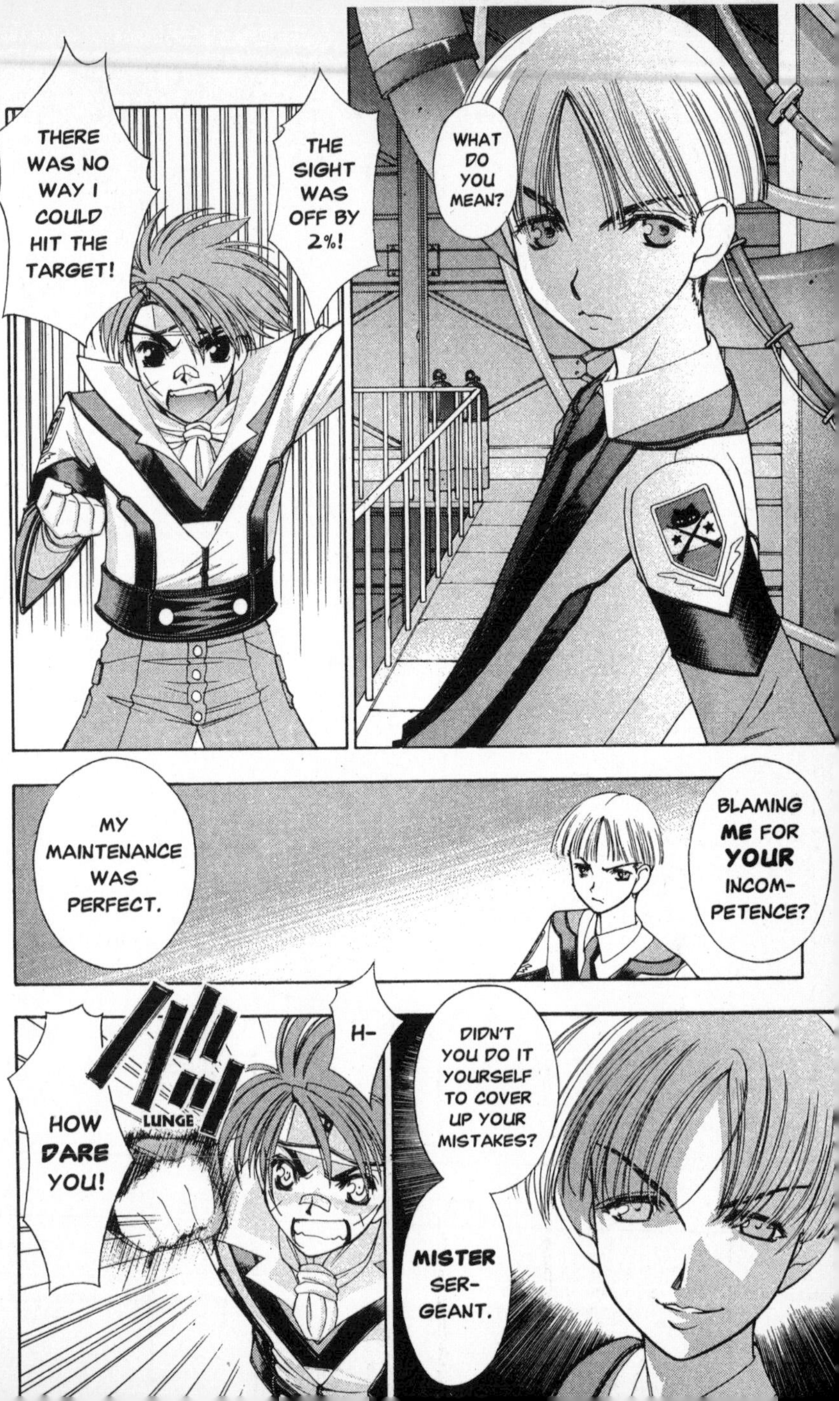
THERE WAS NO WAY I COULD HIT THE TARGET!
THE SIGHT WAS OFF BY 2%!
WHAT DO YOU MEAN?
MY MAINTENANCE WAS PERFECT.
BLAMING ME FOR YOUR INCOMPETENCE?
HOW DARE YOU!
LUNGE
H-
DIDN'T YOU DO IT YOURSELF TO COVER UP YOUR MISTAKES?
MISTER SERGEANT.

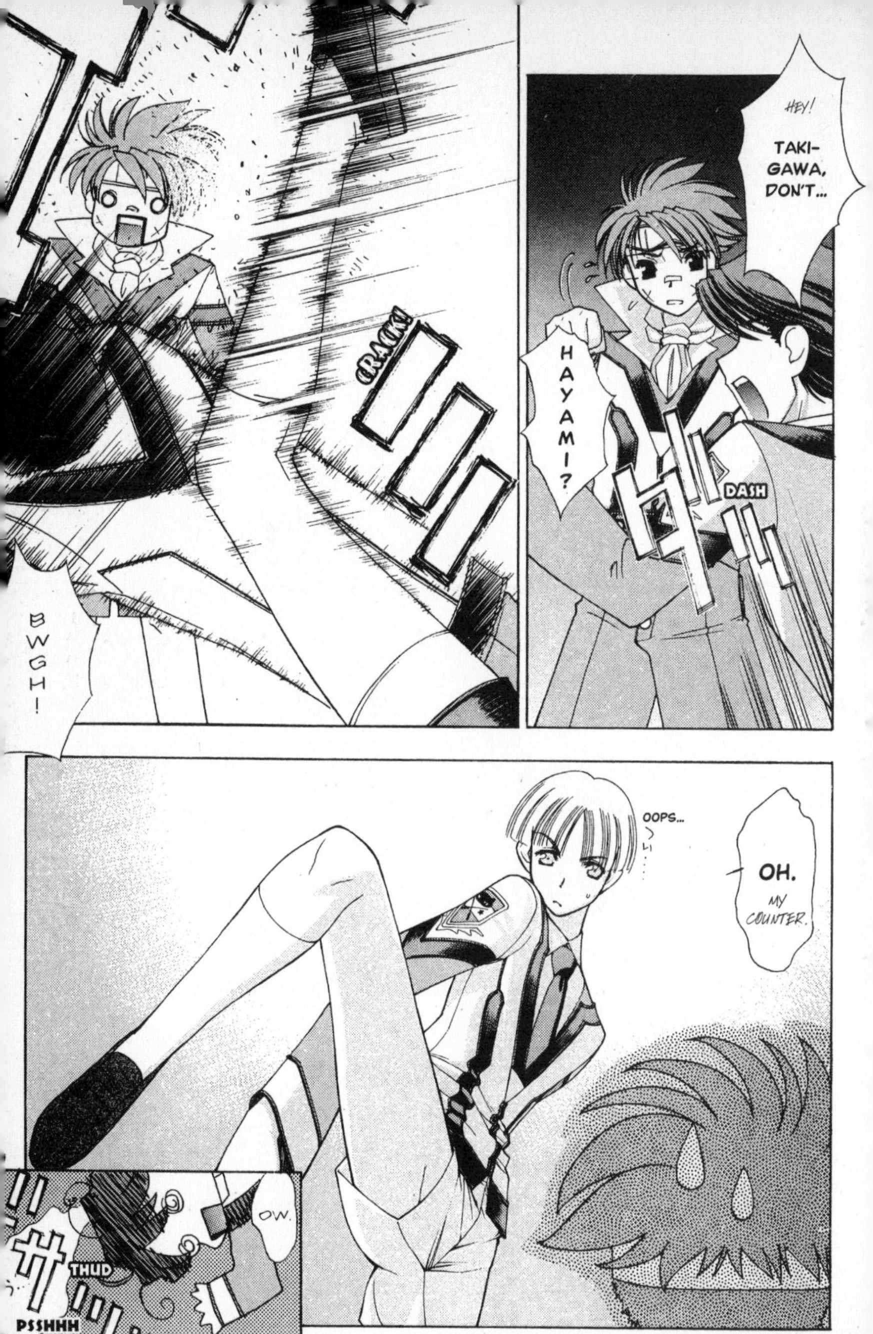
HEY!
TAKI-GAWA, DON'T...
HAYAMI?
DASH
CRACK!
BWGH!
OH. MY COUNTER.
OOPS...
OW.
THUD
PSSHHH

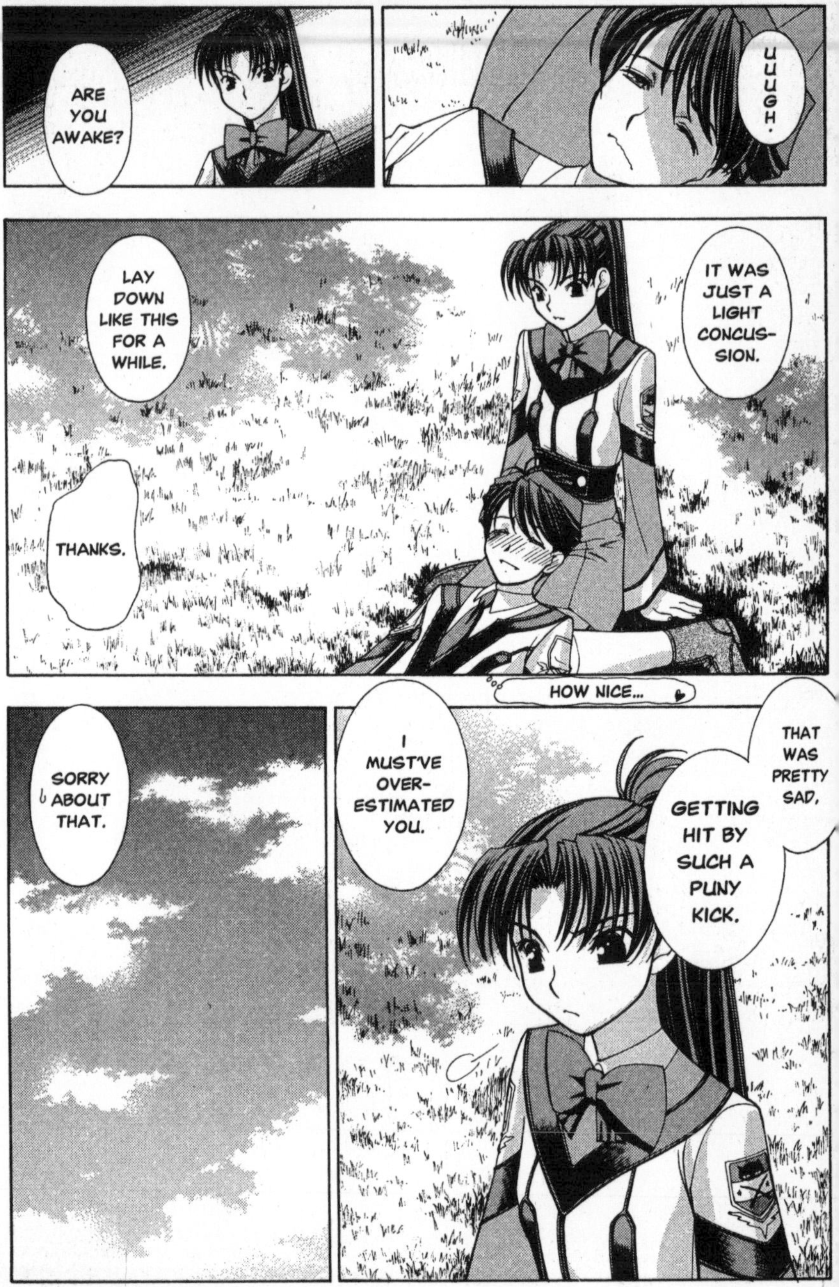

UUUGH.
ARE YOU AWAKE?
IT WAS JUST A LIGHT CONCUSSION.
LAY DOWN LIKE THIS FOR A WHILE.
THANKS.
HOW NICE...
THAT WAS PRETTY SAD,
GETTING HIT BY SUCH A PUNY KICK.
I MUST'VE OVER-ESTIMATED YOU.
SORRY ABOUT THAT.

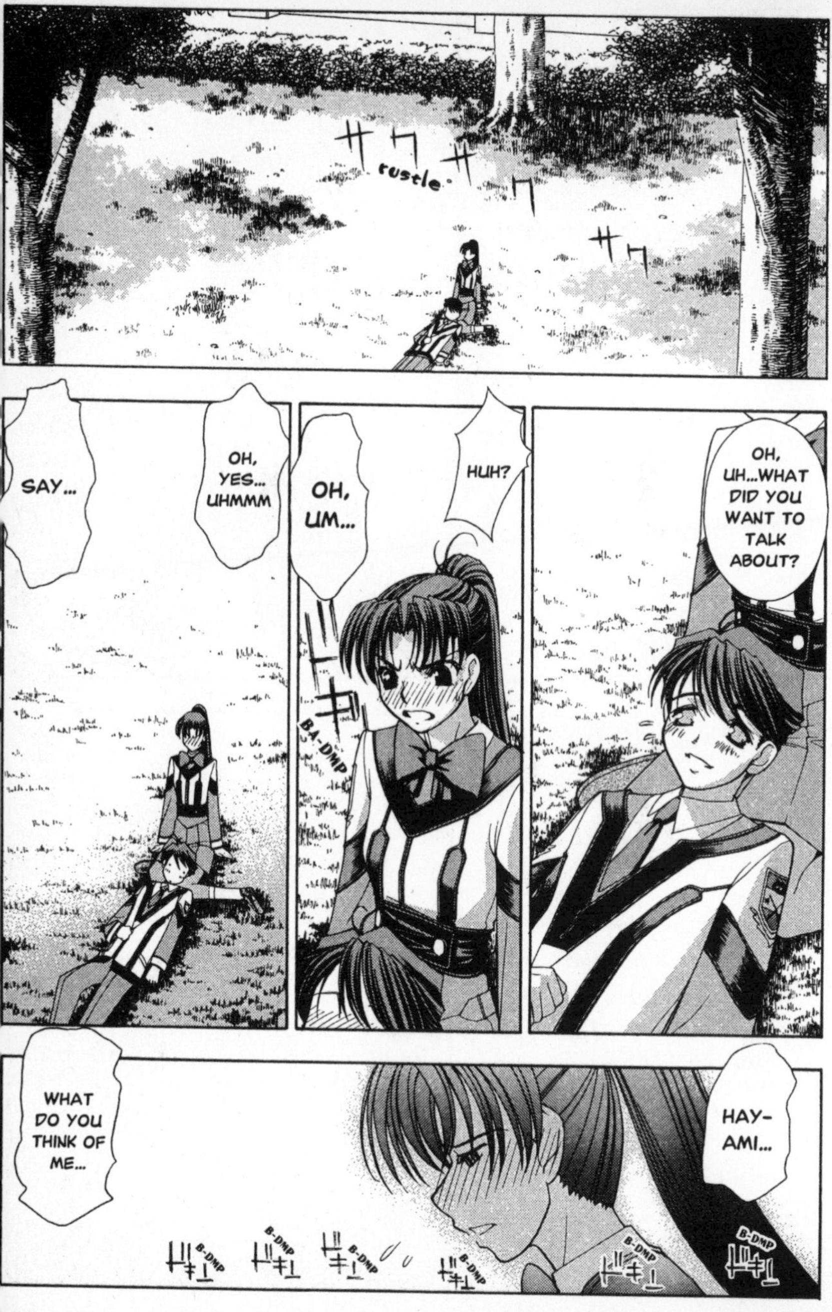
rustle
OH, UH...WHAT DID YOU WANT TO TALK ABOUT?
HUH?
OH, UM...
BA-DMP
OH, YES... UHMMM
SAY...
HAY-AMI...
WHAT DO YOU THINK OF ME...
B-DMP
B-DMP
B-DMP
B-DMP
B-DMP
B-DMP

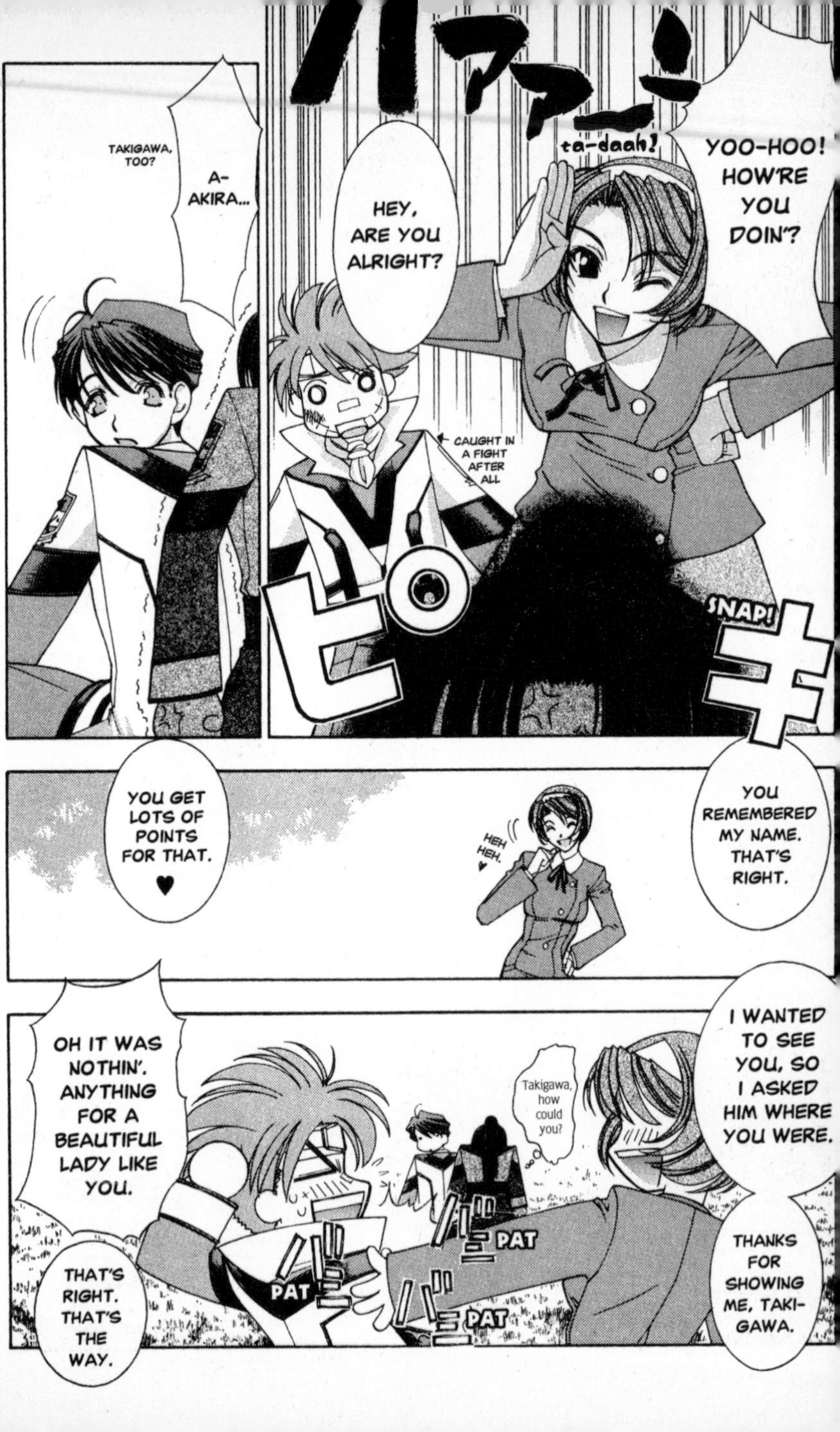
ta-daah!
YOO-HOO! HOW'RE YOU DOIN'?
HEY, ARE YOU ALRIGHT?
CAUGHT IN A FIGHT AFTER ALL
SNAP!
A-AKIRA...
TAKIGAWA, TOO?
YOU REMEMBERED MY NAME. THAT'S RIGHT.
HEH HEH.
YOU GET LOTS OF POINTS FOR THAT. ♥
I WANTED TO SEE YOU, SO I ASKED HIM WHERE YOU WERE.
THANKS FOR SHOWING ME, TAKI-GAWA.
Takigawa, how could you?
OH IT WAS NOTHIN'. ANYTHING FOR A BEAUTIFUL LADY LIKE YOU.
PAT
PAT
PAT
THAT'S RIGHT. THAT'S THE WAY.

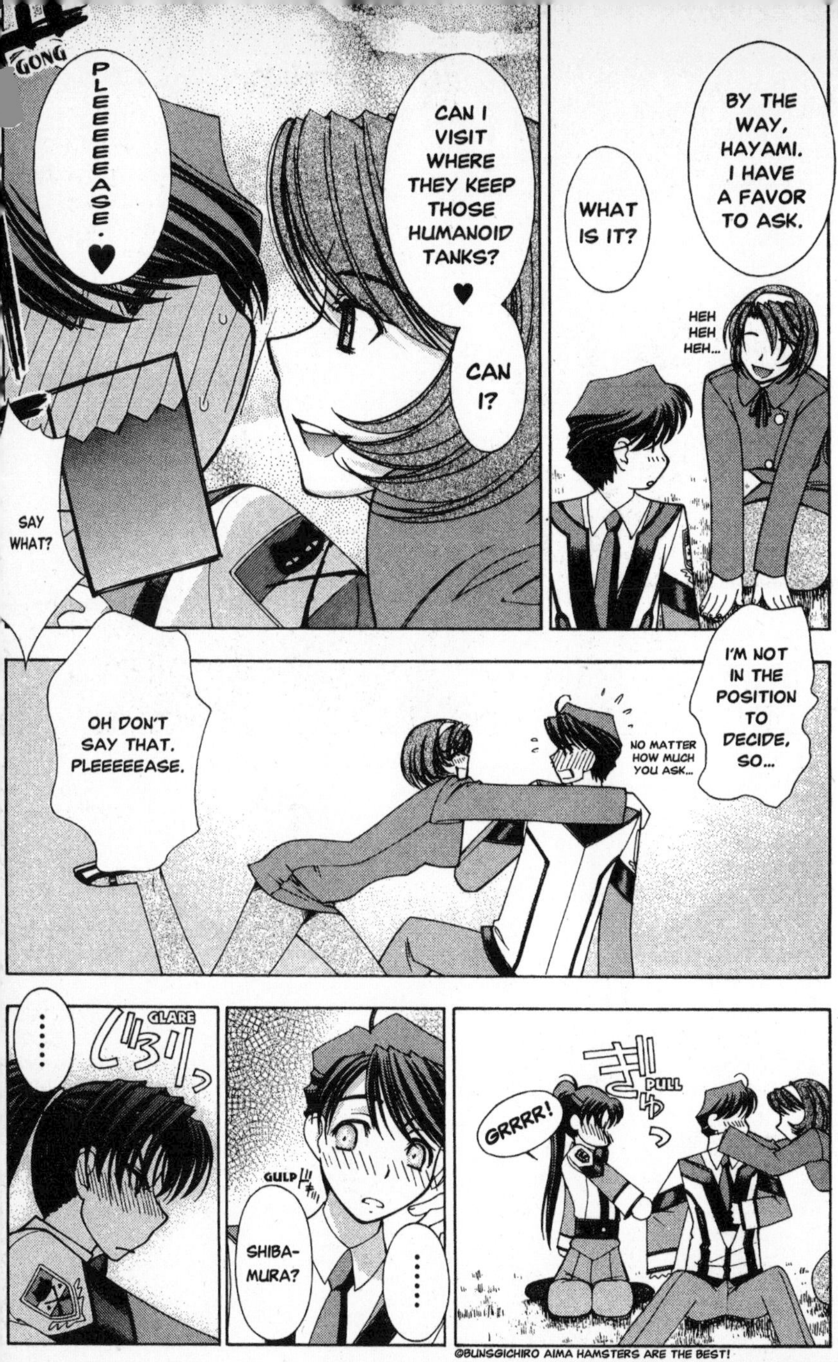
BY THE WAY, HAYAMI. I HAVE A FAVOR TO ASK.
WHAT IS IT?
HEH HEH HEH...
CAN I VISIT WHERE THEY KEEP THOSE HUMANOID TANKS? ♥
CAN I?
PLEEEEEASE. ♥
GONG
SAY WHAT?
I'M NOT IN THE POSITION TO DECIDE, SO...
NO MATTER HOW MUCH YOU ASK...
OH DON'T SAY THAT. PLEEEEEEASE.
GRRRR!
PULL
ぎゅっ
GULP
ドキ
SHIBA-MURA?
......
GLARE
じろりっ
......

©BUNSGICHIRO AIMA HAMSTERS ARE THE BEST!

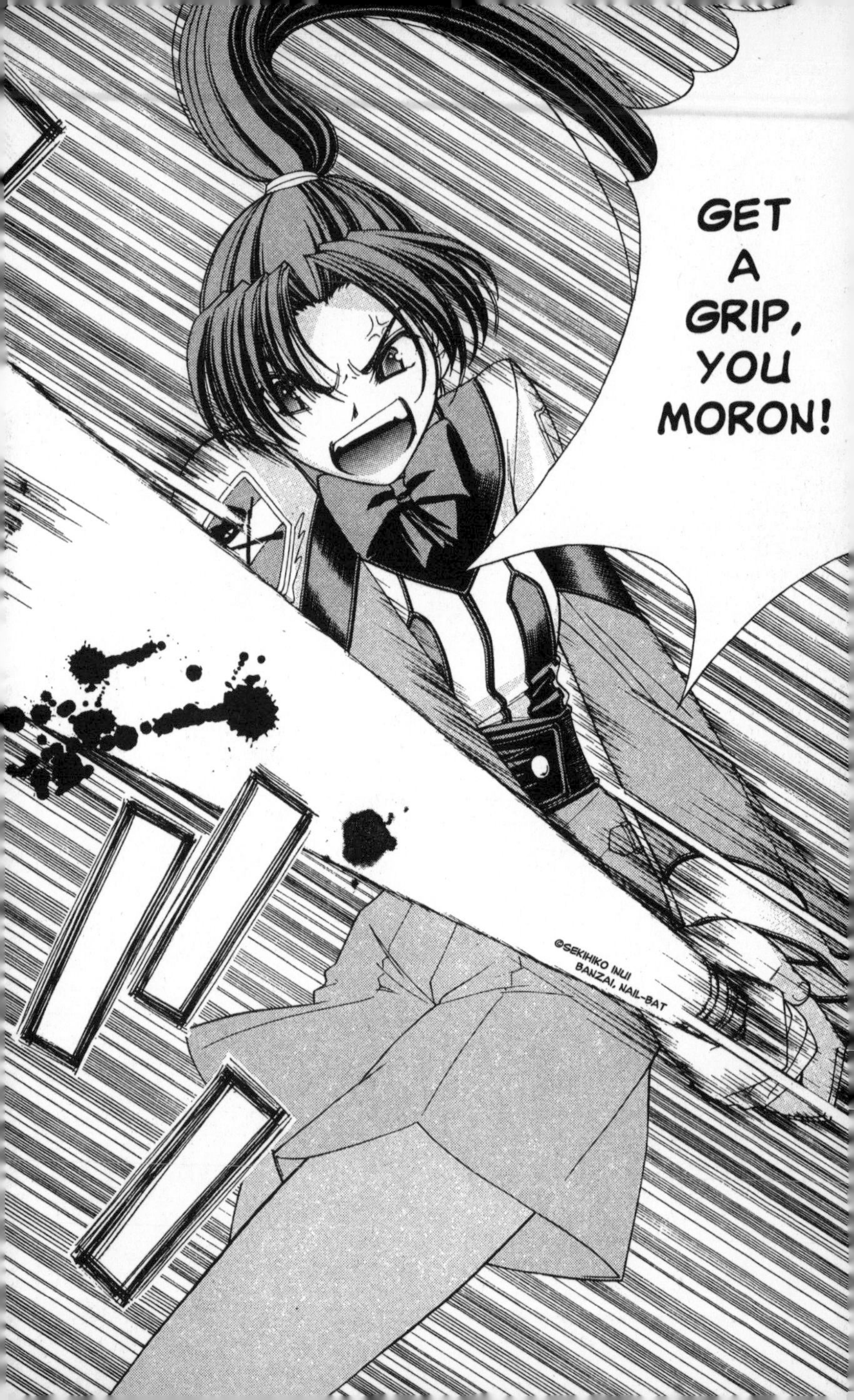
GET A GRIP, YOU MORON!
©SEKIHIKO INUI BANZAI, NAIL-BAT

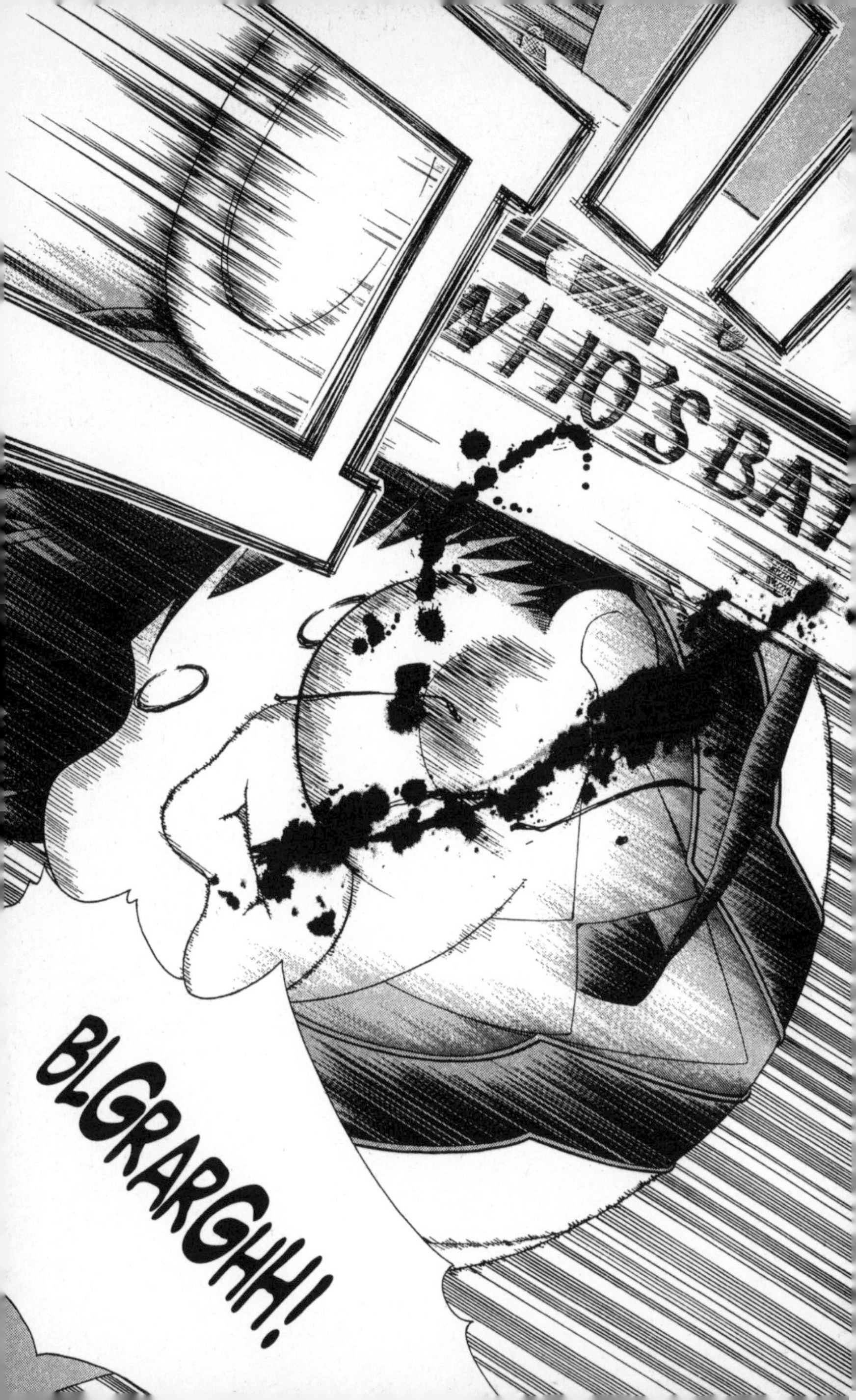
BLGRARGHH!

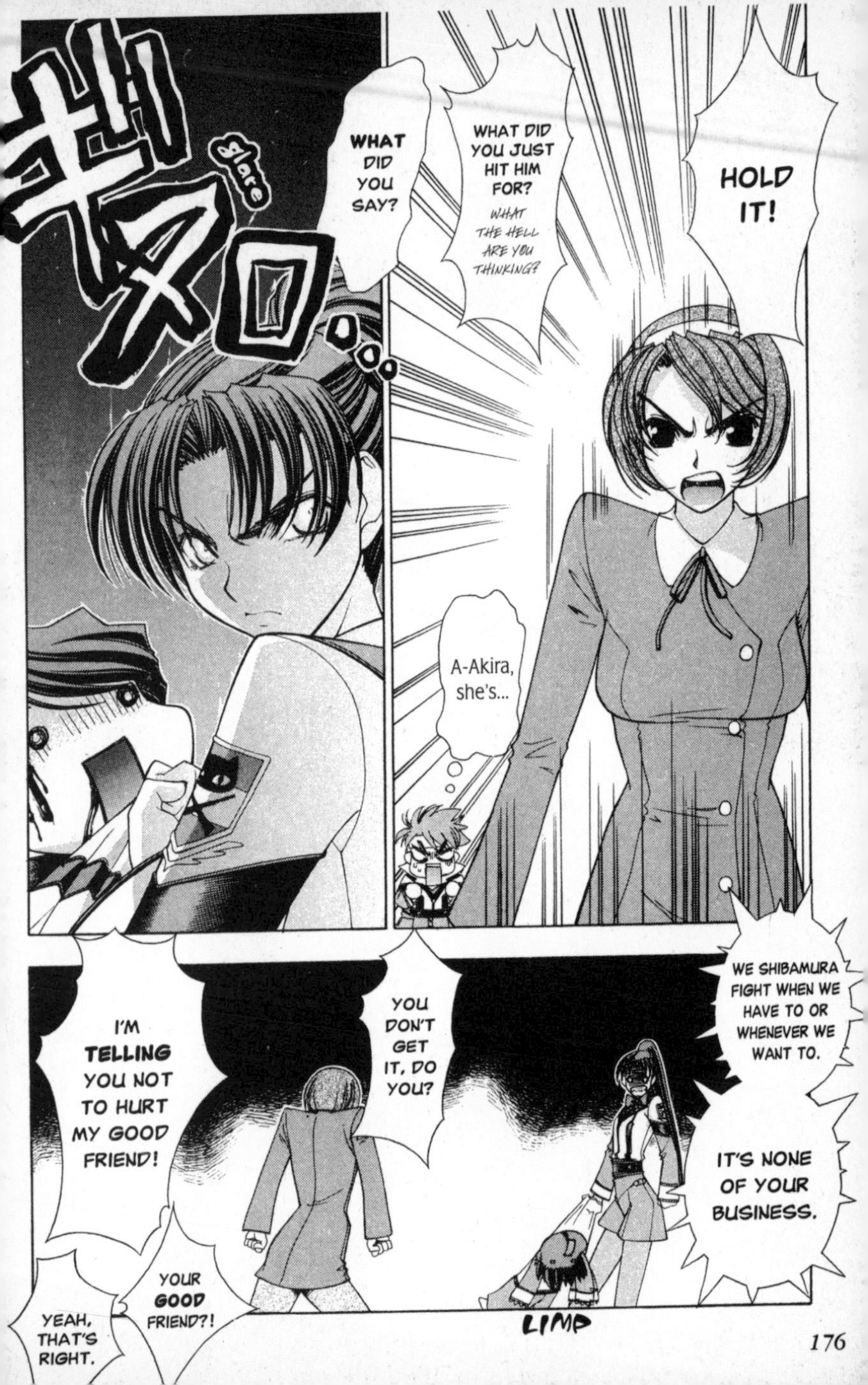
HOLD IT!
WHAT DID YOU JUST HIT HIM FOR?
WHAT THE HELL ARE YOU THINKING?
A-Akira, she's...
glare
WHAT DID YOU SAY?
WE SHIBAMURA FIGHT WHEN WE HAVE TO OR WHENEVER WE WANT TO.
IT'S NONE OF YOUR BUSINESS.
YOU DON'T GET IT, DO YOU?
I'M TELLING YOU NOT TO HURT MY GOOD FRIEND!
YOUR GOOD FRIEND?!
YEAH, THAT'S RIGHT.
LIMP

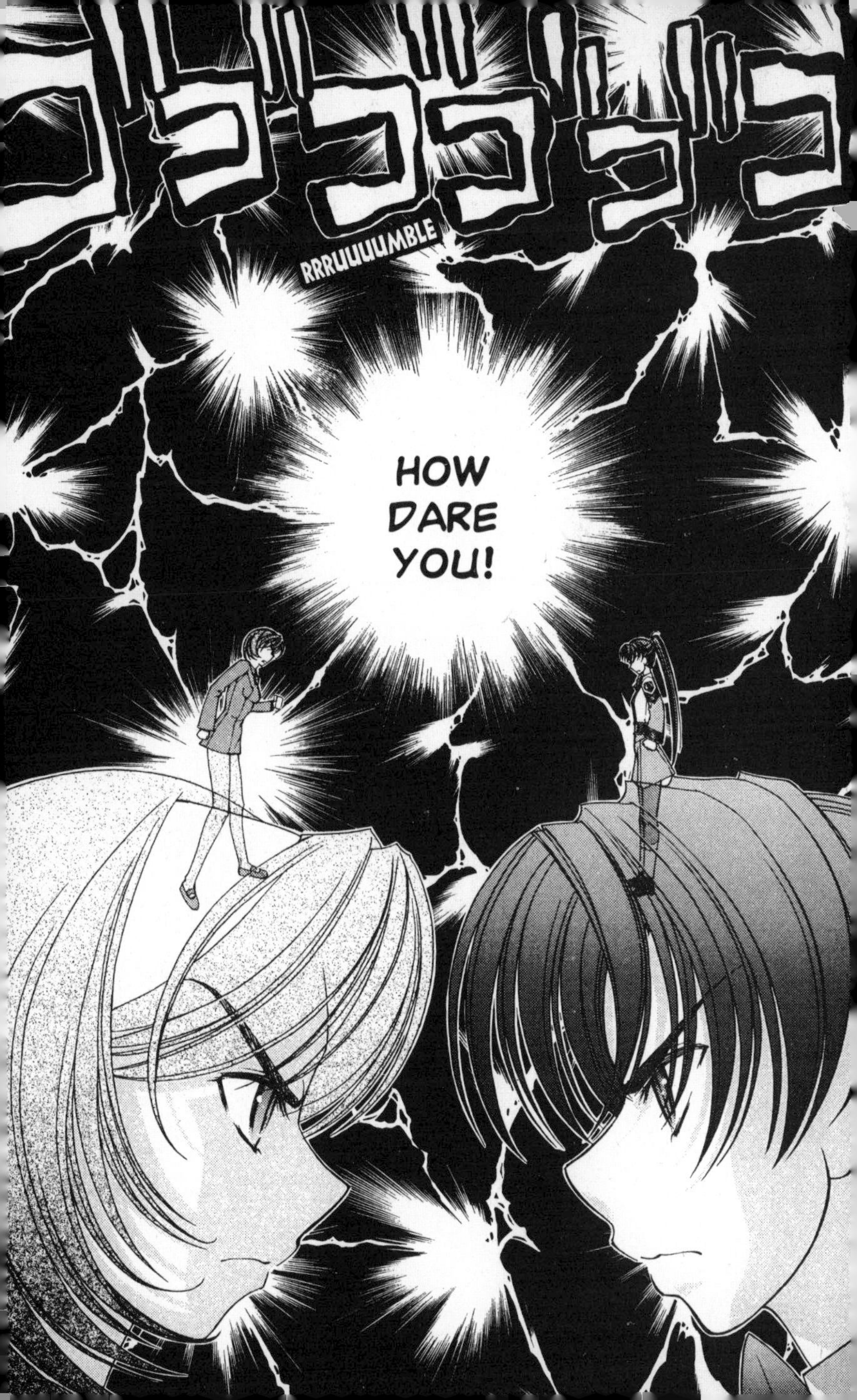
RRRUUUUUMBLE
HOW DARE YOU!

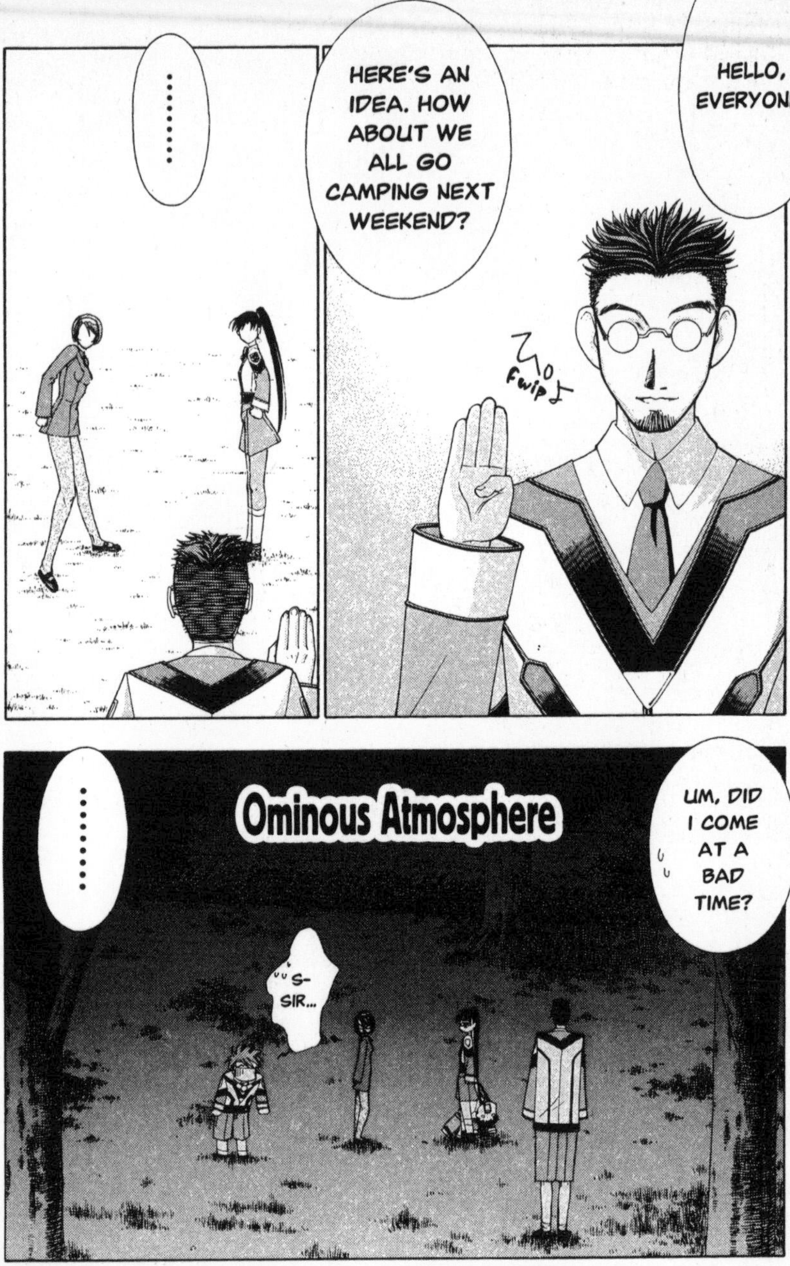
HELLO, EVERYONE.
HERE'S AN IDEA. HOW ABOUT WE ALL GO CAMPING NEXT WEEKEND?
Fwip
....
UM, DID I COME AT A BAD TIME?
Ominous Atmosphere
....
S-SIR...

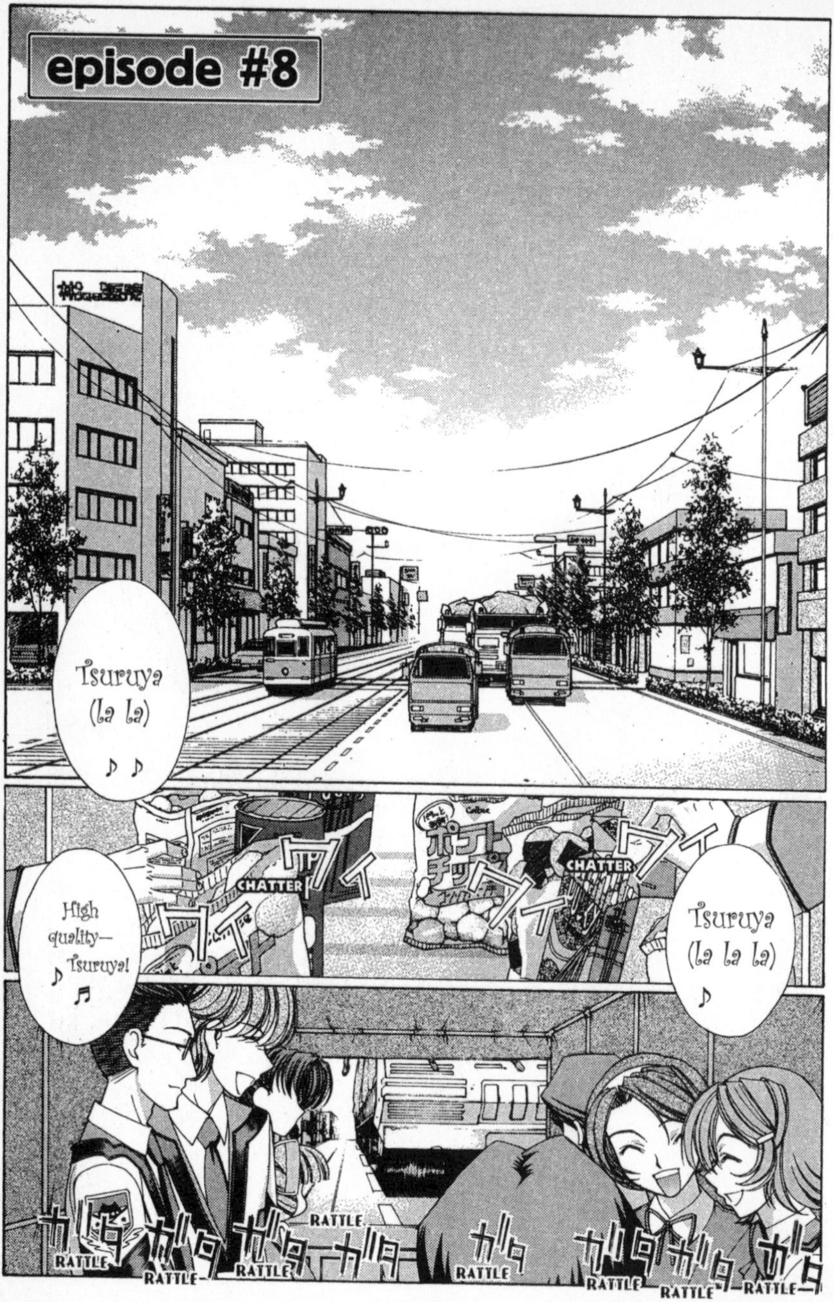
episode #8
Tsuruya (la la) ♪ ♪
Tsuruya (la la la) ♪
CHATTER
CHATTER
High quality— Tsuruya! ♪ ♬
RATTLE RATTLE RATTLE
RATTLE
RATTLE RATTLE RATTLE RATTLE RATTLE

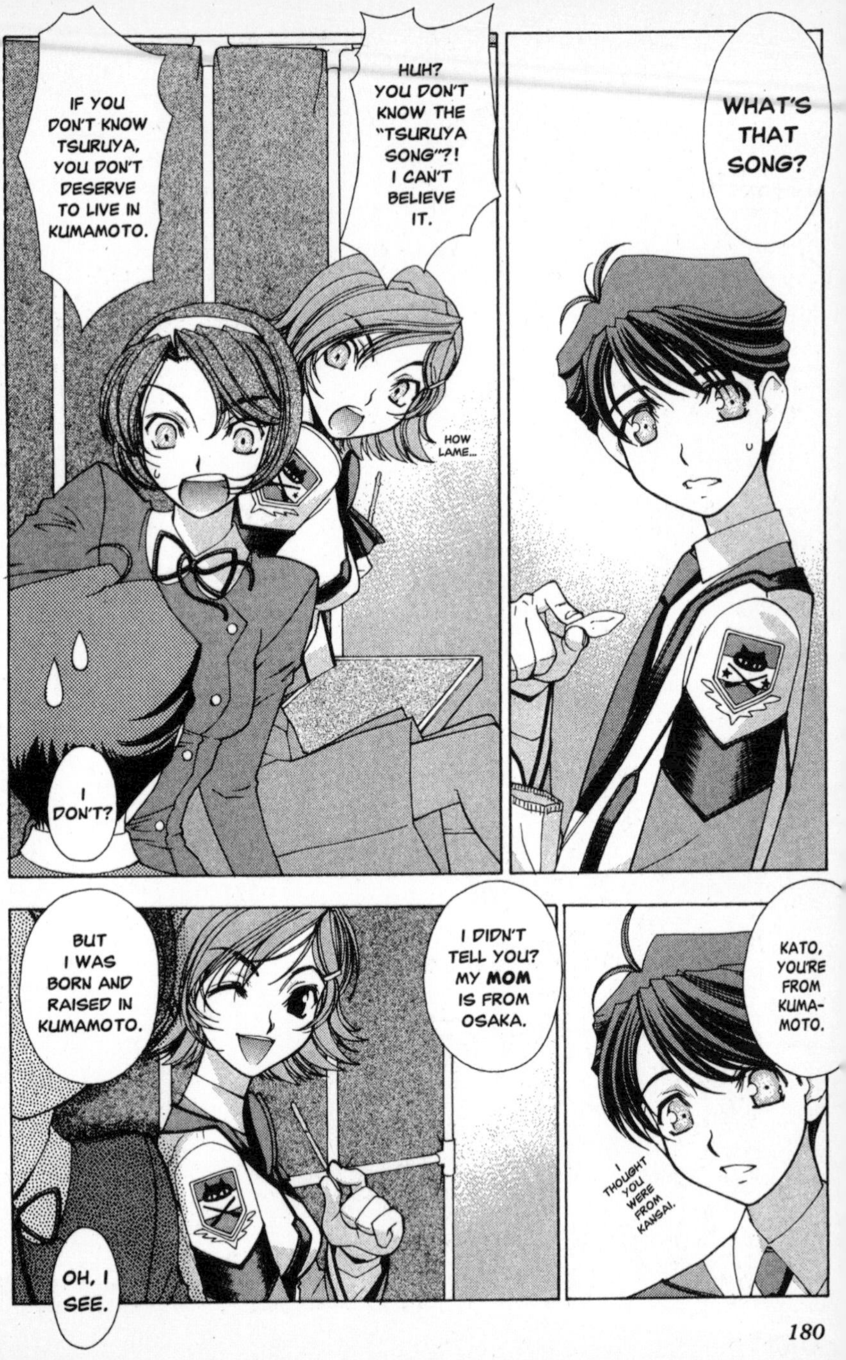
WHAT'S THAT SONG?
HUH? YOU DON'T KNOW THE "TSURUYA SONG"?! I CAN'T BELIEVE IT.
IF YOU DON'T KNOW TSURUYA, YOU DON'T DESERVE TO LIVE IN KUMAMOTO.
HOW LAME...
I DON'T?
KATO, YOU'RE FROM KUMA-MOTO.
I THOUGHT YOU WERE FROM KANSAI.
I DIDN'T TELL YOU? MY **MOM** IS FROM OSAKA.
BUT I WAS BORN AND RAISED IN KUMAMOTO.
OH, I SEE.

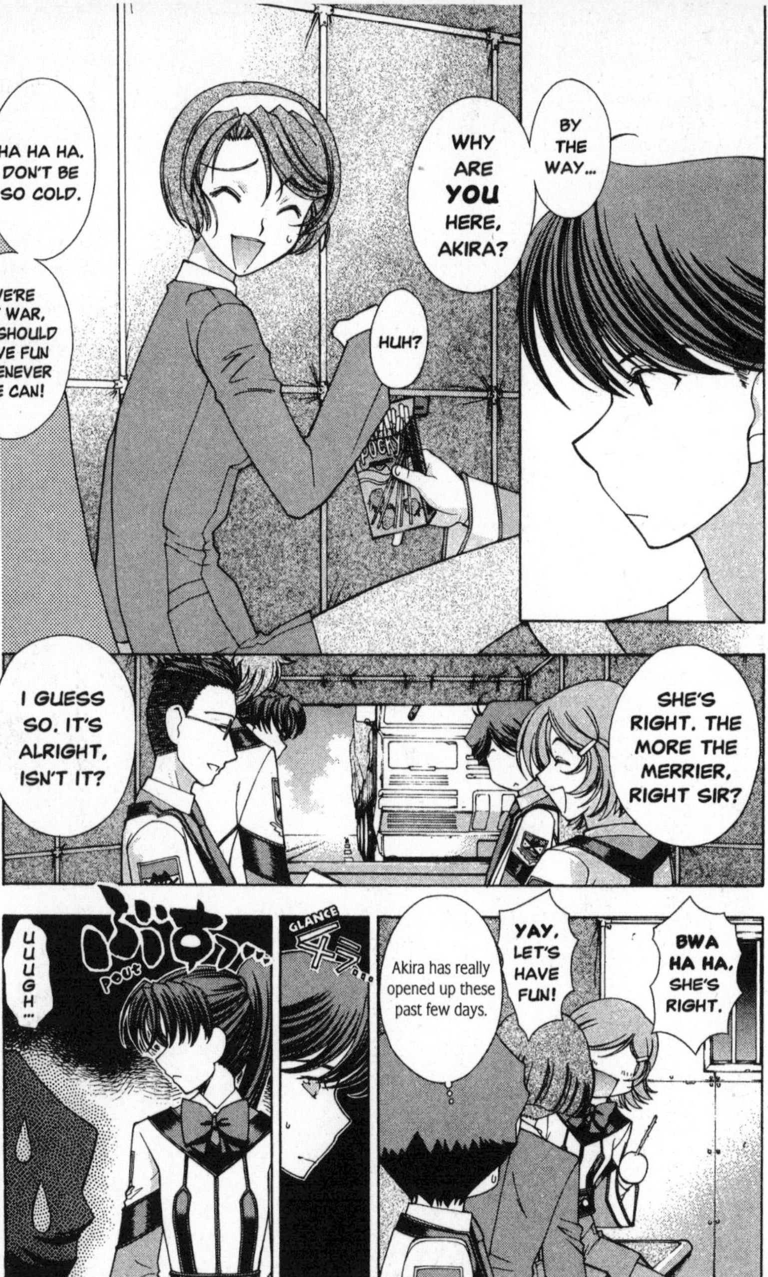
BY THE WAY...
WHY ARE YOU HERE, AKIRA?
HUH?
HA HA HA. DON'T BE SO COLD.
WE'RE AT WAR, WE SHOULD HAVE FUN WHENEVER ♥ WE CAN!
SHE'S RIGHT. THE MORE THE MERRIER, RIGHT SIR?
I GUESS SO. IT'S ALRIGHT, ISN'T IT?
BWA HA HA, SHE'S RIGHT.
YAY, LET'S HAVE FUN!
Akira has really opened up these past few days.
GLANCE
pout
UUUGH...

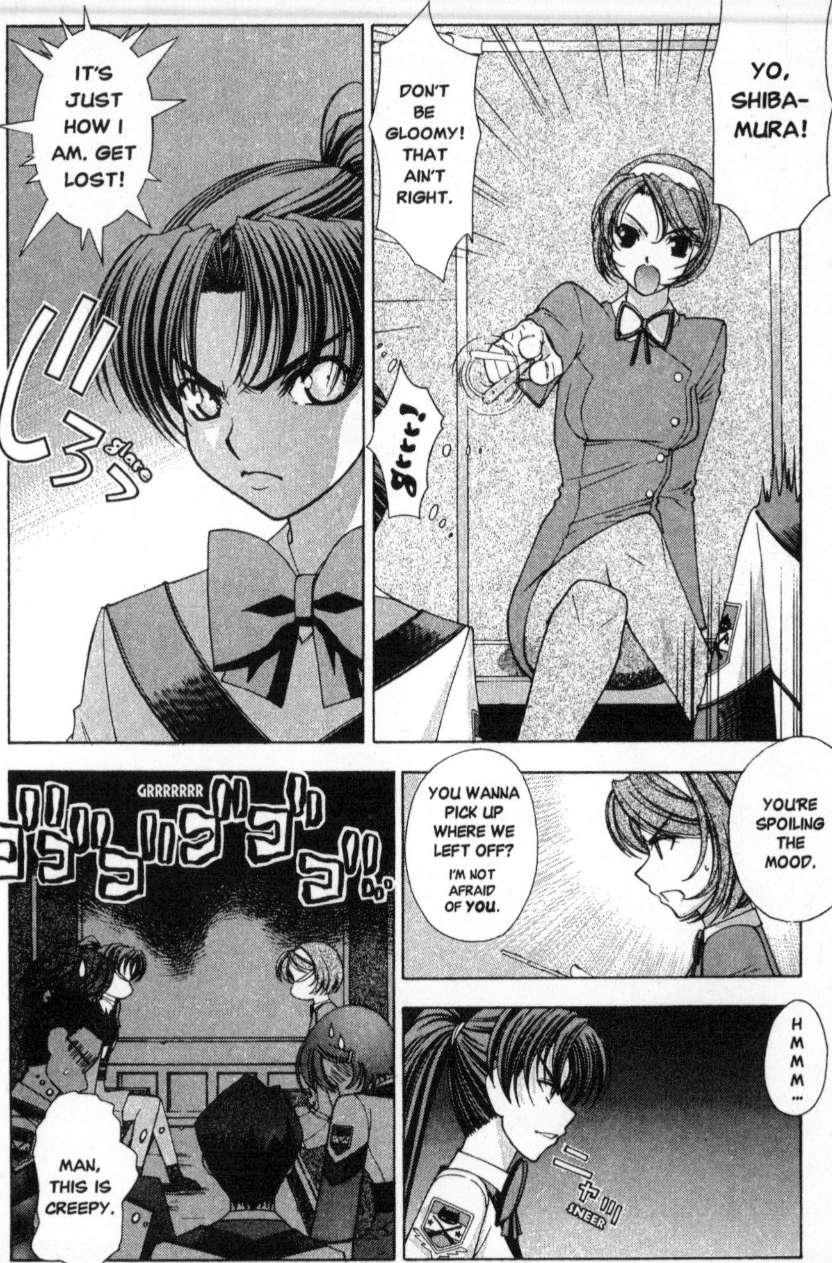
YO, SHIBA-MURA!
DON'T BE GLOOMY! THAT AIN'T RIGHT.
IT'S JUST HOW I AM. GET LOST!
glare
YOU'RE SPOILING THE MOOD.
YOU WANNA PICK UP WHERE WE LEFT OFF? I'M NOT AFRAID OF YOU.
GRRRRRRR
HMMM...
SNEER
MAN, THIS IS CREEPY.

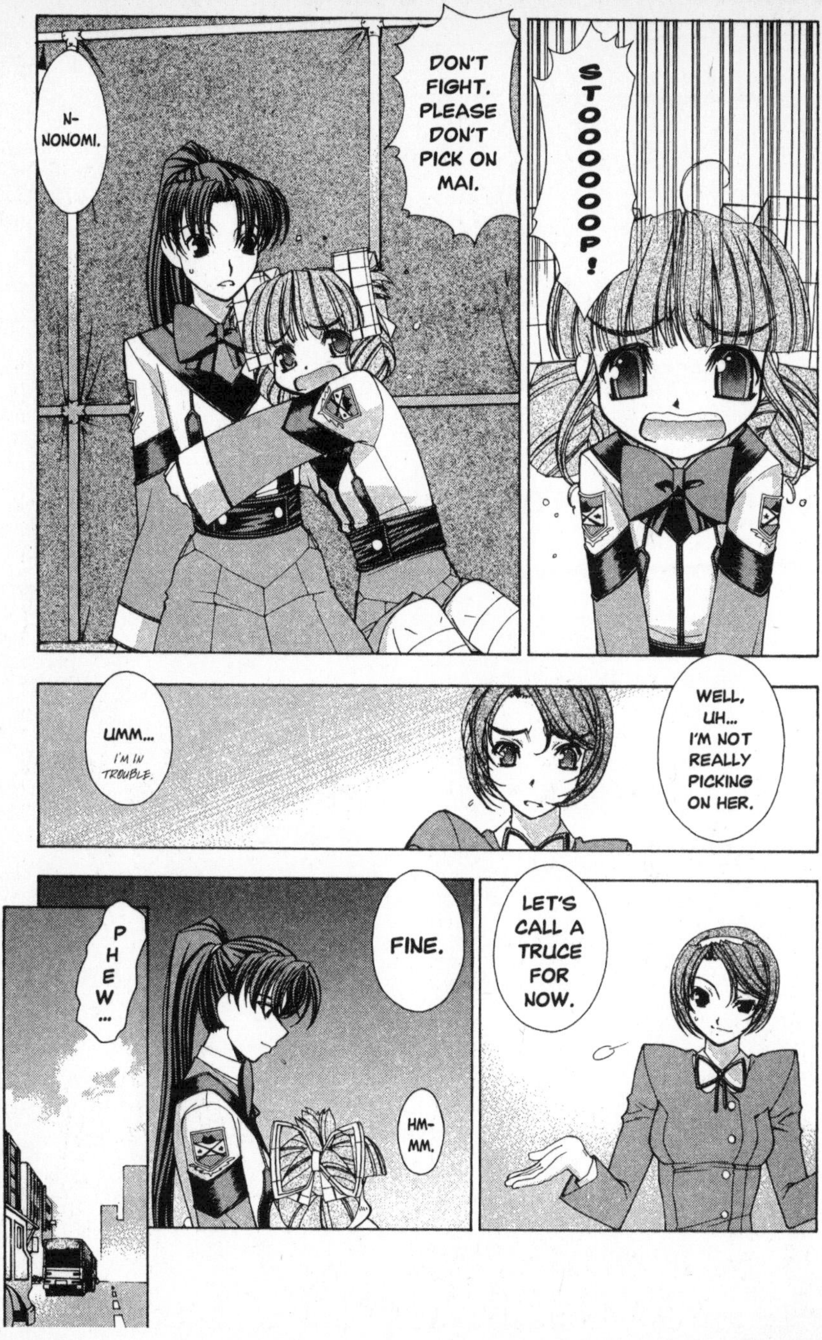
STOOOOOOP!
DON'T FIGHT. PLEASE DON'T PICK ON MAI.
N-NONOMI.
WELL, UH... I'M NOT REALLY PICKING ON HER.
UMM...
I'M IN TROUBLE.
LET'S CALL A TRUCE FOR NOW.
FINE.
HM-MM.
PHEW...

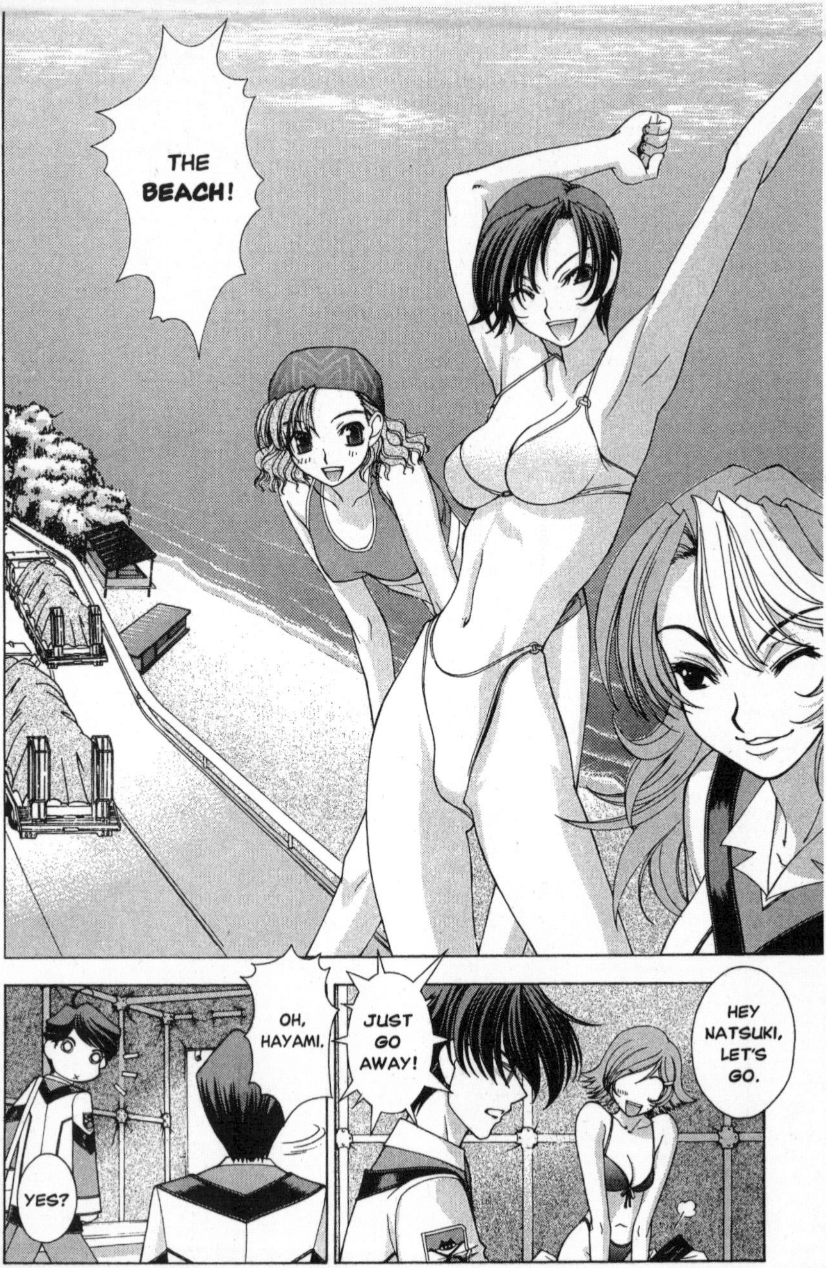
THE BEACH!
HEY NATSUKI, LET'S GO.
JUST GO AWAY!
OH, HAYAMI.
YES?

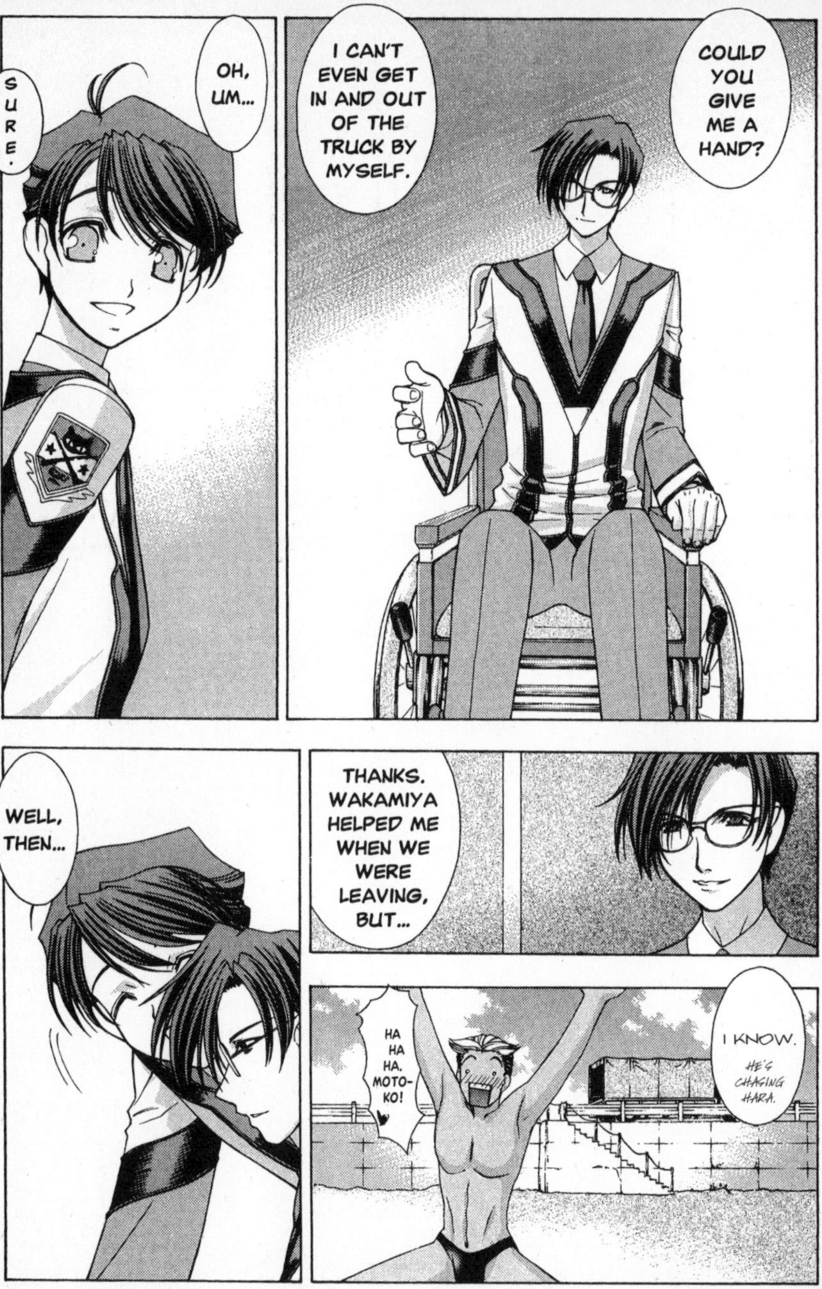
COULD YOU GIVE ME A HAND?
I CAN'T EVEN GET IN AND OUT OF THE TRUCK BY MYSELF.
OH, UM...
SURE.
THANKS. WAKAMIYA HELPED ME WHEN WE WERE LEAVING, BUT...
WELL, THEN...
I KNOW.
HE'S CHASING HARA.
HA HA HA. MOTOKO!

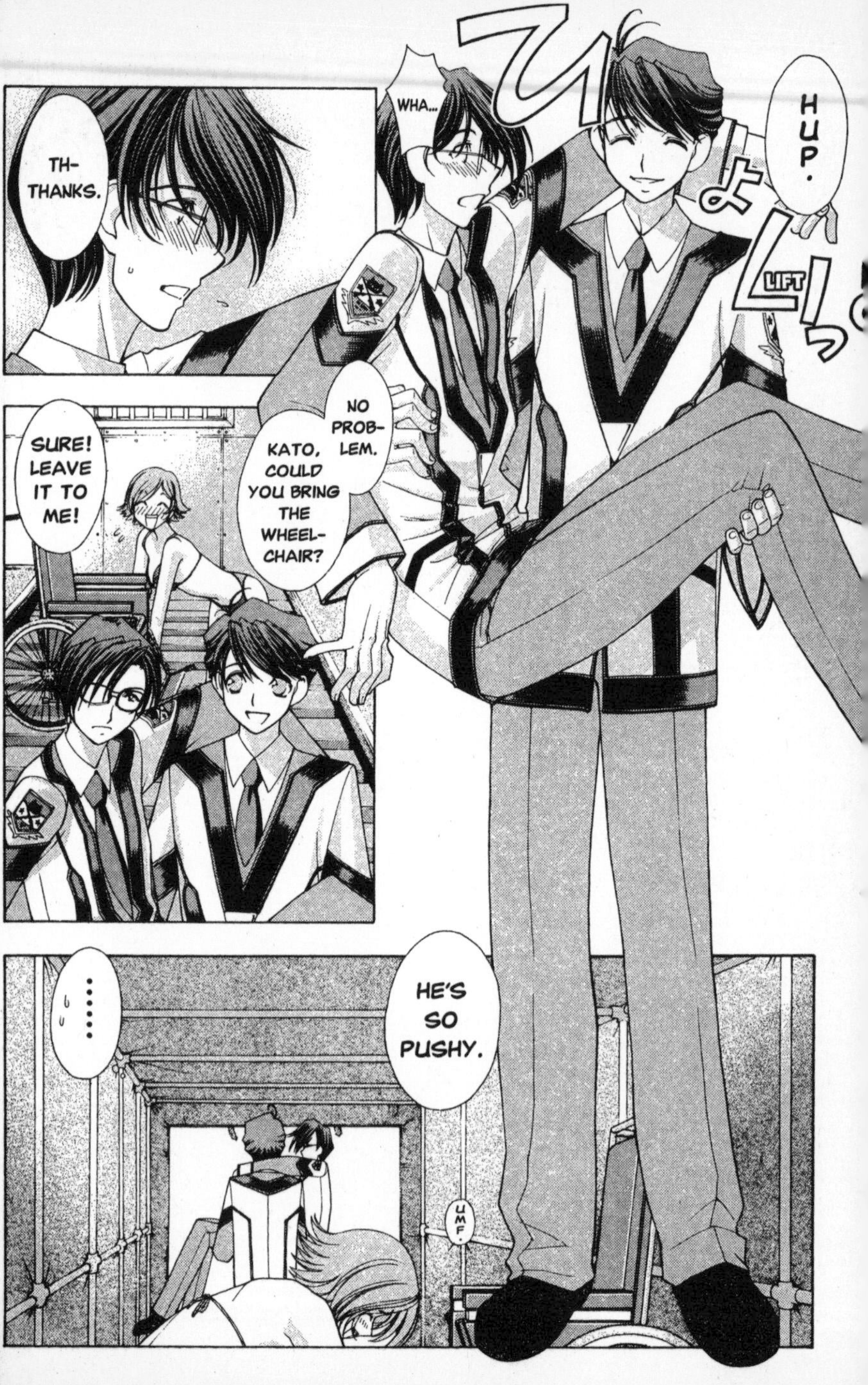
HUP.
LIFT
WHA...
TH-THANKS.
NO PROB-LEM.
KATO, COULD YOU BRING THE WHEEL-CHAIR?
SURE! LEAVE IT TO ME!
HE'S SO PUSHY.
......
UMF.

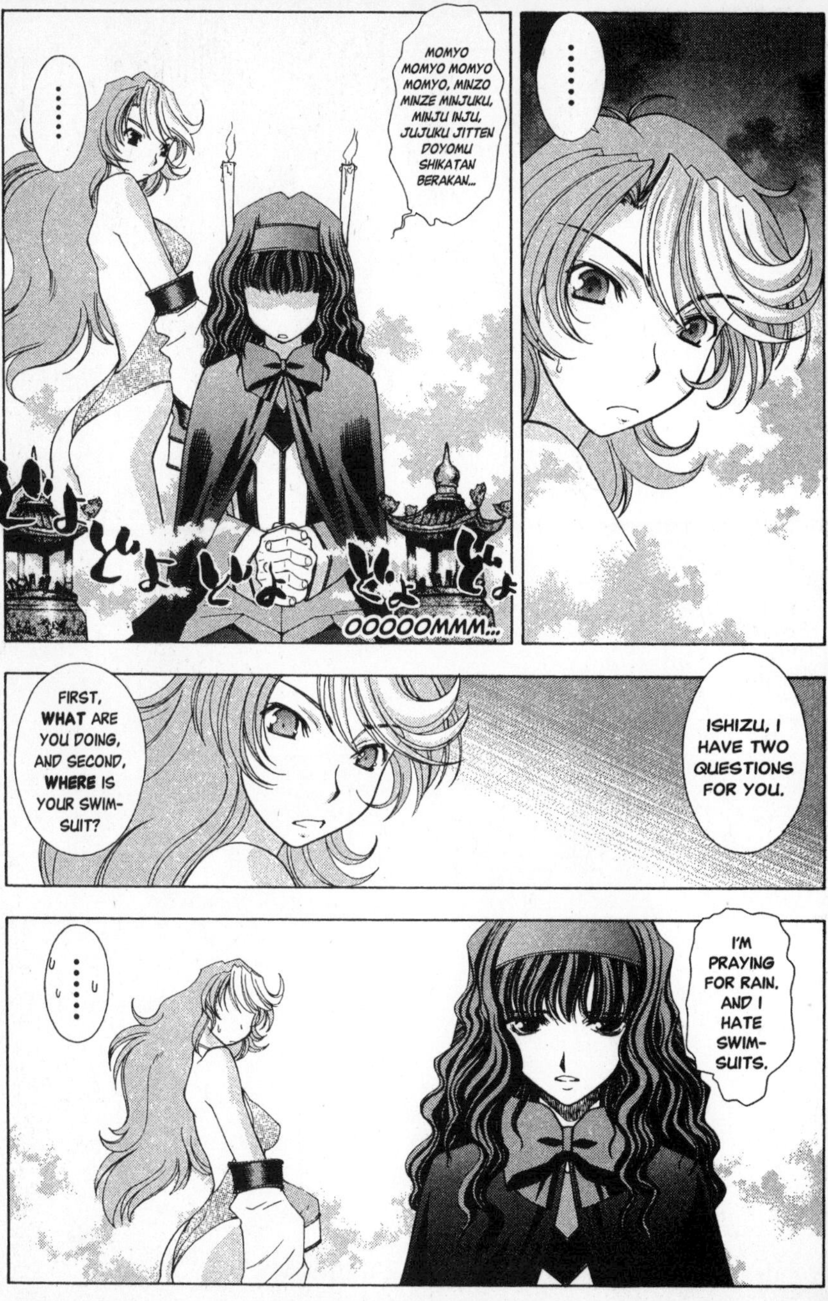
......
MOMYO MOMYO MOMYO MOMYO, MINZO MINZE MINJUKU, MINJU INJU, JUJUKU JITTEN DOYOMU SHIKATAN BERAKAN...
......
OOOOOMMM...
ISHIZU, I HAVE TWO QUESTIONS FOR YOU.
FIRST, WHAT ARE YOU DOING, AND SECOND, WHERE IS YOUR SWIM-SUIT?
I'M PRAYING FOR RAIN. AND I HATE SWIM-SUITS.
......

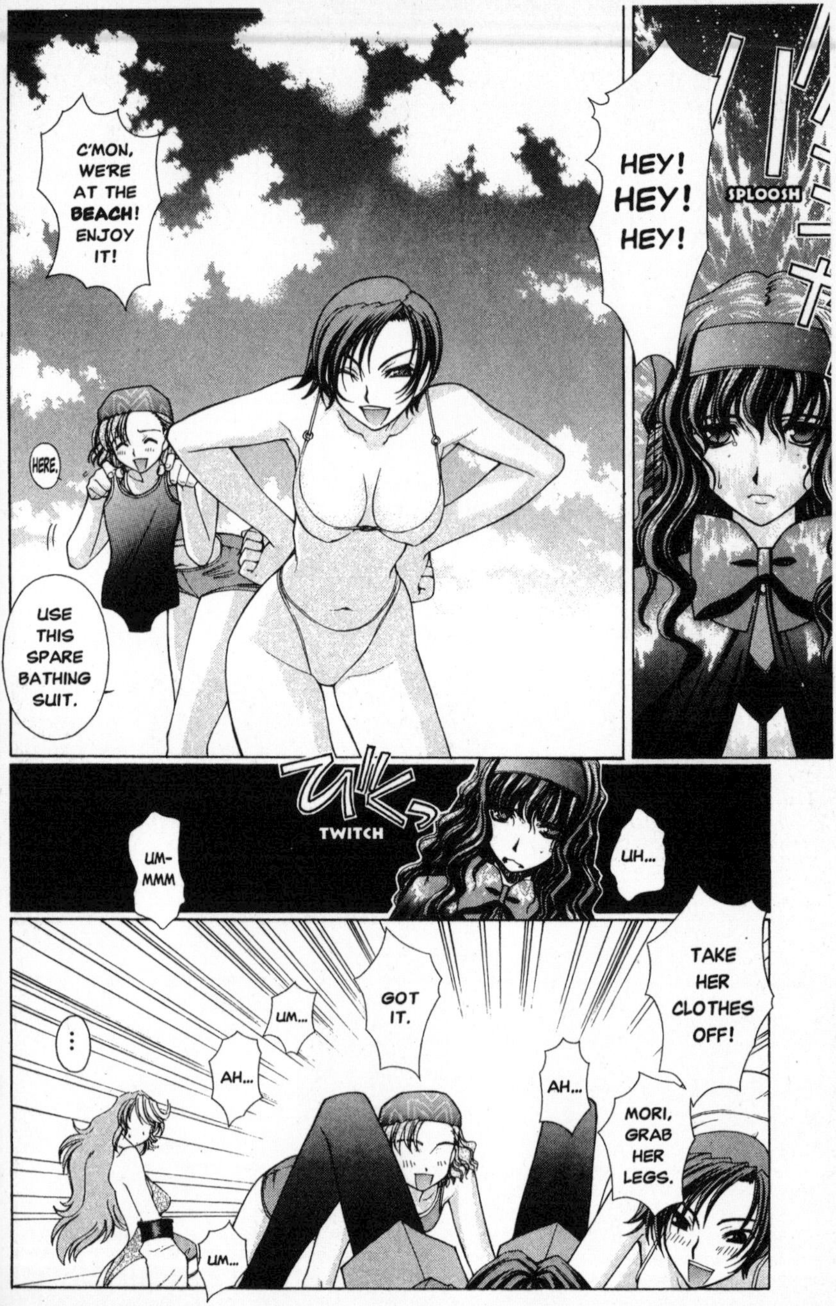

SPLOOSH
HEY! HEY! HEY!
C'MON, WE'RE AT THE BEACH! ENJOY IT!
HERE.
USE THIS SPARE BATHING SUIT.
UH...
TWITCH
UM-MMM
TAKE HER CLOTHES OFF!
GOT IT.
UM...
...
AH...
AH...
MORI, GRAB HER LEGS.
UM...

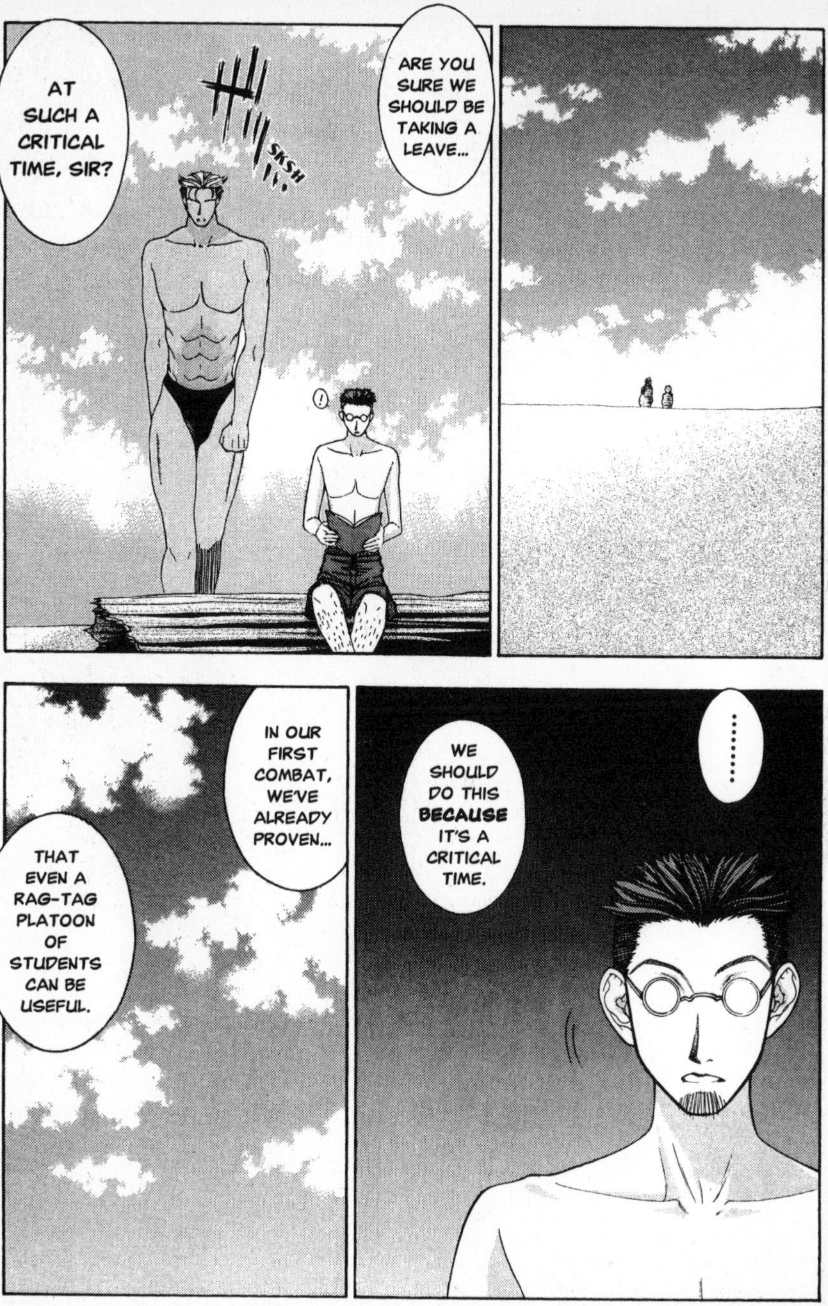
ARE YOU SURE WE SHOULD BE TAKING A LEAVE...
AT SUCH A CRITICAL TIME, SIR?
SKSH
!
......
WE SHOULD DO THIS **BECAUSE** IT'S A CRITICAL TIME.
IN OUR FIRST COMBAT, WE'VE ALREADY PROVEN...
THAT EVEN A RAG-TAG PLATOON OF STUDENTS CAN BE USEFUL.

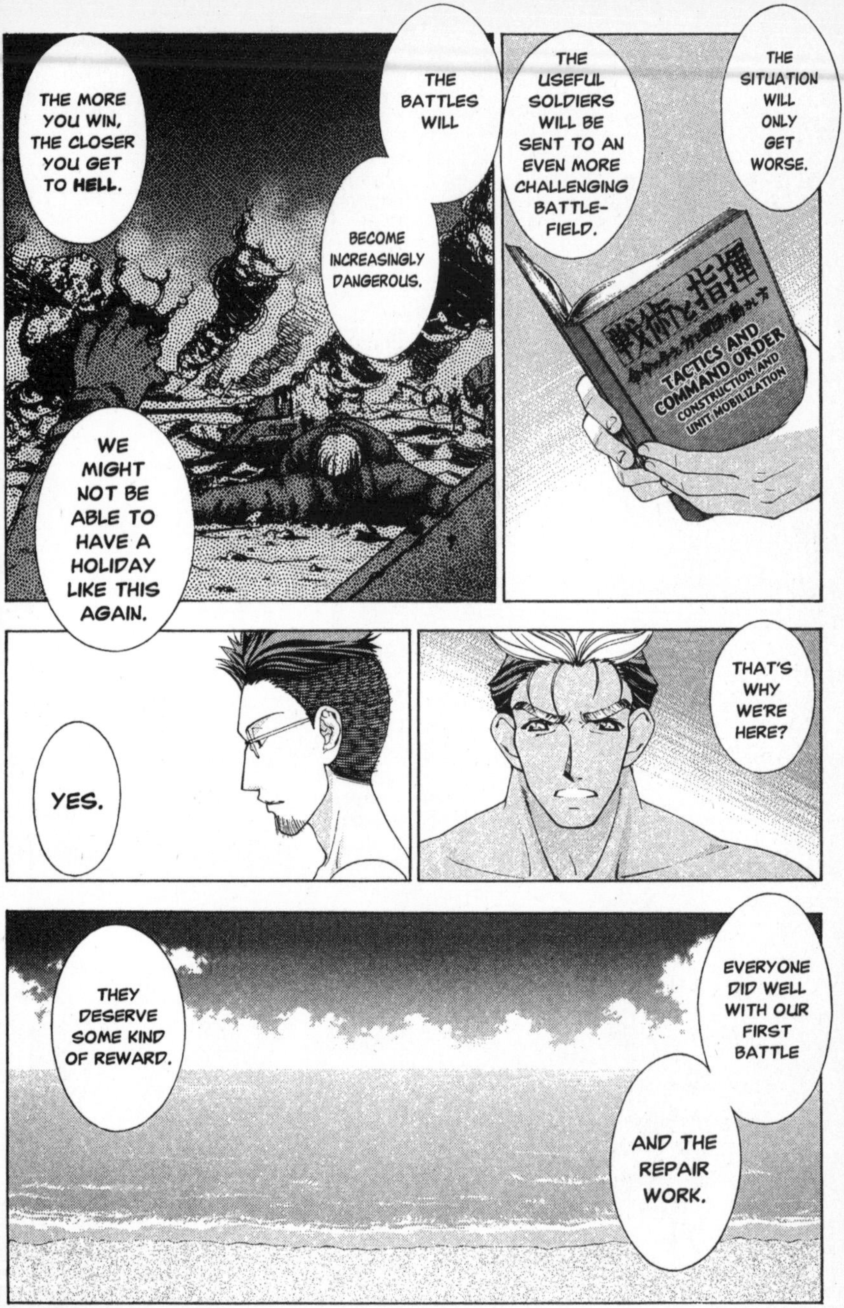
THE SITUATION WILL ONLY GET WORSE.
THE USEFUL SOLDIERS WILL BE SENT TO AN EVEN MORE CHALLENGING BATTLE-FIELD.
戦術と指揮
TACTICS AND COMMAND ORDER
CONSTRUCTION AND UNIT MOBILIZATION
THE BATTLES WILL
BECOME INCREASINGLY DANGEROUS.
THE MORE YOU WIN, THE CLOSER YOU GET TO **HELL**.
WE MIGHT NOT BE ABLE TO HAVE A HOLIDAY LIKE THIS AGAIN.
THAT'S WHY WE'RE HERE?
YES.
EVERYONE DID WELL WITH OUR FIRST BATTLE
AND THE REPAIR WORK.
THEY DESERVE SOME KIND OF REWARD.

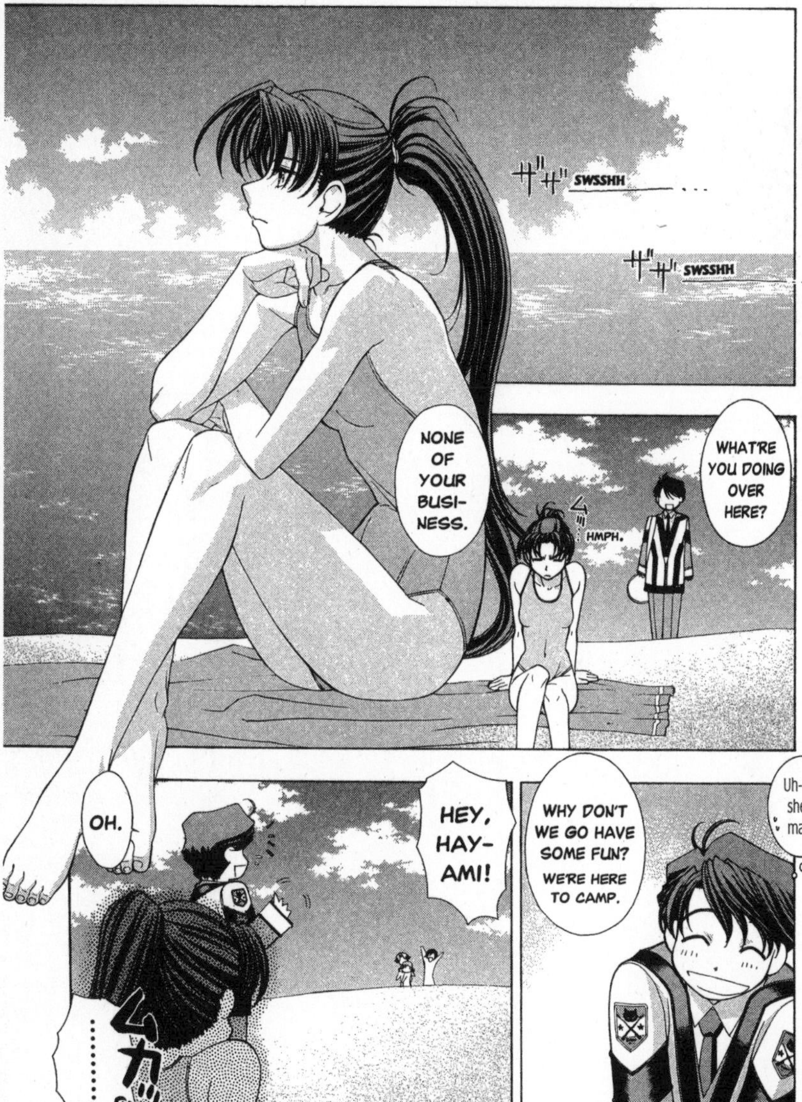
ザザ SWSSHH...
ザザ SWSSHH...
WHAT'RE YOU DOING OVER HERE?
ム HMPH.
NONE OF YOUR BUSI- NESS.
Uh-oh, she's mad.
WHY DON'T WE GO HAVE SOME FUN? WE'RE HERE TO CAMP.
HEY, HAY- AMI!
OH.
ムカッ GRRR
......

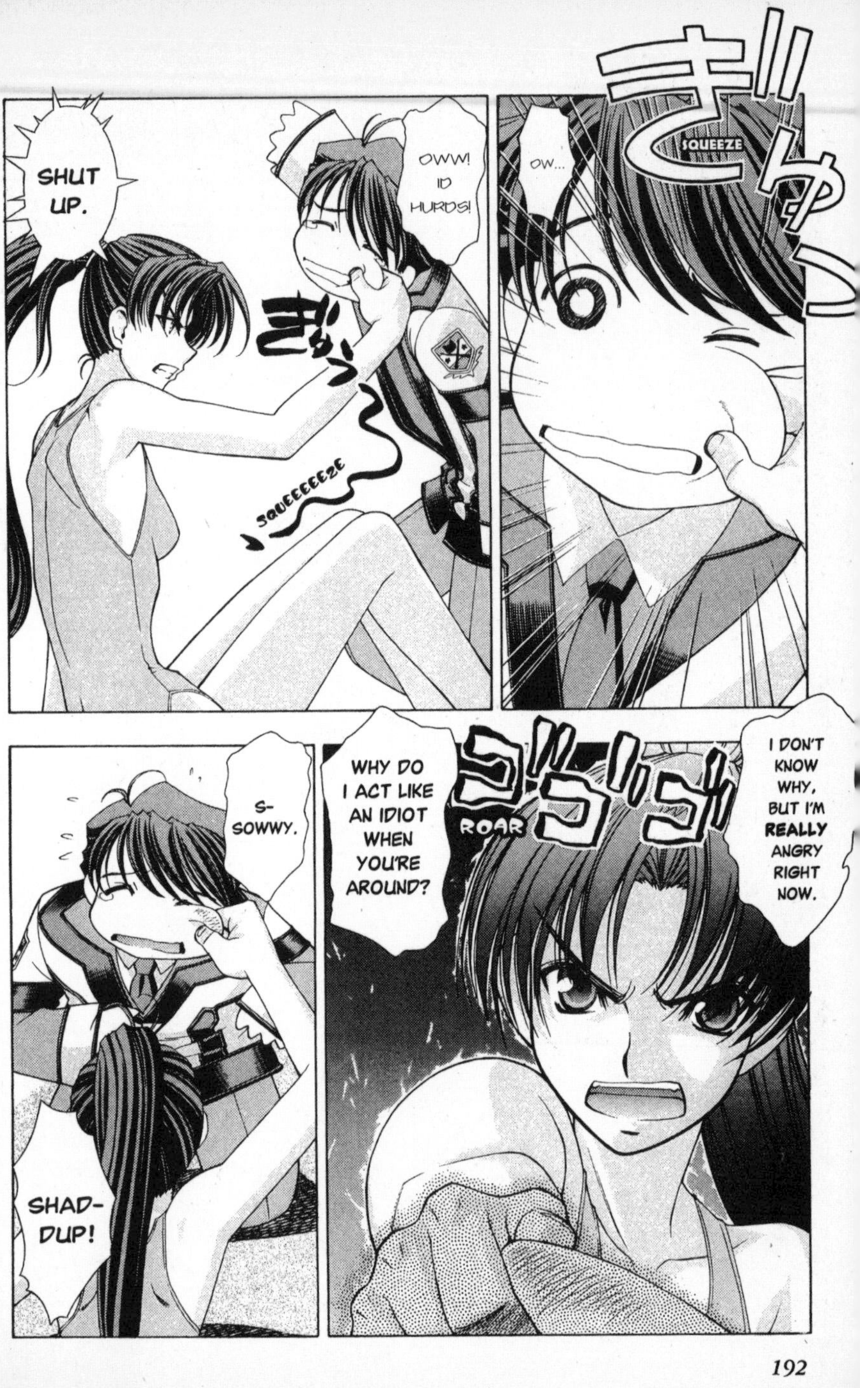
SQUEEZE
OW...
OWW! ID HURDS!
SQUEEEEEEZE
SHUT UP.
I DON'T KNOW WHY, BUT I'M REALLY ANGRY RIGHT NOW.
ROAR
WHY DO I ACT LIKE AN IDIOT WHEN YOU'RE AROUND?
S-SOWWY.
SHAD-DUP!

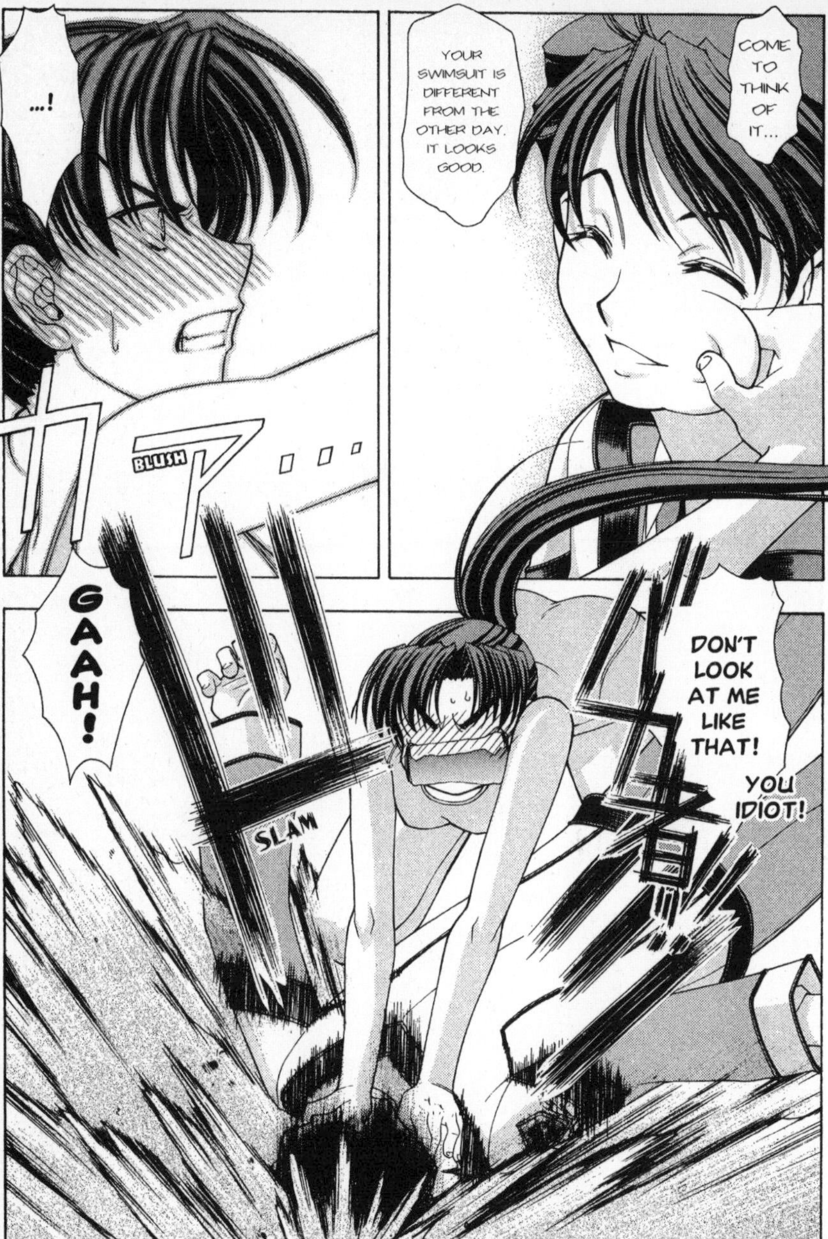

COME TO THINK OF IT...
YOUR SWIMSUIT IS DIFFERENT FROM THE OTHER DAY. IT LOOKS GOOD.
...!
BLUSH
DON'T LOOK AT ME LIKE THAT!
YOU IDIOT!
GAAH!
SLAM

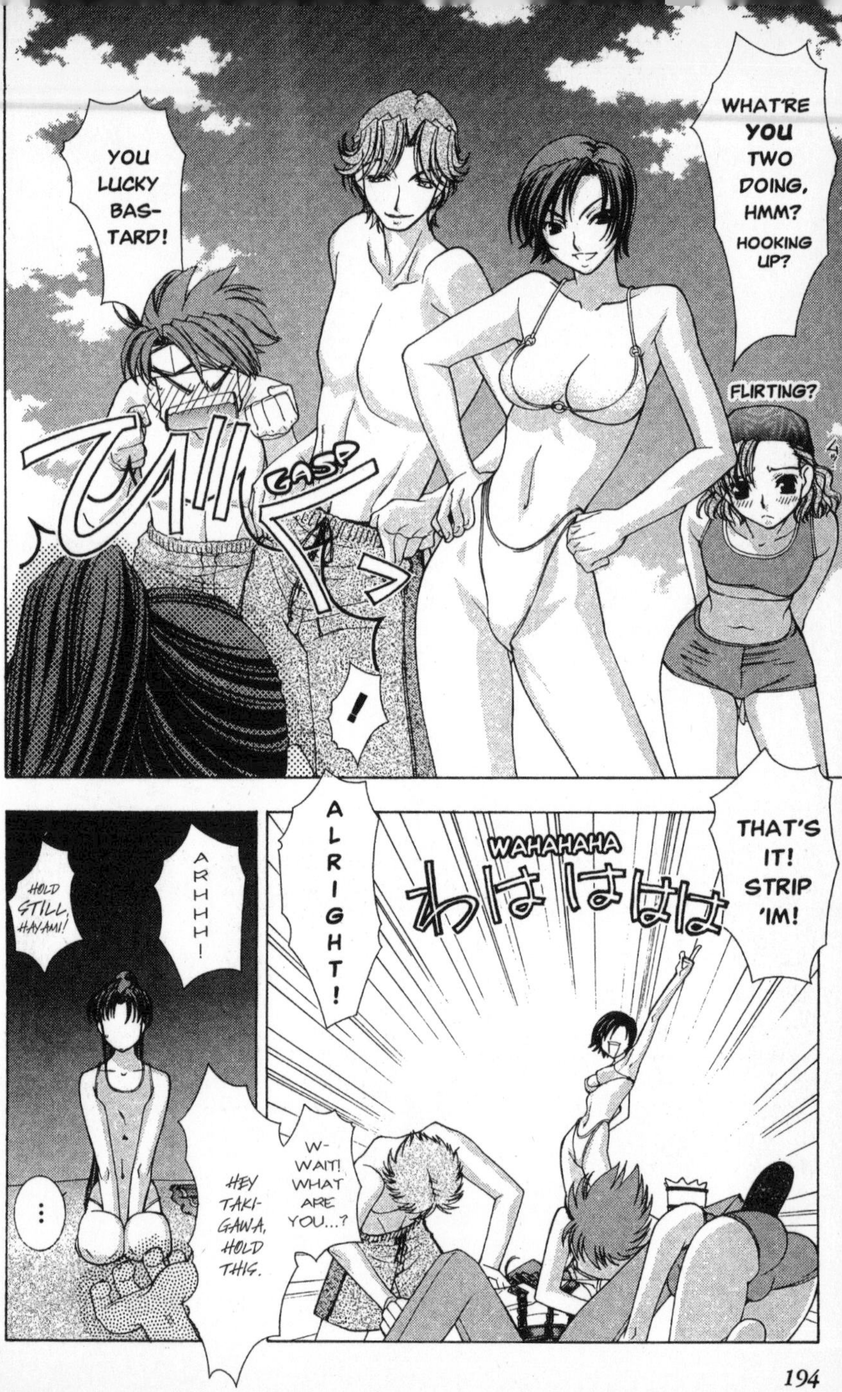
WHAT'RE YOU TWO DOING, HMM? HOOKING UP?
FLIRTING?
YOU LUCKY BAS-TARD!
GASP
!
THAT'S IT! STRIP 'IM!
WAHAHAHA
わはははは
ALRIGHT!
W-WAIT! WHAT ARE YOU...?
HEY TAKI-GAWA, HOLD THIS.
ARHHH!
HOLD STILL, HAYAMI!
...

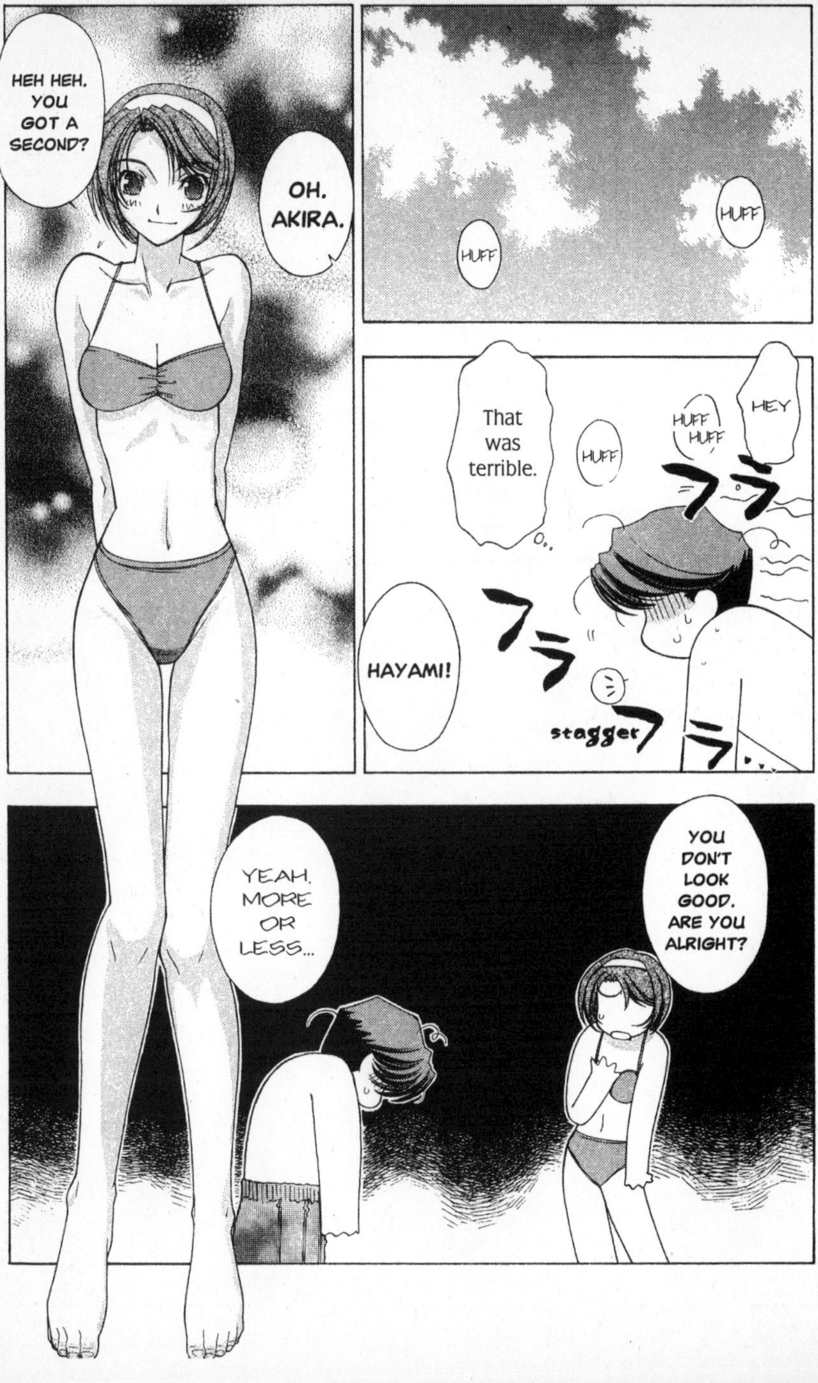
HUFF
HUFF
HEY
HUFF HUFF
HUFF
That was terrible.
HAYAMI!
フラフラ
フラ
stagger フラ
YOU DON'T LOOK GOOD. ARE YOU ALRIGHT?
YEAH, MORE OR LESS...
HEH HEH. YOU GOT A SECOND?
OH. AKIRA.

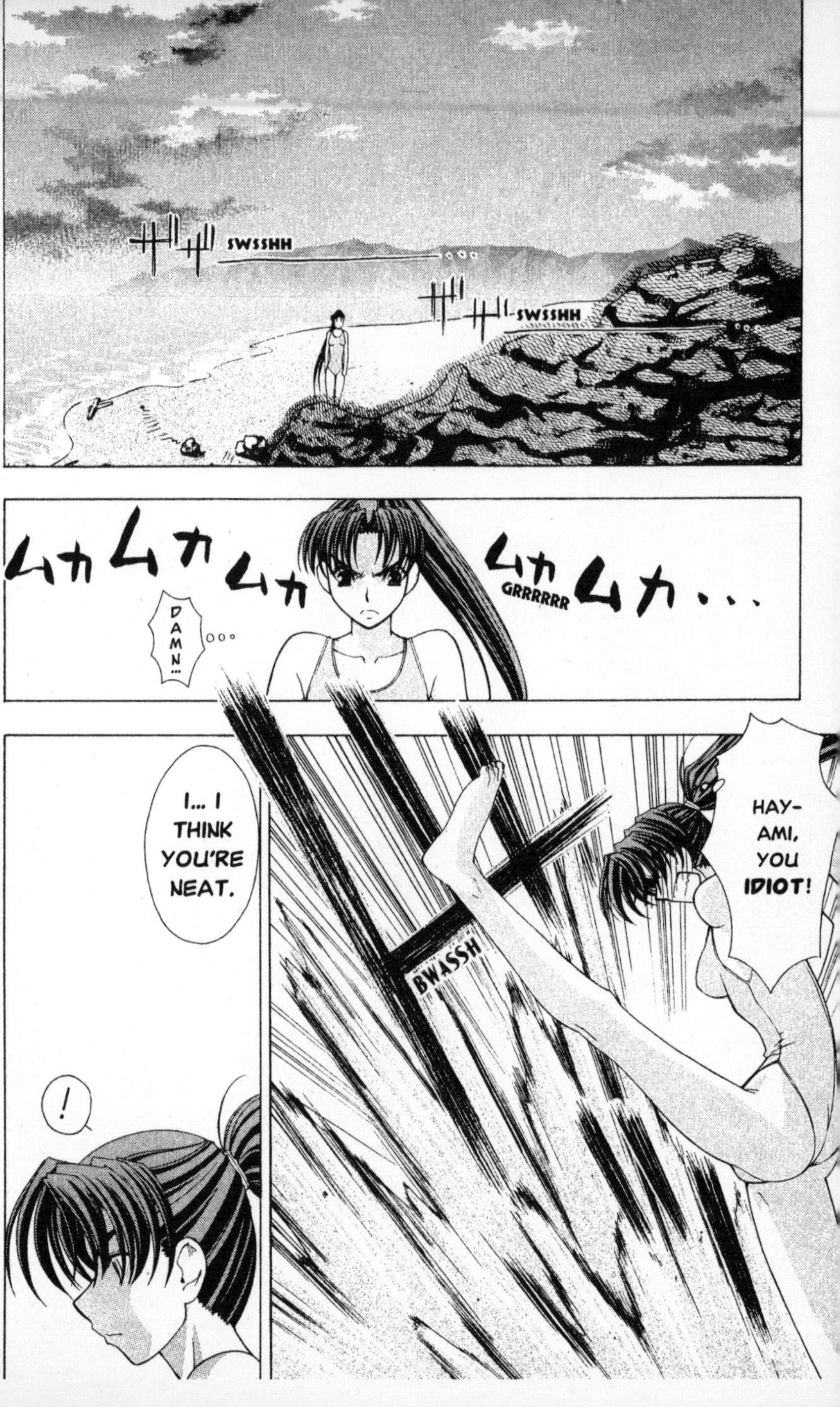
SWSSHH
SWSSHH
ムカムカムカ
ムカムカ…
GRRRRRR
DAMN…
HAY-AMI, YOU IDIOT!
BWASSH
I… I THINK YOU'RE NEAT.
!

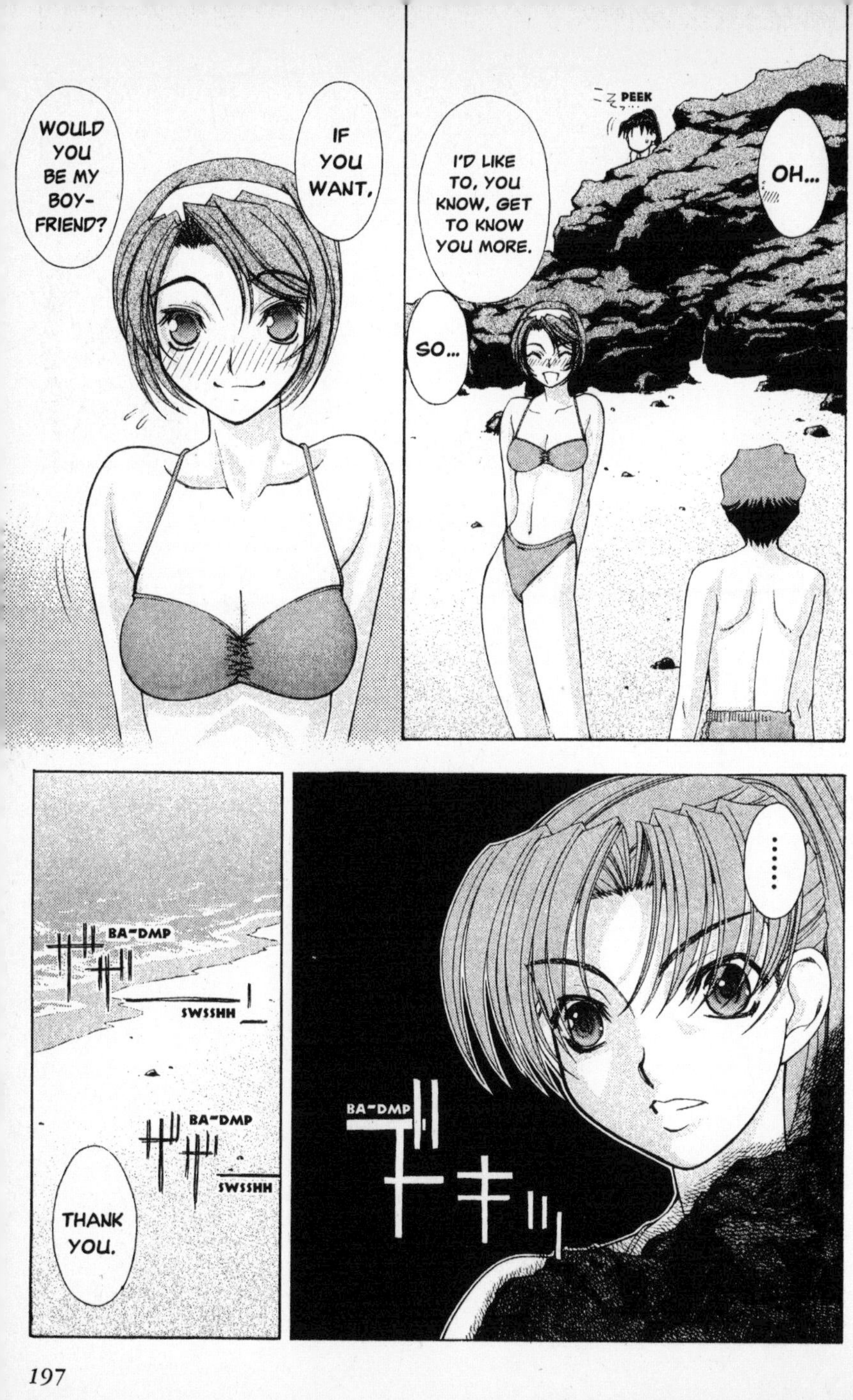
PEEK
OH...
I'D LIKE TO, YOU KNOW, GET TO KNOW YOU MORE.
SO...
IF YOU WANT,
WOULD YOU BE MY BOY-FRIEND?
......
BA-DMP
BA-DMP
SWSSHH
BA-DMP
SWSSHH
THANK YOU.

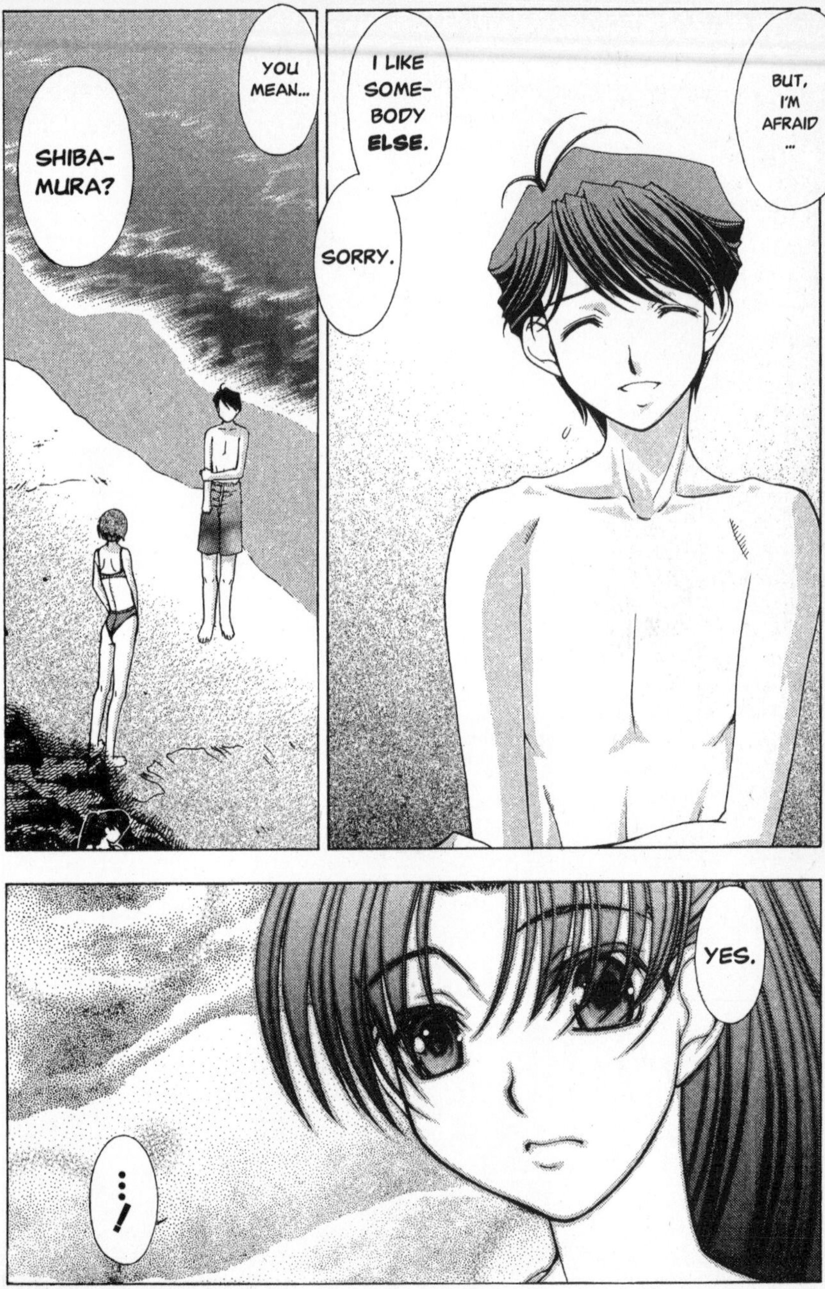
BUT, I'M AFRAID ...
I LIKE SOME-BODY ELSE.
SORRY.
YOU MEAN...
SHIBA-MURA?
YES.
...!

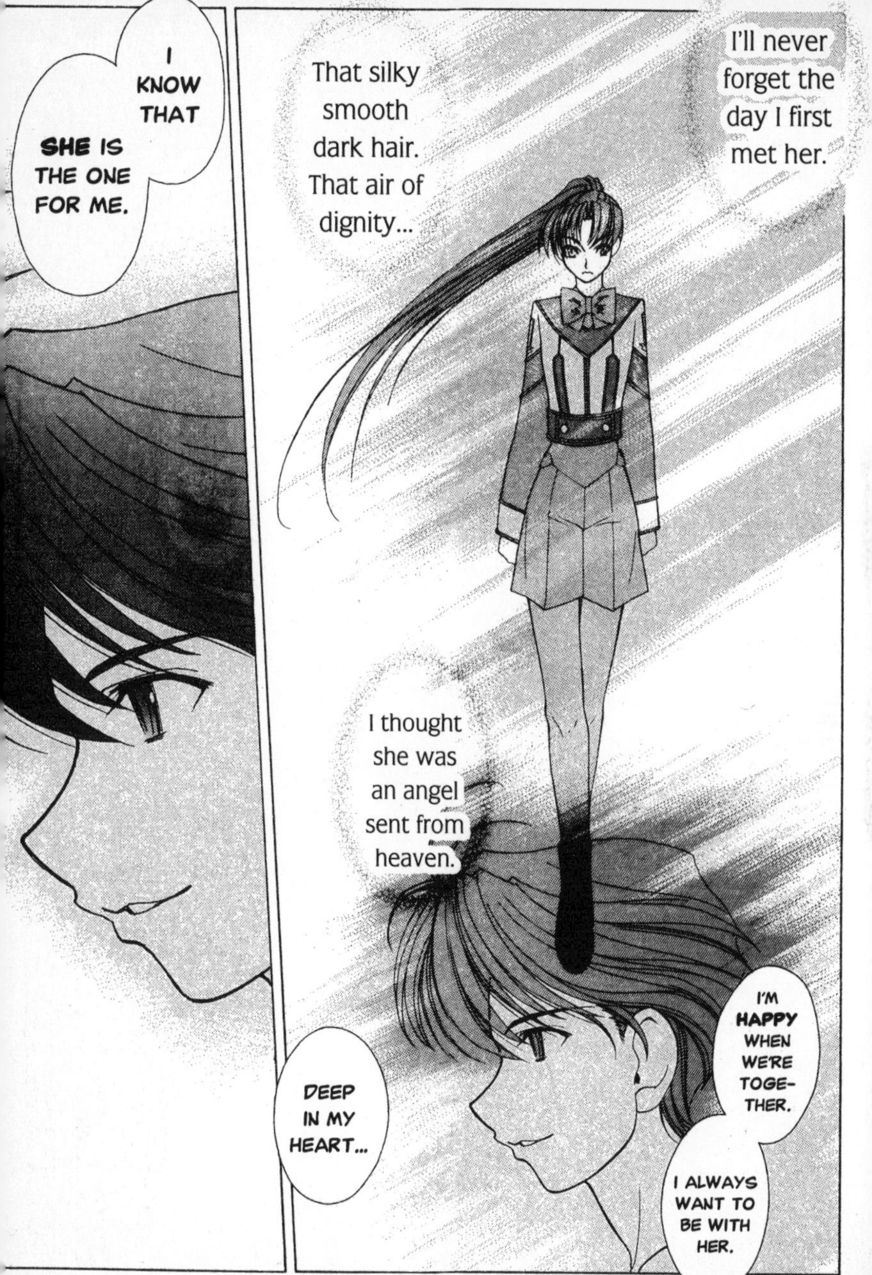
I'll never forget the day I first met her.
That silky smooth dark hair. That air of dignity...
I thought she was an angel sent from heaven.
I'M HAPPY WHEN WE'RE TOGE-THER.
I ALWAYS WANT TO BE WITH HER.
DEEP IN MY HEART...
I KNOW THAT SHE IS THE ONE FOR ME.

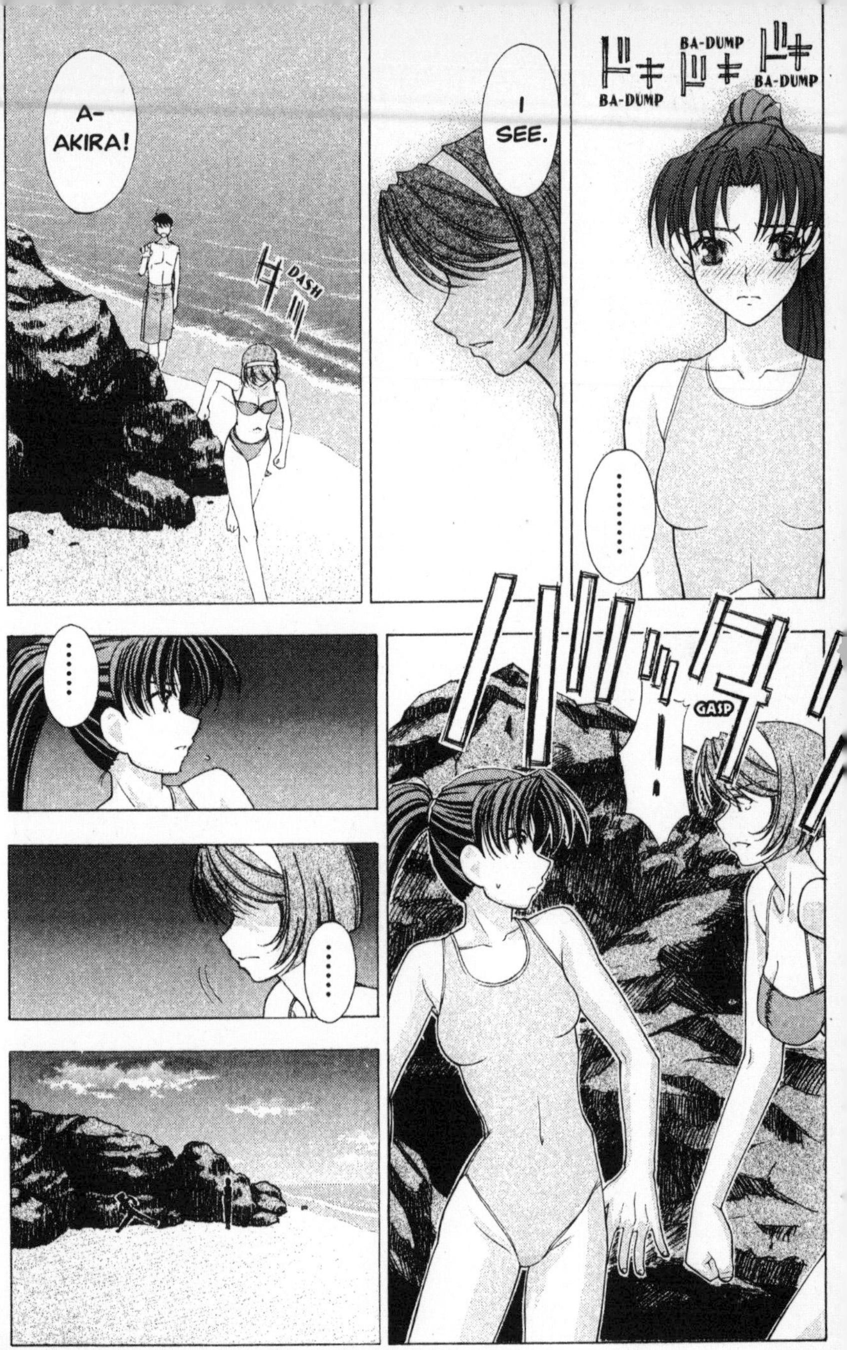
BA-DUMP
ドキ
BA-DUMP
ドキ
BA-DUMP
ドキ
……
I SEE.
A- AKIRA!
DASH
GASP
……
……

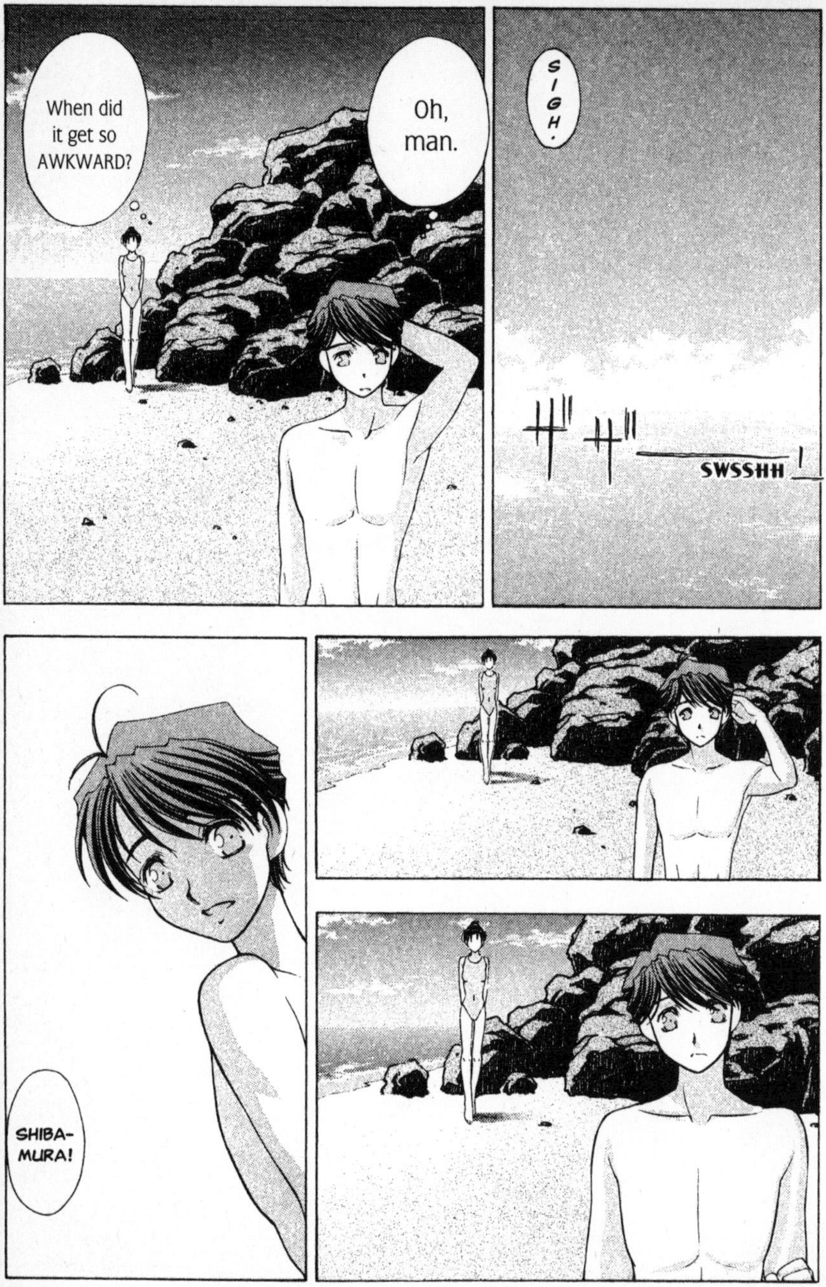
SIGH.
SWSSHH!
Oh, man.
When did it get so AWKWARD?
SHIBA-MURA!

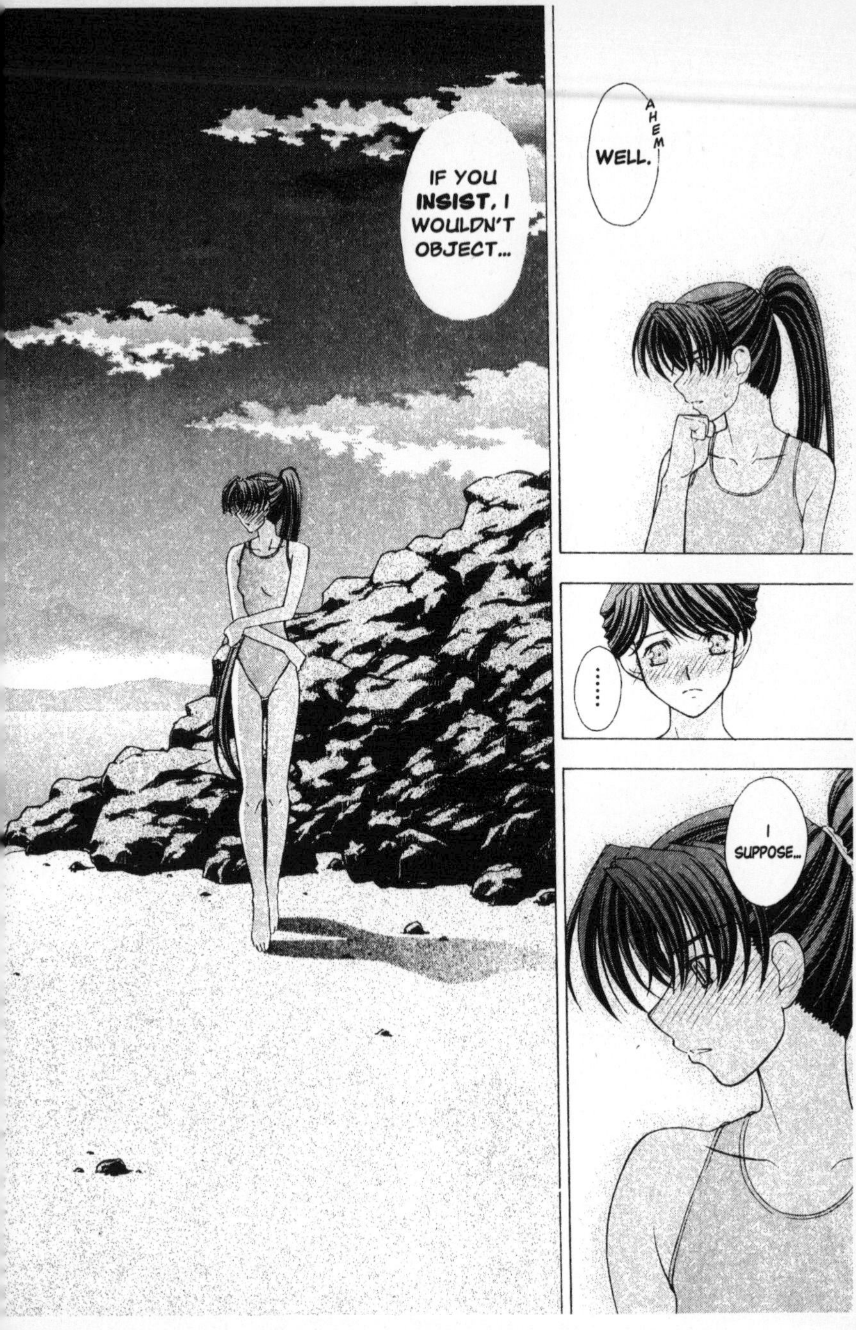
WELL.
AHEM
......
I SUPPOSE...
IF YOU INSIST, I WOULDN'T OBJECT...

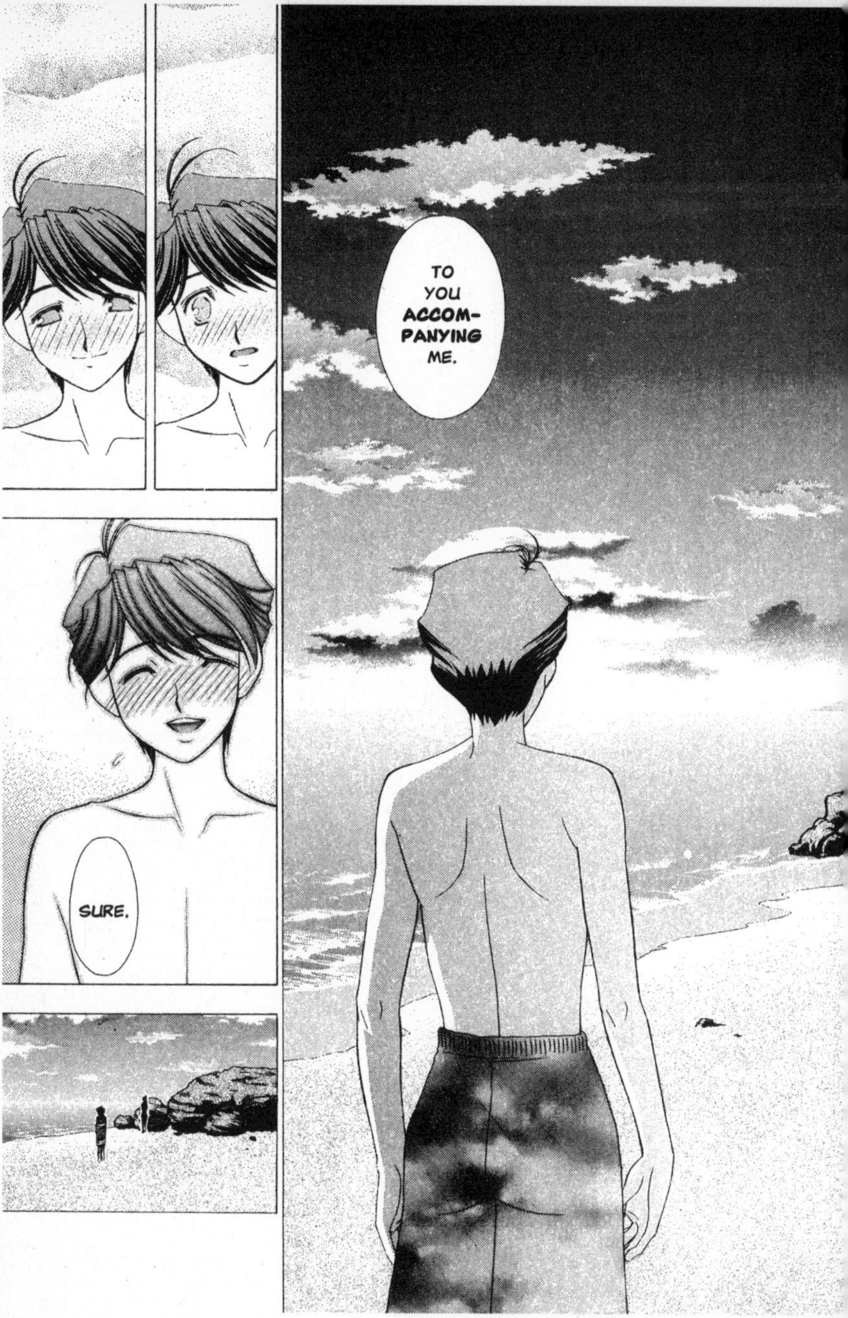
TO YOU ACCOMPANYING ME.
SURE.

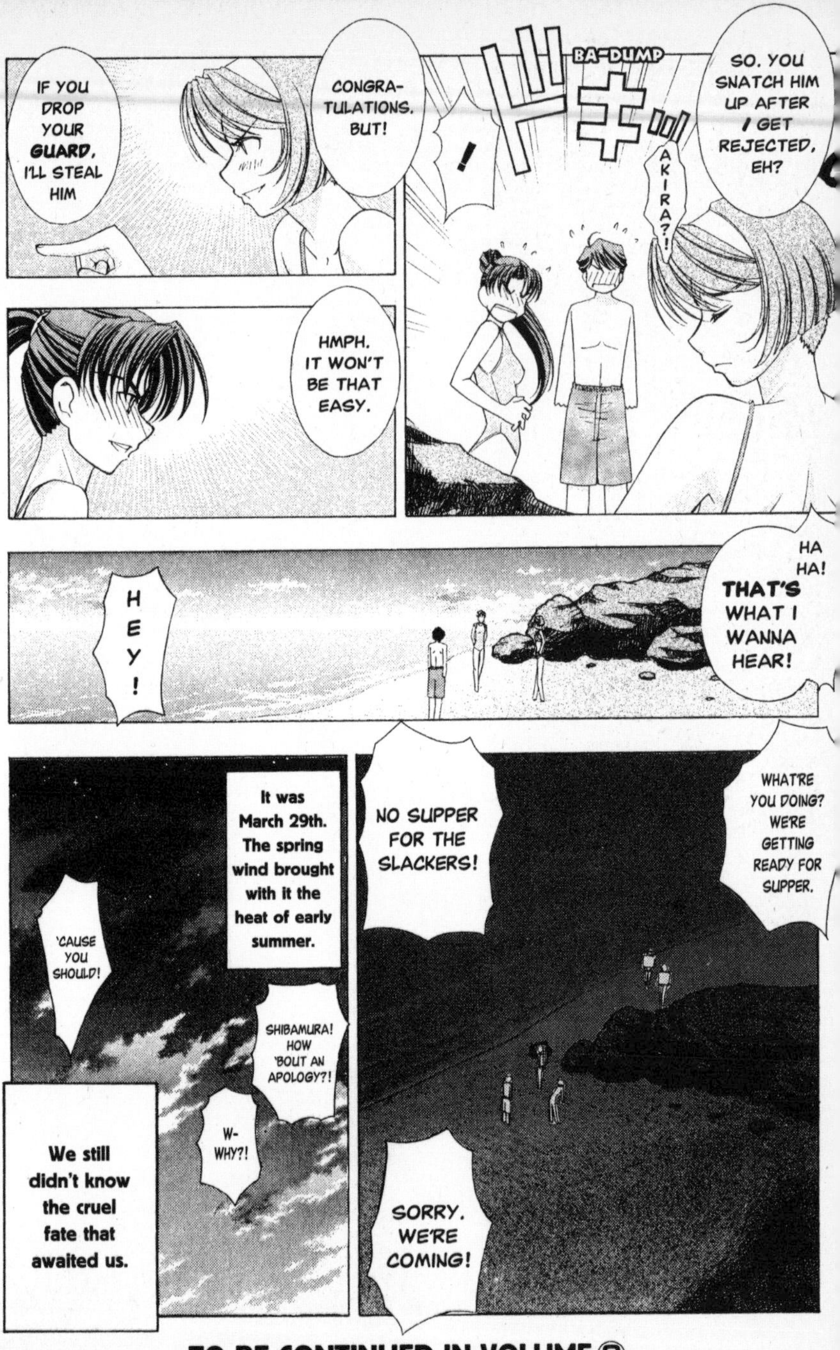

SO. YOU SNATCH HIM UP AFTER I GET REJECTED, EH?
BA-DUMP
AKIRA?!
!
CONGRA-TULATIONS. BUT!
IF YOU DROP YOUR GUARD, I'LL STEAL HIM
HMPH. IT WON'T BE THAT EASY.
HA HA!
THAT'S WHAT I WANNA HEAR!
HEY!
WHAT'RE YOU DOING? WE'RE GETTING READY FOR SUPPER.
NO SUPPER FOR THE SLACKERS!
SORRY. WE'RE COMING!
It was March 29th. The spring wind brought with it the heat of early summer.
'CAUSE YOU SHOULD!
SHIBAMURA! HOW 'BOUT AN APOLOGY?!
W-WHY?!
We still didn't know the cruel fate that awaited us.

TO BE CONTINUED IN VOLUME ②

STAFF
Hakkinen Lopez
Makito Boku
Taayama
Yoshikichimaru
Shuji Ogura
Koishikawa

SPECIAL THANKS (In no particular order)
Saneyoshi Hinaidori
Shigeki Saiki
IONOS
Seiro Touto
Tooru Zekuu
Kyoko Tsuchiya
Alpha System staff

■ HELLO, HIROYUKI SANADURA HERE.

THANK YOU FOR PURCHASING
THIS MANGA. *GUNPARADE MARCH*
WAS MY FIRST SERIAL COMIC, AND
THROUGH A PROCESS OF TRIAL AND
ERROR, I NOT ONLY LEARNED A LOT,
BUT WAS SOMEHOW ABLE TO
PRODUCE THIS VOLUME YOU NOW
HOLD IN YOUR HANDS. THIS MANGA
IS STILL A WORK IN PROGRESS,
SO PLEASE BEAR WITH ME AS IT
CONTINUES TO IMPROVE.

■ FINALLY, LET ME EXPRESS MY THANKS
TO:
  HIROYUKI UTATANE
  REI HIROE
  AND THE STAFF OF ALPHA SYSTEM

THANK YOU AGAIN, BYE FOR NOW...

GUNPARADE MARCH

1

© HIROYUKI SANADURA 2001
© 2001 Sony Computer Entertainment Inc.
First published in 2001 by Media Works Inc., Tokyo, Japan.
English translation rights arranged with Media Works Inc.

Translator **HIROAKI FUKUDA**
Lead Translator/Translation Supervisor **JAVIER LOPEZ**
ADV Manga Translation Staff **KAY BERTRAND, JOSH COLE, AMY FORSYTH, BRENDAN FRAYNE,
HARUKA KANEKO-SMITH, EIKO McGREGOR AND MADOKA MOROE**

Print Production/ Art Studio Manager **LISA PUCKETT**
Pre-press Manager **KLYS REEDYK**
Art Production Manager **RYAN MASON**
Sr. Designer/Creative Manager **JORGE ALVARADO**
Graphic Designer/Group Leader **SHANNON RASBERRY**
Graphic Designer **HEATHER GARY**
Graphic Artists **SHANNA JENSCHKE, KERRI KALINEC, GEORGE REYNOLDS AND CHRIS LAPP**
Graphic Intern **MARK MEZA**

International Coordinator **TORU IWAKAMI**
International Coordinator **ATSUSHI KANBAYASHI**

Publishing Editor **SUSAN ITIN**
Assistant Editor **MARGARET SCHAROLD**
Editorial Assistant **VARSHA BUHCHAR**
Proofreaders **SHERIDAN JACOBS AND STEVEN REED**

Research/ Traffic Coordinator **MARSHA ARNOLD**

Executive VP, CFO, COO **KEVIN CORCORAN**

President, CEO & Publisher **JOHN LEDFORD**

Email: editor@adv-manga.com
www.adv-manga.com
www.advfilms.com

For sales and distribution inquiries please call 1.800.282.7202

ADV MANGA™ is a division of A.D. Vision, Inc.
10114 W. Sam Houston Parkway, Suite 200, Houston, Texas 77099

English text © 2004 published by A.D. Vision, Inc. under exclusive license.
ADV MANGA is a trademark of A.D. Vision, Inc.

ISBN: 1-4139-0035-6
First printing, October 2004
10 9 8 7 6 5 4 3 2 1
Printed in Canada

Gunparade March Vol. 01

PG. 4 **The black moon**
The appearance of the Phantom Beasts was heralded by that of the so-called "black moon," which appeared some 240,000 kilometers between the Earth and the (pre-existing) moon.

PG. 21 **You'd be better off *cat watching*!**
Shibamura, in her own special way, is not only telling Hayami that he'd be better off abandoning such (perceived) flights of fancy and getting himself a new hobby, she's showing us a glimpse her deep affection for felines (as we'll see more of in volume 2).

PG. 22 **Spirit of the samurai**
Shikon is written with the characters for "warrior" and "spirit."

PG. 23 **Synch-op**
The operation wherein a pilot "synchronizes" with his or her *Shikon*.

PG. 24 **Goblin**
A type of Phantom Beast, characterized by its vaguely chicken-like appearance. Each of the different types of Phantom Beasts were named after creatures from various mythologies (incidentally, the word "goblin" is attributed to the Norman French *gobelin* and has been in use since at least the 12th century).

PG. 27 ***Hitouban***
A specter from Chinese mythology that can separate its head from its body to attack unsuspecting victims. It is often compared to the Japanese *rukurokubi*, though the latter stretches its neck rather than disengaging its head. (Trivia: The *ban* in the creature's name, which can mean either "barbarian" or "vulgar/uncouth," is the same as that used for one of the lead characters in *Getbackers*).

PG. 27 **Gorgons**
In Greek mythology, three hideous sisters with bat-like wings and snakes for hair. While Stheno and Euryale were immortal, only the third—Medusa—could be killed. Her head was in fact later lopped off while she slept, and from her blood sprang the winged horse, Pegasus.

Gunparade March Vol. 01 continued...

PG. 38 **(1) CO**
Abbreviation for "Commanding Officer."
(2) NCO
Abbreviation for "Non-Commissioned Officer," an officer appointed from enlisted personnel.

PG. 49 **HWT**
Abbreviation for Humanoid Walking Tank.

PG. 63 **Buta**
The name of this rather obese cat means "pig" in Japanese.

PG. 88 **CV**
Abbreviation of "Command Vehicle."

PG. 98 **That ain't right!**
In the original Japanese (Japlish?), this line was *Yes ja nai naa*, or "Man, that is not Yes." Akira tends to repeat this phrase quite a bit.

PG. 137 **I *will* protect you!**
This phrase traditionally carries with it romantic connotations, and is used as a man's pledge to protect and provide for the object of his affections.

PG. 148 **He used me as a springboard?**
Gundam fans will recognize this as a line (spoken by Gaia) from episode 24 of the original *Mobile Suit Gundam* television series, as well as *Mobile Suit Gundam - the Movie 2*.

PG. 174 **Sekihiko Inui**
Author of *Comic Party*.

PG. 179 **Tsuruya**
A major department store located in Kumamoto and founded in 1951. The song the characters are singing is the store's jingle.

STRUGGLE FOR SURVIVAL CONTINUES IN
GUNPARADE MARCH 2

Having been thrust into the seemingly hopeless war against the Phantom Beasts, the young tank operators of Army Unit 5121 certainly earned some measure of success—even a small victory is a mark in the win column for the human race. And while a day at the beach may be a well deserved reward for these mecha-driving teens, the Phantom Beasts know nothing of rest—their goal is the total annihilation of the human race! Next up for Army Unit 5121 is the front line, where only the bravest and strongest survive. The Phantom Beasts will show no mercy, but do the courageous Humanoid Walking Tank troops have the know-how to defeat the enemy, or will inexperience lead to tragic results? The fight for existence resumes in the next intense volume of *Gunparade March*, Volume 2!

COMING IN
DECEMBER 2004
FROM
ADV MANGA!

ADV MANGA™
www.adv-manga.com

EDITOR'S PICKS

IF YOU LIKED *GUNPARADE MARCH* VOLUME 1, THEN YOU'LL LOVE THESE!

PICK 1

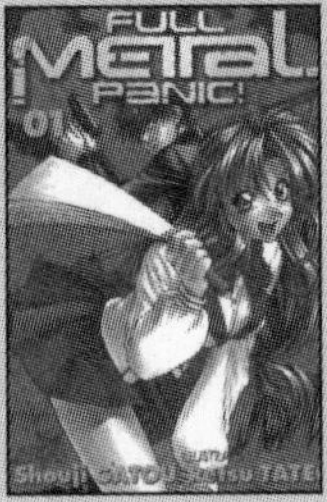
FULL
Metal
PANIC!
01

© 2000 RETSU TATEO · SHOUJI GATOU · SHIKIDOUJI

FULL METAL PANIC!

Kaname Chidori appears to be leading a normal life as a popular high school student, but unbeknownst to her, a group of terrorists believes she possesses the special powers of "The Whispered." When the terrorists' plan to kidnap Kaname reaches the ears of MITHRIL, a secret military organization, they send one of their own to pose as a student while acting as protector to the teenaged social butterfly. This MITHRIL member, Sosuke Sagara, is gung-ho, war-crazed and completely obnoxious, finding his mission as a high school student to be sheer torture. Kaname, on the other hand, finds herself thinking more and more about her undercover classmate, but refuses to own up to it. Her chances are running out! With attempted murders and kidnappings, will these two ever have a moment of truth? It's an exciting blend of fully-loaded action and teenage romance in the thrilling tale of *Full Metal Panic!*

PICK 2

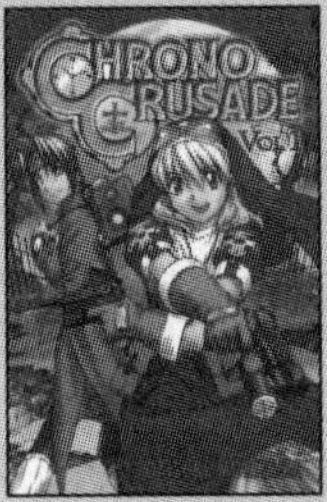
CHRONO CRUSADE

© 1999 DAISUKE MORIYAMA

CHRONO CRUSADE

Villains and demonic creatures are flocking to America and infesting the cities. One woman is fighting the invasion of these damned beings, and she shows little mercy. Flanked by her partner Chrono, Sister Rosette is the one nun who can flatten demonic enemies and save the souls of their prey. Together they are pulling out their tommy-guns to protect the entire population, but with a combination of hellfire and holy water, this nun's rampage might lead to the destruction of more than demons!

PICK 3

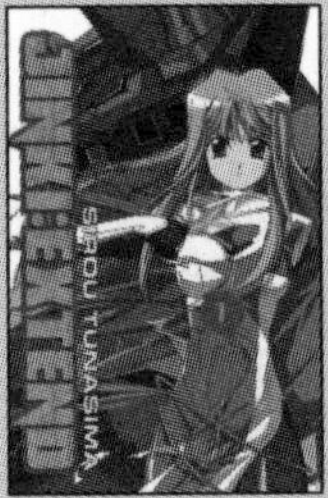
JINKI EXTEND
SIROU TUNASIMA

© SIROU TUNASIMA 2002

JINKI: EXTEND

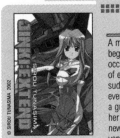

A mysterious explosion rocks La Gran Sabana, Venezuela, marking the beginning of the "Lost Life Phenomenon," a series of strange occurrences ranging from random murders to sudden disappearances of entire populations of villages.Three years later, heroine Akao Hiiragi suddenly finds herself piloting a *jinki*, a gigantic battle robot. But even as this young girl seeks to use her newfound power for good, a group of mysterious masked villains is after her, determined to take her captive. As she stands against these enemies, Akao will only face newer, tougher *jinki*, but as long as young pilots like herself crave vengeance, the struggle will continue.

THE BATTLE TO SAVE THE HUMAN RACE CONTINUES IN *GUNPARADE MARCH* VOLUME 2. COMING SOON FROM ADV MANGA!

ADV Manga™

www.adv-manga.com

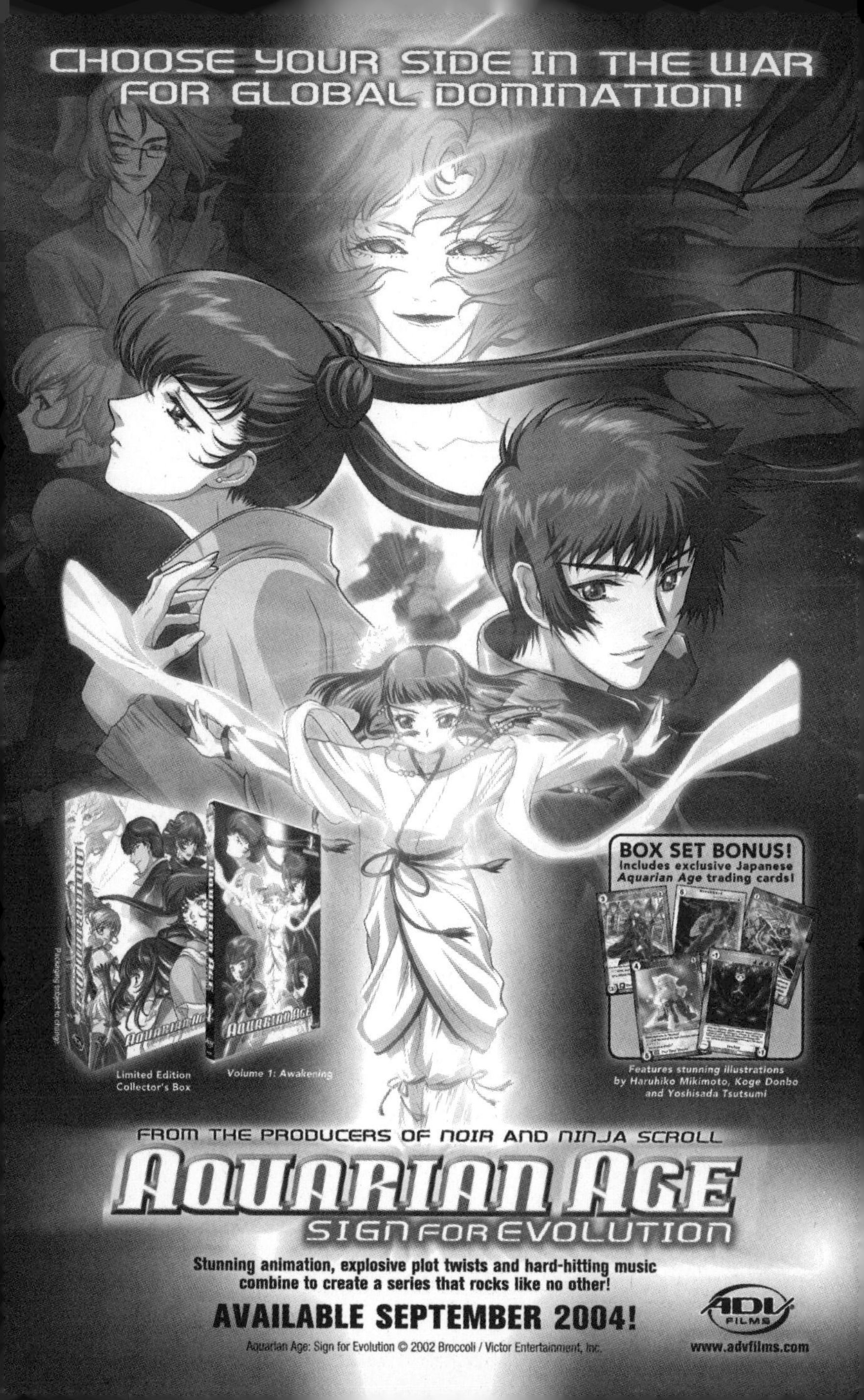
CHOOSE YOUR SIDE IN THE WAR FOR GLOBAL DOMINATION!
BOX SET BONUS!
Includes exclusive Japanese Aquarian Age trading cards!
Features stunning illustrations by Haruhiko Mikimoto, Koge Donbo and Yoshisada Tsutsumi
Limited Edition Collector's Box
Volume 1: Awakening
FROM THE PRODUCERS OF NOIR AND NINJA SCROLL
AQUARIAN AGE
SIGN FOR EVOLUTION
Stunning animation, explosive plot twists and hard-hitting music combine to create a series that rocks like no other!
AVAILABLE SEPTEMBER 2004!
ADV FILMS
Aquarian Age: Sign for Evolution © 2002 Broccoli / Victor Entertainment, Inc.
www.advfilms.com

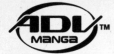

MANGA SURVEY

PLEASE MAIL THE COMPLETED FORM TO: EDITOR – ADV MANGA
c/o A.D. Vision, Inc. 10114 W. Sam Houston Pkwy., Suite 200 Houston, TX 77099

Name: ____________________
Address: ____________________
City, State, Zip: ____________________
____
E-Mail: ____________________
Male ☐ Female ☐ Age: ____________________

☐ ***CHECK HERE IF YOU WOULD LIKE TO RECEIVE OTHER INFORMATION OR FUTURE OFFERS FROM ADV.***

All information provided will be used for internal purposes only. We promise not to sell or otherwise divulge your information.

1. Annual Household Income (*Check only one*)
- ☐ Under $25,000
- ☐ $25,000 to $50,000
- ☐ $50,000 to $75,000
- ☐ Over $75,000

2. How do you hear about new Manga releases? (*Check all that apply*)
- ☐ Browsing in Store
- ☐ Internet Reviews
- ☐ Anime News Websites
- ☐ Direct Email Campaigns
- ☐ Magazine Ad
- ☐ Online Advertising
- ☐ Conventions
- ☐ TV Advertising
- ☐ Online forums (message boards and chat rooms)
- ☐ Carrier pigeon
- ☐ Other: ____________________

3. Which magazines do you read? (*Check all that apply*)
- ☐ Wizard
- ☐ SPIN
- ☐ Animerica
- ☐ Rolling Stone
- ☐ Maxim
- ☐ DC Comics
- ☐ URB
- ☐ Polygon
- ☐ Original Play Station Magazine
- ☐ Entertainment Weekly
- ☐ YRB
- ☐ EGM
- ☐ Newtype USA
- ☐ SciFi
- ☐ Starlog
- ☐ Wired
- ☐ Vice
- ☐ BPM
- ☐ I hate reading
- ☐ Other: ____________________

4. Have you visited the ADV Manga website?

- ☐ Yes
- ☐ No

5. Have you made any manga purchases online from the ADV website?

- ☐ Yes
- ☐ No

6. If you have visited the ADV Manga website, how would you rate your online experience?

- ☐ Excellent
- ☐ Good
- ☐ Average
- ☐ Poor

7. What genre of manga do you prefer?
(*Check all that apply*)

- ☐ adventure
- ☐ romance
- ☐ detective
- ☐ action
- ☐ horror
- ☐ sci-fi/fantasy
- ☐ sports
- ☐ comedy

8. How many manga titles have you purchased in the last 6 months?

- ☐ none
- ☐ 1-4
- ☐ 5-10
- ☐ 11+

9. Where do you make your manga purchases? (*Check all that apply*)

- ☐ comic store
- ☐ bookstore
- ☐ newsstand
- ☐ online
- ☐ other:________________
- ☐ department store
- ☐ grocery store
- ☐ video store
- ☐ video game store

10. Which bookstores do you usually make your manga purchases at?
(*Check all that apply*)

- ☐ Barnes & Noble
- ☐ Walden Books
- ☐ Suncoast
- ☐ Best Buy
- ☐ Amazon.com
- ☐ Borders
- ☐ Books-A-Million
- ☐ Toys "Я" Us
- ☐ Other bookstore: ____________________

11. What's your favorite anime/manga website? (*Check all that apply*)

- ☐ adv-manga.com
- ☐ advfilms.com
- ☐ rightstuf.com
- ☐ animenewsservice.com
- ☐ animenewsnetwork.com
- ☐ Other:________________
- ☐ animeondvd.com
- ☐ anipike.com
- ☐ animeonline.net
- ☐ planetanime.com
- ☐ animenation.com

All information provided will be used for internal purposes only. We promise not to sell or otherwise divulge your information.